Inside Campaigns

CQ Press, an imprint of SAGE, is the leading publisher of books, periodicals, and electronic products on American government and international affairs. CQ Press consistently ranks among the top commercial publishers in terms of quality, as evidenced by the numerous awards its products have won over the years. CQ Press owes its existence to Nelson Poynter, former publisher of the *St. Petersburg Times,* and his wife Henrietta, with whom he founded *Congressional Quarterly* in 1945. Poynter established CQ with the mission of promoting democracy through education and in 1975 founded the Modern Media Institute, renamed The Poynter Institute for Media Studies after his death. The Poynter Institute (*www.poynter.org*) is a nonprofit organization dedicated to training journalists and media leaders.

In 2008, CQ Press was acquired by SAGE, a leading international publisher of journals, books, and electronic media for academic, educational, and professional markets. Since 1965, SAGE has helped inform and educate a global community of scholars, practitioners, researchers, and students spanning a wide range of subject areas, including business, humanities, social sciences, and science, technology, and medicine. A privately owned corporation, SAGE has offices in Los Angeles, London, New Delhi, and Singapore, in addition to the Washington DC office of CQ Press.

Inside Campaigns

Elections through the Eyes of Political Professionals

William J. Feltus
George Washington University

Kenneth M. Goldstein
University of San Francisco

Matthew Dallek
George Washington University

FOR INFORMATION:

CQ Press

An Imprint of SAGE Publications, Inc.

2455 Teller Road

Thousand Oaks, California 91320

E-mail: order@sagepub.com

SAGE Publications Ltd.

1 Oliver's Yard

55 City Road

London EC1Y 1SP

United Kingdom

SAGE Publications India Pvt. Ltd.

B 1/I 1 Mohan Cooperative Industrial Area

Mathura Road, New Delhi 110 044

India

SAGE Publications Asia-Pacific Pte. Ltd.

3 Church Street

#10-04 Samsung Hub

Singapore 049483

Printed in the United States of America

ISBN 978-1-5063-3296-3

This book is printed on acid-free paper.

Acquisitions Editor: Michael Kerns

Editorial Assistant: Zachary Hoskins

Production Editor: Laura Barrett

Copy Editor: Megan Markanich

Typesetter: C&M Digitals (P) Ltd.

Proofreader: Alison Syring

Indexer: Jeanne Busemeyer

Marketing Manager: Amy Whitaker

MIX
Paper from responsible sources
FSC® C014174
www.fsc.org

16 17 18 19 20 10 9 8 7 6 5 4 3 2 1

Contents

Preface

The campaign just becomes a bunch of questions you have to answer.

And once you've answered the questions, you have to follow through on that answer.

Robby Mook, campaign manager,
Terry McAuliffe for Governor, 2013[1]

This book seeks to reveal what really happens inside American political campaigns and to unpeel some myths. During each election season, the contemporary political media tends to hype the latest new campaign technologies and tactics as revolutionary game changers and election winners. In fact, they rarely are. Layered on top of this is the near-single-minded focus among scholars and journalists on presidential elections, a focus that tends to obscure the realities of nonpresidential election contests and the effects that campaigns can have on election results.

To gain a broader understanding of American campaigns, we interviewed more than 100 campaign managers and political professionals using a combination of in-depth conversations and structured questionnaires. Using insights from our research and our own experiences covering, studying, and doing campaigns, this book takes the reader on a tour of modern election campaigns as seen through the eyes of the women and men who run them. "A Textbook on Managing Campaigns, by the Managers Themselves" is how the *New York Times* headlined a 2014 article about our research and writing.[2] This book shows when, how, and why campaigns matter, using the experiences and the words of campaign managers themselves to shed new light on why this distinctly American political process, warts and all, is still the best demonstration of democracy in action.

Based on our research, political campaigns are best described as short-term marketing and communications organizations. As Robby Mook sees it, campaigns come down to asking and answering a series of strategic questions about how their candidate can win more votes than the other candidates. We identify five fundamental strategic questions that are most often asked in campaigns, ranging from "Who are our target voters?" to "What are my opponents and allies doing?"

However, as Mook just pointed out, just answering strategic questions is not enough. The campaign manager must follow through and implement the strategy. We've found that campaign managers must be able to play at least ten specific roles in order to effectively execute their campaign strategies, whether the campaign is a small local effort or a large national juggernaut like Mook's. These ten roles provide the structure for our book and open a window onto the nature of the struggle for political power in America. Depending on the circumstances of a particular campaign, some roles will be more critical than others, but none of the ten are unimportant. We begin with a brief historical case study in American campaign management and argue that the job description hasn't changed that much. This is followed by a chapter presenting a theory of how and why campaigns matter to election outcomes. Then we begin to examine the ten roles of the campaign manager, including chapters such as Political Historian and Data Scientist, Entrepreneur and Chief Financial Officer, Field General, and Candidate Caretaker and Confidant, just to name a few.

Our interviews with campaign managers and other political professionals began in early 2011 and have yielded a trove of original research and fresh perspectives on the electoral process in the United States. Our interviewees are as diverse and as politically balanced as we could make them. To provide generational perspective, we interviewed seasoned hands including those who began their careers in the 1970s and 1980s as well as the most recent class of managers who worked in the 2012 and 2014 election cycles. Some of our interviewees—James Carville, Clinton, 1992; David Axelrod, Obama, 2008, 2012; Ken Mehlman, Bush, 2000, 2004; Sally Bradshaw, Bush, 2016; Robby Mook, Clinton, 2016—are among the most recognizable political names in the country. Others featured in this book—for example, Jen Pihlaja, Kelly Evans, Jarryd Gonzales, Jay Howser—are less well-known, but they have had key roles in helping many of America's most influential members of Congress, governors, mayors, and state and local officials win, or sometimes lose, their elections.

We have thousands of pages of transcribed interviews to date. In them, managers and political professionals offer remarkably candid insights about their experiences working in and running campaigns. To a degree not typically seen in political news reporting, they generously share the personal joys and disappointments of their political lives. We are sorry we could not tell all of their fascinatingly colorful stories in these pages.

Based on our conversations, *Inside Campaigns: Elections through the Eyes of Political Professionals* describes the complex ways in which campaigns can affect election results and, more broadly, how campaigns shape the struggle to win power in American democracy. While much scholarly literature on campaigns is focused on a single presidential election or relies on quantitative data to explore the impact of campaign activities on election outcomes, *Inside Campaigns* takes a holistic look through the managers' perspectives as to when, how, and why campaigns and the people running these multimillion-dollar operations seek to affect, and often do influence, election outcomes.

A great many academics dispute the idea that campaigns can influence election outcomes. These scholars assume that underlying factors either favor a candidate or they do not favor a candidate and that no amount of campaign spending or brilliant strategy or campaign tactics can change the likely outcome. The scholarly skepticism also rests on the argument that even if campaign tactics had the potential to change entrenched minds and outweigh the nature of the times, there would need to be measurable differences in the impact of the competing campaigns. And the overwhelming conventional wisdom among political scientists is simply that such differences rarely exist in competitive US races. In short, in the view of many scholars, campaigns either don't matter because they're dwarfed by the political "fundamentals" or opposing campaigns simply cancel each other out.

None of the campaign managers we talked with would argue that campaigns are always decisive or can turn a sure loser into a winner, but they would also not agree with these arguments. In American political campaigns, the margin—one, two, or three percentage points—can mean the difference between victory and defeat. Our research leads us to believe that campaigns and the people who run them have the power to influence in small, but potentially decisive ways, the direction of an election. There is no one formula—no single play, magic message bullet, or technical wizardry—that guarantees victory. That said, in close races, campaign strategies and day-to-day tactical decision making can matter at the margin, and even a small effect can mean all the difference in the world when it comes to election outcomes.

Ultimately, our research reveals that campaigns continue to be more about the power of personal engagement and persuasion than about technique or technology. Of course, even the most engaging and persuasive campaign will bump up against and be constrained by the fundamental structure of the election, and campaign managers understand the limits on what they can accomplish. But campaign outcomes are not foreordained and winners are not predestined. The campaigns that can target the right voters, find the most effective ways to reach them, develop persuasive messages, and adjust their tactics and strategies according to how they are faring and what their allies and opponents are doing, are going to gain an advantage that is in many instances decisive. Campaign managers who can answer the key strategic questions and who have the management skills to execute their strategies can increase their candidate's share of the vote

David Axelrod told us that the most successful campaign managers and staffers strongly share their candidate's policy positions. Unsurprisingly, the Democrats and Republicans we interviewed had very different perspectives on issues. But we found that Democratic and Republican campaign professionals do share a surprisingly strong consensus on how campaigns work and on how they should be run. Seasoned Democrats are more likely to have moved up through voter contact or field operations while Republicans are somewhat more likely to have press relations or communications backgrounds, although this difference doesn't seem to color their opinions about how to win an election. Our conversations reveal a nonpartisan, shared political language, and we hope that our readers, regardless of their own partisanship, can learn equally from the Democrats and Republicans we've interviewed.

We often heard that working on campaigns is the only way to learn how campaigns really work, although we hope that this book conveys some of that knowledge to our readers. Most political pros told us they started out with volunteer or part-time jobs while in high school, in college, or shortly after graduating. This was certainly the career path for David Plouffe, President Obama's campaign manager in 2008. Plouffe began working on campaigns at twenty-one, with little academic preparation. By forty, he had worked on dozens of them and had developed a wide-ranging skill set that allowed him to direct one of the most unlikely presidential campaigns in history. A similar story describes Karl Rove, the architect of George W. Bush's election in 2000 and reelection in 2004.

Our interviews end by asking "What advice would you give to a young person who's thinking about getting involved in politics?" Of everyone we've talked to, only one said "Don't!" But politics is not for everybody, observed James Carville, noting that many college graduates simply aren't cut out for weeks of unglamorous entry-level grunt work at little or no pay: "They should go get a job in some senator's office," he dismissively advised.[3] For those young people who can do the work, electoral politics can provide a very fast track for twenty-somethings to gain experience and responsibility. "Five years with a company gives you one line on your resume. Five years in the campaign realm gives you several," said Dan Centinello, who managed Chris Christie's 2009 gubernatorial campaign.[4]

While a book cannot teach someone to be a winning campaign manager, we believe that this book will let the reader, young or not-so-young, better understand what campaigns do and why they matter, and perhaps interest them in working in a campaign or advocating for a cause. If our readers do decide to get involved, we hope *Inside Campaigns: Elections through the Eyes of Political Professionals* makes them a more informed student and consumer of civic life and enables them to make a more valuable contribution to our democratic process.

Notes

1. R. Mook, personal communication. March 13, 2013
2. *New York Times*, October 31, 2014, p. A16.
3. J. Carville, personal communication, November 9, 2011.
4. D. Centinello, personal communication, November 2, 2011.

Acknowledgments

This book is the result of a unique collaboration between a small band of academic researchers and more than one hundred political professionals who were willing to share their personal experiences from working inside campaigns. Since 2011, the Campaign Manager Survey under the direction of Jennifer Dubé and Melissa Sharp has produced thousands of pages of transcribed and coded data about the backgrounds, decision-making processes and insights of American political managers. Joan Price, a graduate student of at the University of San Francisco, joined Jennifer in conducting many of the early interviews. Signing on in the final year of the project, MacKenzie Miller rounded out our core team and provided terrific research assistance. This book would never have happened without the diligent and able work of Jennifer, Joan, Melissa, and MacKenzie

Christian Schneider, now at the *Milwaukee Journal*, accepted the assignment of reading through the early interview transcripts and organizing quotes, as well as doing some of his own excellent in-depth interviews and reporting; the authors are indebted to his journalist's perspective and his early contributions. We also want to thank Christopher Blunt of Overbrook Research who assisted in building the Campaign Manager Survey codebook, and acknowledge the work of a team of undergraduate interview coders including Sumner Canfield and Emma Hobson.

Additional research support came from the University of San Francisco and we would like to thank then professor and McCarthy Center director and now, Dean Corey Cook for his help with the project. We are also indebted to the Hon. Mark Kennedy, Dr. Lara Brown, and other faculty and staff in George Washington University's Graduate School of Political Management for giving Matthew Dallek the time, moral support, and encouragement to work on this book.

Robin Roberts, founder of the Washington Media Scholars college scholarship program and president of National Media in Alexandria, Virginia, generously donated office services, computer systems, and staff assistance to the authors and our research team. We are very grateful to Robin and his employees who have supported Will Feltus and our work, including Tracey Robinson who built and formatted the original manuscript document that has served the authors well during four years of research and writing.

We are indebted to those political reporters and journalists who identified and provided interview introductions to campaign managers and consultants. Several were particularly helpful. Elizabeth Wilner, who writes for the *Cook Political Report*, conducted several key interviews and edited early chapters of the book. Reid Wilson, formerly editor of *The Hotline*, also conducted interviews and made introductions. Jenny Barker took on the difficult and time consuming task of quote checking and permissioning, which often included gently cajoling people to go on-the-record instead of on-background. Most of these quotes came from four years of interview transcriptions which were expertly and promptly produced by the politically knowledgeable Easton Sanderson and his colleagues at Scribe Collective.

At CQ Press/SAGE, a team of first-rate editors guided us through the publication process. Sarah Calabi showed enough faith in this project to acquire it, and her excellent edits significantly strengthened the early chapters. Elise Frasier took over for Sarah when she went on maternity leave, providing smart feedback on the manuscript, the book's title, and helping us to navigate the reader reports. Megan Markanich fielded our queries and copyedited the book with skill and patience. Laura Barrett patiently shepherded us through production. Five anonymous outside readers provided detailed, thoughtful insights on the manuscript and helped us to sharpen the book's themes and tighten the prose. We are grateful to all of them for their contributions.

Finally and most importantly, we want to thank all of the political professionals who gave their time, experiences, and insights to this project. Nearly everyone we interviewed enjoyed the process and supported our goal of providing students with a new perspective from inside American political campaigns. Many of those we talked to also provided introductions to other political professionals who were interviewed for the book. Campaign managers are most often comfortable working behind the scenes, so we are particularly indebted to those individuals who were willing to share with students their personal experiences and opinions in print and in their own words. We are also grateful to all those individuals who were interviewed and made a valuable contribution to our research but whose names and insights we were sadly unable to include in our limited pages—we apologize to them. We wish we could have talked with another two hundred political pros and published everyone's campaign war stories. We heard a lot of good ones. Thank you for letting us listen.

List of Tables, Figures, and Boxes

Tables

Figures

Boxes

CHAPTER 1

Losing and Winning

The Craft and Science of Political Campaigns

Political campaigns are not unlike new restaurants: Most of them will fail. Of the more than 100 campaign managers we interviewed for this book, nearly all had lost elections—many more than once. Even the most experienced and successful campaign manager can lose unexpectedly and even spectacularly.

Consider the case of a campaign manager we will call "TW." For three decades, he managed his candidate—who was both his best client and his best friend—from the New York legislature, to the governor's mansion, and on to the US Senate.[1] Along the way, TW had worked for other candidates who were nominated for or won the presidency.[2] TW's skills as a campaign manager had earned him national renown and a very comfortable living. He was the undisputed American political wizard behind the curtain.

Now at the peak of his craft, TW was in Chicago at the Republican Party's nominating convention. His client of thirty years was the front-runner to win the nomination. TW was so certain of the result that he had sent his candidate out of the country on a preconvention tour of European capitals. The news media and the buzz on the convention floor held that TW's candidate was assured the nomination. But when the voting finally got underway, TW and his candidate were stunned when they led the first roll call with only 37 percent of the delegates and were forced into a second ballot.[3] The aura of inevitability so carefully cultivated with the media and party leaders began to dissipate, and there was no Plan B. On the third ballot, a dark-horse candidate wrested the nomination from TW's grasp.[4] The political wizard was no more.

The dark-horse candidate was Abraham Lincoln, and the year was 1860. It was only the second national convention for the Republican Party, and Sen. William H. Seward of New York had been expected to emerge with the nomination. Seward's manager was fellow New Yorker Thurlow Weed, who had earlier worked on the presidential campaigns of William Henry Harrison (1840), Henry Clay (1844),

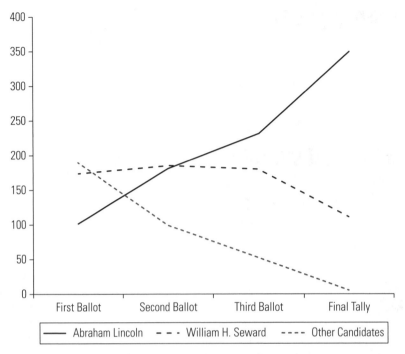

FIGURE 1.1

Presidential Balloting at the 1860 Republican National Convention, Chicago, Illinois

Source: Data from the Proceedings of the Republican National Convention held in Chicago, May 16, 17, and 18, 1860, https://archive.org/details/proceedingsofrep00repulala.

Zachary Taylor (1848), Winfield Scott (1852), and John Charles Fremont (1856) (see Figure 1.1).[5]

Weed was a national figure, but even the most successful managers rarely achieve that status. This book is not about celebrity campaign managers and consultants who achieve notoriety on presidential campaigns—although we've interviewed a number of those. Instead, we aggregate the insights of a wide swath of people who have run winning and losing races for both parties and at all levels of politics—from the courthouse to the White House.

The managers we heard from share a number of common traits and skills, including the ability to play multiple roles in the pursuit of victory on election day. And, in this book, we examine the many responsibilities, decisions, and experiences that managers can—although don't always—use to drive the success or failure of campaigns. This is not a how-to handbook but instead the collected insights from scores of political professionals, supplemented with our own knowledge of campaign mechanics and core scholarly findings about the fundamental factors that influence campaigns and elections in America. Through this synthesis, we can gain not only a greater understanding of what managers do and the array of roles they play but also the workings of the most important mechanism in a democracy—free and fair elections.

A Tale of Two Managers

The science and mechanics of political campaigns have changed since Weed's heyday. Yet many of Weed's skills remain essential in twenty-first-century electoral politics. For example, compare Weed to President Barack Obama's adviser David Axelrod, one of today's best-known political strategists.

Before entering politics, both Weed[6] and Axelrod[7] worked in the newspaper business where they learned the degree to which the news media can shape public opinion. During Weed's career, the printed newspaper was king. In his media world, all newspapers were partisan organs like today's Fox News Channel, Drudge Report, MSNBC, or the Huffington Post. With almost no formal schooling, Weed started out as a teenage typesetter and press operator for the *Albany Register* in the state capital.[8] There, he learned the ways of the political machine that ran the state legislature and government offices of New York. Much like today's political bloggers, Weed launched his own *Evening Journal* in 1830, using the paper and his bylined column to first support the Anti-Mason Party, then the Whig Party, before finally joining the newly formed Republican Party in 1856 in opposition to the Southern-dominated Democratic Party.[9]

Senator Seward himself said, "Weed is Seward, and Seward is Weed, each approves of what the other says or does."[10] No candidate today would publicly say such a thing, but trust and mutual dependence between candidate and manager remains essential in politics. Even after the wrenching 1860 defeat in Chicago, Seward reached out to console Weed and sustain their relationship. "You have my unbounded gratitude for this last [campaign], as for the whole life of efforts in my behalf. I wish that I was sure that your sense of disappointment is as light as my own," Seward wrote in a letter to Weed after their 1860 defeat in Chicago.[11]

Courtesy of the Library of Congress, Prints and Photographs Division, Brady-Handy Photograph Collection.

Thurlow Weed was stunned along with the rest of the political establishment when his candidate, Sen. William H. Seward, was upset at the 1860 Republican convention by a dark-horse member of Congress named Abraham Lincoln.

Thurlow Weed's client, Sen. William H. Seward.

After losing the 1860 Republican nomination to Abraham Lincoln, Seward and Weed both became actively involved in Lincoln's general election campaign. Seward went on to serve as Lincoln's secretary of state.[12] Weed also continued to be politically involved. In fact, Lincoln asked for Weed's help in supporting Republicans in the 1862 congressional elections.[13]

Like Weed, Axelrod's first job was at a newspaper. After graduating from the University of Chicago in 1977, Axelrod worked for the *Chicago Tribune*, becoming the paper's youngest political writer before leaving journalism and joining the 1984 Illinois campaign of Democratic candidate, Paul Simon, for the US Senate.[14] After starting as communications director, Axelrod eventually was named campaign manager. The underdog Simon went on to upset the popular three-term Republican incumbent, Sen. Charles Percy, in a year when Republican Ronald Reagan carried Illinois and every other state except Minnesota. In the same state where Weed lost his final campaign, Axelrod won his first.

Journalism made Axelrod a better manager and strategist, he says now. "Because so much of what modern campaigns involve is about message and communications, having been a journalist was helpful to me." He added, "When I was parachuted into campaigns as a reporter, I went in with some presumptions. But to me the job was to get on the ground and really understand what the political terrain was . . . to figure out what people were thinking, what voters were thinking. Those skills were very helpful as a strategist and as a manager."[15]

Those skills came up short in 1988 when Axelrod, now playing the role of campaign consultant instead of manager, was the chief strategist for Sen. Paul Simon's, D-IL, campaign for the Democratic presidential nomination. Simon's campaign gained early momentum with a stronger than expected second-place finish in Iowa, the first round of the nomination contest. But, in the next round, Simon lacked the cash to put Axelrod's television ads on the air in New Hampshire, which includes the expensive Boston media market. Simon came in third in the Granite State behind eventual nominee Gov. Michael Dukakis of neighoring Massachusetts.

Axelrod also lost with his next presidential candidate, Sen. John Edwards, D-NC. It wasn't until the third try that an Axelrod client made it to the White House. "You have to choose your candidates well. . . . But you also have to go in knowing that none of that guarantees victory in a very dynamic process in which so many factors can impact on the outcome," said Axelrod. "You're never as smart as you look when you win, and never as dumb as you look when you lose."[16]

NBC Chicago

Ron Wade Buttons

David Axelrod lost his first presidential campaign. He is pictured here in 1988 when his client, Sen. Paul Simon, finished a surprisingly strong second in the Iowa caucuses but faltered in the New Hampshire primary.

The Personal Side of Politics

After President Obama's 2012 campaign outmaneuvered challenger Mitt Romney, the postelection coverage and conversation was dominated by talk of campaign mechanics and tools like big data analytics, controlled field experiments, and new methods for targeting media. To be sure, campaigns have more and more data at their fingertips, and they have become increasingly sophisticated in the how they analyze those data. Furthermore, the empirical findings and methodological approaches of political scientists have had a profound influence on what campaigns do and how campaigns budgets are shaped. As we will discuss later in the book, this is especially the case when it comes to the science of voter mobilization and get-out-the-vote (GOTV) efforts.[17]

Still, the campaign managers we've talked with remind us that politics and campaigns remain a very personal business. In today's modern campaigns, after decades of dominance by television advertising and other mass media, personal one-on-one politics has made a comeback. The campaign managers we surveyed were asked to rate the cost effectiveness of various communications methods on a zero-to-ten scale, with ten being the most effective. Direct contact—meaning personal phone calls or door-to-door canvassing by both volunteers and paid workers—was seen as just as effective as broadcast television advertising.[18]

One Obama staffer dedicated to person-to-person contact was David Simas, who learned his retail politics as a successful young candidate for the school board and city council in his hometown of Taunton, Massachusetts, south of Boston. Simas made lists of voters, knocked on doors himself, and tried to gauge the mood of the electorate by interacting with voters.[19] Newly elected Massachusetts governor Deval Patrick recognized Simas' political talent and named him deputy chief of staff in 2007. David Axelrod, who served as campaign strategist for Patrick in his 2006 gubernatorial campaign, brought Simas to the White House as a top aide after the 2008 presidential election.[20]

Presidential aides are often reluctant to leave the comforts of the White House for the rigors of a reelection campaign—but not Simas, who moved to Chicago to run the campaign's focus group and polling operations.[21] Just as he had in Taunton, Simas would spend hundreds of hours listening to and interacting with voters. What Simas and his team learned was used to target voters in the campaign's massive database of voters and passed along to thousands of Obama campaign workers and volunteers who made phone calls and knocked on doors.

Why Campaign Managers Do It

Most managers and staffers suffer lows between the highs—and only a handful enjoy the high of winning a presidential election. They talk about a world in which the news media loves, then hates; supporters believe, then doubt; and campaign decisions are second-guessed by the press and by everyone else. Candidates are subjected to personal attacks that seem unfair, there's never enough money, and there's always a good chance of ending up an unemployed loser. So why do most campaign managers keep coming back for more?

For many, it's the prospect of the thrill of victory. "I mean, it's just sickness, we're all infected with it," said Joe Abbey, who ran Democrat Ned Lamont's unsuccessful campaign for governor of Connecticut in 2010. "The rush of a campaign, man,

Official White House Photo by Pete Souza

David Simas, White House aide and campaign staffer, traveled with President Obama to a 2011 meeting in Portugal where Simas's parents were born. Obama introduced him to the assembled international media: "David's family is watching. This is my friend David Simas."[22]

election night, when you win. There's no other feeling like that in the world. . . . You're exhausted, you haven't eaten real food in months, and you've poured your whole life into a cause and you win."[23]

Win or lose, campaign managers also are rewarded by the chance to develop an uncommon bond like Seward and Weed shared, almost a codependence, with a candidate they believe in. In exchange for investing life and career in electing their candidate, the manager becomes the candidate's whisperer and keeper. This bond provides its own sort of high. "Campaign managers get a bad rap that they're mercenaries. Well, we're not," said Martha McKenna, who ran Democrat Sheila Dixon's winning 2007 race for mayor of Baltimore.[24] "I think of it as the most brave and courageous thing to do to put your name on the ballot. And it's something that I don't think I could do. But when you're the campaign manager and you're entrusted with that person's name and reputation, that comes with seriousness and a responsibility that's both important and exhilarating"[25] (see Box 1.1).

Some campaign managers do it clear-eyed as a career-building investment that can pay off with other professional opportunities. There's always the prospect of a staff job after a winning campaign. Managers also come into close contact with the lawmakers, businesspeople, and wealthy donors who make up a candidate's surrogate bench or inner circle. Losing a race doesn't preclude a campaign manager from making a good impression with these future potential employers or clients. "I can't tell you the millionaires that I know that started doing campaigns," Screven Watson told us.[26] Watson ran Democrat Rod Smith's unsuccessful 2006 campaign for governor of Florida and was later hired as a lobbyist. "I'm not one of them, not smart enough, but the people that got involved in the campaign and got identified as a talent, they got sucked up."[27]

Campaign managers are the field marshals in America's ceaseless war for governing power. Many people understand that elections have significant consequences, but few have any idea of what it takes to win one. Most scholarly work on the subject has focused on factors that drive how people vote. In the process, some

Like Seward and Weed, and Obama and Axelrod, the right relationship between a candidate and their campaign manager is an important part of electoral success.

There were never two men in politics who worked together or understood each other better. . . . Neither controlled the other in any objectionable sense. One did not always lead, and the other follow. . . . They were like two brothers with whom nearly all interests are common.[28]

Thurlow Weed Barnes, grandson of
Thurlow Weed, *Memoir of Thurlow Weed* (1883)

[Thurlow Weed] always thinks I am driving everything to the devil. But throughout my public life he has told me to do this or that particular thing, and I have done it. He told me not do that and I have refrained from doing it.[29]

Senator William H. Seward, R-NY,
speaking of Thurlow Weed in 1857

I think it has to be like a sibling relationship. I think you need to know each other well like siblings do, but also siblings aren't afraid to call each other out.[30]

Adam Bodily, campaign manager, Duane Snow for
Albemarle County Board of Supervisors, 2009

A lot of times, your job is just to [let them vent] when they've had a bad day. . . . But that also means that when I'm getting yelled at [by someone else], they've got my back, which leads to trust. So you [need to] have that relationship where you can speak your mind in private.[31]

James Cauley, campaign manager,
Barack Obama for Senate, 2004 (IL)

You know, it's not about managing the candidate, but it's about having a kind of partnership. You respect the candidate. You each understand what your roles are. And you respect those boundaries. You're in constant communication. You understand what decisions you're going to make, what decisions the candidate will make, and you operate based on those agreements.[32]

Katie Merrill, campaign manager,
Phil Angelides for Governor, 2006 (CA)

You never saw a horse turn around and tell the jockey which way to run. [The] candidate is the horse and the manager is the jockey. And so the manager needs to run the campaign. The candidate obviously has input . . . but at the end of the day, the candidate can't be digging through the research, can't be talking to the hierarchical leadership and the grassroots leadership. The manager's got to do that.[33]

Haley Barbour, chairman, Republican National Committee,
1993–1997; governor of Mississippi, 2001–2009

scholars have concluded that campaigns don't much matter (see Chapter 2: Political Math: Why Campaigns Matter). Other research has been conducted on the effects of big-ticket campaign tactics such as television advertising and voter mobilization.

Until now, almost no attention has been paid to the unique role of the manager and what it teaches us about elections in America. This book is not intended as a substitute for hands-on experience but as a means to constructively share managers' experiences and to understand campaigns and elections through the eyes of those who manage them. This book also serves as a window into how campaigns affect who wins and who loses and the struggle for power in modern American democracy. According to Steven Law, manager of Senate majority leader Mitch McConnell's (R-KY) 1990 campaign and now of American Crossroads, one of the highest spending advertisers in Republican politics today, "You just don't get campaigns until you work on campaigns."[34]

What Campaigns Do

Based on our conversations with campaign managers, we developed a flowchart model describing what happens in campaigns (see Figure 1.2: What Campaigns Do in Five Questions). This is not an organizational chart describing jobs and personnel. Instead, it is a dynamic model showing what campaigns do on a day-to-day basis, describing key activities, five core questions that drive the campaign, and the tracking loops that campaign managers use to measure their expected performance on election day. These feedback loops are critical to the success of a campaign and are another area in which political campaigns differ from consumer marketing campaigns. The consumer brand manager has the luxury of daily sales data, but the political campaign manager can never be sure of which voters are sold on their candidate and will not see any hard sales numbers until election night.

The questions are ones that virtually every candidate running in a competitive election—whether it's a presidential or city council race—must ask and answer in order to be successful: (1) "Who do we need?" represents the coalition that the campaign must assemble in order to reach 50.1 percent of the vote (assuming a two-person race). (2) "How do we reach them?" involves the methods available to a campaign to mobilize and persuade their targeted voters with their limited resources. (3) "What do we tell them?" reflects a need on every campaign to drive a clear message about why its candidate deserves a voter's support and why the opponent would be harmful to the voters' interests. (4) "How are we doing?" encompasses the feedback loop that helps managers track their progress and adjust the campaign's tactics and strategy according to how they're faring. (5) "What are they doing?" sheds light on what the opposing side is doing to target, mobilize, and persuade their own voters and whether or not attacks by the opposition need to be answered; increasingly, nowadays, "What are they doing?" also spurs a conversation

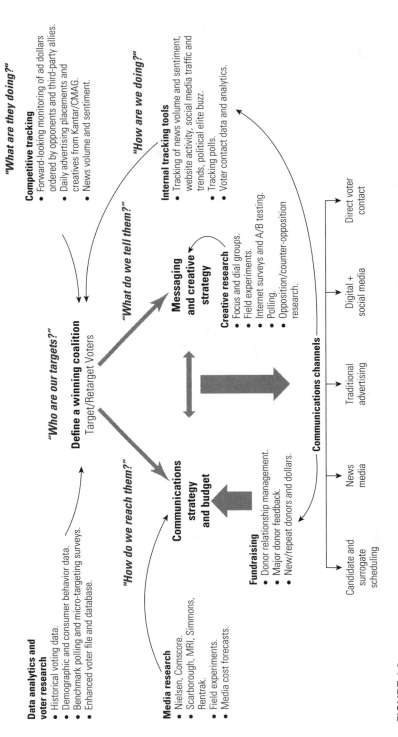

FIGURE 1.2

What Campaigns Do in Five Questions

about the influence of super-PACs (political action committees) (friend and foe) on voters' views of the candidates and the issues. Taken together, these questions guide the strategic decisions and tactical choices that each campaign manager and their team must make. These five questions structure each campaign's quest to win the election.

The Targeting and Retargeting of Voters

What will the candidate's winning coalition look like? This "Who do we need?" question must be the starting point of every campaign. Targeting voters who support a candidate but may or may not vote, as well as targeting likely voters who remain undecided in their choice, remains a central element of any campaign operation. That's why we put "Who do we need?" at the top of Figure 1.2. Without knowing what a winning coalition looks like, the campaign can't create a strategy, refine its message, and allocate its finite resources to conduct its campaign activities. When Thurlow Weed was managing William H. Seward's US Senate campaigns, members of state legislatures—not individual voters—did the electing. Weed could keep a list of all the eligible voters in his coat pocket along with updates on each voter's concerns, when they were last contacted on Seward's behalf, and the latest estimate of how they were likely to vote.

Today's campaign manager also can keep a detailed and updated voter list in his or her pocket, but that list could contain millions of names and be on a mobile device or portable data drive. The growing affordability of computing power and data storage means campaigns can target and track millions of individual voters. They must set aggregate vote goals by precinct and other geography, by party identification, by demographic group, and for other buckets of voters.

Beyond that, today's sophisticated campaigns start by building a voter file that is maintained, enhanced, and updated in a database management program. Based on voting history, party registration (when available), and other individual information, the campaign can describe its winning coalition voter by voter. The voter database is continually updated with results of phone calls, door knocking visits, and other forms of direct voter contact that can include use of online and social media, volunteering and donating habits, and other one-on-one touch points (see "Internal Tracking" feedback loop in the model). The "human touch" in modern campaigns is very much data assisted.

Axelrod and his team of Obama managers invested millions to build the most sophisticated and dynamic voter database in political history. They also built a culture of data analysis-driven decision making, hiring dozens of data analysts who provided Axelrod and other senior staff the daily intelligence they needed. After Romney "won" the first presidential debate in early October 2012, public opinion polls showed the race tightening with Romney moving ahead in some surveys for the first time. Yet at the Obama headquarters in Chicago, confidence was unshaken. Based on thousands of nightly interviews with samples drawn from their voter database, Obama's analysts concluded that Romney's gains were among voters who should have been supporting the Republican in the first place.

Axelrod publicly offered to shave his mustache if Obama lost the election—but only after checking one more time with the campaign's chief data scientist.

Messaging and Creative Strategy

In twenty-first-century American politics, campaigns—for public office or to influence public policy—are often won and lost at the margins by the side that does the best job of developing, testing, and delivering the most compelling messages possible to their targeted voters. Every campaign needs a narrative arc, both about its own candidate and her positions on the issues, and about the opposing side. What traits, experiences, or positions does the candidate possess that appeal to the target voters? How would the candidate improve these voters' lives, and how would the other side affect voters' lives in a negative way? Getting back to the campaign-as-marketing operation analogy, campaigns need to test what sort of branding (in the form of logos and other graphics) and look and feel (for its events) it should have.

All of this occurs through a creative testing process ("What do we tell them?") that involves the manager overseeing a team of advertising consultants, pollsters, graphic artists, and often the candidate and the candidate's family. This process yields the messages that the campaign uses to appeal to its targeted voters. While the overarching message is typically held constant and ideally doesn't change much (think Obama's 2008 "hope and change" message), the campaign can tailor messages to discreet audiences based on their distinct concerns and particular political passions.

Communications Strategy and Budget

This is the "war room" side of the communications operation—the constant grind of media and social media outreach, the rapid response operation, event planning, etc. It's also the purse string side of the operation.

Advertising is typically the single biggest expense of any campaign. Many campaigns deploy a mix of television, radio, and digital along with direct mail. Print advertising is rarely used anymore, though in races in prohibitively expensive media markets, campaigns may forgo TV and invest more heavily in the other forms of advertising.

Opposition research—essentially, a book on the exploitable weaknesses of one's opponent—also falls under this category. The first target for any opposition researcher is the researcher's own candidate. The vastness of the Internet makes this process both easier and tougher: It's easier to conduct extensive research on one's own candidate and identify any potential issues that might be thrown at a candidate. However, one can never be sure she has found everything. Once one has achieved as much certainty as possible, the researcher sets his or her sights on the candidate's opponents.

Fundraising

With advertising typically being the single biggest expense of any campaign, managers can feel at times as though the fundraisers basically exist to pay for advertising.

It's actually a more reciprocal relationship (see the "Donor Development" loop in the model). Advertising, particularly on TV, can be a shorthand way of telling potential big donors that your candidate is "real" or viable.

At the same time, not all advertising is aimed at persuasion; digital advertising has become an effective way to raise smaller contributions because online ads can link through to fundraising forms that appear alongside information, even videos, about the candidate. As critical as those massive contributions from big donors are for building a substantial financial foundation for a campaign, the smaller contributions become the fuel that keeps the campaign going. Small donors can be solicited over and over again before they reach the fundraising cap; small-dollar donors tend to view their contributions as an investment and are more likely to help in other ways, either financially or by volunteering to knock on doors or make phone calls.

Media coverage of the candidate also tends to boost fundraising—and not just when the news is good. Savvy campaign communicators can turn bad news into effective fundraising pitches, especially over the Internet for the kind of small-dollar contributions that are relatively easy for a candidate's faithful to give.

The Roles and Goals of a Campaign Manager

Campaigns are one of the most consistent growth industries in the American economy, with the most recent fundraising and spending totals smashing all records and dwarfing what was conceivable only a few years ago. The total cost of congressional and presidential races combined approached $7 billion in 2012 (see Figure 1.3), and spending will surely exceed that amount in 2016.[35]

Meanwhile, more and more media outlets obsessively cover how much money is being raised and spent, and they minutely track all of the activities that comprise modern campaigning. While the flowchart model (Figure 1.3) captures the dynamism of a campaign's inner-workings, the following chart (Figure 1.4) offers a succinct take of the core activities that appear on any campaign manager's to-do list.

But, stepping back for a moment from the campaign's activities, we must ask some hard questions about the nature of modern elections: Do they matter? Is most of the money raised and spent squandered on useless activities? Do any of the activities referred to in Figure 1.4 have a measurable impact on determining losers and winners? Some political scientists who study campaigns have argued that campaign activities have minimal to zero effect on the ultimate election results. In other words, they say that all of the money raised and spent, and all of the enormous effort expended on electioneering, tend to cancel each other out. They also argue that the fundamentals of the campaign—indicators such as the gross domestic product, presidential approval ratings, the partisan distribution of a given state or district—are the biggest drivers that determine election results.

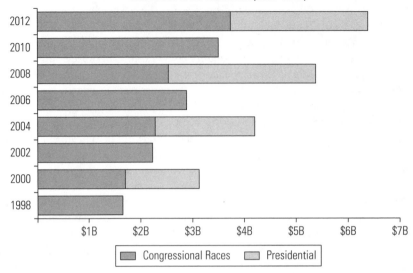

FIGURE 1.3

Costs of Campaigns

Source: OpenSecrets.org, "The Money Behind the Elections: Total Cost of US Elections (1998–2012)," https://www.open secrets.org/bigpicture

✓ Raise Money

✓ Hire Lawyers

✓ Conduct Research on the Electorate

✓ Research Opponent

✓ Research Yourself

✓ Develop Messages

✓ Create Messages

✓ Target Messages

✓ Deliver Messages—Air, Ground, Free, Paid

✓ Gain and Avoid Advantages

FIGURE 1.4

What Do Campaigns Do?

But let's frame the "so-what" issue in a different light: If campaigns are typically humming with activity (raising funds, researching opponents, targeting voters), what does it all add up to? *Do campaigns matter? If campaigns do matter, how do they matter?* Why should we study campaigns? Why *do* campaigns? Why do accomplished women and men devote so much time, sweat, and money to activities that perhaps at best have a meager effect on electing candidates to office?

This is no idle theoretical debate. As you will find in Chapter 2 and elsewhere in this book, campaigns matter—and in particularly crucial ways that depend on the political climate, the nature of the electorate, and other variables, some of them under the campaign's control. Our 100-plus interviews with America's foremost campaign managers yield some insights into how and why campaigns make a difference at the electoral margins and show that pundits are prone to overplaying the effects of campaigns, while the majority of political scientists tend to underestimate the effects of campaigns.

Looked at another way, all campaign managers need to answer the five questions featured in the workflow campaign model (Figure 1.2) and how well a campaign is able to answer these questions can be, and often is, determined on election day: *Who do we need? How do we reach them? What do we tell them? How are we doing? What are they doing?* These core questions, deceptively simple-sounding, are actually rather complicated. They frame the roles that ultimately all campaign managers must fill in order to be effective at their jobs. In addition, campaign managers not only have to answer these questions but these questions are interdependent, and managers must wear multiple hats as they structure their campaigns in order to put their candidates in a position to win their elections.

Campaign managers have to play a series of roles so that they can answer these questions and run their campaigns effectively. Ultimately, the campaign manager is responsible for the smooth and synchronized functioning of the workflow and performance of any campaign. While a manager's particular experiences might make him or her an expert in a certain part of the process, most managers are generalists who can wear many different hats. In their conversations with us, they have described an array of roles they've had to play that may be more varied and complex than the expectations for the average CEO of a Fortune 500 company. We've grouped these roles into the ten buckets (see Figure 1.5) that correspond to the chapters in this book.

These ten "hats" that any successful campaign manager must wear will guide us as we explore how campaigns function and how they can affect the outcome of elections. Managers that excel in these roles and ask and effectively answer the five questions do not guarantee that their candidate will triumph, of course. But they can give their campaigns the kind of organization, messaging, strategic direction, and steadiness that in modern American politics is necessary to compete in some of the hardest contests our society knows, contests with tens of millions of dollars as well as issues of war, peace, the economy, and civic society often riding on the outcome.

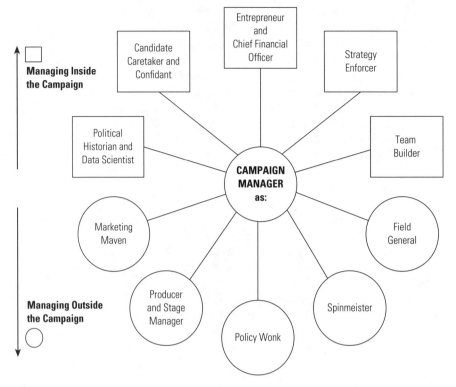

FIGURE 1.5

What Campaign Managers Do: Ten Key Roles the Campaign Manager Must Play

Notes

1. *Encyclopaedia Britannica*, "Thurlow Weed," (n.d.), www.britannica.com/biography/Thurlow-Weed.

2. Ibid.

3. Republican National Convention. *Proceedings of the Republican National Convention Held at Chicago, May 16, 17, and 18, 1860* (Chicago: Albany: Weed, Parsons, and Company, 1860), https://archive.org/details/proceedingsofrep00repuiala.

4. Ibid.

5. *Encyclopaedia Britannica*, "Thurlow Weed."

6. Donn Piatt, *Thurlow Weed (1797–1882)* in New York Historical Society, www.mrlincolnandnewyork.org/content_inside.asp?ID=67&subjectID=3.

7. D. Axelrod, personal communication, March 14, 2013.

8. *Encyclopaedia Britannica*, "Thurlow Weed."

9. Ibid.

10. Gideon Welles, "The Diary of Gideon Welles (1909)," *Atlantic Monthly*, 103, 482.

11. Elbridge Gerry Keith, "A Paper on the National Republican Convention of 1860" (University of Illinois Urbana–Champaign, June 19, 1904), https://archive.org/details/paper onnationalr00keit.

12. Piatt, *Thurlow Weed (1797–1882)*.

13. Ibid.

14. Biography.com, "David Axelrod," 2015, www.biography.com/people/david-axelrod-431900.

15. D. Axelrod, personal communication, March 14, 2013.

16. Ibid.

17. For example, see, Donald P. Green and Alan S. Gerber. *Get Out the Vote: How to Increase Voter Turnout*, 2nd ed. (Washington, DC: Brookings Institution Press, 2008).

18. See the Campaign Manager Survey Questionnaire Library in Appendix A.

19. Michael D. Shear, "Obama's New Political Chief Tries to Reassure Democrats," *New York Times*, March 1, 2014, www.nytimes.com/2014/03/02/us/politics/obamas-new-political-chief-tries-to-reassure-democrats.html?_r=0.

20. Matt Viser, "Taunton Native David Simas Takes on Elevated White House Role," *Boston Globe,* January 25, 2013, https://www.bostonglobe.com/news/politics/2013/01/25/david-simas-taunton-native-and-former-patrick-aide-takes-elevated-white-house-role/Whcr9m9Ol1GsEQii94liRI/story.html.

21. Ibid.

22. Ibid.

23. J. Abbey, personal communication, November 18, 2011.

24. M. McKenna, personal communication, October 26, 2011.

25. Ibid.

26. S. Watson, personal communication, October 7, 2011.

27. Ibid.

28. New York Historical Society, *Memoir of Thurlow Weed*, Vol. II, p. 262, www .MrLincolnandNewYork.org.

29. Ibid.

30. A. Bodily, personal communication, September 30, 2011.

31. J. Cauley, personal communication, November 1, 2011.

32. K. Merrill, personal communication, September 15, 2011.

33. H. Barbour, personal communication, October 30, 2011.

34. S. Law, personal communication, September 29, 2011.

35. Open Secrets.org, "The Money behind the Elections: Total Cost of US Elections (1998–2012)," https://www.opensecrets.org/bigpicture.

CHAPTER 2

Political Math

How Campaigns Matter

> On the margins is where a lot of the important shit in life happens.[1]
>
> Jim Bognet, campaign manager,
> Steve Poizner for Governor 2010 (CA)

Mark Harris ran Rep. Pat Toomey's race for US Senate in Pennsylvania during the 2010 midterm elections. Toomey's opponent was member of Congress and retired navy admiral Joe Sestak. Sestak had defeated Arlen Specter, the incumbent, in a hotly contested Democratic primary. Sestak had strong name recognition in the state; a record of military service; and, most importantly, he was also running in a state where Democrats had more than 1.2 million registered voters on the rolls than Republicans.[2] The last time a Republican had won Pennsylvania in a presidential race was 1988.[3] In short, the electoral math was challenging. Harris knew that beyond simply mobilizing core Republican voters to cast their ballots for Toomey on election day, the campaign was going to need to persuade at least some Democrats and independents to support Toomey.

Beyond the usual challenges of winning when the electoral math was unfavorable, Toomey's reputation as a "right-wing extremist" was going to make it difficult to win over Democrats and swing voters. The news media in the state pinned the label on him at what seemed to Harris like almost every mention of Toomey's name. Harris explained that "all throughout the beginning of the campaign, whenever he was described by the press, there was always the modifier 'ultra-conservative former congressman,' 'extreme conservative former congressman,' 'far-right.' Sort of all these adjectives." In order to make Toomey more palatable to Democrats and swing voters, Harris had to rid Toomey of these negative labels: "We very diligently worked to strip that away," Harris recalled.

> We were fine. We knew we could win if it was just "conservative former congressman," but we had to get rid of the modifier to "conservative." So we spent a lot of time and energy and effort in the beginning of the campaign to highlight things in Pat's record with the press and with the VIPs that they would understand the whole picture of who Pat Toomey was and what he would be like as senator. And for the last, I don't know, nine or ten months of the campaign, I don't think we ever had a single article where it described him in those harsh ideological extremist terms.[4]

Toomey defeated Sestak by two percentage points, 51 percent to 49 percent, pulling in a majority of independents and even a few Democrats. While he clearly benefited from the nationwide Republican wave in 2010 that helped Republicans take control in the House of Representatives, the wave alone was not enough to lift Republicans like Ken Buck (Colorado) and Sharron Angle (Nevada) into the US Senate. They were tarred as too extreme or too conservative and lost in states with Republican-leaning electorates (especially during nonpresidential years when Republicans typically have stronger turnouts than Democrats) that should have been more likely to elect a Republican than Pennsylvania. Harris believes that his strategy worked. Disputing what some political science literature says about campaigns having little effect on election outcomes, he believes that Toomey's campaign mattered.

Debating Campaign "Effects"

Harris is hardly the lone manager who sees campaigns as electoral difference-makers. At the risk of stating the obvious, the vast majority of campaign managers wouldn't have chosen their profession had they not believed that campaigns had an impact on election outcomes. Jim Bognet, who ran Republican Steve Poizner's losing 2010 race for California governor, spoke for a lot of campaign managers when he observed the following:

> Campaigns matter greatly. . . . They tend to matter on the margins. But on the margins is where a lot of the important shit in life happens. You know, in 2008, Republicans probably were not going to win [the presidency]. But in 2012, a Republican could have won. So campaigns do matter. . . . I'd say that what's going on in the world matters the most, and the candidate matters the second most, and then campaigns matter the third most.[5]

The notion that campaigns matter is not uncontroversial, however. In fact, a great many political scientists find that campaigns rarely have effects that decide election results. Many argue that the "fundamentals"—the performance of the economy, an incumbent's approval ratings, and the partisan composition of the electorate—ultimately sort winners from losers, not the hundreds of decisions, large and small, that campaign managers and candidates make. Some of the leading scholars of the field have made claims along these lines:

Almost all politicians and journalists and citizens way exaggerate the effect of the campaign. Most voters don't change their minds, period.[6]

Michael Lewis-Beck, University of Iowa

When you're in the middle of a campaign, there's a tendency for people, especially the media, to overestimate the importance of certain events. [Gaffes, advertising, debates, etc. have no measurable impact on voters' decisions.] The media are interested in getting people's attention, but a lot of the stories you read or see are focusing on things that are trivial. The way campaigns play out is largely determined by fundamentals.[7]

Alan Abramowitz

The assumption is that the major parties basically nominate reasonable candidates that are both well-funded and reasonably well organized. They have equally good pollsters, media advisers, strategists. Therefore, they tend to cancel each other out.[8]

James Campbell

Both sides are pulling very hard. If, for some reason, one side let go—meaning they stopped campaigning—then the other side would soon benefit. But of course the candidates do not let go and that makes it hard to see that their efforts are making a difference. . . . We argue that it means they are equally effective.[9]

John Sides and Lynn Vavreck, *The Gamble* (2013)

The scholarly consensus, specifically on *direct persuasive effects of media on vote choice*—the type of effect that most fascinates the public and the media—is still that media's impact is marginal at most. . . . There is little evidence of direct persuasive effects [on national campaigns from] the slick, highly professional advertising that most Americans think of as powerful.[10]

Diana C. Mutz

There's always more ocean, and there are always more plausible-sounding special explanations for Obama's victory—including demographic shifts, early ads, clever microtargeting, and a fortuitous storm, among many others. Some of them may even have merit. But what all of them have in common is that they are superfluous. In 2012, as in 2008, Obama's electoral performance was quite consistent with what might have been expected on the basis of political fundamentals.[11]

Larry Bartels

Such scholarly doubt—and even exasperation at the way the media cover the tick tock of a campaign—is rooted in several assumptions. Scholars argue that the nature of the times (the state of the economy) and the partisan distribution of likely voters are the key fundamental factors influencing election outcomes. Scholars assume that underlying factors either do or do not favor a candidate and that no amount of campaign spending or brilliant strategy can change the likely election outcome. The scholarly skepticism also rests on the theory that even if advertising had the potential to change entrenched minds and outweigh the nature of the times, there would need to be measurable differences in the impact of the competing advertising campaigns.[12] And the overwhelming conventional wisdom among political scientists is simply that such differences rarely exist in competitive US races. The two sides, in other words, tend to cancel out each other's activities.

Campaign managers, who are on the front lines, tend to roll their eyes at such absolutist scholarly skepticism of campaigns' effects on election results. Consistent with the findings of scores of researchers, they agree that the fundamentals greatly matter, but they also believe that they don't explain *every* last percentage point of election outcomes. Put another way, while a massive effects "fantasy" world may be the reality of cable television news, it is not the reality for most campaign managers we spoke to and is not the reality if one carefully reads much other scholarly research.[13] These scholars realize that the fundamentals leave ample room for marginal effects of turnout or persuasion.

In other words, campaign managers understand that the fundamentals matter, but they also believe that in competitive elections the fundamentals don't point to a clear and obvious winner in more than the occasional case. Based on their extensive practical experiences, campaigns, they conclude, have the ability to mobilize and persuade voters and affect the margins of the vote total. Campaigns have the power to increase in small but potentially decisive ways the number and partisan distribution of voters who show up to cast their ballots, or their side's so-called partisan *share* of the electorate. In addition, they argue that campaigns have the ability to improve their *performance* among persuadable (or swing) voters, convincing undecided voters to vote for their candidate. They add that campaign activities focused on mobilizing partisans (again, referred to as "share") or those focused on persuasion (what we'll call "performance") can often be the difference between winning office and losing a tight election, all while paying attention to the fundamentals shaping the electoral terrain.

Ironically, in the same way that there is a divide among those who say that campaigns matter and those who say it does not, there is also a divide among those who think campaigns can matter. Some managers, journalists, and academics stress the preeminent role played by share (mobilizing one's partisan voters to turn out and vote in greater numbers) in influencing election results. Still, other participants and analysts are more wedded to the theory that performance (again, persuading independent, undecided voters to support their side) is the optimal path to winning elections. Put simply, campaign analysts are divided into three rough camps—those who see fundamentals as all-important, those who claim that share (or mobilization) is the hinge on which elections turn, and a third group that sees performance (persuasion activities) as the most vital driver of election results.

Campaign managers also make a key point about the structure of this debate about campaigns and their effects on election results. They say that although most of the scholarly research is on presidential elections, these are the contests in which fundamentals are likely to matter the most and campaigns are likely to matter the least. Of course, there are many thousands of nonpresidential elections in the United States every year that not only determine control of the US Congress but state legislatures, city councils, city halls, and governors' mansions across the nation.

"Maybe [the notion that campaigns have little effect] has some validity on a presidential level," one campaign manager we talked to argued. "But on state and local levels, I think the campaigns make all the difference. I can point to survey data showing that specific ads and messages moved voters and made differences in almost every campaign I've worked on."[14] Down-ballot races—races for city council, school board, mayor's offices—are more susceptible to campaigns' effects than higher-profile (congressional) races because the quality of the campaigns varies more widely at the local level, according to some campaign managers. And campaigns that are held during off years (when neither presidential nor midterm elections are taking place) can have a bigger impact on elections because there are few national races shaping the political environment and interfering with the state and local campaigns' messages.

Consider how campaign managers replied when asked for their views on how campaigns have the ability to influence results:

I think the further you go down the ballot, the more important it is. I think at the presidential level, it's probably true that 80 percent of what occurs is out of the campaign's control, but the 20 percent that is does matter. As you go farther down, the more impact it has.

Carl Forti, American Crossroads, 2010

There is an idea informed by academic literature that says campaigns don't have a massive effect on [elections]. But I think it's important to drill down to the small number of actual competitive campaigns—and the small number of voters in your persuasion or mobilization universe. Most successful campaigns don't need to involve moving huge percentages of the electorate. For example, I think that field organizing is really important, but field has never been shown, even in super low turnout special elections in awful weather, to move more than 5 to 6 percent of the vote. But that's a huge amount if 20 percent of the electorate's the only part that's up for grabs. Campaigns can make a critical difference when focused appropriately—and real analysis should understand these areas of focus.[15]

Todd Schulte, campaign strategist

I think they have a ton [of impact]. Now I'm in the business to run effective campaigns, so I guess take that with a grain of salt, but to some extent they're right. I mean, you have certain waves. But a campaign's effectiveness is whether they can be in place to catch that wave, whether they've raised enough money to deliver their message, whether they've found enough volunteers and activists to, you know, generate momentum on a grassroots level.[16]

Graham Shafer, Van Hilleary for Governor, 2002 (TN)

Particularly in your open seats and swing state statewide elections, campaigns absolutely matter. In 2010, you look at campaigns like Rick Scott in Florida who was relatively unknown and running against a well-known statewide elected candidate in Bill McCollum. Marco Rubio, nobody knew who Marco Rubio was but they ran a heck of a campaign. If there was no campaign, Charlie Crist would have blown Marco Rubio away. But campaigns, at the highest levels, at the most expensive levels, in the congressional races above absolutely matter. If you're not raising money, executing a paid and earned media plan, others will define you. . . . Say you're a popular governor . . . your approval rating is at 60 percent. Does a campaign really matter if you have a weak opponent? Probably not . . . until something happens and your approval dips into the low fifties or high forties. What if you throw somebody with $50 million, no name ID, and is running against somebody that's teetering on a 50 percent approval rating? Then you have big problems. Absolutely it matters. . . . The higher the profile, the more competitive the state and the stronger people feel like the outcome affects them, in a congressional, senate, governor's, more money will be spent and the more the campaigns matter.[17]

Kyle Robertson, Rick Snyder for Governor, 2014, (MI)

I know they matter. . . . I've run really good races in bad years and we were going to lose no matter what. But do I think that had we run a terrible race, we would have gotten 40 instead of 46 in a race? Probably. It just meant that there was no real way to get to 50+1, you know?[18]

Mark Harris, Pat Toomey for US Senate, 2010 (PA)

What Does "Matter" Mean?

Are the scholars who say fundamentals matter most and campaigns hardly register on the results correct? Are those who say share is most vital right? What about those who say performance is the most important factor? Put differently, do political campaigns matter? If they matter, then do they matter most by share (mobilization) or by performance (persuasion) activities? Do campaigns win by mobilizing their side's partisan voters or by persuading swing voters to vote for them? Or are elections primarily determined by a set of structural, underlying economic, demographic, and partisan fundamentals and almost completely outside the control of the candidates and the campaigns they're running?

This is no idle academic debate. How operatives and academics answer these questions has consequences in the real world. This debate has not only defined how political scientists have explained election outcomes but it also is now shaping how the men and women in charge of campaigns spend their resources and plot and execute their strategies. Yet there is a problem with the way the debate—scholarly and popular—has unfolded through the years and surfaced in the popular press in recent times. By single-mindedly focusing on share (mobilization), performance (persuasion), or fundamentals as the explanatory factor in elections, to the exclusion of almost everything else, some political scientists and journalists are guilty of creating a narrow analytic framework that ignores mounting evidence that all three schools of thought have something important to say about why campaigns matter and how certain candidates win elections. While all three schools of thought uncover truth about why candidates win and lose elections, none of these schools in and of themselves provides a sufficient theoretical model for explaining election outcomes in contemporary American politics.

The campaign managers interviewed for this project tend to understand this complicated reality better than many political journalists. As campaign managers repeatedly argued, there is no pure formula—no single play—that guarantees victory. Thirty-six-year-old Robby Mook, who ran Democrat Terry McAuliffe's 2013 Virginia gubernatorial campaign (and is now Hillary Clinton's 2016 campaign manager), underscored the delicate interplay of fundamentals with persuasion and mobilization activities.

> In virtually every campaign I've done, I've seen public opinion move depending on what information you're putting out there. I think sometimes the question is, does the national or local environment move in such a way that people aren't listening to or aren't receptive to what you're saying?

Mook said that the course of campaign events and news coverage can drown out the effects of advertising:

> What I always used to say in 2010 was [that] our TV ads were like bringing a boom box to a rock concert. Our stuff was out there and people sometimes picked up on it, but for the most part it just never got the reach because the public was so focused on [other] things that we didn't want to talk about. In a vacuum, everything you do has tremendous effect. I think the [first] variable is how much the electorate cares and how much they're plugged into what you're doing. It can sometimes be a lot, can sometimes be not very much. And then secondly, are there prevailing issues, narratives, partisan leanings in the environment that are superseding what you're doing as a campaign?[19]
>
> Robby Mook, Terry McAuliffe for Governor, 2013 (VA)

Let's stay for a moment with Robbie Mook's boom box analogy. Now, let's give it a new twist. If Mook's boom box were in a basketball arena filled with 15,000 screaming rival fans, most wouldn't hear it at all. But if it were placed right in front of the 10 or 20 people in that huge crowd who the campaign most wanted to reach with a particular message, then that boom box would still manage to reach the campaign's targeted audience. A poll taken of the entire audience would likely show the boom box having no effect—most people would say they hadn't heard it and hadn't changed their opinions—but talk to just those 10 or 20 key targeted audience members and the story may be very different.

Campaign managers are actually trying to find and target a relatively small number of people with their messages—those 10 or 20 out of 15,000. To measure a campaign's impact, then, it is much more telling to study each side's targeted efforts to reach the roughly 800,000 persuadable voters in the 2012 presidential election who were up for grabs in nine battleground states, instead of, say, surveying the entire electorate in the 2012 presidential campaign, which would result in a quixotic search for campaign effects.

Josh Ginsberg's experience in Oregon is a nice illustration of why the margins are so instrumental in determining the election results. Ginsberg managed former NBA star Chris Dudley's Republican campaign for governor in 2010. Democrats in Oregon held nearly a 200,000-person registration advantage during that election,[20] yet Dudley lost by just 22,000 votes to his Democratic opponent, John Kitzhaber.[21] The margin was less than 2 percent of the total. Ginsberg told us that although the national Republican wave of 2010 obviously aided Dudley's campaign, their campaign's activities were effective enough to bring Dudley within a relatively small number of votes of pulling off a big upset. Even though Ginsberg's activities ultimately were targeted on a relative handful of Republican partisan voters and swing voters, "the campaign has a huge impact," Ginsberg concluded. While President Obama trounced John McCain by over sixteen percentage points in Oregon during the 2008 campaign, Dudley, the Republican, almost pulled off a major upset two years later. Dudley was a first-time candidate, yet he came closer to winning the election than any Republican in seven consecutive governor's races. The fundamentals of 2010 gave Dudley a shot. But Dudley's campaign was an effort that almost tilted the election in his favor.[22]

The Role of Fundamentals: From Demographics to Party ID

Let's go deeper on the question of fundamentals. How do scholars and nonscholars define them? The fundamentals of race and ethnicity (and, to a lesser extent, gender) are often the metrics by which they segment the electorate into discreet chunks of voters and then from there figure out the odds each side has of victory ahead of election day. To such scholars, the crucial point is to estimate and know the percentages by which each group (blacks, whites, Latinos) turns out at the ballot box.

If a campaign has a certain percentage of, say, white voters show up on election day, then the election will tilt in a particular direction and basically predetermine the result, no matter how adroit a campaign's strategy and tactics. According to this theory, demographics, especially turnout among racial groups, is the linchpin that determines losers and winners.

And, since 2004, the trend has been clear during presidential election years: The sheer number of eligible voters has shifted toward nonwhite groups, favoring the Democrats on the fundamentals. During presidential campaigns, the number of eligible Hispanic- and Asian American voters has risen sharply, while the number of eligible white voters has declined by more than four percentage points between 2004 and 2012. (Meanwhile, the number of African American voters has remained essentially unchanged as a portion of the electorate.)[23]

The trends in who's eligible to vote have corresponded with trends in who turns out to vote, further shaping fundamentals in ways that have advantaged Democrats seeking the White House. Some scholars observe that white turnout rates declined by more than four percentage points between 2004 and 2012, while black, Hispanic, and Asian American turnout increased by approximately six, one, and three percentage points, respectively, over the same time. This matters because while Democrats have lost the white vote by sizable margins in recent national elections, they have won upwards of 90 percent of the African American vote and 70 percent of the Latino vote.[24] Thus, the theory advanced by some political scientists holds that the demographics of the presidential campaigns in 2008 and 2012 gave the Democrats a decisive built-in advantage. And, this so-called twenty-first-century electorate (less white, more diverse, more liberal), some scholars add, will almost certainly continue to favor the Democrats in presidential elections.

Demographics are playing out in other ways, too, some of the scholars are arguing. They point out that the presidential electorate has not only become less white over the past decade but nonwhites are voting in bigger percentages for Democratic candidates (see Table 2.1).[25] As political professionals and scholars try to forecast how future presidential races will unfold, no question is more momentous than whether the surge in minority turnout, the demographics, will continue to favor the Democrats. Will future Democratic presidential nominees enjoy the same advantage in the demographic composition that launched Obama to victory in 2008 and 2012?

But what those who stress the overwhelming role of fundamentals are really talking about when they discuss demographics is *votes generated*, which is simply defined as a function of *eligible voters x turnout x performance*. Campaign managers are looking at the pool of potential voters and multiplying it by their side's turnout and then by their side's performance. Campaign manager Todd Schulte explained his approach to calculating how to assess the potential electorate and how he tries to figure out what percentage of the vote he must move in order to achieve victory for his candidate. "It's important to filter down past the idea that . . . campaigns should be about moving huge portions of the electorate," he argued. "They're not."

TABLE 2.1   The Changing Face of the American Electorate

Ethnic Group	Percentage of Electorate, 2004	Percentage of Electorate, 2008	Percentage of Electorate, 2012
White	77	74	72
Black	11	13	13
Hispanic	8	9	10
Asian	2	2	2
Other	2	3	3

Source: Data from national election pool exit polls.

He went on to say that get-out-the-vote (GOTV) operations "have never been shown . . . to move more than 5 to 6 percent of the vote." Nevertheless, given that only 20 percent of an electorate may be "up for grabs," 5 to 6 percent matters a great deal to determining the outcome in close elections.[26]

Partisan Composition of the Electorate

Demographics are a powerful way to think about the shape and predispositions of the electorate (the number and kind of eligible voters and the breakdown of the voters who actually show up and vote on election day), and demographics can correlate fairly strongly with vote choice and are sometimes used for targeting by campaigns. But *partisan affiliation* is a more proximate cause, more strongly correlates with voter choices, and is the most common metric used for targeting by the campaigns themselves. Party ID is how campaign managers typically look at the fundamentals of the electorate and see which side, based on the fundamentals, holds an edge in any given contest.

Consider the following tables. They demonstrate how elections can be about simple math—calculating how many Republicans, Democrats, and independents will turn out and what percentage of each side needs in order to reach a winning margin. The figures within the parentheses show what percentage of the electorate was Democratic, Republican, and independent. The percentages in the columns represent what proportion of each partisan group voted for the Democratic or Republican candidate. For example, as show in Table 2.2, in 2008, Democrats comprised 39 percent of the electorate, and candidate Obama won the support of 89 percent of these Democratic voters.

In 2012, the election was more competitive, but Obama still won 51 percent of the popular vote.[27] Romney improved on McCain's (and Bush's) showing, winning independents by five percentage points. But these gains weren't enough to offset the ultimately decisive six percentage point advantage that Obama held over Romney in Democratic vs. Republican share of turnout, as Table 2.3 illustrates.

TABLE 2.2   Party ID by Vote for President in 2008

Party (Percentage)	Percentage of Votes for Barack Obama	Percentage of Votes for John McCain
Democrats (39)	89	10
Independents (29)	52	44
Republicans (32)	9	90

Source: Data from national election pool exit polls. Retrieved from http://www.cnn.com/ELECTION/2008/results/polls/# USP00p1.

TABLE 2.3 Party ID by Vote for President in 2012

Party (Percentage)	Percentage of Votes for Barack Obama	Percentage of Votes for Mitt Romney
Democrats (38)	92	8
Independents (29)	45	50
Republicans (32)	7	93

Source: Data from national election pool exit polls. Retrieved from http://www.cnn.com/election/2012/results/race/president.

TABLE 2.4 Party ID by Vote for the House in 2010

Party (Percentage)	Percentage of Votes for the Democratic House	Percentage of Votes for the Republican House
Democrats (35)	91	7
Independents (29)	37	56
Republicans (35)	5	94

Source: Data from national election pool exit polls. Retrieved from http://www.cnn.com/ELECTION/2010/results/polls/#USH00p1.

TABLE 2.5 Party ID by Vote for the House in 2014

Party (Percentage)	Percentage of Votes for the Democratic House	Percentage of Votes for the Republican House
Democrats (35)	92	7
Independents (29)	42	54
Republicans (36)	4	94

Source: Data from national election pool exit polls. Retrieved from http://www.cnn.com/election/2014/results/race/house #exit-polls.

The 2010 and 2014 House election results (see Tables 2.4 and 2.5), in contrast, demonstrated how the partisan split of the electorate worked to benefit the Republicans during recent midterm congressional campaigns. Unlike the turnout advantage Democrats held in 2008 and 2012, the midterm electorates were evenly divided between Republican identifiers and Democratic identifiers, and this evenly distributed partisan composition ultimately helped the Republicans to big midterm victories.

Clearly, fundamental factors—partisan composition of a district or state, incumbent approval ratings (basically, a voter referendum on how an officeholder is performing his or her duties), or economic performance (voters' sense of how the economy is affecting their lives)—are key drivers in most presidential and congressional campaigns. No one really controls these factors; hence, they are called fundamentals. And, as some campaign managers acknowledge, the underlying circumstances (described in this paragraph) explain almost every last percentage point of recent election results.[28]

Share and Performance

But, as much as the fundamentals help us understand election outcomes and shape campaign strategies, the fundamental factors such as demography, party ID, and economic performance are in most cases not enough by themselves to explain fully why one side loses and the other side wins. Both *share* (mobilizing one's partisans to vote) and *performance* (persuading swing voters to vote for one's candidate) can and often do influence election outcomes; in other words, the campaigns' activities to try to improve their share of the electorate and their performance among swing voters are often difference-makers on election day. In a basic calculus every campaign manager must make, elections can be won or lost by how well the campaign succeeds at the following five goals:

1. **Get a large share of the votes from your own identifiers.** Democrats, for example, need to lock down the Democratic base and must shoot to get at least 90 percent of the Democratic vote. Republicans must do the same with their own partisans.

2. **Get high turnout from one's own identifiers.** Most Democrats are going to vote for Democrats, and most Republicans are going to vote for Republicans. But it is crucial for both political parties to generate as much turnout from their side as possible in order to maximize their vote totals.

3. **Get some of the other candidates' supporters.** It is very difficult to convince members of the opposite party to vote for one's candidate. But if it happens, it can make a big difference; not only do these votes count for one's candidate but they are also subtracted from the total of the opponent.

4. **Lower turnout among the other candidate's identifiers.** If the opponent's base is angry or unenthusiastic, it can cost him or her votes. Getting one's opponent's supporters to vote for one's candidate is the best possible scenario, but getting them to refrain from voting at all is the next best option. That's why laws governing elections and absentee ballots and registration rules matter so much to parties and their strategists. When Republicans and Democrats battle over voter ID rules, the Democrats are not simply fighting to protect democracy and Republicans are not protecting integrity; both sides have a direct electoral stake in such rules because the rules affect the composition of the electorate.

5. **Win swing votes.** Even if one believes that there are relatively few swing voters, there are not *zero* swing voters, and their behavior can be decisive at the margin in a close election. The main driver of partisan loyalty, voter turnout, and the division among independent or undecided voters (no matter how few there may actually be) is the nature of the times. But having said that, most campaign managers are trying to get *a little more* turnout of their supporters or persuade *a few* "undecideds" to come their way.

Another way that campaign managers approach this problem is to think in terms of possible Democratic and Republican targets, as Figures 2.1 and 2.2 illustrate. Democrats aim to mobilize their party members (to get them involved in the campaign and to come out to vote on election day—share), to persuade independents to support their side (performance), and to ignore Republican voters. Republicans aim for the inverse.

Consider just how hard it is for a campaign manager to assess the electorate and chart a winning path. Say the candidate is a Democrat running for statewide office in a heavily Republican state. The campaign manager must employ a strategy that draws on multiple strategies that involve both turnout and persuasion, share and performance. For example, having lost Senate seats in Alaska and North Carolina in 2014 and also having lost both states in the 2012 presidential election, Democrats

		Direction of Vote		
		Democrat	**Independent**	**Republican**
Propensity to turn out	Likely Voter	Mobilization	Persuasion	
	Possible Voter	Mobilization		
	Unlikely Voter			

FIGURE 2.1

Expected Targeting by Democrats in Competitive Races

		Direction of Vote		
		Democrat	**Independent**	**Republican**
Propensity to turn out	Likely Voter		Persuasion	Mobilization
	Possible Voter			Mobilization
	Unlikely Voter			

FIGURE 2.2

Expected Targeting by Republicans in Competitive Races

cannot hope to win Senate seats in either state in 2016 simply by recreating the composition of the 2012 or 2014 electorates. If they choose to focus solely on their base, they will somehow need to make these two electorates *more Democratic* than they were in earlier cycles, which is unlikely to happen because Obama will not be on the ballot. And if they focus solely on winning swing voters, there will not be nearly enough of them to give the Democrats a shot at picking up Republican-held seats. Instead, they will need to turn out their own identifiers in high numbers, get a large share of their partisans to vote for them, win swing voters, and either depress turnout on the other side or persuade some of the other side's supporters to vote for them. Even the most astute campaign manager would have a tough time pulling off such a feat.

Ultimately, each manager in a competitive race faces a series of hard choices, illustrated by the five goals and two tables described previously.

Campaign managers recognize that the structure of a state or district (and thus the predispositions of the electorate) influences which and how many of these strategies will be utilized. While there might be a variety of theoretical solutions to the algebra word problem of 50-percent-plus-one, realistically, campaign managers have limited time, money, and resources. After evaluating the fundamentals, a campaign manager must decide on the best strategy: How strongly should they pursue each of the five goals listed previously? Should they try to get people who are going to vote for their candidates—but may not be inclined to show up—to go to the polls on election day? Or should they attempt to win over people who are going to vote but who may vote for the opposition? If a candidate gets a very high percentage of the vote from her own identifiers and they show up to the polls in droves, then she may not even need to worry about winning over swing voters or members of the opposing party.

Campaign Math

Typically, campaign managers have to solve some basic election math in order to figure out how best to achieve the marginal edge that will carry their candidate to victory. Remember that the goal is to win, of course, and that winning means earning 50.1 percent of the vote. Therefore, campaign managers can solve the basic algebra problem by looking at the following table (Table 2.6) and then solving the mathematical formulation that follows.

TABLE 2.6   Campaign Manager Algebra Problem

Party (Percentage)	Percentage of Votes for the Democratic Candidate	Percentage of Votes for the Republican Candidate
Democrat (X)	A	B
Independent (Y)	C	D
Republican (Z)	E	F

$$Democratic\ total = (X^*A)+(Y^*C)+(Z^*E)$$
$$Republican\ total = (X^*B)+(Y^*D)+(Z^*F)$$

Managing campaigns and winning elective office can be seen as exercises in influencing the letters, solving, in other words, some of the above algebra problems. And this math is far from a theoretical undertaking. Democratic campaign operative Steve Rosenthal, for example, summed up his approach to influencing the letters as illustrated by the equations just highlighted:

I start in any campaign [trying] to begin to visualize a state or a district in terms of how many people voted here. Is this a presidential year, is it a midterm year, is it an off year? How many people have voted in each of the last several elections in those presidential, midterm, off-year elections? What's happened to the population over the last few years? Is it going to change? What's the turnout likely to be? What's 50% plus one of that turnout? We generally set a vote goal of 52% and then begin to work from there. . . . Let's take a look at a state like Ohio, for example, and understand Barack Obama won it, Ted Strickland won it and lost it, Sherrod Brown won it. Can we overlay the results of those elections and begin to understand the difference between what the path was that each of them took to get there. And now I'm approaching the state with a new candidate. What's the path that I'm going to use? Where are the votes, geographically, demographically, that are going to get me the majority that I need to win?[29]

Steve Rosenthal, founder,
The Atlas Project

In other words, Rosenthal is seeking to improve one side's performance among those voters open to being swayed and/or expanding one's share of partisan voters who show up to the polls. The mathematical functions underscore the dynamism of the interdependent factors that make up the marginal variation in many close races—a difference between losing and winning. While these math formulas may seem relatively straightforward (i.e., solve the algebra problem and win first place), winning 50.1 percent of the vote requires influencing the letters through any number of distinct ways. The choices managers make depend on the predispositions of the electorate, the political environment, which voters campaigns need to reach, and what the most effective messages will be. Turnout is crucial, but turnout alone is often not enough to win an election. Consider some of the election simulations that follow: If the partisan composition of the 2012 electorate was similar to 2010, the White House would have been up for grabs.

The battles for Congress and president are of course not decided by a national vote, and one could do the following analysis state by state. But this simple analysis

TABLE 2.7 2012 Presidential Election Results: Share and Performance

Party (Percentage)	Percentage of Votes for Barack Obama	Percentage of Votes for Mitt Romney
Democrats (38)	92	8
Independents (29)	45	50
Republicans (32)	7	93

Source: Data from national election pool exit polls. Retrieved from http://www.cnn.com/election/2012/results/race/president.

makes the point that the composition of the electorate is crucial. Table 2.7 again shows the national party share and performance data in the vote for president from the 2012 exit polls.

If we do a little math and multiply the proportion of the electorate by each candidate's performance, we get a three-point Obama victory.

$$Obama\ total = (.38)(.92) + (.29)(.45) + (.32)(.07) = .3496 + .1305 + .0224 = .5025$$
$$Romney\ total = (.38)(.08) + (.29)(.50) + (.32)(.93) = .0304 + .1450 + .2976 = .4730$$

$$Obama\ total = 50.25\%$$
$$Romney\ total = 47.30\%$$

And Table 2.8 again shows the party share and performance data from the 2010 exit polls. If we do the math here and multiply share by performance, we see that Republicans won the national House vote by a little less than seven percentage points. Two factors contributed to this ten-point swing between Obama's 2012 performance and House Democrats' 2010 vote share: the electorate was more Democratic in 2012 than it was in 2010, and while Obama lost among independents, he performed better among them than House Democrats did in 2010.

TABLE 2.8 2010 Midterm Election Results: Share and Performance

Party (Percentage)	Percentage of Votes for the Democratic House	Percentage of Votes for the Republican House
Democrats (36)	92	7
Independents (28)	39	55
Republicans (36)	4	95

Source: Data from national election pool exit polls. Retrieved from http://www.cnn.com/ELECTION/2010/results/polls/#USH00p1.

Now, what happens if the 2012 election is replayed with 2010 turnout, assuming 2010 composition with 2012 performance? Do the math, and multiply share by performance for each cell. Contrary to what the persuasion camp argues, turnout did matter in 2012. If the composition of the 2012 electorate looked as it did in 2010 and Obama's performance was what it was, Obama's three-point victory (in the exit polls) in the 2012 national vote count would have become a two-point loss. One could do the same exercise in all states, or in all battleground states, but it is virtually certain that a two-point loss in the national vote would have translated into enough Romney victories in swing states for him to win the White House (see Figure 2.3). The key points here are that election outcomes in competitive races are often decided at the margins and rarely boil down to a single explanatory factor. See Figure 2.4.

Now let's say the candidate is a Republican running for statewide office in Utah, which is one of the most solidly GOP states. The only options the manager will need to focus on are getting a large share of the voters from your own identifiers and getting high turnout from your own identifiers. In simpler terms, make sure Republican voters support the candidate and get them to the polls. There is no need to worry about Democratic turnout or party loyalty, since there are vastly more Republicans than Democrats. In fact, in this scenario, there is not even any need to worry about independents. The same math works in states like Rhode Island or Massachusetts, only with Democrats as the dominant party.

BOX 2.1 Hypothetical Performances

Democratic House total = (.36)(.92) + (.28)(.39) + (.36)(.04) = 45.48%
Republican House total = (.36)(.07) + (.28)(.55) + (.36)(.95) = 52.12%

FIGURE 2.3A   Hypothetical 2010 Composition with 2012 Performance

Composition (Percentage)	Percentage of Votes for Barack Obama	Percentage of Votes for Mitt Romney
Democrats (36)	92	8
Independents (28)	45	50
Republicans (36)	7	93

Obama total = (.36)(.92) + (.28)(.45) + (.36)(.07) = 48.24%
Romney total = (.36)(.08) + (.28)(.50) + (.36)(.93) = 50.36%

FIGURE 2.3B 2012 Performance in Colorado

Composition in Colorado (Percentage)	Percentage of Votes for Barack Obama	Percentage of Votes for Mitt Romney
Democrats (34)	96	3
Independents (37)	45	49
Republicans (29)	5	94

Obama Colorado total = (.34)(.96) + (.37)(.45) + (.29)(.05) = 50.74%
Romney Colorado total = (.34)(.03) + (.37)(.49) + (.29)(.94) = 46.41%

FIGURE 2.3C Hypothetical 2010 Composition with 2012 Performance in Colorado

Composition in Colorado (Percentage)	Percentage of Votes for Barack Obama	Percentage of Votes for Mitt Romney
Democrats (36)	96	3
Independents (28)	45	49
Republicans (36)	5	94

Obama Colorado total = (.36)(.96) + (.28)(.45) + (.36)(.05) = 48.96%
Romney Colorado total = (.36)(.03) + (.28)(.49) + (.36)(.94) = 48.64%

FIGURE 2.4 2010 Share and 2012 Performance = Romney Victory

Party (Percentage)	Percentage of Votes for Barack Obama	Percentage of Votes for Mitt Romney
Democrats (36)	92	8
Independents (28)	45	50
Republicans (36)	7	93

The Case of Nevada

Let's consider how some recent elections in Nevada reveal that share and performance combined can, and often do, decide election results. In 2012, Barack Obama beat Mitt Romney by nearly seven percentage points in the state, but Democratic

Senate candidate Shelley Berkley lost to Republican Dean Heller by one percentage point, as over 85,000 people voted for the Democrat for president but not for Senate.[30]

Obama handily won Nevada because Democrats turned out in sufficient numbers and overwhelmingly voted for him, and independents (those not registered with either party) gave him enough support to give him a majority. Berkley lost because she failed to persuade Democrats and independents to support her at the same levels that they voted for Obama. Clearly, the campaign and the candidate mattered. The *Las Vegas Sun* reported that Heller crushed Berkley in rural counties by a 4–1 margin and that he was able to persuade some of Obama's voters to punch the hole for him, splitting their tickets, voting Democratic for president and Republican for Senate.[31] With a smaller turnout, Obama might still have prevailed but by a much tighter margin. Turnout clearly mattered, yet the persuasion activities of the Obama campaign were also crucial, spelling the difference between Obama's victory and Berkley's loss.

Now take the cases of Harry and Rory Reid in 2010. According to voter records, that year the composition of the Nevada electorate was less friendly to Democrats. They made up a slightly smaller proportion of the electorate compared to the 2008 and 2012 presidential electorates (41 percent, compared to 42 percent and 43 percent in the presidential years). At the same time, the 2010 midterm electorate in Nevada included a higher proportion of Republicans than it had during the presidential contests. Indeed, contrary to the wide advantages Democrats had in the partisan composition of presidential years, 42 percent of the electorate in 2010 was registered as Republican, and 41 percent was registered as Democratic.[32] Thus, in 2010, the electoral terrain was much less favorable to Democrats. There were two major statewide races in 2010. Both were won by comfortable margins.

But here's the wrinkle illustrating why the campaign can matter. One contest was won by a Democrat, and the other contest was won by a Republican. Embattled Democrat Harry Reid beat Republican Sharron Angle in his bid for reelection to the US Senate 50.3 percent to 44.5 percent, and Republican Brian Sandoval beat Reid's son Rory 53.4 percent to 41.6 percent to become governor.[33]

What happened? According to exit polls, in the US Senate race, Harry Reid won self-identified Democrats 91 percent to 5 percent and lost self-identified independents/others 44 percent to 48 percent, while, importantly, managing to win 11 percent of the self-identified Republican vote (compared to 84 percent for Angle). Reid's ability to mobilize Democrats, who overwhelmingly supported him, and persuade many independents and a disproportionate number of Republicans to vote for him was not matched by his son. While the father was able to keep Democrats in his column in overwhelming numbers, he was also able to persuade enough Republicans and independents to vote for him or against his opponent.[34]

With the same electorate, however, Rory Reid faltered. The son managed to win only 86 percent of self-identified Democrats (compared to 10 percent by Sandoval) and 32 percent of self-identified independents/others (compared to 60 percent by Sandoval). In contrast to his father's relative success with Republicans, Rory Reid was able to draw the support of only 4 percent of Republicans (compared to 92 percent by Sandoval), a figure that was even more important in 2010 than in presidential year elections because Republicans were accounting for a greater proportion of the electorate.[35] The fates of the two Reids show how candidates of the same party with the same electorates (and sometimes even with the same last names!) can draw vastly different vote shares.

The motivation of citizens to vote for candidates of different parties comes from evaluations of those candidates, and voter judgments come in no small measure from the persuasion activities of the campaigns. One difference was the quality of the Republican candidates squaring off against the father-son duo. Harry Reid's opponent, Sharron Angle, was a deeply controversial figure. She ran ads depicting Latinos as blights on Nevada and called for harsh crackdowns on undocumented immigrants. Harry Reid was able to turn the campaign into a referendum on Angle's qualifications for office as well as her views of such hot-button issues as immigration reform and Social Security.[36]

In contrast, Rory Reid's opponent, Brian Sandoval, ran a better, more inclusive campaign, and Rory Reid suffered because his last name reminded voters of his father, who was relatively unpopular at the time of the election. Republicans should have won both the gubernatorial and Senate races in 2010, but the persuasion and mobilization activities of Harry Reid's campaign (and Angle's flawed persuasion activities) enabled the father to survive the national Republican wave while his son went down to defeat.[37]

The exit polls from Nevada show that the difference in performance is partly due to how candidates are supported or opposed by independents. But it is also a function of how well they do with their own (and opponents') partisans. This is particularly important in nonpresidential elections, where independents historically make up a smaller proportion of the electorate. Higher partisan turnout can clearly help, but it should not necessarily be assumed that partisans will uniformly or universally support candidates of their preferred party, something that is made even harder when structural difficulties (such as lack of party registration) make finding likely partisans even trickier.[38]

Ask Al Gore if the Margin Matters

No presidential election was closer—and no result more hotly contested in recent times—than Gore's 537-vote loss in Florida to Bush in 2000. After 2000, does anybody think that Gore or Bush would ever say that marginal differences in the vote don't matter? Or that they don't affect election results, let alone the course of history? Virtually every campaign manager has been on the losing and winning sides of some narrowly decided elections. Although these contests were not as high profile as the Gore-Bush race, they were seared into the brains of the managers who ran the races, convincing them that marginal differences in performance and share, all structured by the fundamentals, absolutely were, and still are, the difference-makers in whether they lost or won.

The fact is, the Gore-Bush result was not even all that much of a freak occurrence, either. The political landscape is strewn with the names of would-be victors who lost by excruciatingly tight vote margins and sure winners who became ignominious losers. Gore and Kerry led Democrats to two bitterly close defeats in the 2000 and 2004 presidential races, while Republican Senate candidates experienced something similar when they lost where they should have won in Nevada and Delaware in 2010 and in Indiana and Missouri in 2012.

We saw how Sharron Angle fumbled in Nevada. In Delaware, a moderate Republican Michael Castle was well known and well liked by state voters and was widely expected to win the Senate seat before losing the GOP primary to Christine O'Donnell, a Tea Party candidate with a record of controversial remarks who was ultimately unacceptable to general election voters. In Indiana and Missouri, Republicans nominated right-wing candidates Richard Mourdock and Todd Akin. They talked flippantly and offensively to many about abortion and rape. They lost races in Republican states that the GOP were widely expected to win.

In Colorado in 2010, to cite another example, Republican Ken Buck stood a good chance of defeating Democrat Michael Bennet in a state that routinely elected Republicans statewide. They were running in a midterm election that favored Republican candidates nationwide. During the primary, however, Buck referred to Tea Party members as "jackasses." He urged a group of voters to support him "because he doesn't wear high heels" (a reference to Buck's defeated Republican primary opponent, Lieutenant Governor Jane Norton). In a very good year nationally for Republicans, Buck lost by less than 1 percent.

It's safe to assume that if we asked any of them—Buck, Mourdock, Akin, Gore, or Kerry (to name a few losing candidates)—and all of their campaign managers, that none of them would hesitate to say that the campaigns made a difference at the electoral margins and helped determine their fates. Actually, that might be the only thing they agree on. The vast majority of campaign managers believe that those campaigns that are able to alter even slightly one side's share (mobilizing one's partisans) and performance (persuading swing voters) can be decisive in highly competitive elections.

Kelly Evans, who managed Washington governor Christine Gregoire's 2008 reelection campaign, is a case in point. She worked for a candidate who in 2004 had won her election (after both machine and manual recounts) by an impossibly thin margin of 261 votes out of nearly 3 million votes cast.[39] Evans believed that 2008 was going to be a replay of 2004: Both Gregoire and her same opponent, former state senator Dino Rossi, were locked in a race that the polls showed to be dead even. But when Rossi said in a debate during the campaign's final weeks that he wanted to lower the state's minimum wage by $1.50 an hour because "it's not meant to be a family wage," Evans helped cut an ad that highlighted Rossi's remarks and sank his campaign. Gregoire notched a 6 percent victory, an uncommon example of a single moment that turned a neck-and-neck race into a clear victory. Evans reflected that the fundamentals combined with share and performance was decisive: "There are some things that sometimes influence campaigns that are larger

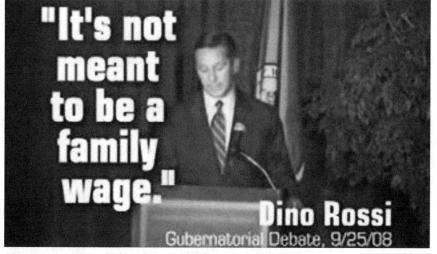

Christine Gregoire for Governor, 2008

"We knew we had struck gold," said the manager of Washington governor Christine Gregoire's reelection campaign after their opponent Dino Rossi said he wanted to lower the state's minimum wage by $1.50 an hour because "it's not meant to be a family wage."[41]

than the campaigns," such as "the economic condition of the country and the state. . . . But the candidates have to communicate what they will or won't do given all of those circumstances to people in a way that makes sense to them."[40]

In the end, the complex array of factors that determine election outcomes has implications for those running campaigns and students hoping to understand how campaigns matter. The three schools—fundamentals, share, and performance—all help to explain how candidates fight, win, and lose American elections. But none of these camps by themselves allows for a wide-enough telescope that sufficiently captures the complex angles and dynamics that constitute national election campaigns. In most races, campaign managers are targeting their side's own voters, seeking to persuade a small minority of swing voters, and trying to depress turnout or win votes from the other side. Their hope is to win an additional one or two percentage points—a small margin at first blush—but as Al Gore or John Kerry and countless losing congressional candidates and campaign managers well know, even a tiny margin can mean the difference between the Oval Office or a House or Senate seat and nothing.

Notes

1. J. Bognet, personal communication, June 11, 2013.

2. Gant Local News Team, "Nearly 8.5 Million Registered to Vote in PA," *Gant Daily*, November 2, 2012, http://gantdaily.com/2010/11/02/nearly-8-5-million-registered-to-vote-in-pa.

3. Pennsylvania. *270 to Win*, http://www.270towin.com/states/Pennsylvania.

4. M. Harris, personal communication, June 20, 2014.

5. J. Bognet, personal communication, June 11, 2013.

6. Jesse Singal, "Wait, Campaigns Don't Work?" *Boston Globe*, September 23, 2013, www.bostonglobe.com/ideas/2012/09/22/wait-campaigns-don-work/vuZ4ZrAL6xMIo2D9iyDsVO/story.html.

7. Paul Fahri, "Do Campaigns Really Change Voters' Minds?" *Washington Post*, July 6, 2012, https://www.washingtonpost.com/opinions/do-campaigns-really-change-voters-minds/2012/07/06/gJQAEljyRW_story.html.

8. Ibid.

9. John Sides and Lynn Vavreck, *The Gamble: Choice and Chance in the 2012 Presidential Election* (Princeton, NJ: Princeton University Press, 2013).

10. Diana C. Mutz, "The Great Divide: Campaign Media in the American Mind," *Daedalus* (Fall 2012): 83–97, https://www.amacad.org/multimedia/pdfs/publications/daedalus/12_fall_mutz.pdf.

11. Larry Bartels, "Obama Toes the Line," The Monkey Cage, January 8, 2013, http://themonkeycage.org/2013/01/obama-toes-the-line.

12. John Zaller, *The Nature and Origins of Mass Opinions* (Cambridge, UK: Cambridge University Press, 1992).

13. See James E. Campbell, "The Revised Theory of Surge and Decline," *American Journal of Political Science* 31, no. 4 (1987): 965–979; Steven Finkel, "Reexamining the 'Minimal Effects' Model in Recent Presidential Elections," *Journal of Politics* 55, no. 1 (February 1993): 1–21; Sunshine Hillygus and Todd Shields, *The Persuadable Voter* (Princeton, NJ: Princeton University Press, 2008); Michael D. Martinez and Jeff Gill, "The Effects of Turnout on Partisan Outcomes in U.S. Presidential Elections 1960–2000," *Journal of Politics* 67, no. 4 (2005): 1248–1274; William G. Mayer, "The Swing Voter in American Presidential Elections," *American Politics Research* 35, no. 3 (2007): 358–388; Jack H. Nagel and John E. McNulty, "Partisan Effects of Voter Turnout in Senatorial and Gubernatorial Elections," *American Political Science Review* 90, no. 4 (1996): 780–793; Samuel Popkin, *The Reasoning Voter* (Chicago: University of Chicago Press, 1991); Daron R. Shaw, *The Race to 270: The Electoral College and the Campaign Strategies of 2000 and 2004* (Chicago: University of Chicago Press, 2006).

14. Anonymous, personal communication, June 20, 2014.

15. T. Schulte, personal communication, November 9, 2011.

16. G. Shafer, personal communication, September 20, 2011.

17. K. Robertson, personal communication November 3, 2011.

18. M. Harris, personal communication, June 20, 2014.

19. R. Mook, personal communication, March 14, 2013.

20. Oregon Secretary of State Elections Division, "Voter Registration by County," December 13, 2010, http://sos.oregon.gov/elections/Documents/registration/nov10.pdf.

21. Oregon Secretary of State, "Official Results—November 2, 2010," http://sos.oregon.gov/elections/Documents/results/results-11-2010.pdf.

22. J. Ginsberg, personal communication, October 19, 2011.

23. William H. Frey, "Minority Turnout Determined the 2012 Election," Brookings, May 10, 2013, www.brookings.edu/research/papers/2013/05/10-election-2012-minority-voter-turnout-frey.

24. Ibid.

25. Ibid.

26. T. Schulte, personal communication, November 9, 2011.

27. CNN.com, "Election Center—Races and Results," http://www.cnn.com/election/2012/results/race/president.

28. John Sides, "There Is No Wave Coming in the 2014 Election," *Washington Post*, December 4, 2013, www.washingtonpost.com/blogs/monkey-cage/wp/2013/12/04/there-is-no-wave-coming-in-the-2014-election.

29. S. Rosenthal, personal communication, December 9, 2013.

30. CNN.com, "Races and Results—President," 2012, http://www.cnn.com/election/2012/results/state/NV/president. CNN.com, "Races and Results—Nevada Senate," 2012, http://www.cnn.com/election/2012/results/state/NV/senate.

31. Karoun Demirjian, "Heller Fends Off Berkley in Bitter Senate Race, *Las Vegas Sun*, November 6, 2012, http://lasvegassun.com/news/2012/nov/06/berkley-heller-battle-expected-be-closest-night.

32. Nevada Secretary of State, "Close of Registration Statistics—2010 General Election," 2010, www.nvsos.gov/index.aspx?page=794.

33. *New York Times*, "Election Results—Nevada," 2010, http://elections.nytimes.com/2010/results/nevada.

34. Ibid.

35. Real Clear Politics, "Nevada Governor—Sandoval vs. Reid," 2010, www.realclearpolitics.com/epolls/2010/governor/nv/nevada_governor_sandoval_vs_reid-1137.html.

36. *New York Times*, "Election Results—Nevada."

37. Real Clear Politics, "Nevada Governor—Sandoval vs. Reid."

38. Ken Goldstein, Matthew Dallek, and Joel Rivlin, 2014, "Even the Geeks Are Polarized: The Dispute over the 'Real Driver' in American Elections, *The Forum* 12, no. 2 (2014): 211–222.

39. Washington Secretary of State, "Elections & Voting," 2004, https://www.sos.wa.gov/elections/2004gov_race.aspx.

40. K. Evans, personal communication, September 20, 2011.

41. Ibid.

CHAPTER 3

Political Historian and Data Scientist

Charting a Path to Victory through Information and Analysis

> The whole is greater than the sum of its parts. When it comes to data, that's really true. . . . It's bringing together the quantitative and the qualitative that really is the strategic exercise. You've got to have both. It's the context along with the statistics that give you the best insight.[1]
>
> Laura Quinn, cofounder and CEO of Catalist, a leading data services provider to progressive organizations and candidates

Ever since precinct captains first made handwritten lists of how their neighbors were likely to vote, data has been the DNA of campaign strategy, shaping how campaign managers approach virtually every aspect of their jobs. Campaigns need access to data, research, and other forms of information to guide key decisions such as the candidate's message and the best ways to target the campaign's winning voter coalition. In order to answer the five questions on our campaign flowchart, managers must have access to data. Today's analytically enhanced voter files and computer models can be used to figure out in advance the people who are most likely to vote and for whom, and can suggest the best ways to mobilize and persuade them. Driven by technology, the amount of political data available to today's campaign managers has exploded. But the path to victory doesn't necessarily begin with "big data." More often it starts with mastering the recent voting history of the local political geography. As political pros often tell us, the best predictor of the next election is what happened in past elections.[2]

Tough Numbers in the Big Easy

Running Democratic senator Mary Landrieu's 2008 reelection campaign in Louisiana, Jay Howser had to figure out where his target voters in the state were living and how best to reach them. This wasn't a new question for Howser. The Landrieu campaign was actually Howser's second Bayou State race in 2008. Earlier in the year, he'd run a Democratic primary campaign for governor, but Howser's candidate had failed to make it to the runoff in Louisiana's unusual election system that pits Democrats and Republicans together in one big bipartisan primary.[3]

Howser had been doing campaigns for ten years and had learned that the voters in the next election didn't always look like the voters in the last election. That was certainly the case here in post-Katrina Louisiana. In 2005, Hurricane Katrina had displaced tens of thousands of Louisianans, including 9 percent of the African American population, and Landrieu's reelection bid was clearly going to be more akin to an off-balance three-point shot than an uncontested slam dunk. Like other southern states, Louisiana had steadily been trending Republican (so much so that by 2009 Louisiana Democrats would hold a minority of state and federal offices). Howser saw the trend and knew he had to have his numbers right if Landrieu had any shot of bucking it.

Landrieu had first won the seat in 2002 partly as a result of her opponent Rep. John Cooksey's slipup and not because she was such a strong candidate.[4] Cooksey had said during the campaign that "if I see someone's coming in and he's got a diaper on his head and a fan belt around that diaper on his head, that guy needs to be pulled over and checked."[5] Cooksey's campaign imploded, and Landrieu won easily.

Six years later, Landrieu was no shoo-in for a second term. She had championed charter schools, angering the state's teacher unions, a powerful Democratic constituency.[6] She had also crossed trial lawyers, who were among her party's most reliable sources of campaign funds.[7] But, as Howser noted, Landrieu had acquitted herself well in the aftermath of Katrina. "Every politician in the state except for Bobby Jindal and Mary Landrieu were vilified over Katrina," he recalled.

> And Mary's . . . effort post-Katrina . . . to help rebuild the suburban part of the community, but also New Orleans and just her constant presence on TV and her working to bring back funds for Katrina repair, . . . built an image of . . . someone who would stand up to the federal government [and] stand up to anybody to fight for Louisiana.

Still, Howser had to find a strategy and make a plan that would maximize the turnout for Landrieu and overcome some of the skepticism facing her in her own party. So he studied the data and did the numbers (see Box 3.1). He estimated that the African American vote would make up anywhere from 25 to 29 percent of the electorate. Landrieu had to win an overwhelming share of the African American

- Historical Louisiana parish (county) and precinct level election returns
- Pre- and post-Katrina lists of registered voters with voters' past election turnout behaviors
- Updated individual voter contact information collected by teams of Landrieu telephone and door-to-door canvassers
- Polling and focus groups to assess voters' candidate perceptions, issue positions, and current voting intentions

vote. In addition, Howser estimated, she would need to claim approximately 32 percent of the white vote in order to assemble a winning coalition. The Democratic nominee Barack Obama was polling 9 percent among the state's white electorate, so Landrieu had to more than triple Obama's performance among white voters. She also had to overcome suspicion of her record in an African American community that saw her as an unreliable ally.[8]

Howser helped her negotiate all of these landmines. To African Americans, Landrieu stressed her efforts to rebuild minority neighborhoods hit hard by Katrina. She reminded African American leaders that Landrieu's father, former New Orleans mayor Maurice Edwin "Moon" Landrieu, had hired African Americans on his staff and helped integrate the city. Working with Howser, she persuaded potential antagonists such as New Orleans Mayor Ray Nagin and ex-congressman Cleo Fields to campaign for Landrieu or not work against her.[9]

At the same time, Howser and his team sought to remind Louisiana's white voters that her positions were consistent with the policies they shared.

> We targeted the electorate. With older voters, I mean that obviously older white voters were scary because we knew they weren't going to be punching the card for Obama, so . . . a lot of our communication both on TV and radio was targeted towards older white voters and especially older white women. But they weren't separate. I mean, we called them, we ID'd them, we gave them messages, we knocked on their doors with messages about Mary. We ran radio ads that certainly were geared towards older white women. We ran negatives on our opponent that we knew older white women would respond to.[10]
>
> Jay Howser, campaign manager, Mary Landrieu
> for Senate 2008 (LA)

When the results came in and all of the Democratic wards had reported, the race was even. But then, the largely white Republican wards in southern Louisiana reported their results. Howser realized that they had voted for Landrieu in larger numbers than ever. When the final votes were tallied, Landrieu had increased her vote total by 58,000 over her 2002 victory. She had won 200,000 more votes than Obama received in the state, winning reelection by six percentage points.

Howser's estimates were dead-on. He had expected the African American vote to be between 25 and 29 percent; in fact, African Americans made up 27.5 percent of the total, up 6 percent over 2004 largely due to Obama's popularity in the African American community.[11] Landrieu took 96 percent of the African American vote.[12] At the same time, she won 33 percent of the white vote—one point more than Howser had hoped to win. Data science helped Howser and Landrieu lock up their core voters and reach persuadable voters. Howser had mapped the electorate, seeing what it would look like, well in advance of election day. Then, he helped his candidate mobilize and persuade those citizens to vote for Landrieu in sufficient numbers to retain her seat. In brief, Howser had charted the path that led to Landrieu's winning a second term in the Senate.

Like most campaign managers we interviewed, Jay Howser has statistical and data analytics skills that don't go beyond making Excel spreadsheets. Yet he and other campaign managers have learned how to use numbers to answer strategic questions and make decisions. Based on our research, the five big questions campaign managers most often ask and answer are shown in Figure 3.1. In this chapter, we take a first look at each question before revisiting them in later chapters of the book. In order to answer these questions, campaign managers must use data analysis and historical information to chart a path to victory.

Defining a Winning Coalition: Who Are Our Targets?

Although Howser knew how many votes Mary Landrieu needed in order to win, that's not always the case according to Republican campaign veteran David Carney. "You'd be surprised how many times I've asked candidates, managers, consultants how many votes they need on election day and they don't know," said Carney, a New Hampshire native who got his first political paycheck in college while working on John Sununu's unsuccessful US Senate campaign in 1980. "I mean, they can't give you a number, like 'I need 2 million and one votes out of the 4 million votes on election day from 7 million people registered to vote.'" Once the campaign knows that number, Carney said, they can then begin to break it down by groups of voters, such as Howser's 25 to 29 percent target from African American, and by smaller units of geography. Ultimately, the campaign can target individual voters on a computerized voter file.[13]

A large man whose physical appearance and personality is often compared to a bear, Carney followed up Sununu's 1980 Senate loss by working in Sununu's successful 1982 New Hampshire gubernatorial campaign. Sununu was an early supporter of Vice President George H. W. Bush's 1988 bid for the presidency. Carney went to work in grassroots field operations for the Bush campaign and remembers

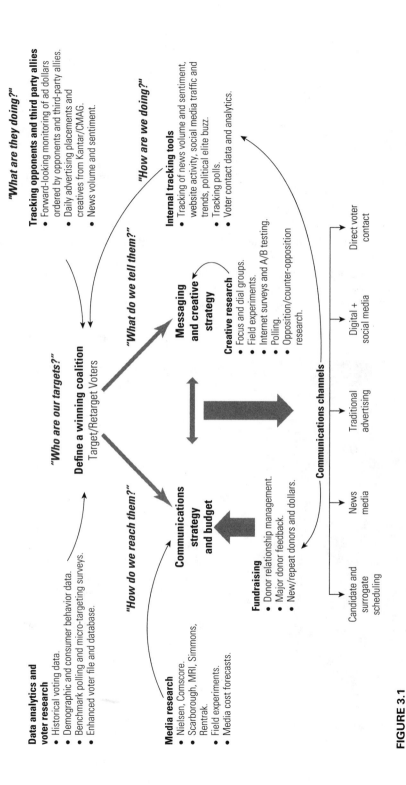

FIGURE 3.1

Five Big Questions Campaign Managers Ask

what state-of-the-art voter targeting looked like in those days. "The technology [now] is totally different, but even back then we did have a voter file," said Carney, who recalled collecting giant magnetic tapes from different state governments and delivering them to a mainframe computer facility somewhere on Long Island where the files were cleaned and formatted and phone numbers were added so volunteers could make canvassing calls. "That was really [all the data] you had." It was the big data of the day, and it came on very big reels of magnetic tape. "Today, there's infinitely more data, which is not necessarily better," observed Carney.[14]

After Bush defeated Michael Dukakis in 1988, Sununu was named White House chief of staff, and Carney moved up to the major leagues as the White House deputy political director with a large office in the Executive Office Building next door to the West Wing. Only 29 years old, Carney included in his office furnishings a 1960s era pinball machine, which would occasionally administer electric shocks to unwary visitors. It was in the White House political shop where Carney first began to learn about the politics of Texas, President Bush's home state where the capital Austin had a larger population than Carney's entire native state of New Hampshire. "Because of President Bush's interest in Texas, I spent a lot of time with Texas [while] at the White House," said Carney. "So I just basically ended up—you know, I knew a lot of

Dave Carney leaves the Texas State Capitol in 2006 while serving as the top political adviser to Republican governor Rick Perry.

Texans."[15] One of the Texans Carney got to know was political data junkie and strategist Karl Rove who during the 1980s and 1990s ran a successful direct mail and voter list company based in Austin. The two stayed in touch after President George H. W. Bush lost his 1992 reelection campaign to Bill Clinton. Carney went to work for Sen. Bob Dole, the Senate Republican leader from Kansas who was planning his own bid for the presidency in 1996. Carney gained more Texas experience when he helped Dole beat back a Republican primary challenge in the state from the more conservative Pat Buchanan. In the general election, Dole carried reliably Republican Texas but lost the national race to President Bill Clinton.

Carney, who had moved from Washington back to New Hampshire, got his big Texas political break in 1997 courtesy of Karl Rove. A Rove client named Rick Perry was the state's elected commissioner of agriculture and was planning to run in the Republican primary for lieutenant governor in 1998. Rove's top

Texas client was Gov. George W. Bush, who was running for reelection in 1998 and contemplating a 2000 campaign for president. "The story goes that Bush didn't want any of his consultants or folks working in the primary," remembered Carney, who said that the governor didn't want to appear to be indirectly endorsing one Republican candidate over another. "Karl [Rove] suggested Perry hire us for that race and I ended up working for Perry for almost 15 years," said Carney, who kept his home and family in New Hampshire while he commuted from Manchester to Austin on Southwest Airlines.[16]

In November, Carney helped guide Perry to a narrow two-point victory in the lieutenant governor's race while Governor Bush cruised to a thirty-seven-point victory. Two years later, George W. Bush was in the White House, Rick Perry was in the Texas governor's mansion, and Dave Carney was plotting Perry's 2002 reelection campaign.

The closeness of the 1998 race reinforced Carney's belief in the potential value of political data and analysis to add one or two or three percentage points in a tight contest. "You've got to prove that something works," said Carney. Knowing whether something worked and was worth the money would be particularly important to Perry in his 2002 reelection campaign. He would be running against Democratic millionaire businessman Tony Sanchez, and Carney feared that Governor Perry was likely to find himself in the unusual position of an incumbent who is outspent by the challenger.

That's exactly what happened. The Sanchez campaign outspent Perry by more than two to one, and their negative anti-Perry ads dominated Texas television. But on election eve, it appeared to Carney that none of it had made any difference. Perry had been reelected with a landslide twenty-point margin. "Does any of this fucking matter?" Carney was reported to have told a 2002 campaign colleague.[17]

In an interview with the authors, Carney said the 2002 experience convinced him to do something different with data when the governor ran again in 2008. In fact, what Carney did in 2008 was so different that it became the subject of a 2011 e-book, *Rick Perry and His Eggheads: Inside the Brainiest Political Operation in America*. The volume was Sasha Issenberg's prequel to the 2012 release of his authoritative *The Victory Lab: The Secret Science of Winning Campaigns*. The type of data analytics practiced by Carney and described by Issenberg has become increasingly prevalent in campaigns. The most advanced data arts are practiced at the national level as evidenced by the 2012 Obama employment ad in Box 3.2.

How Do We Reach Them?

Ask campaign professionals how they reach their target voters (see question number 2 in Figure 3.1), and most of them will start talking about television or digital advertising. Laura Quinn, who has spent her career working for Democrats and

BOX 3.2 The Highest Art of Political Data Analytics Takes Place in Presidential Campaigns

This is an online employment advertisement placed by the 2012 Obama reelection campaign:

We are looking for Predictive Modeling/Data Mining Scientists and Analysts, at both the senior and junior level, to join our department through November 2012 at our Chicago Headquarters. We are a multidisciplinary team of statisticians, predictive modelers, data mining experts, mathematicians, software developers, general analysts and organizers—all striving for a single goal: reelecting President Obama.

Using statistical predictive modeling, the Democratic Party's comprehensive political database, and publicly available data, modeling analysts are charged with predicting the behavior of the American electorate. These models will be instrumental in helping the campaign determine which voters to target for turnout and persuasion efforts, where to buy advertising and how to best approach digital media.

Our Modeling Analysts will dive head-first into our massive data to solve some of our most critical online and offline challenges. We will analyze millions of interactions a day, learning from terabytes of historical data, running thousands of experiments, to inform campaign strategy and critical decisions.

Responsibilities Include:

- Develop and build statistical/predictive/machine learning models to assist in field, digital media, paid media and fundraising operations
- Assess the performance of previous models and determine when these models should be updated
- Design and execute experiments to test the applicability and validity of these models in the field
- Create metrics to assess performance of various campaign tactics
- Collaborate with the data team to improve existing database and suggest new data sources
- Work with stakeholders to identify other research needs and priorities

Required Experience:

- B.S degree (M.S/PhD for scientist and senior positions) in statistics, machine learning, mathematics, quantitative methods, computer science, or related field
- Experience with political, Nielsen/Arbitron, fundraising or digital media & online advertising data
- Application of advanced statistical, machine learning, and/or data mining techniques (i.e. classification, clustering, association mining, forecasting), to real-world problems with massive data
- Experience with text data, search, natural language processing, social media analytics is a plus - we're also hiring for text mining positions
- Proven creativity and problem-solving skills

Required Software:

- Applicants must have demonstrated, extensive experience (professional or academic) with any major statistical or data mining package (R, STATA, SPSS, SAS, Enterprise Miner, Matlab, KNIME, Weka). Other desired software skills would include:
  o Any SQL-based query language (MySQL, PostgreSQL, etc.)
  o Programming skills desirable but not required for all positions (C#, C++, Java, Python, Ruby, Perl)
  o Strong MS Excel skills also desired

progressive causes, is different. She is more likely to talk about old-fashioned phone calls and door knocks instead of electronic media. For her, campaigns begin with making a list of voters and putting them in order from the most likely supporter to the least likely. "I really like to have all my lists lined up from the best guy down," said Quinn. "I'm calling my best prospect and working down the list."[18] When Quinn talks about phone calling and door knocking, she can sound old school and old-fashioned. She admits that some of the young Democrats she works with have compared her to Granny, the shotgun-toting, country-come-to-town character from the 1960s hit sitcom *The Beverly Hillbillies*.[19]

In fact, Quinn is far from being old-fashioned. She's the chief executive officer of Catalist, one of the country's most successful political technology and data agencies. The lists she talks about getting "lined up" are drawn from her data files that include almost every adult in America. Catalist's mission is "To provide progressive organizations with the data and services needed to better identify, understand, and communicate with the people they need to persuade and mobilize."[20] Headquartered in modest offices in downtown Washington, the firm's clients include Democratic candidates, Democratic campaign committees, and independent advocacy organizations that typically support Democratic candidates.

If Quinn is old-fashioned, it's her belief in the political power of direct contact, one of our five campaign communications channels (see Figure 3.2). Despite words like *cutting-edge* and *dynamic modeling* found on the Catalist website, Laura Quinn holds firm to the belief that "at the end of the day, the exercise is still an exercise in persuasion."[21]

Catalist provides data and analytics services to campaigns, civic organizations, and advocacy groups to get their message to broad target audiences, but in the end,

Candidate and surrogate scheduling | News media | Traditional advertising | Digital + social media | Direct voter contact

FIGURE 3.2

Communications Channels

Laura Quinn runs the Democratic data agency Catalist. Here is the company's mission statement: "To provide progressive organizations with the data and services needed to better identify, understand, and communicate with the people they need to persuade and mobilize" (http://catalist.us/about).

the data always points them toward individuals. Specific unique transactions like voting history, civic information, and commercial behavior all add up to understanding people and their participation in civic life, Quinn said.[22]

One of the biggest changes Quinn has seen in the past thirty years is the exponential growth in the amount of information available to political marketers. It has increased tremendously due to cheaper data processing and advances in technology, allowing political organizations, commercial entities, and companies like Catalist to listen and understand people in a more refined way. This change has given groups the capacity to target messages to subsections of populations in ways they never have before. However, Quinn said, "It requires more discipline now to personalize a message, but still to have it in service to a larger narrative. . . . You've got to be saying something in a way that meets them where they live and demonstrates you really have been listening to them."[23]

While this idea of personalization is not new to political campaigns, the capacity to do so has expanded not only horizontally to a greater number of campaigns but also deeper to a more minute, individual level. Today, state or party voter files can be augmented with door-to-door responses and then quickly categorized, all through the same company and program. Yet, Quinn said, "It's even more challenging now because the expectation of personalization has gone way up."[24] With continually clearer images of individual voters, all types of organizations have begun using these personal connections in marketing their products and ideas.

Even in the political off-season, Catalist keeps up with millions of personal political behaviors not only for nonprofits and advocacy groups still working but also to maintain an up-to-date universe of data—a feature that sets them apart from other voter file vendors who gather their database just before election cycles.

Nonetheless, Quinn made it clear that it is not data alone that carries you across the finish line but insisted, "You have to be able to ask the data the right questions. You have to see the numbers against the context." She continued to explain that advances in data storage and analytics isn't the end, but instead that, "bringing together the quantitative and the qualitative that really is the strategic exercise . . . that gives you best insight."[25]

From the first computers and fax machines in campaign headquarters, campaign managers have had to adjust and learn new technology and techniques to keep a clear path to victory. Yet, campaign managers across the country agree that it's the campaign that utilizes the combination of historical knowledge and cutting-edge technology that wins. Quinn recognized that there may be "a whole new set of tools" but that "ultimately the same sort of ability to bring qualitative context to the numbers . . . that's not going to change at all."[26]

What Do We Tell Them?

Mitch Daniels didn't want to waste money putting ineffective ads on televisions. Back in early 1983, Daniels—who would later become governor of Indiana and president of Purdue University—had just become the executive director of the National Republican Senatorial Committee (NRSC) and was charged with protecting the GOP's narrow majority in the US Senate. Daniels was looking for a way to test political television ads before they were aired. In the 1984 elections, Daniels would be responsible for allocating millions of television advertising dollars to Republican Senate campaigns across the country, and he wanted a research-based method for evaluating the countless TV spots that would be produced by campaign media teams in key Senate races. Daniels made it clear to Republican Senate campaign managers that he wouldn't release any money to air a spot unless it passed muster with his political ad testing system.

But first Daniels had a problem: In 1983, there was no systematic research methodology for testing political TV ads. Some campaigns, when they had the money or the time, would screen spots for focus groups of eight to twelve voters, but Daniels considered focus groups too subjective and unstructured. Watching the focus group behind a one-way mirror, the campaign media consultant could usually convince campaign management that their spots "would work" even in the face of negative feedback from group participants. Daniels wanted a less subjective approach and thought he could find his answer on Madison Avenue where large consumer advertisers used more rigorous quantitative methods to "copy test" alternative creative executions before they invested millions in a new media campaign. Copy testing methods were either "forced exposure" where ads were shown to people in groups or individually, or "in-home exposure" where test spots were aired in television programs followed by telephone interviews with those who said they had watched the program. Both methods had advantages and drawbacks, and a large consumer marketer was likely to use both of them.

To help develop and manage his new political ad testing program, Daniels hired Paul Curcio, a young Madison Avenue adman. Daniels and Curcio prepared requests for proposals (RFPs) and sent them to several consumer ad research firms as well as to some Republican polling companies. Looking at the responses, they first discarded the in-home exposure method because of the long turn-around time. It could take several days to arrange this kind of research, get the test ads on the air, and then conduct telephone surveys with target voters who might have seen the test ads. Political campaigns needed a much faster turn-around time than did consumer advertisers. Daniels and Curcio would have to go with forced exposure.

The winner of the contract wasn't located in New York City or Washington, D.C., but in Detroit, Michigan. Detroit was the home of Market Opinion Research headed by pollster Robert Teeter. Teeter's firm had just completed a successful 1982 focus group program testing ads for the National Republican Congressional Committee (NRCC). The NRCC methodology emphasized the use of preprinted questionnaires. Instead of beginning with focus group participants talking about ads they'd just seen, the NRCC focus groups started out with a written question-naire. Focus groups were given questionnaires with 0 to 100 thermometer scales printed on them. Participants used the scales to rate TV, radio, and print advertis-ing on believability, likability, information content, and on whether the ad would have a positive or negative impact on other viewers. Written questions asked what the main message of the ad was and allowed participants to comment on why they liked or disliked the ad. Other thermometers were completed before the groups began and after the groups were finished in order to measure shifts in attitudes that might be attributable to the advertising. No discussion or comments were allowed until the end of the sessions in order to keep participants from influencing each other.

Building on their 1982 experience, Teeter's Detroit ad test team won Daniels' and Curcio's 1983–1984 Republican Senate contract by proposing to take the newest data processing technology to each ad test site. The Compaq had just been released in the spring of 1983 and would become the first commercially successful portable computer. A statistician and computer programmer on Teeter's staff, Dr. James Leiman, wrote a custom data entry and data analysis program that would run on the Compaq and also on the IBM personal computers that were used at the NRSC Capitol Hill headquarters in Washington. Ad test participants would complete their written questionnaires. These would be immediately collected and manually entered into the traveling Compaq. The results would be assessed that night by Curcio and the ad test team and then the results delivered to Mitch Daniels at NRSC headquarters.

Paul Curcio, the ad tester, is now a political ad maker. He remembers that the NRSC tests were most useful for pointing out potential problem ads—the "dogs" that shouldn't be aired. Negative spots always received lower scores than posi-tive spots, although that didn't necessarily disqualify the spots from being aired,

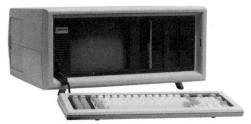

Evolving data technologies have enabled new political research methods. In 1983, the new portable Compaq computer made it possible for traveling Republican ad test teams to enter focus group data on-site, resulting in much faster turnaround times. Called a "suitcase computer," the Compaq weighed more than thirty pounds and relied on floppy magnetic disks for data storage.

This was followed in the mid-1980s by the development of the Perception Analyzer, a handheld dial device used by ad test participants. This eliminated the need for manual entry of paper questionnaires and gave researchers the ability to gauge moment-to-moment reactions to political television ads and radio ads.

Dials are still in use today, although the development of low-cost video streaming has made Internet ad tests a viable alternative to more expensive in-person advertising research.

particularly if the negative ad was seen as believable and people could remember the ad's message when they were telephoned to measure message recall after the tests.

One thing that quickly became apparent was that the ad makers weren't always big fans of the ad testing process, and Curcio said that's true today: "It may be mildly uncomfortable for the media consultant to have their client sitting behind the mirror and looking at the data and having these people respond poorly." Some media consultants feel that their judgment is more valuable than how fifty or so target voters respond to an ad in an artificial environment. "It's a threat to their power," said Curcio.

How Are We Doing?

"How am I doing?" was the well-known political slogan of three-term New York mayor Ed Koch, who would ask the question of city residents he encountered on sidewalks and subways.[27] Personal feedback—from voters, political activists, donors, and others—has always been offered to candidates and campaign staffers. Whether welcome or not, word of mouth remains a key source of political information, particularly for smaller campaigns that are unable to afford regular polling.

Word-of-mouth feedback has been augmented with the growth of the Internet and social media, which offer campaign managers new ways to continually monitor the vital signs of their campaigns. This can be as simple as tracking daily visits to the campaign website or watching the trend of online donations. Campaigns can tally and track positive and negative comments on Facebook, Twitter, and other social media platforms. More sophisticated methods involve the computer-assisted collection and analysis of tens of thousands of daily news items, commentaries, blog posts, social media interactions, and other content harvested from the Internet. This type of analysis increasingly is used by consumer marketers to monitor positive and negative "buzz" about their brands and can also be used by political campaigns that are able to afford it.

Polling remains the primary method used by campaign management to answer the "How are we doing?" question. While a consumer marketer can track daily sales volumes, the political marketer is left to ask a sample of voters, "If the election was being held today, would you vote for Candidate A or Candidate B?" Polls are a staple of American politics, and the hiring of a polling firm is seen as one of the most important decisions a candidate and campaign manager will make. Pollsters tend to be one of the first consulting hires in campaigns, and the relationship between pollster and candidate is comparable to that between a physician and a patient who asks, "Doctor, how am I doing?"

The pollster tells the candidate how they are faring in the head-to-head ballot matchup, but they must also be able to describe what voters know about the candidate and their opponent, whether they like or dislike them, and why. Pollsters test potential messages for or against a candidate; ask if the respondent has seen or read any news or advertising about a candidate; and collect data on the respondent's issue positions, demographics, and past voting behaviors.

The first campaign pollster of prominence was Lou Harris, who worked for over 240 political campaigns from 1956 to 1963, including the 1960 presidential campaign of John F. Kennedy.[28] In his 1992 book *The Superpollsters*, author David W. Moore says that the rise of the modern pollster actually began in the 1970s.[29] In those days, before the introduction of the personal computer, there were high barriers of entry into the polling business. A polling firm had to have its own mainframe computer, its own sampling department, its own phone facility, data entry department, and other support staff. As a consequence, there were only a handful of political pollsters. Democrats like Peter Hart and Pat Caddell along with Republicans Robert Teeter and Richard Wirthlin became campaign superstars known both for the accuracy of their data and for their sage ability to interpret the results to the political advantage of their clients.

More recently, political polling has fallen on harder times. As people have moved away from the use of the traditional at-home landline telephone, they have also become more reluctant to share their opinions with strangers.[30]

According to Dave Carney, traditional random selection polling methods are increasingly being supplemented by tracking a campaign's contacts with its targeted voter file. "Say you get 20,000 field reports a week, 20,000 or 30,000 online sign-ups a week, maybe 1,000 new donors a week," said Carney, talking about his work with Gov. Greg Abbott's campaign in Texas. On top of that, the campaign's pollsters did 1,000 weekly interviews with voters drawn from the voter file. "That's 50,000 to 60,000 new data points a week," said Carney. Based on the new data points, each week the campaign would run statistical models, called Monte Carlo simulations, to predict likely election outcomes. "Each week the models will get smarter," said Carney. In the closing weeks of the campaign, there were 1,000 interviews conducted each day with respondents drawn from the campaign voter file. The data let Carney know not only where they stood in the head-to-head ballot but also allowed them to target their volunteer contacts and messaging more effectively.[31]

What Are Our Opponents and Allies Doing?

To answer this question, campaign managers use what they often call competitive research or competitive tracking. Competitive research data can come from many sources, ranging from macro-data about advertising spending and ad occurrences down to microtracking what the opposing candidate says or does at their public campaign appearances.[32, 33]

"Competitive [research] used to be a lot simpler," says Brian Baker, remembering his first campaign job as a twenty-two-year-old junior aide in Senator Bob Dole's unsuccessful 1996 challenge to incumbent president Bill Clinton. "If we knew what the Clinton campaign and [Reform Party candidate] Perot campaign were doing, plus maybe the DNC [Democratic National Committee] and a couple of labor unions, that was pretty much the whole competitive picture."[34]

By 2014, the competitive picture was a lot more complicated and harder to see. At the time, Baker was running the Ending Spending Action Fund, one of the larger and more highly regarded super political action committees (PACs) that had sprung up across the country after a 2010 US Supreme Court ruling in the case of *Citizens United v. Federal Elections Commission*. The ruling made it legal for individuals, corporations, and unions to fund, out of their own pockets, unlimited independent expenditures relating to campaigns and candidates. These super PACs could run ads or do any of the other things the campaigns were doing themselves. The catch was that the independent super PACs were prohibited from communicating with a candidate or their campaign. Super PACs could, however, communicate with one another. The Ending Spending Action Fund was established in 2010 and initially funded by Joe Ricketts, a Wyoming resident and founder of Ameritrade, the online stock trading giant. Baker, an attorney, had served as the group's executive director since the group was launched.[35]

The proliferation of both Democratic and Republican super PACs by 2014 was making Baker's job more difficult. "Just like the other super PACs, we were tracking what everybody else was doing in sixteen or seventeen Senate and House key races," said Baker, who had to make recommendations about where and when the Ending Spending Action Fund should spend their money, primarily on television, radio, and digital advertising or on direct mail and direct voter contact operations.[36] To do this, Baker needed intelligence on where other super PACs and the campaigns they supported were spending or planning to spend their money.

Some of the information Baker could get by talking with the managers of other friendly Republican-allied super PACs. "I needed to know where the money was going," said Baker, who was looking for opportunities or "holes" where his super PAC might make a difference. To get a more detailed picture, he tapped into the informal intelligence network maintained by political media buyers and media sellers, like television stations, radio stations, cable operators, and digital media vendors. "One of the secrets of political advertising is that there aren't that many secrets," says Baker.[37]

Unlike consumer advertising spending, most political advertising spending is a matter of public record. Federal regulations have long required television and radio broadcasters to place political orders in their "public file." Local cable operators followed the same practice. In 2012, the Federal Communications Commission (FCC) mandated that television operators put their public files online.[38]

In fact, the political media industry was well ahead of the Federal Election Commission (FEC). For years, political ad sellers and buyers have used informal e-mail networks to collect and share information about the dollar amounts of orders placed. Since political media buys will ultimately become public information, media sales representatives for decades have shared the dollar amounts of Republican buys with Democratic media agencies and vice versa. The total dollar amounts of television and radio buys are available up to several days before the actual detailed order appears in the public file where reports must list the names of programs purchased and the cost of each spot. In the political media business, getting these early dollar spending estimates is known as getting "the competitive." Political media agencies compile competitive reports and provide them to their clients.

Competitive ad spending reports have joined polling as must-have daily information for campaign managers. "If the polls are the first thing you look at, competitive is the next thing," said Baker, who received daily e-mail reports of new ad spending. The proliferating number of political advertisers made the job more difficult in 2014. "In most of these big races there might be a dozen or more players [to track]," said Baker. The reports Baker received would break down spending amounts by media type and media market. "The forecasted spending amounts were always changing," said Baker. "For example, a candidate we were supporting might have only a light media buy in place for the next two or three weeks. So we would go in and start spending to help them and then suddenly another super PAC opposing our candidate would place a buy for the next two weeks and we'd have to rethink. It never stopped."[39]

Campaigns and their allied super PACs cannot directly communicate with one another. But they can indirectly signal what they are planning to do by placing media orders that will be picked up and circulated in competitive tracking reports. "Of course your opponents are going to see it too, but that's the way it's done these days," said Baker. The political press has gotten in on the competitive game, and reports of new media buys appear daily in insider publications like *Politico* and *National Journal*. Some campaigns try to game the system by placing large orders for future dates, hoping to generate favorable press. "Some [political advertisers] try to look bigger than they are by placing a large future order but they don't send a check," said Baker. "Unless you actually send money, the order doesn't mean [anything]. You can't reserve [political media time] without actually paying cash in advance."[40]

The Secret Ballot Problem

There is an apocryphal story that Haley Barbour, the former Mississippi governor and Republican National Committee chairman, tells about a small Mississippi town in the 1930s and 1940s when the South was solidly Democratic.[41, 42] The town prided itself on being solidly Democratic. In fact, in every recent presidential election, there had been only one single Republican vote cast in the whole town, but no one would confess they had done it and—thanks to the secret ballot—there was no way to find out. For years, speculation centered on the town's aging postmaster who had been appointed by Republican president Calvin Coolidge. Finally, the postmaster passed away. But when the next presidential election rolled around, the single Republican vote was still there. "Damn it!" said the town's Democratic mayor. "We've buried the wrong Republican."

The secret ballot is the foundation of American democracy, but it's a problem for campaign managers who are making voter targeting decisions. When someone votes in an election, the fact that they voted is recorded by election officials on the precinct voter rolls. While campaigns are able to see who did and did not turn out to vote in the past, they can never really know who they voted for. So campaigns are forced to make informed guesses. In the past, precinct captains made judgments based on their past conversations with their neighbors. Today, these predictive guesses are more likely to be made by a computer analysis of data drawn from voter data files that are either purchased from a commercial vendor or provided to a campaign by political parties and friendly political organizations.

At the core of virtually all the new techniques used in modern political campaigns is the voter file—lists of registered voters that contain the identities, contact information, demographic characteristics, and voting turnout history of virtually every registered voter in the country. Consider just a few examples of how campaign managers can use the voter file, bulging with data and information, for core campaign tasks: The voter file is the scaffolding of all the "big data" methods of modern campaigns. When it comes to microtargeting, campaign managers use models built off the voter file to prioritize certain voters over others for contact and to better allocate their resources. Furthermore, it is the source employed by on-the-ground field organizers to find and contact the chosen voters. And the file also plays a role in the massive juggernaut that is political advertising. Campaign professionals integrate vast amounts of information on television viewing habits with the voter file to provide insight for media buyers on which shows they should place advertising to target particular sets of voters.[43] And, finally, the voter file is used to help find the money to pay for all the things that campaigns must do. In other words, an analysis of a voter file may suggest that certain voters are not turnout targets, but that they may be ripe for fundraising appeals.

For the past decade, the two major national parties have also been working on assembling large databases with information about individual voters. These lists contain records of individuals, with information added in to describe their voting patterns and consumer habits. Oftentimes, parties will cold-call voters on their lists to determine whether they are Democrats or a Republicans and code them as such in their database. Other times, parties will look to see if a voter voted in an election that had, say, only a Democratic primary and make an educated guess that the voter in question is a Democrat.

Once the records are established, those voter entries can be merged with other publicly available information about them. For instance, if a voter applied for a hunting license, that voter might be coded as a "hunter" or put in a "pro-gun" category. If the state keeps a database of public teachers, a voter on that list might be coded as "pro-public education." One campaign manager interviewed for this book was surprised at the sheer number of categories included in his state's voter target list. His campaign, he said, was able to target motorcycle riders by assuring them that his candidate had fought a law requiring riders to wear helmets. Once all the information is merged into a master database, it can give campaigns a fairly accurate profile of a voter, so the campaign can tailor a message specifically to the voter's interests and preferences.

Looked at another way, campaign manager Jen Pihlaja said all campaigns need to rely on "research" from start to finish if they are going to find success. The data hat worn by campaign managers involves them learning "the patterns of what's happened in campaigns before and [about] the voters and the numbers," she added. All managers need to assess a candidate's strengths and flaws and figure out who will actually go to the polls. At every level, research and data is crucial, and nowhere more so than in presidential campaigns.[44]

Presidential and Congressional Campaigns: The Art and Science of Data Analysis

Since 2000, presidential campaigns have taken the use of data to unprecedented levels of precision. Ken Mehlman, President George W. Bush's 2004 reelection campaign manager, described how he and his team pioneered the use of "big data" in the presidential election process: In the early 2000s, Mehlman concluded that targeting certain demographic groups could add up to a winning coalition for the Bush campaign, and he used new tools to reach this goal and demonstrated the power of data-driven strategies.[45]

We used the 2002 election cycle as a giant laboratory for how we would identify more effective tactics, going forward. And it's one of the things that ultimately led to the use of essentially data analytics, which was, at the time, called microtargeting, which was very important to our success in 2004. And it also convinced us the importance of person-to-person, of me as your neighbor talking to you about the candidate, rather than relying simply on paid operations, paid calls or paid efforts. So the two critical pillars of the 2004 campaign, which was more precise targeting of voters, through all kinds of means including data analytics, big data, as they say today, and, secondly, mobilizing a giant army, or person-to-person persuasion, were much more effective than more anonymous persuasion, both were born out of the lessons we learned from 2000, that we thought we could do better in four years.[46]

Ken Mehlman, campaign manager,
George Bush for President, 2004

The result was indeed impressive. Bush became the only Republican since 1988 to win the popular vote for president. He won 27 percent of nonwhite voters, including 44 percent of Latino voters. Bush's performance among minorities exceeded the performance of past Republican candidates. By targeting these blocs, Mehlman helped chart the path that led to a second term for Bush.[47]

Data also shapes presidential campaign managers' decisions, as they ultimately are trying to reach the magic number of 270 Electoral College votes. The Electoral College is in some respects a math problem for campaign managers. The Electoral College grants the winning candidate in each state all of its votes (with the exception of Nebraska and Maine), and the number of electoral votes each state casts is equal to the number of US House seats plus US Senate seats a state holds. Thus, Wisconsin has eight congressional districts, plus two US senators, for a total of ten electoral votes. During the 2004 presidential campaign, Sen. John Kerry and President George W. Bush had 180 electoral votes apiece without campaigning (each of them easily lead in firm blue and red states).

In 2004, the most contested battlegrounds were Florida, Ohio, and Pennsylvania. Bush won Florida and Ohio, earning 286 electoral votes, but the margin was quite close. If Kerry had won 70,000 more votes in Ohio, he would have defeated Bush 272 to 262. Figure 3.3 represents the Electoral College map in the 2004 presidential election, while Figure 3.4 shows the even more razor-thin result in the 2000 contest between Bush and Vice President Al Gore. In that contest, the switch of a single state—New Hampshire, Tennessee, or Florida—would have made Gore the forty-third president.

Congressional campaign managers face their own set of data-related challenges. Relatively few House and Senate seats are actually competitive in any two- or six-year election cycle. Redistricting and incumbents' ability to raise money and bring infrastructure projects back to constituents give them an inherent advantage over their rivals, limiting the number of competitive congressional seats. Inside the national campaign committees, campaign managers and strategists are constantly using data to figure out which seats should be targeted in the next cycle so their side can reach legislative majorities in the Senate (51 seats) and in the House (218 seats).

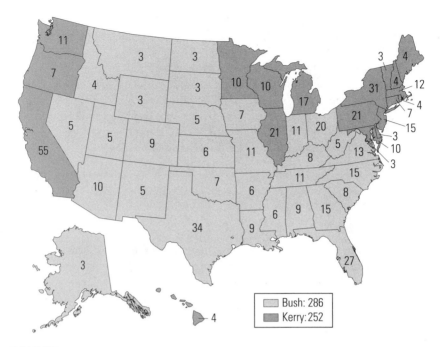

FIGURE 3.3

Electoral Votes by State Election Results, 2004

Ever since Republicans took control of the House in 1994, the partisan fight to control Congress has intensified, as numerous political scientists have shown. Both sides now know that the party switch of a handful of seats could change control of either chamber. The stakes are especially high in each race as a result of these tight margins.[48] Political analyst Charlie Cook created the Cook Partisan Voting Index, which rates the partisan makeup of each of the 435 congressional seats in America, revealing how razor thin the margins are. Rating a district's level of partisanship, Cook combines the voting patterns of past presidential elections in each district and then determines whether the district is safely partisan, moderately partisan, or a "toss-up." For instance, a district with a PVI score of D+2 means that in the 2004 and 2008 presidential elections, the district preformed an average of two percentage points more Democratic than the whole nation. A district is considered even if it performed within half of a percentage point of the national average.

Figure 3.5 illustrates a dearth of toss-up districts in any one congressional election cycle. With a mere two- to three-dozen House and Senate seats competitive during every two-year election cycle, campaign managers in the national committees search for other forms of information. They have to learn which

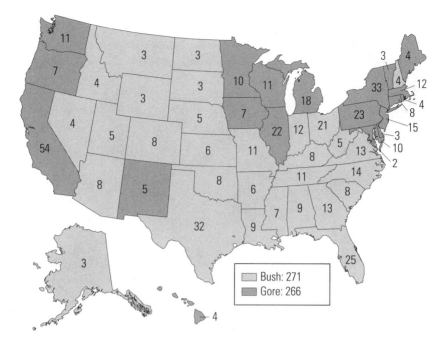

FIGURE 3.4

Electoral Votes by State Election Results, 2000

local and statewide media outlets are influential, which reporters and pundits have the most important platforms, which are the most important business interests, who are the most likely donors, which civic and nonprofit organizations including churches and synagogues are influential, and which organizations (local labor unions, Chamber of Commerce, and so forth) carry weight among key voting blocs.

Redistricting offers another dimension of the problem of data in the eyes of campaign professionals. Every ten years, seats are reapportioned based on new census figures. In the 2010 census, states that were traditionally more Republican or more moderate picked up more population and, thus, increased their share of congressional seats. In the most recent reapportionment, Texas gained four seats; Florida gained two; and Arizona, Georgia, Nevada, South Carolina, Utah, and Washington all gained one seat. Primarily cold weather states like Illinois, Iowa, Massachusetts, Michigan, Missouri, New Jersey, and Pennsylvania lost a seat. (Louisiana also lost a seat, primarily because of the exodus following Hurricane Katrina.) Ohio and New York lost two seats apiece. Table 3.1 shows the changes in the number of House seats as a result of the most recent redistricting plan.

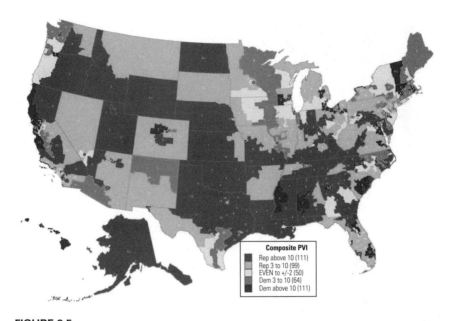

FIGURE 3.5

Cook Partisan Voting Index for the 111th Congress

Source: Composite PVI based upon the average for the 2004 and 2008 elections. Districts of the 111th Congress (2008 General Elections), April 2009. Data from Polidata ® Demographic and Political Guides.

TABLE 3.1 **Apportionment Population and Number of Representatives, by State, 2010 Census**

State	Apportionment Population (April 1, 2010)	Number of Apportioned Representatives Based on 2010 Census	Change from Census 2000 Apportionment
Alabama	4,802,982	7	0
Alaska	721,523	1	0
Arizona	6,412,700	9	+1
Arkansas	2,926,229	4	0
California	37,341,989	53	0
Colorado	5,044,930	7	0
Connecticut	3,581,628	5	0
Delaware	900,877	1	0
Florida	18,900,773	27	+2

State	Apportionment Population (April 1, 2010)	Number of Apportioned Representatives Based on 2010 Census	Change from Census 2000 Apportionment
Georgia	9,727,566	14	+1
Hawaii	1,366,862	2	0
Idaho	1,573,499	2	0
Illinois	12,864,380	18	-1
Indiana	6,501,582	9	0
Iowa	3,053,787	4	-1
Kansas	2,863,813	4	0
Kentucky	4,350,606	6	0
Louisiana	4,553,962	6	-1
Maine	1,333,074	2	0
Maryland	5,789,929	8	0
Massachusetts	6,559,644	9	-1
Michigan	9,911,626	14	-1
Minnesota	5,314,879	8	0
Mississippi	2,978,240	4	0
Missouri	6,011,478	8	-1
Montana	994,416	1	0
Nebraska	1,831,825	3	0
Nevada	2,709,432	4	+1
New Hampshire	1,321,445	2	0
New Jersey	8,807,501	12	-1
New Mexico	2,067,273	3	0
New York	19,421,055	27	-2
North Carolina	9,565,781	13	0
North Dakota	675,905	1	0
Ohio	11,568,495	16	-2
Oklahoma	3,764,882	5	0

(Continued)

TABLE 3.1   (Continued)

State	Apportionment Population (April 1, 2010)	Number of Apportioned Representatives Based on 2010 Census	Change from Census 2000 Apportionment
Oregon	3,848,606	5	0
Pennsylvania	12,734,905	18	−1
Rhode Island	1,055,247	2	0
South Carolina	4,645,975	7	+1
South Dakota	819,761	1	0
Tennessee	6,375,431	9	0
Texas	25,268,418	36	+4
Utah	2,770,765	4	+1
Vermont	630,337	1	0
Virginia	8,037,736	11	0
Washington	6,735,369	10	+1
West Virginia	1,859,815	3	0
Wisconsin	5,698,230	8	0
Wyoming	568,300	1	0
TOTAL APPOINTMENT POPULATION*	309,183,463	435	

Source: US Department of Commerce/US Census Bureau.

*Includes the resident population for the fifty states, as ascertained by the Twenty-Third Decennial Census under Title 13, United States Code, and counts of overseas US military and federal civilian employees (and their dependents living with them) allocated to their home state, as reported by the employing federal agencies. The apportionment population excludes the population of the District of Columbia.

Targeting and Microtargeting

Against these macro forces that structure presidential and congressional campaigns (among other races), campaign managers must find the best tools and make the best use of data to target their core voters with campaign messages. Nowadays, campaign managers are debating the impact of microtargeting and various other targeting tools. Some managers argue that technological advances empower them to send specific and highly personalized messages to particular segments of the electorate in more efficient ways than ever. Managers can thus appeal to voters' highest priorities on a whole range of issues. Jarryd Gonzales, the George W. Bush victory coordinator in 2004 (CA), says microtargeting has enabled campaigns to slice the electorate into such granular detail that he can reach specific voting blocs with messages tailored to their passions.

Before microtargeting, most campaigns would send voters direct mail with the following mind-set: "This is a Republican Primary, we have limited resources to identify voters by issue, so let's blanket the district with a 40,000 piece pro-life or antitax mailer."

The problem with that mind-set is that it is terribly flawed. Not all Republicans care about that issue enough to actually motivate voters to go to the polls. Microtargeting dramatically improves the way campaigns talk to voters. By overlaying voter history and consumer marketing data, a campaign can look at the same 40,000 voters and find clusters of them that are grouped together by issues they care about. Based upon this data, campaigns can send direct mail to voters that will connect with them personally. Microtargeting can be expensive, but so is not communicating effectively with voters. In the end, the cost to acquire a vote will be less if a campaign is armed with better ways to connect with voters.[49]

Jarryd Gonzales, victory coordinator,
George W. Bush for President, 2004 (CA)

Julie Petrick, who ran Gary Peters' 2008 campaign for Congress in Michigan, underscores the increasingly data-driven nature of voter targeting:

We ran a really aggressive direct voter targeting program on both the paid and volunteer sides. And we started very early. One of the tools we used to identify our targets for the field program was the VAN (Voter Activation Network), which was populated with data from the Michigan secretary of state. It was a presidential year, so we knew we wanted to communicate to Democratic voters and make sure they voted down the ballot for our candidate.

Gary had been in the state senate, and he had run for attorney general, losing statewide by less than 5,000 votes. And then he had been lottery commissioner for seven years. So he definitely had a strong presence among Democratic voters. But considering we were trying to unseat a 16-year incumbent, we needed to communicate with a large bloc of persuadable voters. So we targeted a considerable part of our grassroots effort, which was door-to-door canvassing and phones, to those persuadable voters. That program started very early—we started building it in February, and we were out knocking on doors consistently from March to election day.

In 2004, we used an Access database to manage the local voter file—and we blew up maps on copy machines. Then in 2005 and 2006, we walked door-to-door with Palm Pilots. But back then, different states were using different technology to access their individual voter files. Now we have a national voter file and the VAN, which cuts its own turf and targets its own maps. So in less than a decade, we went from blowing up driving maps on a copy machine to using a national voter file that you can access from your iPhone.[50]

Julie Petrick, campaign manager,
Gary Peters for Congress, 2008 (MI)

During his candidate's run for a California Assembly seat, campaign manager Erik Weigand targeted "high propensity" Republican voters during the primary. These included social conservatives and voters opposed to immigration reform. The specific nature of the campaign messages targeted to receptive audiences helped Weigand's candidate sail to victory. Targeting decisions depend on available resources, the coalition campaigns hope to create, and the balance of persuadable and base voters they are trying to bring to the polls. Weigand's assembly campaign also focused on the area where the candidate had been a country supervisor and a retirement community led by an enthusiastic backer of Weigand's candidate. Weigand estimated that voters in both communities voted ten to one for his candidate.[51]

Not all campaign managers see microtargeting as the Holy Grail of modern politics, however. Republican manager Kelly Evans, who ran Washington governor Christine Gregoire's 2008 reelection race, doubts that microtargeting is the omnipotent tool that others describe. She argues that the amount of information out there about each voter is a little "creepy," adding that consumer habits are fundamentally different from voter interests and not necessarily useful when mobilizing and persuading an electorate. Under her theory, the practice of voting is far different from convincing customers to buy a commercial product such as Coke or Burger King french fries.

It's just like all the modeling and microtargeting and stuff that's out there now, like you know, you can figure out that people who move the easiest for your candidate are people who, you know, own guns and have pets. Well, that's great. But how are you going to find people who own guns and have pets? They're not traditionally on the big voter files that we have access to, right? I mean, it's really interesting that you can take commercial data and layer it over a voter file and do a big modeling microtargeting survey and stuff, and all that stuff's really super fascinating, but unless you can find that voter and tell them why they should vote for your candidate, it's irrelevant. And I just think campaigns get sometimes lost in all of the new bells and whistles. And it's one thing to market a product to people based on all that stuff. It's another thing to sell a candidate. And people make their voting decisions differently than what kind of peanut butter they're going to buy.[52]

Kelly Evans, campaign manager,
Christine Gregoire for Governor, 2008 (WA)

Campaign managers also must contend with the challenge of data originating in social and digital media, and this terrain is shifting yearly and shaping campaign managers' strategies and approaches. Campaigns are having trouble keeping up. Ever since Obama's 2008 presidential campaign, it's become increasingly clear that e-mail is an effective fundraising tool. E-mail can target core supporters with emotional, urgent appeals for funds at a moment's notice. The Obama campaign ran experiments to see which e-mail subject lines would raise the most money ("I will be outspent" won, raising more than $2.5 million). But now some campaign managers believe that the next step for digital and social media will be to improve field operations and increase each side's share of the vote. Rather than physically going door-to-door to turn out one's voters, campaigns will rely on digital media and data to mobilize and persuade key supporters to go to the polls. Steven Law, Mitch McConnell's 1990 Kentucky Senate campaign manager, describes the impact of digital media on "retail level politics."

I think it enjoyed a renaissance during the Bush years with the emphasis on microtargeting techniques and door-to-door outreach. The Obama reelection campaign added a sophisticated social media overlay to that. Even with the industrial strength of mass communications, there always needs to be a place for reaching the individual. Both technology and our culture are leading us to look at the electorate in much more sophisticated and nuanced ways. The culture itself is creating many new and different flavors of people. It used to be that what you needed to know is somebody was a Republican from a certain region of the country or a Democrat from another region of the country. Now the demographic distinctions are vastly more significant and the party labels are becoming much less significant. Not only do you have cultural developments that make the electorate more interesting—I don't want to use the word *Balkanized* because that sounds negative—but people are divided among lots of different lines. At the same time, new technologies and data techniques enable you to get a much closer look at these different kinds of voters and focus unique messages on them.[53]

Steven Law, campaign manager,
Mitch McConnell for Senate, 1990 (KY)

But there's no consensus. Steve Bell, who ran Heather Wilson's campaign for Congress in 1998, says basic campaign strategies and tactics remain essentially unchanged by social and digital media advances. The key to winning an election, he said, still requires "find[ing] every person who'll vote for you, identify that person precisely, and make sure that person gets to the polls. Not much has changed."[54]

Targeting voters by party identification and organizational membership presents another kind of data-related hurdle facing campaign managers. Bell recalled, for example, how Wilson's campaign persuaded the NRA and anti-abortion groups to support her candidacy—and to help her win the primary.[55]

> We were able to reach [them] because of Sen. Pete Domenici's record and because they had always supported Domenici overwhelmingly in the past. But [for] the rest of it, we went through voter lists, and we went through people who tend to vote in primaries . . . Republican primary—people who cared about the primary. We went through . . . we had the support of the state party, we had the support of the county party, because most of her district is Bernalillo county, not all of it, but most of it. . . . This was an act of will. This was not an act of genius.[56]
>
> Steve Bell, campaign manager, Heather Wilson
> for Congress, 1998 (NM)

Focus Groups, Polls, and Other Forms of Information Gathering

In order to assemble a winning coalition, campaign managers also rely on metrics generated from focus groups, public opinion surveys, opposition research, and other sources of information. The insights gleaned from these sources guide campaign strategies and voter outreach efforts. Democratic campaign manager Jen Pihlaja argued that interviews conducted with small groups of voters, especially those who are undecided, independents, and of various ages and backgrounds—focus groups—yield invaluable qualitative information that inform her campaign recommendations. It is useful, she said, when voters watch visual clips of her candidate or view campaign advertisements that have not yet aired. She can learn how voters perceive her candidate and the opposition candidate, how effective particular messages are, and gain a window into the minds of persuadable voters, who are among the most crucial audience in a lot of close elections. Pihlaja described how findings from focus groups have helped her present her candidates in a more positive light and figure out how much to use the candidate to communicate with voters directly. In brief, the results of focus groups enable her to maximize the impact of the campaign's message.[57]

While consultants, pollsters, field operatives, and other political specialists tend to be well represented on the typical campaign for high office, the campaign "manager has to be in charge" of the flow of information and the personnel, said Democratic campaign manager Martha McKenna. McKenna, who started as a campaign manager at EMILY'S List, which seeks to elect women leaders to public office, described polls as even more useful than focus groups, and said that finding a top-tier pollster is one of the most crucial tasks facing campaign managers. Polls, she argued, help campaign managers analyze candidates' strengths and flaws, give managers snapshots of a candidate's unfavorable and favorable ratings, measure popular views of their job performance, and reveal head-to-head matchups. Most managers prefer to see a series of polls showing trends over time (rather than seeing a single snapshot in a particular moment), and campaigns now are even using automated dials to test candidates' pluses and minuses.[58]

Not all campaign managers see as much value in public opinion surveys, however. Jim Bognet, who ran David Dewhurst's 2012 Senate campaign in Texas, cautioned about internal campaign polls conducted by the campaign's pollster:

[They] can be frankly so misleading. You know, in the US Senate race, my candidate for twelve or thirteen months of the election was always ahead, but yet he ended up losing the runoff because, among other things, some candidates that are not politically savvy candidates don't know how to read the whole poll. You know, the topline numbers only show you where you are, not where you're going. So my candidate saw that he was ahead, was complacent about it, not realizing that the internals showed really bad stuff in the outlook. So I would say that oftentimes polling is misread, by the candidate especially, and it has a very deleterious effect. Polling can unfortunately show the width of support instead of the depth, and unfortunately give a lot of false positives to candidates and cause them to be complacent.[59]

Jim Bognet, campaign manager,
David Dewhurst for Senate, 2012 (TX)

California-based campaign manager Erik Weigand suspected that one pollster under him had asked leading questions that wound up creating the false appearance that their candidate was performing better than he really was. When polls find unexpected nuggets of data, they often force campaigns to shift their strategy. During one of his races, Weigand received polling that revealed a tighter contest than had been foreseen, and this result, he said, "brought . . . a little bit more . . . attention to the race" and lit a fire under the candidate and his team.[60]

Research also helps campaign managers craft their messages and decide how to spend the campaign's limited resources. Indeed, Weigand observed that one of the most crucial pieces of information was "any dirt on other candidates. . . . Most of the research that we did was on just strictly going after our opponents, trying to find out any dirt." One of Weigand's campaigns discovered that its opponent had voted to raise taxes, while claiming that the vote occurred late at night and he didn't know what he was voting for. The research led to an effective line of attack: their opponent became "a sleepy" politician who was unable to "focus when it's too late."[61]

Campaign managers with a deeper, more sophisticated research effort tend to have the upper hand over their rivals. Research involves not just studying up on the other side's vulnerabilities but also coming to grips with one's own weaknesses. Candidates are typically uncomfortable with the idea of having others sort through their potential weaknesses, and some campaign managers we interviewed were themselves reluctant to go on the record about examples from a specific campaign in which they had been involved. The process can often require negotiation between the candidate and their manager and sometimes can involve lawyers, accountants, and others familiar with the candidate's personal lives. Candidates need to be assured that the counter-opposition research dossier or "self-book" is necessary to help their campaigns prepare for and parry attacks from their political opponents.

A "self-book" was especially important to Jeb Bush's successful 1998 campaign for Florida governor. This was Bush's second try for governor. In 1994, the Democratic candidate Lawton Chiles had unleased a series of attacks on Bush's business career and investments. Anticipating more of the same in 1998, campaign manager Sally Bradshaw and a team of researchers prepared a detailed pre-campaign document that catalogued likely attacks and responses, along with supporting documentation. "How do we build a sort of firewall for him on those issues?" said Bradshaw. "We spent a tremendous amount of time." [62]

Determining Voter Blocs

As the electorate grows racially and ethnically more diverse, campaign managers increasingly rely on assembling key constituencies to form winning coalitions. In the 2008 Colorado Senate race, Democrat Mark Udall's campaign manager placed a premium on turning out Latino voters for his side. In order to push the Latino vote up so that it became 9 percent of the electorate, Udall's campaign manager hired Latino staffers, sent out postcards in Spanish, and campaigned in Latino neighborhoods. Conversely, Udall's opponent, Republican Bob Schaffer, made no such attempt to court the Latino vote, which some GOP campaign managers believe is an untapped pool of potential Republican voters. Prominent Hispanic Republicans urged Schaffer to target Latino votes. But Schaffer, thinking his stances on taxes and education would naturally appeal to Latinos, refused.[63]

The results on election day underscored how data and voter turnout intersected to assemble a winning coalition. Udall carried Latino voters by a 63 percent to 30 percent margin.[64] Further, 123,000 more Latinos voted in Colorado than in 2004, a jump of 70 percent. Udall won by 240,000 votes statewide, with nearly 32 percent of his victory total coming from Latinos showing up to vote for the first time.

Barack Obama's 2004 Senate campaign manager James "Jimmy" Cauley was recruited partly because of his record of success in knitting diverse constituencies into victorious electoral coalitions. Cauley helped elect the first African American mayor in Jersey City in 2001, a city that was roughly one-third white, one-third African American, and one-third Latino. He recalls Obama's chief strategist, David Axelrod, assuming that Cauley could navigate black Illinois politics while reaching out to non-African American voters, too. Targeting segments of the electorate proved invaluable to Obama's candidacy. Obama was running in a congested seven-person primary, so Cauley's goal was to win about 35 percent of the vote, including 23 to 25 percent of the African American vote, while drawing the rest of Obama's support from college-educated white women and liberals living in Chicago's North Shore and "the collars." Hitting these targets would have led to a runoff where Obama, Cauley hoped, could be expected to prevail. But Cauley's plan was over-taken by events on the campaign trail. Facing a formidable self-funded candidate in Blair Hull (who was spending $32 million of his own money on his campaign), Obama had a stroke of luck: Records of Hull's divorce became public shortly before election day, and Hull's campaign never recovered. Obama took 53 percent of the primary vote, winning the nomination outright; in a Democratic state such as Illinois, he now had a clear path to winning a seat in the US Senate. Though they benefited from the accident of timing and the contents of the divorce records, Cauley's plan—to bring African Americans, Hispanics, white women, and liberals into Obama's camp—succeeded.[65]

Using data to target blocs of the electorate also means sending different messages to different people in different geographic regions. This can be tricky when trying to drive out the candidate's base, as not all members of a specific party might see eye to eye with other factions within the same party. As one Colorado political operative put it, the more bohemian, environmental liberals in Boulder may be completely different from the blue-collar, pro-union Democrats who populate a city like Pueblo. In states with a number of large cities, it is possible to send different messages to different media markets, but this, too, requires segmenting the state and sending distinct messages into distinct markets. This was a strategy employed in 1994, when Lawton Chiles ran for Florida governor and targeted voters by region. Here, too, data shaped the campaign manager's decision-making process.

Florida's a big state, and we broke down a lot of our advertising by geographic region. And clearly the tone and the message in the north Florida campaign, although always consistent, were very different than the way we'd do it in south Florida. I mean, we had Sam Nunn, the senator from Georgia, and lots of people like that doing testimonials for Chiles on the north Florida televisions. And in south Florida, it would be much more urban-centric focus in terms of what our message was. I mean, in Florida, whether it's a luxury or a burden, you have the ability to talk about several different things in several different markets.[66]

Karl Koch, Lawton Chiles for Governor, 1994 (FL)

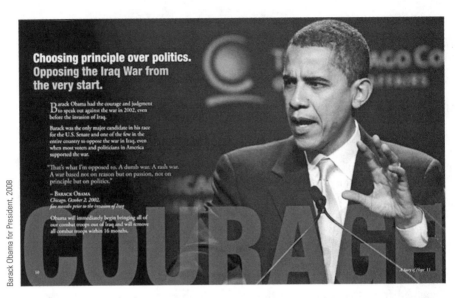

Choosing principle over politics. Opposing the Iraq War from the very start.

Barack Obama had the courage and judgment to speak out against the war in 2002, even before the invasion of Iraq.

Barack was the only major candidate in his race for the U.S. Senate and one of the few in the entire country to oppose the war in Iraq, even when most voters and politicians in America supported the war.

"That's what I'm opposed to. A dumb war. A rash war. A war based not on reason but on passion, not on principle but on politics."

– BARACK OBAMA
Chicago, October 2, 2002,
five months prior to the invasion of Iraq

Obama will immediately begin bringing all of our combat troops out of Iraq and will remove all combat troops within 16 months.

In 2007, Barack Obama used this mail piece in New Hampshire to stress his opposition to the Iraq War.

Koch further mentioned that at the end of the campaign, Chiles brought in both African American and Hispanic consultants to make sure the campaign was properly targeting those groups. That year, Chiles defeated future governor Jeb Bush by barely more than 1 percent.[67]

Aside from tailoring mass media messages for specific groups (there is a full chapter in this book about advertising targeting) and going door-to-door, campaign managers can use the Internet, direct mail, and mass phone calls (i.e., "robocalls") to target voters. According to China Gum, campaign manager for Raul Labrador for Congress, direct mail is the best targeting tool, as it can be tailored and mailed very specifically. "Direct mail is my preferred method of voter contact," Gum said. "It's effective and efficient, as the campaign can target particular groups with a more defined message."[68]

Direct mail is usually done through a mail vendor, which will help design the piece and mass mail it. Sometimes, a campaign may want to obtain its own postal mailing code in order to receive cheaper bulk rates; other times, a mail vendor will simply use their code.

One longtime campaign manager suggested doing direct mail early in the campaign, to cut through the clutter:

> I'm a huge direct mail fan, but I'm also a huge microtargeting fan. I like getting mail that's tailored to me. I like seeing that you may be Obama or you may be Bill Nelson, but that you realize that I'm in north Florida.

I'll give you an example. It was a statewide, but I had regional mail pieces that were trying to build a hospital. You find an issue that has regional appeal. And in north Florida, there was this big issue in these seven particular counties about trying to have a regional medical center. Well, we mailed those seven counties about that issue. Nobody six counties away gives a rat's butt about it, but it mattered to those seven counties. It takes time. It's work. It may cost you a little more.

Or maybe it's point number one and point number two are the same issue around the state, but point number three—it is a regional point. So you're doing a gang print. But point number three is different on this set other than that one, you know. But even more than that, and what I'm saying to you is more theory than I ultimately practice because sometimes the hassle of it becomes too much. I love early direct mail. I do not like late direct mail when every judge candidate, every mosquito district candidate's in the mailbox.[69]

Screven Watson, Rod Smith for Governor, 2006 (FL)

As discussed earlier in this chapter, targeting voters through the Internet is much more art than science—and it's likely to remain that way for the foreseeable future. Large search engines are just beginning to explore the ways specialized content can be delivered to viewers:

[Campaigns are] getting a lot better at targeting people on the Internet. Before, I feel like it was more of a buckshot. And now, it's a pinpoint shot at certain demographics and whatnot.

When you think about it, I don't think it would be long before you see campaign ads on Hulu, you know? I actually recently opted not to buy cable at my apartment. I just have broadcast TV and I've got an Xbox that streams Hulu through it. So I can watch my shows on Hulu and I'm getting the same sort of commercials as television. There's not a wide variety of commercials on there and I don't think it'll be long before we start seeing more people spending money on commercials on Hulu and you start seeing political campaigns putting commercials on there.

Michael Sullivan, Patrick Hughes for US Senate, 2010 (IL)

Finally, campaign managers can deploy robocalls in which a company is paid to automatically dial voters and leave a voice message with them. These prerecorded messages are oftentimes notable people supporting a candidate's campaign—such as Bill Clinton endorsing a Democratic candidate. Some campaign managers, however, think robocalls are a nuisance to voters and can backfire:

> Robocalls are dead 30 days out, maybe 45 days out. Just don't even use them. People are pissed they're getting so many of them. And that's not just the urban areas. Now it's more event-driven. It's more "push 1 if you'd like to be on an email list" or get a polling sample. I'm trying to collect data.
>
> It's a waste of money unless it's Bill Clinton or Bono or some rock star. I still get seniors [who say], "You're not going to believe who called and left me a message." Really? Bill Clinton called you today? Jesse Jackson. Yeah, you know, and the candidates cannot exist without them.[70]
>
> Screven Watson, Rod Smith for Governor, 2006 (FL)

Get Out the Vote

At the same time, data serves a purpose in the final days of a race when campaign managers set their sights on getting out the vote—colloquially known as GOTV. Once campaign managers have identified the groups they want to mobilize, they then need to persuade those specific voters to show up at the polls. Years have passed since Thomas Jefferson once turned out his voters by providing them with beer. Campaign managers above all prefer volunteers and campaign workers actually seeing voters and bringing them to the polls. Matt McDonald, who worked on Elia Pirozzi's California congressional campaign in 1999, wants his campaign to physically turn out 10 percent of their entire vote:

> I do campaign schools now, and I basically teach prospective candidates that their grassroots plans need to be about generating turnout for 10 percent of their entire vote goal. During the last four or five days of the election, when they're doing GOTV, they need to be driving 10 percent of everything they need to the ballot. And all of the grassroots work that they do before that needs to prepare and build toward that goal. I tell them that all grassroots is GOTV.
>
> They should focus on 10 percent because that tends to be a fairly manageable number, which can change depending on how large or small a race you're

running. If you have a bad candidate who has a bunch of personal issues and financial problems, bankruptcies, liens, cheated on his wife, whatever, if it's a close election, something like 2004 when Bush only won by a couple points and both sides are very motivated, the only way that you can win is by having a ton of organization. And if you don't have that, then you probably lose. But I would say that 10 to 15 percent of the final outcome is something that you have legitimate control over through a strong grassroots operation.[71]

> Matt McDonald, deputy campaign manager,
> Elia Pirozzi for Congress, 1999 (CA)

Data assumptions drive turnout strategies. A prime example of data-driven voter mobilization is the "72-Hour Task Force," implemented by Republicans in the 2002 midterm elections and 2004 presidential election. The 72-hour plan trained GOP volunteers in GOTV techniques then sent them out to targeted races throughout the country where they were likely to do the most good. Some campaign managers credited the plan for Republican electoral success in 2002 and 2004:

I can tell you I know '04. You look at the presidential campaign, you know, that was basically a fifty-fifty country at that time. There was no wave. So what was the genius of that race? The genius was four years earlier, you had the leadership—the Bush leadership—say, "Hey, you know, 2000 was way too close. Look what happened. We ended up at the Supreme Court and blah blah blah. We need to make sure that we're going to run an effective campaign next time around." So what came out of that? The 72-hour program. In fact, if the 72-hour program wasn't enacted and fully functioning for the '04 presidential campaign, you know, there might have been a very different outcome than George Bush winning.[72]

> Graham Shafer, campaign manager, Van Hilleary
> for Governor, 2003 (TN)

In the 2008 Udall-Schaffer Colorado Senate race, the Republican GOTV effort had grown so large that it reported 2.4 million voter contacts between June 1 and election day, including 600,000 door knocks and 1.8 million phone calls. While that wasn't enough to overcome Udall's winning coalition, it provided a GOTV template to campaign managers running Colorado races after 2008. The data has become so detailed that campaigns rely on it to tailor their GOTV efforts all the way down to the ward and street level:

We obviously had our overall vote goal, we had that—and then we had it by county and we actually had our vote goal at the precinct level as well. And off of using that set of metrics, we built out weekly and daily voter contact goals in terms of calls and doors. And, of course, that became kind of the bible as well, then, for all of our GOTV efforts, making sure we were hitting those goals. If we weren't hitting those goals, figuring out why we weren't and making sure that we fixed it before it became kind of a fatal blow.[73]

Jon Reedy, campaign manager,
Scott Bruun for Congress, 2010 (OR)

Money can certainly help GOTV efforts, and the amount of money can determine how many GOTV workers a campaign hires and where the GOTV effort is targeted. So campaigns need to decide how many GOTV workers to hire. Cauley reported the following in Obama's 2004 Senate primary race:

I spent close to a million dollars turning out a base vote for a base vote candidate. So that was all hand to hand. I mean, I had probably 180 vans on my payroll on election day. I hired 3,000 people to flush a vote. So I spent a large amount of money trying to turn out the base for him in that primary.[74]

James Cauley, campaign manager,
Barack Obama for Senate 2004 (IL)

Summary

Of the fundamental factors that determine election outcomes, the most fundamental is the composition of the likely electorate. Campaign managers start their races by trying to determine what that composition will need to look like in order for them to win the election. They study how they might influence that composition and where their most plausible path to victory lies. Campaign managers have to find their universe of voters and determine where their votes will come from. Data, research, and information allow them to achieve all of these goals. Armed with data, campaign managers are able to strategize more effectively and envision a winning coalition before any votes are even cast. Data presents the candidate with a road map by enabling campaign managers to assess their candidate's strengths and their opponent's flaws as well as targeting campaign messages to various voting blocs that both mobilize core supporters and persuade swing voters.

Notes

1. L. Quinn, personal communication, June 1, 2015.
2. A. Spillane, personal communication, September 30, 2011.
3. J. Howser, personal communication, November 9, 2011.
4. Allison Stevens, "Reversal of Fortune," *The American Prospect*, December 12, 2002, http://prospect.org/article/reversal-fortune.
5. Sunil Ahuja et al., in *The Roads to Congress 2008*, ed. Robert P. Watson and Robert Dewhirst (Lanham, MD: Lexington Books, 2010).
6. J. Howser, personal communication, November 9, 2011.
7. Aside from figuring out where minority voters were, there had been some discomfort between Landrieu and black voters since her brother, Mitch Landrieu, had run for mayor of New Orleans in 2006 against the African American incumbent, Ray Nagin. In January of 2006, Nagin stoked the city's racial embers by promising a "chocolate New Orleans." Nagin won the election by a 52 percent to 48 percent margin. (Mitch Landrieu would be elected New Orleans mayor in 2010 after Nagin had to leave office due to term limits.)
8. Ibid.
9. During the 1995 campaign, Fields accused Mary Landrieu of trying to garner support by telling voters that a black candidate couldn't win statewide; Landrieu had to hold a press conference to deny the charges. When Landrieu first ran for the Senate in 1996, Fields refused to endorse her. In 2008, Fields still wasn't excited about supporting Landrieu but agreed to avoid causing any problems for her with the Baton Rouge African American vote.
10. Ibid.
11. Ibid.
12. Melinda Deslatte, "Mary Landrieu's Challenge: Turn Out the Black Vote," NBC News, October 30, 2014, www.nbcnews.com/politics/meet-the-voters/mary-landrieus-challenge-turn-out-black-vote-n237731.
13. D. Carney, personal communication, March 25, 2015.
14. Ibid.
15. Ibid.
16. Ibid.
17. Sasha Issenberg, *The Victory Lab: The Secret Science of Winning Campaigns* (New York: Broadway Books, 2012).
18. L. Quinn, personal communication, June 1, 2015.
19. Ibid.
20. Catalist Mission, www.catalist.us.
21. L. Quinn, personal communication, June 1, 2015.
22. Ibid.
23. Ibid.
24. Ibid.
25. Ibid.
26. Ibid.
27. Steve Almasy, "New York's Brash Former Mayor, Ed Koch, Dies at 88," CNN.com, March 7, 2013, www.cnn.com/2013/02/01/us/ed-koch-obit.
28. Harris Interactive Inc., "International Directory of Company Histories," Encyclopedia.com, 2001, www.encyclopedia.com/doc/1G2-2844500060.html.

29. David W. Moore, *The Superpollsters: How They Measure and Manipulate Public Opinion in America* (New York: Four Walls Eight Windows, 1995).

30. Drew Desilver and Scott Keeter, "The Challenges of Polling When Fewer People Are Available to Be Polled," Pew Research Center, July 21, 2015, www.pewresearch.org/fact-tank/2015/07/21/the-challenges-of-polling-when-fewer-people-are-available-to-be-polled.

31. D. Carney, personal communication, March 25, 2015.

32. Many campaigns now hire or retain the services of a "tracker" who is always present at the opponent's campaign events and armed with a video camera to record any mistake or misstatement.

33. Mark Kaste, "When Politicians Slip, Video Trackers Are There," NPR, April 23, 2012, www.npr.org/2012/04/23/151060718/behind-the-scene-to-the-next-debacles-video-trackers.

34. B. Baker, personal communication, April 1, 2014.

35. The launch of the group in 2010 was controversial.

36. Ibid.

37. Ibid.

38. Federal Communications Commission, https://stations.fcc.gov/about-station-profiles.

39. B. Baker, personal communication, April 1, 2014.

40. Ibid.

41. When Barbour started out as a staffer at the Mississippi Republican party in late 1960s, no Republican had been elected to statewide office since Reconstruction after the Civil War.

42. H. Barbour, personal communication, October 30, 2011.

43. Jim Rutenberg, "Secret of the Obama Victory? Rerun Watchers, for One Thing," *New York Times*, November 12, 2012, www.nytimes.com/2012/11/13/us/politics/obama-data-system-targeted-tv-viewers-for-support.html?_r=0.

44. J. Pihlaja, personal communication, October 25, 2011.

45. K. Mehlman, personal communication, November 9, 2011.

46. Ibid.

47. Ibid.

48. Sam Wang, "The Great Gerrymander of 2012," *New York Times*, February 2, 2013, www.nytimes.com/2013/02/03/opinion/sunday/the-great-gerrymander-of-2012.html?pagewanted=all.

49. J. Gonzales, personal communication, November 18, 2011.

50. J. Petrick, personal communication, November 9, 2011.

51. E. Weigand, personal communication, October 27, 2011.

52. K. Evans, personal communication, September 20, 2011.

53. S. Law, personal communication, September 29, 2011.

54. S. Bell, personal communication, June 20, 2014.

55. Ibid.

56. Ibid.

57. J. Pihlaja, personal communication, October 25, 2011.

58. M. McKenna, personal communication, October 25, 2011.

59. J. Bognet, personal communication, June 11, 2013.

60. E. Weigand, personal communication, October 27, 2011.

61. Ibid.

62. S. Bradshaw, personal communication, October 17, 2011.

63. Jason Kosena, "Schaffer's Latino Voter Strategy Could Bring Election Day Peril," *Colorado Independent*, October 13, 2008, www.coloradoindependent.com/11121/schaffer-ignores-latino-voters-at-his-own-election-day-peril.

64. Colorado Secretary of State, "Official Publication of the Abstract of Votes Cast for the 2008 Primary 2008 General," 2008, www.sos.state.co.us/pubs/elections/Results/2008/2008_Abstract.pdf.

65. J. Cauley, personal communication, November 1, 2011

66. K. Koch, personal communication, October 20, 2011.

67. Ibid.

68. C. Gum, personal communication, October 17, 2011.

69. S. Watson, personal communication, October 7, 2011.

70. Ibid.

71. M. McDonald, personal communication, November 7, 2011.

72. G. Shafer, personal communication, September 20, 2011.

73. J. Reedy, personal communication, November 11, 2011.

74. J. Cauley, personal communication, November 1, 2011.

CHAPTER 4

Entrepreneur and Chief Financial Officer

Launching and Sustaining the Campaign

Start-ups are very difficult. In my business life, I found that acquiring and growing an existing company is easier than starting something from scratch. From finding the office space, installing phones and computers, even arranging details like cleaning services: in these and many other ways, a campaign goes from zero to sixty in a matter of days. And the campaign manager is the one that pulls that off. The job is part logistics, part hiring, part strategy, and part management.[1]

Mitt Romney, 2012 Republican presidential nominee

Spending and Margins

The early days of a campaign are hectic, intense, and crucial. A manager must plan, budget, hire, raise funds, and strategize, doing all these things simultaneously. The strength of a campaign's fundraising operation often determines the kind and number of core activities (persuasion and mobilization) the campaign can undertake. While money alone does not determine election outcomes, campaigns need enough resources to reach voters with their messages, and in close contests, the amount of money each side accumulates—and how each side spends its money—can shape the political landscape and even affect the results on the margins. And, as Chapter 2 illustrated, the margins matter. Structure and finance can have an outsized effect on the closest races, ratcheting up the pressure on campaign managers to excel as the entrepreneur who must lead in both of these fields.

In short, campaigns are super-costly start-ups—and start-ups need plans; budgets; staff; and, most of all, financing. Consider how Ken Mehlman saw the role of money and structure in President George W. Bush's 2004 reelection campaign. In early 2002, Bush invited Mehlman, his White House political director, to Camp David for the weekend. Mehlman had talked to Karl Rove, Bush's chief strategist, and Rove had "explored me a little bit to see if I was interested [in running Bush's reelection campaign] because if I wasn't, the last thing you want to do is have the president be told no by some guy he invited to Camp David for the weekend."[2]

Mehlman agreed to manage the campaign on two conditions. Mehlman insisted that he—not anyone in the White House, not even Rove—must have the power to hire and fire everyone on the campaign and that he alone would have the authority to sign off on campaign expenses:

> Look, I get how the world works . . . I don't need my name in the paper. I don't need to be identified as the guy who is calling the shots. I don't actually love that stuff. But if you were deciding who's hired and what's spent and everyone knows that and you cannot be vetoed, then you're going to be in a good place. And that was important to me.[3]

He wasn't looking for the high-profile status many campaign managers attain during national elections; he primarily wanted "to be a good manager."

"'You're smart to ask for that,'" Bush replied. "'You got it.'"[4]

Mehlman did not believe that money alone, or simply controlling the campaign's purse strings, was how he could lead Bush's campaign to victory. Just outraising Kerry hardly guaranteed a win for the Republican side. But Mehlman did believe that the money mattered. He believed that the money—if he could spend it effectively on core campaign activities—would indeed affect the margins of a race that was likely to be close.

In March 2003, Mehlman launched the campaign. He opened the campaign's bank account (finance) and began hiring people to help in the enormous undertaking of reelecting a sitting president (staff). He crafted a budget and laid out a month-by-month spending plan (spending priorities). He spent several months studying both the 2000 Bush-Gore campaign and past reelection campaigns (research). Funding the campaign and spending the right resources in the right areas to maximize Bush's chances of success were crucial early steps for the campaign, in Mehlman's view.[5]

When he made a hire, he typically presented the new employee with a budget and offered the chance to change it. He sat down with his employees every month to figure out how they did against their budget. He called the budget a "critical" element that forced the campaign to put its intentions in writing—to make hard choices. He explained the reality:

> [I] probably spent 20 percent of my time on budgeting. . . . I viewed my job as being the CEO of a company whose business happened to be politics. First and foremost was not politics. It was not, you know, schmoozing. It was CEO. It was leading a business. It was management. The most important part of my job was management.[6]

Mehlman eventually hired a whole team to comb through the budget "religiously" and "relentlessly." And his pioneering efforts at microtargeting, which were discussed in Chapter 3, were made possible partly by the campaign's successful budgeting, fundraising, and spending decisions. Combined, the Bush and Kerry campaigns raised more than $880 million, shattering all records up until then.

Mehlman's tactics—enabled by his ability to spend in the right places on activities that mattered—were highly effective on the campaign's margins, as the narrow election results (also described in Chapter 3) illustrated. By spending wisely, Mehlman helped make it possible for Bush to eke out a victory in his hard-fought reelection campaign.[7]

And by standing up the organization as the campaign's undisputed entrepreneurial leader, Mehlman also supported and enacted the activities that helped Bush do what his father couldn't do—win a second term. Mehlman described himself as an "obsessive planner." He figured that if he could take care of 80 percent of the issues that could come up in the next week, then he could devote his full energy to "the 20 percent that needed to be decided during the week and the rest could be executed."[8] While some political scientists have shed fresh light on how events outside the candidates' control (economic conditions, war and peace, a candidate's background) are key drivers of presidential election results, campaign managers reveal that, in primaries and general elections alike, their entrepreneurial activities and spending decisions give them some often-unseen leverage over the fate of their races.[9] By establishing the infrastructure and ensuring that the campaign has adequate resources to carry out their priorities, campaign managers influence the campaign's strategy, tactics, and direction as well as help their candidates to victory.

The Money Advantage

While this was a presidential race and budgets were exponentially higher than in congressional, state-level, or local elections, budget and money are reality. The fact is that almost all campaigns cost a lot of money, sometimes tens of millions of dollars, and the core question of this book—how do campaigns matter?—is really just another way of asking, how and when does money matter? As you'll remember from Chapter 2, political scientists often argue for a variety of reasons that campaigns have minimal to null effects on the election result, especially presidential contests.

Thus, we are left with this paradox: campaign managers put a big premium on fundraising, describing it as their most vital job. And candidates, many of whom detest "dialing for dollars," spend inordinate amounts of time doing just that, what is known as "call time," talking to potential donors, urging them to give as much money as legally possible. At the same time, some political scientists say money tends to flow to the side that already has the upper hand and that in any case, each side has enough resources (especially in presidential general election races) to cancel each other's activities out.[10] Both political scientists and campaign managers provide us with important insights on the effects of campaigns on election results—and the role of campaigns in our electoral democracy. Scholars have demonstrated that money is not the decisive factor, and that the most well-funded campaigns don't necessarily win the election. At the same time, campaign managers point out, money funds the activities that can, and often do, give one side or another a marginal advantage over the opposition, and because campaigns are often decided on the margins, the money advantage can have a real impact on election day. Thus, the question is not simply how much money a campaign is able to raise but, more importantly, how effectively that money is being spent, which can influence the margins of competitive elections. Thus, the ability to raise enough sums; budget wisely; identify a campaign's spending priorities; execute; and efficiently find, reach, mobilize, and persuade voters—all of which requires money—affects election margins.

In Chapter 1, we showed you a chart that highlighted how presidential and congressional campaigns were now in total costing many billions of dollars. Thus, with no end in sight to the fundraising arms race, another way to think about the impact of money on campaigns is, what's all that money actually buying? Why are campaign managers so focused on fundraising as their highest priority? Money is *not* the primary driver of election outcomes; money does not buy elections. Money ultimately doesn't predetermine which side loses and which side celebrates. As political scientists have demonstrated, the person with the most money often gets beat, and wealthy candidates using their own money (so-called self-funders), such as Meg Whitman of California, outspend their opponents by large sums, but more often than not, they, too, lose their elections.[11]

At the electoral margins, having enough money to fund the campaign's core activities, laid out in the campaign's budget, can often move the electorate in decisive ways in close elections. In order to be competitive in presidential, congressional, many statewide, and even local races, campaigns need to raise enough money to find and reach their voters and, most crucially, must spend that money on activities that are likely to influence the electoral margins to their advantage. Thus, when assessing campaigns, campaign managers think not only in terms of *how much* they need to raise but also in terms of *what* they are spending their money on. How are my core activities influencing voters? Have my spending decisions reached and engaged the electorate? How am I doing?

Campaign managers we interviewed said that grit, hard work, and grassroots excitement are important but hardly sufficient. Campaign managers must put together a budget, make tough spending choices, and assemble a staff and structure to affect the vote margins.

While the budget decisions and spending priorities of each campaign vary from race to race, all managers are seeking to answer the five questions featured in the campaign model (see the Preface). They must decide who they need, how they reach them, what they will say, how their campaign is doing, and what "they," including outside groups, are doing. But understanding the political climate, identifying their campaign's targets, figuring out the right mix of persuasion and mobilization activities, crafting a message, delivering the message to their targets, and ensuring that their voters go to the polls are all tasks that require money—*a lot of money*. Furthermore, managers need to establish a solid organizational foundation led by dedicated professionals to carry out all of these activities. Mark Harris, Pat Toomey's 2010 Pennsylvania Senate campaign manager, said that "the tricky thing about campaigns is that you need to both build and sail the ship at the same time."[12]

Whether the candidate is running for president or a seat on the city council, managers must establish the campaign organization and have enough funds on hand to support the campaign's core activities. In 2007, David Plouffe told then senator Barack Obama and a group of his friends that any campaign they ran would need to "launch a cutting-edge website, recruit talented senior staff, develop a plan and budget." Plouffe wrote in his memoirs that the campaign manager's job "encompasses a lot more than just developing electoral theories, obsessing about metrics, and spending lots of money creatively."[13]

> It also requires dealing with myriad personnel issues, mediating internal disputes, and worrying about things like office air conditioning costs and how much to reimburse staff for mileage—stuff I had not had to worry about for a long time but remembered as a grind. The manager has to be on top of every aspect of the campaign—when the candidate calls, he or she can't say, "I haven't been paying much attention to (fill in the blank). Let me talk to the staffer who has." As I had told Obama, there are no shortcuts. The manager's ass is on the line every minute of every day. The campaign has to be all-consuming.[14]
>
> David Plouffe, campaign manager,
> Barack Obama for President, 2008

How Money Matters (Decisions)

If money buys the stuff that can win elections, then campaign managers must write detailed budgets reflecting a campaign's goals and priorities. One campaign manager we spoke with was concerned when he joined a campaign and found the budget was simply scribbled on the back of a napkin. One of the first things he did was identify spending priorities, write a specific budget for each month and quarter and determine how they wanted to spend for the rest of the campaign.[15]

As we discussed in Chapter 2, pure claims that money buys elections or that money is inconsequential miss the boat. Campaigns can matter at the margin and none of the things campaigns do to influence the shape and performance of the electorate can be done without resources. Money matters and budgets matter because margins matter; money funds the key activities that enable campaigns to find, mobilize, and persuade voters in the hopes of moving the margins a bit in their favor—and answering some of the core questions (Who do we need? How do we reach them? What do we say?) will drive virtually all campaign decision making.

As entrepreneurs, the campaign managers we interviewed recognized that money was vital to launching and then sustaining the operation.

While flush campaigns are not always victorious, financially strapped campaigns are typically losing campaigns. Campaigns don't need to raise more money than the other side to win, but they do need to raise enough to be competitive and to conduct the core voter activities that matter at the margins. That's why managers work so hard to prepare a detailed budget, set up a strong fundraising operation, and spend the campaign's funds on core activities judiciously. Ultimately responsible for a campaign's fundraising strength, managers are also, typically, signing the campaign's checks and making crucial decisions on spending the campaign's finite resources. But how, specifically, does the money matter? In which particular ways can money affect the electoral margins? As some of the qualitative evidence in this chapter illustrates, money is important to campaign managers on several levels. They know they need enough money in the bank to fund the core activities that will make them not just competitive but potentially give them a decisive edge. Money can make a candidate viable (who might otherwise not be), and campaigns that use it effectively may not even need to have the most money in the bank. Deciding how to spend the money is arguably more important than the sheer number of dollars raised. Virtually every campaign manager told us of instances in which raising money—and spending it wisely or poorly—affected the election result. Money can give relatively unknown candidates a lift in recognition and respect; help a campaign break through with its message in a crowded primary field; refute negative attacks on the candidate; and maximize the campaign's ability to find its core voters, reach its voters, and get them to the polls. In a competitive primary, money can enable a candidate trailing in the polls to gain earned and paid media and reach voters with his message in ways that ultimately give him a decisive advantage.

Joe Abbey (How Money Matters: Name ID and Message Delivery)

Put differently, the amount of money in a campaign's coffers drives and constrains the ability of the campaign manager to deliver the candidate's message to the electorate. Consider how Joe Abbey, campaign manager during Creigh Deeds' 2009 run for the Democratic nomination for Virginia governor, used a surprise infusion of funds to reach voters and influence the electorate. Abbey assumed that Deeds, a relatively unknown state senator, would never raise enough to be able to afford television ads in costly media markets such as Richmond, Norfolk, and Washington, D.C. "I originally had no money for broadcast TV in the budget. We couldn't afford the big three," Abbey explained. But Deeds performed well overall, and the campaign received an infusion of cash, presenting Abbey with a set of decisions he had never anticipated at the outset.[16]

Raising $100,000 and $200,000 at a fast clip, Abbey had to decide how to spend the windfall. He held daily calls with his consultants. Abbey realized that there was so much money that, "Oh my God, we think we could go up on D.C. TV," and that "was going to blow everybody's minds." But in order for Abbey to buy ads in the D.C. market, he had to funnel resources from the field operation into the media buy. He fired some "great kids" who as field operatives "were doing their job." Forty thousand dollars determined whether Abbey could sustain a televised campaign in Northern Virginia or "go up and go dark, which obviously you do not ever want to do." So Abbey let the entire field staff go, a decision he described as "the worst experience as a manager I've had including losing races."[17]

Abbey had seen polls showing Deeds down by fifteen points. Deeds' pollster told Abbey, "Field gets you two points, it doesn't get you fifteen." Abbey agreed. As Chapter 5 will show you, television advertising, especially in some of the nation's larger states and pricier media markets, is the best way that campaigns can reach voters with their messages. Abbey knew that the only way to win the Virginia primary was "to do it on TV. And so we just dumped it and we went up on D.C. TV, and suddenly we're up on Richmond and suddenly we're up on Tidewater and suddenly we're surging [in] public polls." Abbey made another hard choice, arguing to Deeds that the campaign had to go into debt to keep the TV ads on the air.[18]

"Even if we lose, you'll still be a state senator," Abbey reasoned with Deeds. "I think even if you're a state senator you can probably raise a hundred grand after the primary. And I think the nominee would probably want to help because, you know, we haven't attacked anybody and there was a general goodwill toward our candidate." Deeds replied that he was comfortable going $80,000 but not $100,000 into debt. Abbey spent until the campaign was "80 in the hole on election day, but we won the primary."[19]

On top of it, Abbey was able to hire back all of the kids who were fired and who wanted to rejoin the campaign. The episode was a case "where it was really about managing your money" in ways that maximized the campaign's odds of winning. "That was the truest, I think, example of really day-to-day budgeting on a campaign." When the returns came in, Deeds handily defeated his two better-funded, better-known rivals. His victory stunned political observers in Virginia and Washington, D.C. Not only did Abbey help raise enough money but he also spent it in a way that aided Deeds' cause, maximizing the impact of the dollars they had raised. Money—spent in ways that helped Deeds reach Democratic voters in a low-turnout primary election—added up to a come-from-behind primary victory for the underdog.[20]

"The Nightmare of All Campaigns" (Fundraising)

It is worth understanding how campaigns are able to raise so many millions of dollars and why campaign managers in particular put such a premium on fundraising activities. If their goal is to win the election, they typically told us that victory is extremely difficult without raising enough money to fund the campaign's core activities. These activities, furthermore, will vary, depending on the state, the amount of money available, the cost of television advertising in the relevant media markets, the candidate's name identification, the campaign's vote targets, and numerous other fast-changing factors. Because campaigns are looking for any edge they can gain to influence the margins of the election result, they have to make tough choices, but they prefer to make those choices on a campaign that has enough money to target their voters, reach them with their message, respond to the other side's activities, and assess how they are doing as the campaign progresses.

All of this leads to the following question: How are campaign managers able to help candidates raise so much money in the first place? And, why do they insist that candidates devote so much of their time to asking donors to give them money? Members of Congress, for example, typically walk or drive the few blocks between their offices and the offices of their party's respective campaign committees. There, they engage in call time, soliciting funds from any number of wealthy donors, most of whom have a track record of donating either to the member or her party. Generally speaking, the fundraising environment is a hostile, unforgiving place for campaigns and campaign managers.

Legal, political, and personal obstacles to fundraising are ubiquitous. Major donors are receiving calls from virtually every candidate, every super political action committee (PAC) (more on super PACs in Chapter 9), and every party committee to which they might consider donating, and everybody is pitching their cause aggressively and consistently. Campaign managers have the challenge of showing potential donors that their campaigns are a wise investment for them. Donors, managers say, most often contribute to incumbents with a track record they admire, candidates who share their ideologies, and those who are likely to advance their economic interests once in office. Donors typically prefer to spend on a candidate with a serious shot rather than a candidate who is almost surely going to lose. But that doesn't necessarily mean that money always flows to the ultimate winner. Donors, according to campaign managers, have varied motivations for giving. Another challenge facing campaign managers is that they also must learn the campaign finance rules in order to ensure they don't run afoul of the law. It's easier said than done. At the federal level, as of the 2016 election cycle, campaigns are prohibited by law from taking corporate contributions, and individuals are restricted to $2,700 individual donations to a single candidate for each election (primary and general elections each count as individual elections).[21] The Federal Election Commission (FEC) governs campaign fundraising in congressional and presidential (federal) races, while campaigns for governor, state legislatures, and local offices such as mayor need to follow the campaign finance laws of the state. (The secretary of state typically enforces the state laws.) But state laws vary widely, and while some states present stricter restrictions than federal elections, some states permit unlimited individual donations for candidates.[22]

Campaign managers who were new to a state and unfamiliar with the state's laws had to take crash courses in finance regulations. "It's really, really difficult to go state to state and get a good grasp on what the election laws—they're different in each state and they change regularly," one manager, who wished to remain anonymous to speak candidly about her experiences, reported. "And making it even harder, in some states the laws differ county to county. It's really important, I think, before you start writing your campaign plan, to have a really good understanding of what the laws are."[23]

Once, this manager was running an absentee ballot program in Iowa, having just arrived from Ohio. Knocking on doors for three days, the operative encountered a woman who said, "Oh, do you mind taking my ballot and dropping it off?"[24]

"Absolutely, sure," she replied. The manager returned to the car. Her colleagues told her that it was illegal in Iowa to submit a ballot on behalf of somebody else. "You can't take those," they warned her. The manager went back to the voter, apologized, and gave her back her ballot.

"Especially in the world where you're bouncing state to state, I don't know how you can't get super familiar with [the laws] first," the manager reflected. "It just impacts everything you do and how you design your program," as she had to learn the hard way.[25]

Campaign managers have several tools they use to help raise the funds necessary to make smart investments in order to fund core activities and gain marginal advantages. While direct mail used to be the method of choice for soliciting small donations, campaigns now heavily rely on email and online contributions through a campaign's website.

Above all, though, campaign managers stress that candidates must be willing to spend hours of their day calling donors, asking supporters for money in face-to-face meetings, and asking for contributions at fundraising events. Call time is especially crucial for most candidates. James "Jimmy" Cauley, Obama's 2004 campaign manager, summed up his approach to Obama's finance plan pithily: "Put him on a phone and let him beg." While Creigh Deeds was little known and running against better-funded candidates in a large state with costly media markets, Barack Obama was also up against a self-funded front-runner in an even larger state with even costlier media markets. Cauley's plan for the campaign required enough funds to reach the campaign's targeted voters (especially African Americans and white liberal women in and around Chicago's suburbs) with the campaign's message.[26]

James "Jimmy" Cauley (How Money Matters: Reaching Voter Targets)

At first blush, Cauley was an unlikely person to manage the campaign to elect the third African American to the US Senate since Reconstruction. Raised in Pikeville, Kentucky, in the Appalachian Mountains, Cauley was the son of Democrats; his father, James, was Pike County's property valuation administrator, and his mother, Deloris, was a Democratic campaign worker.[27] During college at the University of Louisville in 1990, Cauley began working on a US Senate campaign for Kentucky Democrat Harvey Sloane.[28] Upon graduating in 1992, he gravitated toward the world of campaigns, and as he rose through the ranks, he won a series of races including electing the first African American mayor of Jersey City in 2001.[29]

Obama's chief strategist, David Axelrod, called Cauley in 2003 when Cauley was working as chief of staff to Congressman Dutch Ruppersberger, D-MD. Cauley wanted to do a top-tier Senate race that cycle, and Obama seemed like a midtier candidate, but Axelrod pressed him hard to manage Obama's campaign.[30]

"You fly up here, you meet with the guy, and if you don't see what I . . . see, then we'll call it even. You get a free trip to Chicago for the day," Axelrod offered.[31] Cauley flew to Chicago, a city he had never visited, figuring he'd get a free trip but that Obama probably lacked both the money and name identification to prevail in a crowded eight-person Democratic primary.[32] After talking with Obama for an hour at a tiny bakery across the street from the campaign headquarters, Cauley did an about-face. He concluded that Obama's "got the juice."[33]

When Cauley became manager in July of 2003, Obama had raised about $700,000. Obama was calling donors for funds in a tiny room with his finance director, Claire Serdiuk, who was the campaign's first hire. The start-up campaign had a closet full of Obama's memoirs, *Dreams from My Father*, and Cauley recalled that "if somebody wrote us a $1,000 check, we gave that shit away all the fucking time." Obama would sign the book; send it to the donor; and that, said Cauley, "was the biggest finance plan we had. It was just call-time."[34]

Cauley had a simple rule about candidate fundraising. If his candidate was not spending at least four hours a day on the phone asking for donations, they were not doing their job. Cauley wanted Obama to connect with eight to ten people an hour over four hours of call time each day. And, "if you're not doing twenty hours of call time a week, I've got no use for you. You're not going to get elected." Obama kept focused on the task. Cauley pointed out that another of his clients, Kentuckian Steve Beshear, actually relished the fundraising task. "He was ambitious," Cauley recalled. "He'd call anybody and everybody and ask them for a grand. He didn't give a shit. If he'd met you on the street, he'd ask you for a grand, no shame." Finance was so central to Obama's campaign operation that by primary day, around eight of Cauley's sixteen staff were working in finance. The hotter Obama became, the more delicate the fundraising operation became.[35]

Robert Gibbs, who later became Obama's first White House press secretary, joined the campaign and urged Cauley to vet the donors who were now giving to Obama's campaign in droves. "Robert made me invest all this money in vetting," said Cauley, "hadn't vetted a damn check. We took it, if it came through, we took it." But now the stakes were higher, and the operations had grown substantially, and as Cauley and his team vetted hosts of fundraisers, he realized, "'Oh my god, this guy's been indicted. You got to take him off as a host. . . .' All of a sudden, I was doing a lot of vetting that I didn't do in the primary. But Robert was right" because as Obama "became bigger and bigger, people were coming out of the woodwork to give." Cauley hired four staffers to handle the vetting, heading off any potential fundraising scandals.

Cauley ultimately helped Obama raise $6 million for the primary. Although he was vastly outspent by Hull, Obama was able to start advertising on Illinois television three weeks before the election, and he stayed up. As Hull's campaign imploded, Obama easily won the election. But if he had raised, say, only $1 million, would he still have prevailed? Would he have then been asked to keynote the Democratic National Convention a few months later, the speech that made him a national star?[36]

Campaign managers believe that candidates insufficiently committed to fundraising are not even worth working for. If they want to win the election, then they simply have to spend the time raising the money that will enable them to affect share and performance. Brandon Waters, Rick Clayburgh's manager in his 2002 North Dakota Republican congressional campaign, called fundraising not just the biggest priority but also "the nightmare of all campaigns."[37] "Getting candidates to fundraise is always extremely difficult to do," he explained, and putting "the potential donor lists in place and getting a structure to the fundraising process" adds to the size of the challenge.[38] Democratic manager Martha McKenna, who runs a campaign firm with Jen Pihlaja, explained that when one campaign she was running failed to hit its fundraising targets, she made every staffer spend at least one hour a day calling donors. Her program helped turn the operation around, and McKenna described her fundraising philosophy as "everyone's in it together."[39]

Still, running for office and soliciting contributions was just a "dreadful" process, she admitted. Candidates would rather talk to voters, shake their hands, and hold meetings than "be in a room, dialing for dollars," which is "a hard and lonely thing to do." She added that managers who were personally invested in the fundraising operation were typically going to have successful fundraising campaigns.[40] Indeed, managers need to expand the network of campaign donors; maintain good relations with a campaign's financial supporters (donor maintenance); and ensure that the entire campaign is doing the right things to raise enough money to conduct its core activities, with all eyes firmly fixed on affecting the margins. Campaign managers argued that they worked hard to broaden a campaign's donor network, launch a bundling program (in which individuals raise funds through their own networks), and sustain small-donor programs that not only generate dollars but also build grassroots enthusiasm.[41] (In 2012, Obama's presidential campaign raised more than $200 million from small-dollar contributions.[42])

Persuading would-be donors to part with their money is more art than science. Some pitches work better than others, depending on the type of campaign that's being run, the political environment, the candidate, and the would-be donor. Campaign managers often have to steer and coach candidates in order to help them become more effective fundraisers. One campaign manager we talked to argued that a good pitch should blend attacks on one's opponent with a positive message from the candidate.[43] Fear is "a very good motivator," he said.[44] Others stressed that more positive pitches could also be effective, while still other managers observed that candidates needed to call donors directly because the candidate is the person best positioned to ask for donations, and they have to start with their family and friends and then go beyond their comfort zone. Even during so-called "wave" elections (when one party benefits from a national trend in its direction), candidates, managers told us, need enough money if they are going to catch the wave.

Fundraising often involves a dance between the manager and the candidate, in which the candidate wants to meet voters and community leaders and the campaign manager is pushing the candidate to spend more time raising money. Brad Beychok, who served as Democrat Charlie Melancon's 2010 campaign manager for a Louisiana congressional seat, agreed with his colleagues that candidates disliked sitting in a room calling friends and strangers and asking for money for hours at a time. It was vital, he explained, to balance that distasteful part of the process by incentivizing candidates, so with some candidates, he made them a deal, offering, "Look, will you call until five o'clock? At five o'clock, you can go do whatever you want. You can go to Walmart and shake hands."[45] Campaign managers took their fundraising roles—the budget and money aspect of being the entrepreneur—seriously because, again, the activities that the money funds matter. "It is your job, as manager, to make sure that there is a comprehensive fundraising plan in place and that it is being effectively executed," Stuart Roy, Republican Ben Nighthorse Campbell's campaign manager on a 1998 Colorado Senate race, told us.[46] Campaign managers, Jen Pihlaja argued, had to hold everybody accountable for fundraising goals and ensure that if the plan gets off track that the campaign "adjust and correct."[47] Campaign manager Todd Schulte, who ran Democrat Scott Murphy's 2010 New York congressional race, insisted that candidates should be warned that skipping an activity as vital as "call time" meant the loss of "days of TV" ads.[48] Parades, reaching a relatively small number of voters, were worthless, but fundraising, campaign manager Casey Phillips declared, can help candidates ultimately win votes by supporting activities that reach voters on a large enough scale to affect the election at the margins.[49]

Hiring the Right Team (Staff)

Campaigns that are seeking to gain a competitive advantage over their rivals not only need the money to fund the activities that affect the margins but also the structure and team that can work effectively toward the single goal of winning 50.1 percent of the vote. Other aspects of the campaign beyond money contribute to its running smoothly. Some things that need to be done are basic, but they are also important pieces of the infrastructure that enable campaigns to find, reach, mobilize, and persuade voters. Campaigns, for one, require a physical space, a headquarters; Bill Lattanzi, Republican Andy Harris's Maryland congressional campaign manager in 2010, said finding a campaign office was the first thing he did (followed by a budget and campaign plan).[50] Casey Phillips, who led Republican Delbert Hosemann's 2007 run for secretary of state in Mississippi, captured the multifaceted tasks facing a campaign manager at the outset of the race. He argued that identifying his priorities is a hard chore whenever he has to start up a campaign.[51]

> When I got to the district there was no organization whatsoever. The first thing that I had to kind of do was find a place to live, find a place to have an office, and start laying the groundwork for the campaign. I started by doing a lot of research to familiarize myself with the state so I could begin to understand the quirks of the area and learn about what makes people tick there. Next, I began to build a media contact list and a list of county chairmen and activists. Then, I hit the phones to familiarize myself with the local players.[52]
>
> Casey Phillips, campaign manager,
> Delbert Hosemann for Secretary of State, 2007 (MS)

Another thing a campaign needs immediately is lists, which will help the campaign identify some of its most committed supporters, its potentially winning coalition, and how it plans to reach those voters. Thus, the lists include names of people to start calling to ask to volunteer, people to ask for money, and lists of professions that the campaign can microtarget. Oftentimes, lists can be obtained from past candidates for the same seat. Other voter lists (which usually contain age information, to target seniors) can be obtained from individual municipality clerks or from statewide election boards. Many states are required to issue their lists of registered occupations (doctors, realtors, etc.) upon request. Many campaign managers are dropped into new states with little knowledge of the political landscape. In these cases, getting to know the major political players is also a must, because they better than most typically know how to find, mobilize, and persuade voters in their state or district:

> I think it's really important when you get to a new state to establish a really good relationship with the local operatives and activists. When I get sent out to help on a campaign at the end of the election cycle, I'm often looked at as the bad guy from D.C. It's really easy to get past that if you know who to talk to and who to reach out to. Talking to the state party, labor leaders, other campaign operatives—or the county parties if you're running a congressional race—can be really helpful. At the end of the day, you need these folks to be bought in to the program you're running and engaging with them from the outset is the best way to achieve this. I think for me, most of the time I'm successful because I take the time to listen to people on the ground about who's important to touch and what's important to do.[53]
>
> Ashley Spillane, senior adviser,
> Tim Walz for Congress, 2010 (MN)

Building the ship also required hiring the right people. The people who decide how to spend the money and implement these spending decisions affect share and performance on the margins. That's why we came across remarks like this one from Republican campaign manager Jon Reedy: "The two most valuable assets that you have on a campaign are your money and your people."[54] The key for many managers was less that they find the most experienced people with the best reputations; rather, they said they were looking for people who understood the candidate and the campaign's culture—aides who would complement a manager's strengths and understood the candidate and the campaign's values and goals, thus making them more effective in carrying out the activities that would influence the final vote tally.

The 2012 Republican presidential nominee Mitt Romney told us that on his campaigns the manager was indeed responsible for hiring the right staff.

> If you're lucky, the campaign manager has been in the political arena long enough to know some of the players that will make up the campaign. Some he will want to bring onto the team, others he will approach for references. After my campaign manager had identified key players, he said, "I think you ought to hire this person. I've worked with them before. If you like them when you meet them, I want you to sell them on joining." Finding and recruiting the team is a big part of the campaign manager's responsibility.[55]
>
> Mitt Romney, 2012 Republican presidential nominee

Managers also emphasized the importance of finding and hiring individuals who knew what their roles were and focused on achieving the ultimate objective, responsibly and ethically. Jeb Bush's 1998 campaign manager Sally Bradshaw said her criteria for hiring people was that they would be exceptional team players, rather than arrive at headquarters with sterling resumes.[56] "I mean, a communications director who was not trying to be the media guy. . . . A scheduler who was really focused on scheduling of events and building crowds. . . . People who could be real team players. Nobody who goes, 'I don't have a lot of time for that,'" as she put it.[57] Brad Beychok looked to hire people who were "loyal, tireless, and aggressive."[58] Republican campaign manager and now senior vice president at Stoneridge Group, Kyle Robertson, who ran the 2008 congressional campaign in Missouri's ninth district and the successful campaigns for governor in Indiana (Mike Pence 2012) and Michigan (Rick Snyder 2014), stressed his desire to find utility players "committed to a team concept," arguing that every staffer had to do every job, from fundraiser to field operator.[59] Matt McDonald said the bulk of his staffers should "be worker bees" who were eager to do whatever it took to win.[60] They had to have "a lot of energy and enthusiasm" because the jobs required staffers to work twelve to fifteen hours a day, seven days a week, for three or four months, and at paltry pay.[61]

In Herman Cain's offbeat 2012 White House run, manager Mark Block described his "number one challenge was to find people to hire that understood what we were trying to do and that is to run a national campaign, a nontraditional campaign," that prioritized local control and "was going to be from the bottom up."[62]

Jen Pihlaja

Raised in Michigan's Upper Peninsula as a diehard Green Bay Packers' fan, Jen Pihlaja learned that finding the right people for her campaigns was an art that the best managers were able to master. Right after college, she ran a program for undergraduates who wanted a semester-long experience in politics during the 1996 election cycle.[63] She worked as a field director and a campaign manager on congressional races, spent three years on Capitol Hill as a legislative assistant, conducted opposition research for EMILY'S List, and spent five years total at the organization advising its leaders on recruiting candidates and then helping the candidates run their campaigns. She eventually became the political director of the DCCC.

She argued the following:

A first-time manager will often have been a communications director or field director or research director or some other, finance director. And so they have strengths. I think one of the things that is really important that they do is not hire people who mirror their strengths, but mirror their weaknesses, and empower them to do their jobs. You know, I think that's an incredibly important piece of what a manager can do is recognize what they are good at and what they're not.[64]

She argued that hiring staff too quickly could undermine the campaign's planning, and she has seen campaigns have to fire volunteer coordinators who, it turned out, "really [didn't] like volunteers" and weren't actually "people people." Another time, a research consultant failed to produce the research, so Pihlaja stopped payment for the work and found a replacement. But Pihlaja blamed herself for hiring the wrong people as much as the individuals who performed poorly. Paying attention to the candidate's strengths and finding people to complement those strengths were all high on her list of priorities. But she also admires resumes from people who had worked as waiters or waitresses. She wants people "who don't give up, who are flexible, resourceful, fun, trustworthy, but they don't necessarily have to have political experience." She also prefers a team member who is "smart and exercises good judgment and who is having fun and who wants to be a part of it than somebody who has a particular pedigree."[65]

Screven Watson, who managed Rod Smith's 2006 bid for Florida governor, approached hiring through a somewhat different set of priorities. "The biggest pain in my ass in any campaign has been scheduling," he told us. Bad scheduling "can eat you alive." One candidate called Watson at 11:30 p.m. one night in tears "because she had just driven two hours from one event to the other in a rural county."[66]

"I've got a family. I can't do this," she told him. The scheduler had screwed up, and Watson now had a mini-crisis. But in building his team, something else weighed even more heavily on Watson: He had to find the right lawyer who would keep the campaign within the letter and spirit of campaign law and prevent a PR debacle, which, in the worst cases, can fatally wound a campaign. "You cannot screw up the legal part of it," he said.[67]

Conclusion

Losing campaigns can often have enough money and sufficient organization, but it is hard to win a race when the campaign lacks the resources it needs to mobilize and persuade targeted voters. If the organization isn't set up and resourced appropriately, it is harder for it to find the people it needs to achieve victory. Thus, campaign managers prize money and organization. Money matters because the campaign's activities can affect share and performance on the margins. Structure and finance are not the sole factors determining election outcomes, of course. But without the right structure and enough money to conduct core campaign activities, campaigns are unlikely to be successful. Almost all campaigns need entrepreneurs at the top able to raise the funds, hire the right people, organize the team effectively, and execute plans—ultimately launching the campaign on a winning course.

Notes

1. M. Romney, personal communication, November 7, 2014.
2. K. Mehlman, personal communication, November 9, 2011.
3. Ibid.
4. Ibid.
5. Ibid
6. Ibid.
7. Ibid.
8. Ibid.
9. John Sides et al., *Campaigns and Elections: Rules, Reality, Strategy, Choice* (New York: W.W. Norton & Company, 2011).
10. Paul Farhi, "Do Campaigns Really Change Voters' Minds?" *Washington Post*, July 6, 2012, www.washingtonpost.com/opinions/do-campaigns-really-change-voters-minds/2012/07/06/gJQAEljyRW_story.html.
11. For an empirical, detailed investigation of how self-funders are unable to spend their way to victory, see Jennifer A. Steen, *Self-Financed Candidates in Congressional Elections* (Ann Arbor: University of Michigan Press, 2006).
12. M. Harris, personal communication, June 20, 2014.
13. David Plouffe, *The Audacity to Win: How Obama Won and How We Can Beat the Party of Limbaugh, Beck, and Palin* (New York: Penguin Books, 2009).
14. Ibid.
15. Anonymous, personal communication, 2011.

16. J. Abbey, personal communication, November 18, 2011.

17. Ibid.

18. Ibid.

19. Ibid.

20. Ibid.

21. Federal Election Commission, "Contribution Limits for 2015-2016 Federal Elections," 2015, www.fec.gov/info/contriblimitschart1516.pdf.

22. National Conference of State Legislators, "State Limits on Contributions to Candidates 2015-2016 Election Cycle," 2015, www.ncsl.org/Portals/1/documents/legismgt/elect/ContributionLimitstoCandidates2015-2016.pdf.

23. Anonymous, personal communication, 2011.

24. Ibid.

25. Ibid.

26. J. Cauley, personal communication, November 1, 2011.

27. Jack Brammer, "Two Kentuckians Reflect on Their Time with Barack Obama," *Lexington Herald-Leader*, January 19, 2009, www.kentucky.com/2009/01/19/663459/two-kentuckians-reflect-on-their.html.

28. Ibid.

29. David Remnick, *The Bridge: The Life and Rise of Barack Obama* (New York: Alfred A. Knopf, 2010).

30. J. Cauley, personal communication, November 2011.

31. Ibid.

32. US Election Atlas, "Summary Data," 2015, http://uselectionatlas.org/RESULTS/state .php?year=2004&off=3&elect=1&fips=17.

33. Brammer, "Two Kentuckians."

34. J. Cauley, personal communication, November 1, 2011.

35. Ibid.

36. Ibid.

37. B. Waters, personal communication, November 17, 2011.

38. Ibid.

39. M. McKenna, personal communication, October 26, 2011.

40. Ibid.

41. J. Ginsberg, personal communication, October 19, 2011; G. Shafer, personal communication, September 20, 2011.

42. "Barack Obama—Candidate Summary 2012," *Open Secrets*, 2012, http://www.open secrets.org/pres12/candidate.php?id=N00009638.

43. B. Beychok, personal communication, November 8, 2011.

44. Ibid.

45. Ibid.

46. S. Roy, personal communication, June 20, 2014.

47. J. Pihlaja, personal communication, October 25, 2011.

48. T. Schulte, personal communication, November 9, 2011.

49. C. Phillips, personal communication, October 18, 2011.

50. B. Lattanzi, personal communication, October 18, 2011.

51. C. Phillips, personal communication, October 18, 2011.

52. Ibid.

53. A. Spillane, personal communication, September 30, 2011.

54. J. Reedy, personal communication, November 11, 2011.

55. M. Romney, personal communication.
56. S. Bradshaw, personal communication, October 13, 2011.
57. Ibid.
58. B. Beychok, personal communication, November 8, 2011.
59. K. Robertson, personal communication, November 3, 2011.
60. M. McDonald, personal communication, November 7, 2011.
61. Ibid.
62. M. Block, personal communication, December 17, 2011.
63. J. Pihlaja, personal communication, October 25, 2011.
64. Ibid.
65. Ibid.
66. S. Watson, personal communication, October 7, 2011.
67. Ibid.

CHAPTER 5

Marketing Maven

Reaching the Campaign's Target Voter Audiences

> Television advertising, both broadcast and cable, is the only way to significantly move the dial in a state as large as California.[1]
>
> Brian Brokaw, Kamala Harris for Attorney General, 2010 (CA)

California is the country's most expensive political advertising battleground, as Katie Merrill knows well, and navigating its media landscape is one of the more daunting tasks for even an experienced campaign manager like Merrill. She is a twenty-year veteran of Democratic politics who has worked on more than twenty campaigns in California alone. The 2010 election cycle found her running the Democratic primary campaign for state attorney general contender Chris Kelly, a young, wealthy Facebook executive and Harvard Law graduate. Her story on his campaign illustrates a paradox of politics and marketing in the digital age.

Here's what happened: Kelly was an unknown first-time candidate challenging a field of established elected officials in a state with fourteen media markets. Given the lesser-known candidate's Internet expertise, the campaign turned to online advertising to help Kelly break away from the pack in the June primary. "During the last seventy-two hours, we set off an Internet advertising bomb on Google and major Internet news sites," said Merrill. The objective was to reach late-deciding, high-turnout Democrats who were less familiar with the candidates running for so-called "down-ballot," lower-profile statewide offices such as attorney general and treasurer. "At the time, it was probably one of the largest Internet advertising expenditures ever made in California politics," Merrill added.[2]

Yet, despite the Kelly campaign's Internet savvy and heavy online ad buy, where did most of Merrill's advertising budget go? "Television got between $10 million and $11 million of the $12 million we spent," she told us. As in nearly all California statewide and most congressional elections, the Kelly campaign spent the vast majority of its advertising dollars on television, primarily on thirty-second spots that aired on local broadcast stations.[3]

Merrill was hardly an expert in the artisan craft of selling and buying television advertising. She came from a grassroots organizing background. Like numerous other campaign managers, she started out as a volunteer knocking on doors, making phone calls, and putting together e-mail lists and meetings. When it comes to media buying, she is self-taught by experience. Merrill recalls the first time she ever heard a media consultant talking about television gross rating points, or GRPs, in 1996. "It was a congressional race and the first time I'd ever dealt with TV, so I didn't know what a [GRP] was." Merrill said she asked the campaign's media consultant what they were, and has re-asked the question several times over the years.[4]

Like most of the managers we interviewed, Merrill never learned the math of GRPs but feels she has developed a sense about how much advertising weight she needs on any given campaign. "In 1996, 500 [GRPs] a week was a perfectly reasonable threshold for breaking through. Now it's a minimum of 1,000. And in L.A., it's probably 1,200." And she observed that the political media landscape has changed, noting the rise of "a bazillion different stations" through the explosion of cable options and multiple platforms through which people now experience programming. "It just takes more to break through. They're on their computers, plus they've got TIVO or DVRs and they're fast-forwarding through the commercials . . . [but] you've still got to go heavy broadcast. It's still where most people are. And then if you have target groups that you're going after, seniors for instance, then you use your cable in certain markets to target them."[5]

The Paradox of Politics and Marketing in the Digital Age

In answering the "how do we reach them?" question, the paradoxical fact is that campaigns devote the vast majority of their budgets to broadcast television, so-called old media, despite the growing ubiquity and power of digital communications. Moreover, campaigns continue to depend on traditional over-the-air radio to reach key demographics and for final get-out-the-vote (GOTV) pushes. But why would campaign managers rely on such a seemingly outdated communication tool? Wouldn't they be better off using Twitter, e-mail, and Instagram to reach their voters? Couldn't they spend millions of dollars more wisely on something else besides broadcast television?

Well, actually, it's not so simple. The fact is that most campaign managers still see television advertising as their most powerful tool to reach voters. You're not "real" until you're on TV, they argued.[6] And early in a campaign, they reported, just "being on TV" can build credibility among political activists and donors and with the news media and opinion leaders.[7] Late in a campaign, broadcast television is also the quickest way to reach the largest numbers of potential voters, they added.[8]

Take Barack Obama before he became a household name. When he was running for US Senate in Illinois, he was still a state senator struggling for recognition amid a crowded Democratic primary field. His campaign manager, Jimmy Cauley, budgeted enough funds to spend heavily on television ads in Chicago three weeks before the primary election.[9] And those spots made Obama a public figure—at least in the Windy City.

"Jimmy, people noticed me in the store the other day," a startled Obama told Cauley.

"Yeah," replied Cauley matter-of-factly. "You're on at about a thousand [GRPs] in the Chicago media market. Of course, they do."[10]

Campaign managers typically described broadcast television as hands-down the best, most useful form of political communication in any competitive race. (While ads on cable TV also appeal to campaigns, they tend to reach fewer voters and are seen as less impactful.) Matthew Arnold, who managed Democrat Doug Gansler's campaign for governor in Maryland in 2014, told us that "[Broadcast television is] the thing that moves people. It's the thing that wakes people up to your election. It's incredibly important, incredibly valuable. It is what establishes the frame around your race."[11] Brad Beychok, who ran Charlie Melancon's, D-LA, 2010 Senate campaign, echoed Arnold. "What we would try to do is set our polling schedule to coincide with the ad schedule. . . . So after we maybe did 3,000 points and 4,000 points in, then you can go kind of see what that ad did by taking a trend poll. So I think good campaigns are able to maximize their data," tracking the effects of televised advertising on the electorate.[12]

Well-run campaigns are about any number of things. They are about convincing people who are definitely going to vote for you to go to the polls. They are about persuading people who you know will vote, but may not vote for you, to vote for you. And, they are about using finite resources in efficient ways to reach the campaign's vote targets. Generally speaking, once a campaign manager has identified what a winning coalition will look like (Chapter 3: Political Historian and Data Scientist) and set up a nascent organization and fundraising operation (Chapter 4: Entrepreneur and Chief Financial Officer), she must address this core question: How is the campaign going to reach the targeted voters? One campaign manager argued that those persuadable voters need to be found in almost any close race, and having a "data and analytics program that can help you target your advertising to the shows and time that . . . persuadable voters are watching will save time and money."[13]

Figuring out the most effective way to reach voter targets over the air is among the least appreciated and most misunderstood features of campaigns and elections. Typically, the media considers the mechanics of selling and buying television ads less consequential than, say, the ads themselves, rallies, gaffes, and other sensational events.

But the media errs when it skates past the subject of ad buying. Campaigns use the basic statistics of media, track voters' use of a wide variety of media platforms, and figure out how to reach voters most efficiently through these platforms. Most campaigns devote much time to this endeavor, for good reason. They conduct media research; estimate cash flows and media cost forecasts; track television audiences through Nielsen and other services; and run field experiments to determine when, where, and how much they should run television ads. Such decisions take on special importance in the biggest states, where television, managers agree, is still by far the most effective communications platform. The bottom line is that a campaign that creates a smart, snappy message has to match its creativity with a sound television ad plan. Campaigns that leverage ad buying to their advantage can achieve separation from their opponents, thus having an impact on the electoral margins.

Political Brand Management: Knowledge Is Power

Now, taking a step back, let's consider the importance that private sector marketing leaders put on reaching potential customers with advertising about their commercial product. Worldwide, an estimated $557 billion was spent in 2012 selling branded goods and services.[14] Each of these products has a brand manager who is given a marketing budget and the responsibility for meeting sales and revenue goals. Men and women who become brand managers have knowledge bases built during years of training and experience. Procter & Gamble (P&G), which manages almost 100 brands,[15] starts potential future brand managers in the aisles of grocery stores, superstores, drugstores, and other retail outlets. Like campaign workers going door-to-door and talking to voters, the young P&G future executives talk to store managers and staff, negotiate shelf space and product placement, and watch consumer behavior at the point of purchase. Those selected for further grooming will spend time in other marketing related disciplines, learning about distribution, pricing, market research, product development, and advertising.

Such marketing campaigns last for years whereas political campaigns have lives measured in months. Unlike P&G's brand managers, most campaign managers lack the training or years of experience in making marketing or advertising decisions. But on the day they are hired, they become the key decision makers in an industry that saw an estimated $3.2 billion spent on political advertising in the 2012 election cycle. Many of the campaign managers we talked to admitted that they were not experts on how media is measured, bought, and sold, but they typically had some feel for how to buy television and radio ads effectively. And managers were even less familiar with the growing science of targeting voters over new media.

Selling commercial products on television is different from selling a candidate's message in some important respects. While most consumer advertising is national and can include the heavy use of network television, nearly all political advertising consists of "spot market" buys placed on local television stations, local cable systems, radio stations, newspapers, and Internet sites. Campaigns look for media coverage areas that very roughly conform to boundaries for states, congressional districts, legislative districts, and local government jurisdictions.

Network political advertising is rare, even in today's presidential elections. It was not always this way, however. Historically, presidential campaigns spent most of their money on national network advertising, first on radio and then on television, including buying half-hour blocks of time for broadcast candidate speeches. (Richard Nixon's 1952 "Checkers" speech and Ronald Reagan's 1964 "A Time for Choosing" address lasted many minutes and appeared on network broadcast television, to cite two examples.) Local spot market advertising was relegated to a secondary role and used as a way to "heavy-up" media exposure in swing states and media markets.

But all that changed in 1992 when victorious challenger Bill Clinton emphasized spot advertising in battleground states, while the incumbent George H. W. Bush continued to spend more heavily on national network ad buys.[16] Since then, presidential advertising wars have been fought in the media markets of key swing states.

Almost everyone claims to hate political advertising—except for the owners and sales employees of local television stations, cable systems, radio stations, newspapers, and websites. They love it. "It's a Christmas that comes at least every two years, and Santa Claus really shows up in presidential years," said a salesman who works for a group of local television stations, most of which happen to be located in presidential battleground states. But campaign managers who understand the business of local television advertising will have a significant competitive advantage over managers who do not.[17] States with small geographic areas, like New Hampshire, are allocated relatively few broadcast television licenses. WMUR, an ABC affiliate, enjoys near-monopoly status in the state. Its only other major broadcast competitors are located in Boston, where a television spot typically costs ten times as much as a spot on WMUR. Especially during New Hampshire's "First in the Nation" primary campaigns for the major-party presidential nominations, spots on WMUR are a limited-supply commodity coveted by campaigns.

Campaign managers also need to understand that television advertising is a market driven by supply and demand.[18] The result is that political advertisers, competing for scarce ad time, bid up the price of spots on WMUR (see Figure 5.1). A spot bought in the week before a presidential primary can cost more than twice as much as a spot bought during the same period in a non-presidential year. As Figure 5.1 underscores, the cost differentials to the campaigns are hardly insignificant; given that some candidates have been forced to withdraw from their races due to funding shortages (see, e.g., Republican governors Rick Perry and Scott Walker during the 2016 presidential primary), campaign managers have strong incentives to harvest their resources as effectively as possible.

Under rules established by the Federal Communications Commission (FCC), television stations are required to offer candidates for federal office something known as the "lowest unit rate," or LUR. The LUR is the amount a station charges

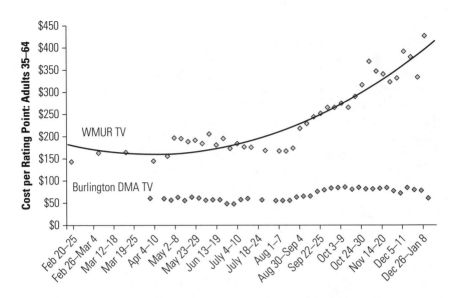

FIGURE 5.1

Political Advertisers Bid Up WMUR Rates during 2007–2008 Presidential Primary Campaign

Source: Analysis of advertising rates prepared by National Media Research Planning and Placement LLC.

its best advertisers, for example, a large local automobile dealership. The LUR rule goes into effect forty-five days before a primary election and sixty days before a general election.

Noncandidate advertisers, such as issue advocacy groups like the progressive MoveOn.org or the conservative Crossroads GPS, do not qualify for the LUR. They are required to pay so-called "issue rates," which in the 2012 presidential campaign ended up being two to three times more expensive than the LURs charged to candidates. For this reason, television stations have a particular financial fondness for independent expenditure advertising (typically highly negative spots) run by these organizations. Viewers may complain about the high volume of negative ads, but noncandidate advertising can be an important revenue stream for a local station.[19]

As we have seen in the case of WMUR, the lowest unit rule does not prevent advertising rates from rising over the course of a campaign and campaign managers need to plan for this cost inflation when they develop their television advertising budgets. The amount of advertising time or "inventory" a station has to sell is relatively finite, so as with every other sort of commodity, rising demand for time drives up the price. The law ensures that candidates pay lower rates than other types of political advertisers, but those rates still rise through the summer and fall of an election year. Campaigns can buy airtime early—for example, a campaign in

June can buy time in October—but the campaign might still be asked to pay any difference between the rate at which they reserved the time and the rate at which the station ultimately is selling it. As a general rule, the longer a campaign waits to buy airtime, the more it will pay.

What Are Gross Rating Points?
Learning the Basic Language of Media

"I don't feel like I really ever have asked the media consultant exactly what GRPs are. I can just know the numbers and what's good and what's bad," one senatorial campaign manager told us. "I knew that 1,000 GRPs meant twice as much television and money as 500 GRPs, but I never asked anyone what a GRP actually was. I was probably embarrassed that I didn't really know, and it didn't seem that important to get bogged down in the technical details. That was the media consultant's job."[20]

This manager was one of many in our survey who could not precisely describe the definition of *GRPs*, which is one measure of the size of advertising audiences. The media statistics of political advertising lack the sex appeal of the creative side (see Chapter 6). Put differently, "what do we say?" (content) receives the lion's share of media and scholarly coverage, while "how do we reach them?" (ad-buying strategy) remains a distant, unloved cousin among political observers. And, unsurprisingly, most campaign managers would rather try to write a blockbuster ad than to do the numbers on a cost-effective media plan. But with big-dollar media budgets under their control, effective managers must learn the quantitative details of how television and other media are sold and bought, and must figure out how to integrate voter media targeting into their overall campaign plans. As Chapter 2 demonstrated, the margins matter by fundamentals, turnout, and performance, so even a slight edge in the ad wars can boost turnout and/or persuade some voters to vote for your side, potentially making the difference between defeat and victory. Box 5.1 illustrates how campaigns use ad-buying concepts to spend their resources wisely and target voters, in the hopes of gaining separation from their opponents.

And for campaigns to maximize the reach, frequency, and impact of their messages, they need to understand the concept and make good practical use of their GRPs. GRPs are actually percentage points. Simply put, let's say we are in a media market with an adult population of 1 million people who are above the age of eighteen and eligible to vote, and assume our advertising campaign is targeting all of them. During the week, we paid for 200 thirty-second TV spots that generated 4 million advertising "impressions," or opportunities for adults to be exposed to our advertising. Simple math—100 percent times 4—shows that my 4 million target impressions are equal to 400 percent of our target audience or, in media-speak, we bought one week of 400 GRPs with adults eighteen and over. Since we got the 400 GRPs from a schedule of 200 TV spots, we can see that the average TV spot in our schedule had a rating of 2, meaning that 2 percent of all adults eighteen and over in the media market were watching the program.

BOX 5.1 Basic Media Vocabulary

These are key terms in the vocabulary which campaign managers use to plot and then measure their media buys as they try to reach targeted voters.

Impressions: An impression is said to occur each time a person *has the opportunity to be exposed to an ad*. Impressions are most often expressed as thousands (000). For example, the "Metro City" local news broadcast on channel 5 averages 7,500 adult (eighteen and up) viewers from 5:00 to 5:30 p.m., according to Nielsen. An ad on the show is described as delivering 7,500 adult impressions whether or not that many people actually saw the ad or paid attention to it.

Program rating: Ratings are the audience size expressed as a percentage of a given population. The adult eighteen and over population of Metro City is 500,000. Metro City channel 5 local news averages 7,500 adult (eighteen and up) viewers from 5:00 to 5:30 p.m., so Nielsen gives the program a 2.5 rating among adults eighteen and up (7,500 audience divided by 500,000 population = 2.5 percent).

Gross rating points: GRPs are the sum of all program rating points in an advertising schedule. Mathematically, a schedule of 1,000 GRPs means 1,000 percent of the target population. For example, Metro City has an eighteen and up adult population of 500,000. If a Metro City advertiser buys 500,000 TV or radio impressions, they have 100 A18+ GRPs. (500,000 impressions equals 100 percent of the population.) If the advertiser buys 5,000,000 impressions, they have 1000 GRPs. See *Reach* and *Frequency*.

Cost per thousand (CPM): This is the cost to make 1,000 impressions. CPMs are used to compare media vehicle or program efficiencies in terms of costs. A $15 CPM means that for every $15 spent in the defined media, the media plan will generate an average 1,000 impressions among a defined population.

Cost per point (CPP): This is the cost to reach 1 percent of a given population. Similar to CPM, CPPs are derived by dividing a media cost by its respective rating. For instance, if a thirty-second TV spot costs $800 and has an adult eighteen and up rating of 5.0, then the A18+ CPP is $160.

Reach: Reach is the percentage of a given population that has the opportunity to be exposed to an ad at least one time. A 1,000 GRP schedule might produce a target audience reach of 90 percent, meaning that 90 percent of the target population was exposed or had the opportunity to be exposed at least one time.

Frequency: Frequency describes the average number of times people will have the opportunity to be exposed to an ad. Many people will be exposed above and below the average. A 1,000 GRP schedule in a particular media market might have a reach of 85 to 95 percent with an average frequency of roughly ten to twelve exposures (*Reach * Frequency = GRPs*). The average frequency number can be misleading—significant percentages of people will be exposed much less often and others exposed much more often.

Demo (Demographic): Media users can be measured and categorized in many different ways. In media-speak, "demo" traditionally referred to age and sex characteristics of an audience since age and sex are the two demographic variables always reported by ratings companies like Nielsen. Advertising schedules that want to reach voters might focus on all adults over the age of eighteen, expressed as Adults 18+, or A18+. Other examples are W25-54 (women between the ages of twenty-five and fifty-four) or M18-34 (men between the ages of eighteen and thirty-four). Since older people are more likely to vote, A35+ has been the traditional political target demo, although some political media planners have turned to younger target demos such as A35-64 to avoid over-delivering older audiences who typically watch much more television.

Target audience ratings points: The target audience is a more descriptive profile of an advertiser's desired consumer. Political target audiences are most accurately expressed in terms of partisanship and voter turnout—for example, a campaign might target W18+ who are high turnout independents or soft party leaners. New data methodologies are enabling political advertisers to directly target different categories of voters without relying on traditional age-sex demographics. These estimated target impressions can be expressed as target audience ratings points (TARPs).

To repeat, GRPs are actually percentage points. But campaign managers sometimes ask their media consultants, "Percentage of what?" Here's what they're told: There are no such thing as generic GRPs. When people are talking about GRPs in a campaign meeting, the manager is responsible for making sure everyone knows what kind of GRPs they are talking about. Are they talking about adult eighteen and over points; adult "thirty-five to sixty-four" points; household points; high-turnout voter points; or independent, Democratic, or Republican points? The same advertising campaign will deliver significantly different GRP levels for each of these groups. Most political media consultants like to target big age or gender groups—adults thirty-five and over is the most common political demographic—because this is the traditional approach and easier for media buyers to execute. But new research methods make it possible to move beyond simple demographics and more accurately target actual voters to generate higher target voter GRP levels for each dollar spent on media.

The following table shows the audiences delivered by a $150,000, 10-day political advertising buy on broadcast television in the West Palm Beach, Florida, media market. The advertiser, who was advocating a vote on a statewide ballot issue, purchased 297 thirty-second spots, but as Table 5.1 suggests, the number of GRPs varied drastically across different audience groups. The advocacy effort focused its advertising on the audience of high turnout voters and achieved an estimated 1,300 GRPs with this group.

In the next West Palm Beach example, the "No on 4" campaign—opposing an amendment that would have required changes in land use to be subjected to public approval—was seeking to reach all high-turnout voters, regardless of their ages or party affiliation. Media buyers used data from Scarborough Research to identify television programs with high percentages of likely voters in the audience. Research showed, for example, that likely voters make up 64 percent of *60 Minutes* viewers in West Palm Beach but only 44 percent of *American Idol* viewers (see Figure 5.2). The beneficial results of the targeting can be seen in the GRP table—the ten-day buy got 850 GRPs among all adults but received a much higher rating of 1,300 GRPs among the target group of adults who actually vote.

TABLE 5.1 Audiences for a $150,000 Ten-Day Political TV Ad Buy in the West Palm Beach, Florida, Media Market Compared across Different Target Groups

Target Groups	Group Population	Advertising Impressions With Group	Cost Per 1,000 Impressions (CPM)	GRPs	Cost Per GRP (CPP)
		Advertising Impressions		**Gross Rating Points (GRPs)**	
Adults 18+	1,503,000	12,775,500	$11.74	850	$176.47
Adults 35-64	720,000	6,192,000	$24.22	860	$174.42
Adults 35+	1,149,000	11,604,900	$12.93	1,010	$178.51
Adults 55+	652,000	7,824,000	$19.17	1,200	$125.00
High turnout voters	720,000	9,360,000	$16.03	1,300	$115.38

Source: Florida "No on 4" campaign, October 2010, used with permission.

How Many Gross Rating Points Does a Campaign Need? Exploring the Conventional Wisdom of "1,000 GRPs per Spot"

"How many GRPs do I need in order to reach them?" This is the bottom-line media question asked and re-asked by every campaign manager. There is no simple, universal answer. But before a campaign can even try to answer that question, it's necessary to understand what actually happens when a campaign buys GRPs.

The conventional wisdom is that a political television spot needs at least 1,000 GRPs to be effective, according to our survey of campaign managers, with the ideal baseline level at 1,000 GRPs per week. This level of advertising is much heavier than even the largest consumer advertising campaigns.

For example, let's say we have a new thirty-second TV spot and have purchased 1,000 target GRPs to show it over the next seven days. This is 1,000 percent of our target audience, so we might assume that we have reached 100 percent of the target ten times each. But that's actually incorrect. Some people will see our ad twenty plus times and get annoyed, while others, alas, won't see it all. These exposure levels are what media professionals call the *frequency distribution*.

The other key variable in the media equation is *reach*, the percentage of the target population that is exposed to your advertising at least once. Taken together, reach and frequency realistically tell you what you are getting for your advertising dollars.

Figure 5.3, a reach and frequency curve, shows a one-week political television buy in the St. Louis media market. It represents the typical, moderately high ad buy in which the campaign would like to achieve 1,000 GRPs per week. The demographic target groups for the buy are adults over the age of thirty-five—the most common demographic targeted by political media consultants because older voters

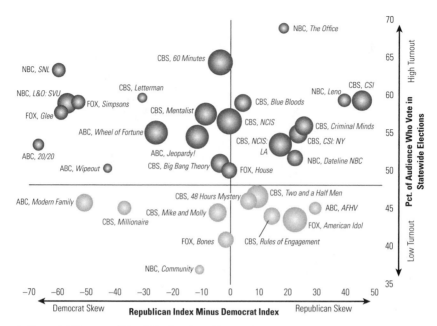

As Figure 5.2 illustrates, West Palm Beach *60 Minutes* viewers are more likely to vote than fans of *American Idol*. The efficiency of political media buys can be improved by using consumer research to better understand the political characteristics of media audiences. In this example, programs in the upper left are more likely to attract high turnout Democrats, while programs in the upper right are more likely to be watched by high-turnout Republicans.

FIGURE 5.2

Political Profile of Prime-Time Television Audiences in the West Palm Beach Designated Market Area

Source: Authors' analysis of Scarborough Research data, 2011 survey of 2,709 adults in the West Palm Beach, Florida, designated market area.

are more likely to turn out. Some consultants use a thirty-five-to-sixty-four age demographic to avoid overexposing older voters at the expense of younger voters.

As Figure 5.3 shows, our buy reaches 94 percent of adults thirty-five and over (35+), meaning nearly all of them have had the opportunity to see our television ad at least once. The average number of opportunities to see our ad—the average frequency—is 10.25 for the entire 35+ population. The average frequency can be highly misleading. In fact, there is a huge variance in voters' levels of exposure to our television advertising simply because some people watch more television and some people watch less.[21] Many political professionals have traditionally talked about the need to "burn in a message" on television, but that approach cannot work with voters who are lighter television users. In our St. Louis buy, those who are most "burned" are the unfortunate 28 percent who have been exposed to our ads thirteen

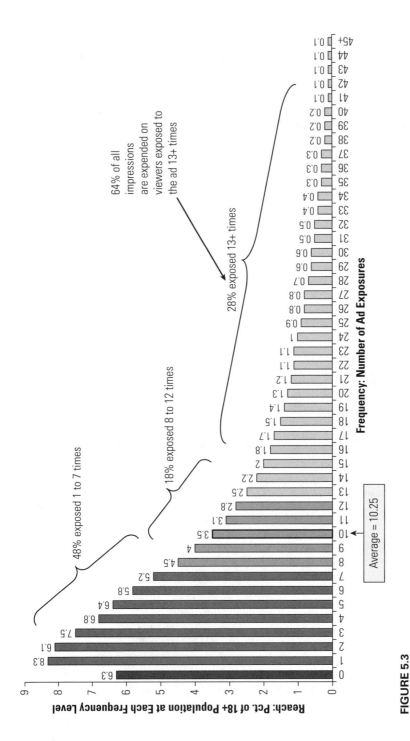

FIGURE 5.3

Reach and Frequency for a 951 Gross Rating Point (Adults 35+) TV Buy, St. Louis Designated Market Area: Reach = 94 Percent; Average Frequency = 10.25

Source: Analysis of a broadcast television buy using PRIME NExT media software and a beta-binomial distribution model. Used by permission of National Media Research Planning and Placement, LLP.

or more times over the course of a week. Slightly less burned are the 18 percent in the eight-to-twelve exposure group. Least exposed are the 48 percent who have the opportunity to see the ad one to seven times.[22]

Unfortunately for campaign managers, those who are least likely to see a campaign ad often include members of the candidate's family, the candidate's biggest supporters, and the candidate herself. "Sometimes it's October and the candidate or the spouse is on the phone with me asking about their six o'clock news schedule, and I'm thinking they should have something more important to do," said one political media buyer. Another manager recalled how a statewide candidate's wife complained about always seeing competing commercials but never her husband's. The manager found out the name of the cable news channel the wife watched each morning while working out and told the media buyer to insert spots on that channel—but only on the local cable system that served the candidate's house.

Ultimately, in an effort to reach those who may be underexposed and pressed for time, political campaigns end up spending much more each week than a consumer advertiser ever would. But, how do campaign managers decide how much volume to put on the air at any given moment?

Having a rule of thumb is useful when it comes time for campaign managers to plan the advertising budget. For example, the campaign manager might estimate that she will be able to afford roughly 8,000 television GRPs with adults age thirty-five to sixty-four over the course of the campaign. If she, depending on her campaign media consultants, wants to have 1,000 points behind each TV spot, that means she will need to budget for the production of eight ready-to-air spots. On the other hand, if the campaign manager believes that most television spots began to "wear out" after 400 to 700 GRPs, she would budget for and produce a higher number of spots. The campaign manager typically hopes to arrive at some consensus with her advertising consultant about how many spots will need to be produced over the course of a campaign, and how much time and resources the consultant can expect to provide.

According to some of the managers who spoke to us, not all ad placements need to reach 1,000 points. Paul Tencher, who managed Joe Donnelly's, D-IN, 2012 US Senate campaign, recounted how their campaign "made the gamble . . . to go up on television very, very early."[23] Even though they were buying fewer than 250 points in most of the state's media markets, their ads were reaching the voters because "we were all by ourselves in all of July, all of August. I mean, Joe and I would say to each other every day, yeah, we won another day."[24] But then again, depending on the state or district and what's happening in the world, even 1,000 GRPs "might not necessarily get heard," said Robby Mook, Terry McAuliffe's, D-VA, campaign manager for the 2013 Virginia governor's race.[25] Ultimately, there is no one-size-fits-all answer.

It is beyond the scope of this book to settle the metaphysical questions of how much weight should be put behind a particular TV ad or how many times a voter must see my ads in order for them to be effective. Billion-dollar consumer advertisers have spent millions trying to answer these questions for years but never seem to reach consensus. Campaign managers will spend many hours in meetings with their hired media experts and pollsters arguing whether there have been "enough points behind a spot" and when the next spot should be prepared and deployed. At the same time, campaign managers also strive to look beyond these details and see television and other forms of advertising within the big-picture context of their overall communications strategy.

Just as in other marketing organizations, campaigns use multiple communications channels. Television advertising is a critically important function, but the candidate's message is also communicated through door knocking, phone calls, radio, e-mail, events, candidate appearances, news coverage, and other channels. The campaign message must be managed across all these platforms. And in some instances, as campaign manager Robby Mook told us, television is simply not a realistic option for a campaign due to budget constraints.[26] Mook argued that if the campaign's budget was unable to cover the costs of television advertising, the campaign's strategists simply had to find alternative ways to reach their vote targets:

> You do your research and you figure out, okay, I know I need to communicate X, Y and Z to win this race. I know I'm going to win them over if I do that. So what tactics fit within my budget to get that job done? And sometimes TV isn't going to fit in there. Sometimes TV fits in quite nicely and that's all you need to do. . . . It just depends.[27]

Let's pause for a moment and think back to the campaign manager model that appeared at the end of Chapter 1. As the model shown in Figure 5.4 reminds us, political campaigns are about so much more than just marketing the candidate's message over the television airwaves. And yet, for those campaigns that can afford it, television ads enable a campaign to reach persuadable voters, especially in campaigns waged in the nation's biggest states with multiple media markets. Old-fashioned televised ads remain the most popular method of political communication in most circumstances. A well-managed television ad strategy can thus keep a campaign on a winning course, flowing in the direction of victory.

In the Internet Age, Television Is Still King

Many college students reading this book will be surprised to learn that broadcast television continues to dominate campaign advertising. Many readers under the age of thirty are likely to be watching their favorite TV programs online instead of on traditional linear television. But our survey of campaign managers shows that broadcast television consistently rates as the most cost-effective advertising tool in political campaigns. Still, a debate has begun about the merits of putting so much weight behind broadcast television ads.

Some campaign managers describe themselves as doubters, and their comments suggest that the typical media mix may slowly be starting to shift ever so slightly away from the reliance on television, first and foremost. Such skeptics point out that

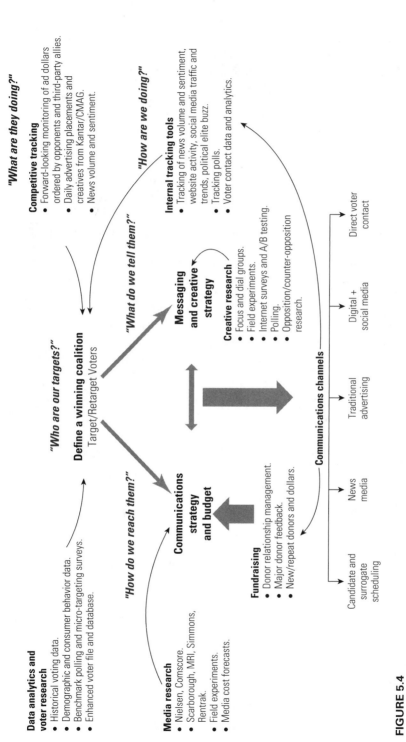

FIGURE 5.4

What Campaigns Do: A Model

Source: Copyright 2015 W. Feltus & NMRPP LLC.

television is not the kind of "mass" media it used to be. When Richard Nixon was running for president against Hubert Humphrey in 1968, a top-rated prime-time program like *Laugh-In* was watched in one-third of all American households with televisions.[28] The stiff, conservative Nixon actually used *Laugh-In* to his advantage on September 16, 1968, when he made a surprise cameo appearance to say, "Sock it to me," the program's signature gag line. Humphrey declined the same invitation, a decision his campaign is reported to have regretted after losing one of the closest presidential races in history.[29]

But, of course, nowadays prime-time shows no longer have the large mass audiences once enjoyed by shows like *Laugh-In*. Ratings for popular shows have continued to decline. These days, broadcast networks are happy if their top-rated prime-time shows attract only about 5 percent of Americans.[30] TV advertising doubters say broadcast is no longer the megaphone that it offered campaigns during the mid- to late-twentieth century.

The ratings decline has also affected local television news, which is where political advertisers continue to place the lion's share of their campaign commercials. Even as local stations have expanded the number of hours they devote to newscasts, the percentage of Americans who watch them has dropped. Local news remains a key profit center for television broadcasters, but average ratings for early evening and late evening newscasts have fallen by more than 50 percent since 1996.[31]

Studies show that a typical American still spends five hours per day with television compared to just one hour on the Internet.[32] So why are broadcast program audiences declining? The reason is not the new media growth of the Internet but rather the rise of a "bazillion different stations," as Katie Merrill put it, which includes the growth of cable television programming, much of which began in the 1980s.[33] In 1986, Americans spent less than 10 percent of their total television viewing time with ad-supported cable programs.[34] Today, ad-supported cable programming accounts for about 60 percent of television viewing.[35] The result is a highly fragmented audience spread across many more channels (see Figure 5.5). When Bill Clinton ran for the White House against George H. W. Bush in 1992, the typical American household received 32 channels; during the 2012 elections, the average number of channels was 187.[36] In sum, for all of television's importance in communicating a campaign's message, the media world has fractured so much in recent years that campaigns that neglect non-television advertising platforms risk missing some of their most-desired voters.

And yet, paradoxically, although cable enjoys the most viewers, local television stations still receive the most campaign ad dollars.[37] With cable's share of the audience growing, it may be surprising that cable typically gets only 10 to 20 percent of most campaign TV ad spending.[38] Campaign managers and their advertising consultants are courted just as aggressively by PowerPoint-equipped salespeople from local cable systems as they are by salespeople from local broadcast stations. But according to a confidential analysis of spending in competitive 2010 congressional and statewide races, broadcast stations received 85 percent of total campaign television spending, leaving cable with only fifteen cents of every dollar.[39]

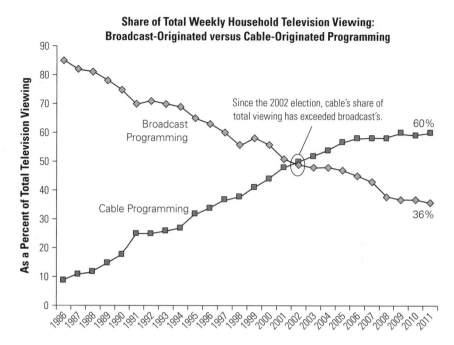

FIGURE 5.5

The Television Audience Fragmented with the Growth of Cable-Originated Programming

Source: Analysis of Nielsen ratings by National Cable Communications.

"Campaigns are about more than just television advertising," said Sally Bradshaw, who managed Gov. Jeb Bush's successful 1998 gubernatorial campaign. "But in Florida, where there are ten media markets and millions of registered voters, unless you have a viable television advertising campaign in place, all of the other things you do in a campaign won't matter."[40]

The Media Mix: Beyond TV

In the final analysis, while television continues to capture the largest share of advertising budgets, most campaign managers agree that it should be part of a larger portfolio of media used by the campaign to communicate with voters. As we saw earlier, traditional broadcast TV has been losing its share of the voter audiences. Voters spend time with many media, including traditional media such as newspapers and radio and the newer media of the Internet and social networking. Thus, almost any successful campaign manager will develop a "media mix" that cost-effectively reaches the campaign's target voter audience across media platforms and leverages each medium to its particular strengths, such as the Internet for ads with a fundraising component or radio for GOTV pushes.

Veteran Republican operative Roger Stone argued that in our fragmented media world, campaigns had a harder time reaching the voters with their messages and that the media mix had become a more complicated calculation than in earlier campaigns.

> There's so much competition in the marketplace in terms of information. There's information overload. There's 100 cable channels, there's digital TV, there's your tablets, your Netflix type sites, your Twitter, your Facebook. I mean, we're bombarded now with information from everywhere. There's a magazine for every discipline you can think of. You want a magazine for biking? There's a biker's magazine. You want a motorcycle magazine? There's a motorcycle magazine. If you're into fly-fishing, there's a fly-fishing magazine. Knitting, there's a knitting magazine. So I mean, it's a lot harder to reach people because they have all this information at their fingertips, and therefore everything takes greater repetition, far greater than it used to, say, when television was in its infancy. I remember in the days when I worked with Roger Ailes on some campaigns, and we would buy 500, 600 points of television in New York, and we thought we were big shit.[41]
>
> Roger Stone, former adviser to 2016 presidential candidate Donald Trump

For a big-picture, national perspective on how voters use media, we can refer to the bubble chart shown in Figure 5.6. This figure demonstrates Stone's argument that reaching voters with targeted communications has become a far more complex endeavor in recent years. In other words, "How do we reach them?" has become a multiple-answer question that must feature elements beyond broadcast and cable television advertising.

In this rapidly shifting media climate, it's hard for campaign managers to predict what the future of political advertising holds. For her part, campaign manager Katie Merrill (see Appendix C for profile) said she expects the traditional reliance on broadcast television advertising to change "pretty rapidly over the next few cycles. Given that voters are now multitasking with their media so much, e.g. on their iPads while watching TV shows that they have recorded on their DVR or are streaming on their TV, there will be an increased need to create a layered effect" with complementary broadcast TV, cable TV, and online ads.[42] Whether or not the billions of dollars spent on broadcast television shift substantially toward digital and cable platforms remains an open question. But, according to dozens of America's leading campaign pros, thirty-second broadcast television ads will likely continue to be a key element in any effort to target voters and build a winning coalition. Even in the age of digital politics, traditional broadcast is still, and will probably remain, number one.

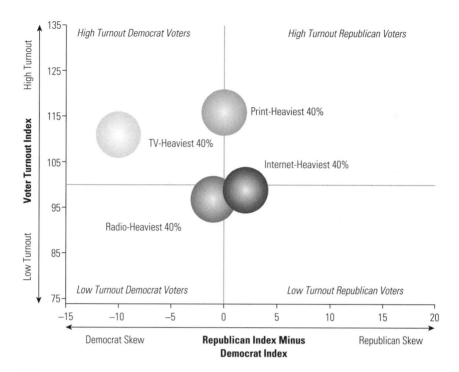

FIGURE 5.6

Media Heaviness—USA

Source: Author analysis of Scarborough USA+ Data, 2014 Release 2.

N = 203,921

Notes

1. B. Brokaw, personal communication, June 20, 2014.
2. K. Merrill, personal communication, September 15, 2011.
3. Ibid.
4. Ibid.
5. Ibid.
6. B. Brokaw, personal communication, June 20, 2014.
7. J. Abbey, personal communication, November 18, 2011.
8. M. Arnold, personal communication, October 25, 2011.
9. J. Cauley, personal communication, November 1, 2011.
10. Ibid.
11. M. Arnold, personal communication, October 25, 2011.
12. B. Beychok, personal communication, November 8, 2011.
13. Anonymous, personal communication.
14. Nielsen, "Global Adview Pulse Lite Q4 2012," 2012, www.nielsen.com/us/en/reports/2013/global-adview-pulse-lite—-q4-2012.html.
15. Procter & Gamble, "All Brands," 2015, www.pg.com/en_US/brands/all_brands.shtml.

16. Howard Kurtz, "Clinton, Bush Ads Go Separate Ways," *Washington Post*, September 23, 1992, https://www.washingtonpost.com/archive/politics/1992/09/23/clinton-bush-ads-go-separate-ways/c22680ec-d930-4840-b60e-1850b0698be0.

17. G. McGavick, personal communication.

18. Ibid.

19. Deborah Potter, Katerina-Eva Matsa, and Amy Mitchell, "Local TV: By the Numbers," The Pew Research Center's Project for Excellence in Journalism, 2013, www.stateofthemedia .org/2013/local-tv-audience-declines-as-revenue-bounces-back/local-tv-by-the-numbers.

20. Anonymous, personal communication.

21. Larry Powell and Joseph Cowart, "Campaign Communications in the Mass Media," in *Political Campaign Communication: Inside and Out* (New York: Routledge, 2016).

22. Travis N. Ridout et al. (2004), "Evaluating Measures of Campaign Advertising Exposure on Political Learning," *Political Behavior* 26, no. 3: 201-225, https://www.journalism .wisc.edu/~dshah/PB2004.pdf.

23. P. Tencher, personal communication, February 13, 2013.

24. Ibid.

25. R. Mook, personal communication, March 14, 2013.

26. Ibid.

27. Ibid.

28. On the NBC network from 1968 to 1973, *Laugh-In* starred the host comedians and was one of the first programs to feature satirical political humor. Much like *Saturday Night Live*, the program reached an upscale, more urban viewer, many of whom were younger. See also James L. Baughman, *The Republic of Mass Culture: Journalism, Filmmaking, and Broadcasting in America since 1941* (Baltimore: The Johns Hopkins University Press, 1992).

29. All Things Considered, "Humor a Key Part of Presidential Campaign Toolbox," NPR, July 30, 2012, www.npr.org/2012/07/30/157613417/humor-a-key-part-of-presidential-campaign-toolbox.

30. Jim Edwards, "Brutal: 50% Decline in TV Viewership Shows Why Your Cable Bill Is So High," *Business Insider*, January 31, 2013, www.businessinsider.com/brutal-50-decline-in-tv-viewership-shows-why-your-cable-bill-is-so-high-2013-1.

31. Potter et al., "Local TV."

32. Nielsen, "The Cross Platform Report: Free to Move between Screens," March 2013, www.nielsen.com/content/dam/corporate/us/en/reports-downloads/2013%20Reports/ Nielsen-March-2013-Cross-Platform-Report.pdf.

33. K. Merrill, personal communication, September 15, 2011.

34. "Where Did the Primetime Broadcast TV Audience Go?" *TV by the Numbers*, April 12, 2010, http://tvbythenumbers.zap2it.com/2010/04/12/where-did-the-primetime-broadcast-tv-audience-go/47976. Ad-supported cable refers to cable programming sponsored by commercials, as opposed to premium cable such as HBO or pay-per-view cable shows and movies.

35. Ibid.

36. Media Dynamics, Inc., "Distribution of Channels Receivable per TV Home," TV Dimensions, 2015.

37. Elizabeth Wilner, "On Points: Our 2016 TV Ad Spending Projection," *The Cook Political Report*, July 20, 2015, http://cookpolitical.com/story/8685.

38. Ibid.

39. Wilner, "On Points."

40. S. Bradshaw, personal communication, October 13, 2011.

41. R. Stone, personal communication, August 25, 2015.

42. K. Merrill, personal communication, September 15, 2011.

CHAPTER 6

Producer and Stage Manager

Creating and Presenting the Campaign's Messages

> In this country, I am convinced that people secretly love gossip and negative and nasty campaigns, but they just can't admit it to themselves. Football games and boxing matches draw huge crowds, and they are rough. How many people could you pack into a stadium for a hugging contest? The future of our country is at stake. Don't be afraid to figuratively punch your opponent in the face.[1]
>
> Casey Phillips, campaign manager,
> Delbert Hosemann for Mississippi Secretary of State, 2007

Part scripted and part reality, campaigns are like live improvised theatre. The candidate is the star of show, and the campaign manager is the producer handling the business side and making sure that the show goes on every day. In smaller campaigns, the campaign manager is not only the producer and marketing manager of the show but also must be able to help with the "creative" side of the production. For managers in small campaigns, the creative role can include everything from writing a major speech or television script to negotiating a debate stage arrangement as well as small details like helping the candidate pick out clothes or putting on makeup.

In larger campaigns, managers focus on the producer role and subcontract the creative function to outside media consultants who have experience creating campaign messaging and content. While campaigns might hire a variety of creative consultants—including digital video producers, speech writers, debate and media coaches, photographers, graphic artists, web designers, and others—the dominant creative consultant is most often the television ad maker. Much more so than any other type of political professional, media consultants are likely to be covered by the popular political press with many becoming political celebrities themselves. Some media consultants have developed reputations (and occasionally egos) comparable to those of their client candidates. The campaign manager—who is often younger and less experienced than the media consultant—can find themselves mediating between the opinions of creative consultants outside the campaign and the opinions of those inside the campaign, including the candidate and his closest advisers.

This was the situation facing a campaign manager we'll call Chet who was running a Democratic gubernatorial campaign in Pennsylvania. With less than a week until the election, the campaign's media consultant and pollster were arguing that the campaign should run a new and highly negative television ad about the Republican candidate's background. Chet agreed on the need for a hard-hitting spot, but the candidate wanted to avoid anything that could potentially backfire. Chet would have to work with the advertising consultant, the candidate, and ultimately the candidate's family to reach a decision.

The Making of the "Guru Spot"

It was just days before the 1986 election, and Chet needed a win. A few years prior, he'd quit his job as a lawyer to pursue his passion for politics and a new career as a campaign manager, but so far all he had to his credit were two losses. Despite the losses, Chet was developing a reputation within national Democratic circles as a competent, hard-charging, and colorful campaign manager. Earlier in the year, Chet had been given his third chance as campaign manager when he took over the long-shot Pennsylvania gubernatorial campaign of Bob Casey. Chet knew his third chance at winning could be his last.

Like his campaign manager, Casey also desperately needed a win—he'd already run for governor three times and failed. Media consultant Bob Shrum, who was already working for Casey, had introduced Chet to Casey during the Democratic primary campaign in hopes that Casey would replace his existing campaign manager (whom Shrum thought was "out of his depth").[2] According to Shrum, the straitlaced northerner Casey immediately hit it off with the foul-mouthed southerner Chet. Despite the fact that Chet knew nothing about Pennsylvania politics, Casey hired him as his new campaign manager. Under Chet's guidance, the Casey campaign won the Democratic primary by sixteen points.

But Casey was still the underdog in the general election where he faced the state's young, attractive lieutenant governor, Republican Bill Scranton III. Twenty years earlier, Scranton's father had been a popular governor of Pennsylvania and had unsuccessfully run for the Republican presidential nomination in 1964. Young Bill Scranton was more freewheeling than his father and a practitioner of transcendental meditation. Despite his mustache and an admission that he had used illegal drugs, Scranton still managed to become Pennsylvania's youngest-ever lieutenant governor in 1978. Here's how Shrum remembers the 1986 matchup for governor:

Our opponent, Lieutenant Governor Bill Scranton, was the thirty-nine-year-old son of a former governor, a Yale graduate, and a self-confessed 1960s "hippie." Casey's hometown was named for the Scrantons; they'd been the bosses living on the hilltop, while Irish immigrants like the Caseys lived in the valley and worked in the utilities and the railroad equipment factories owned by the Scrantons. Casey had a visceral sense that a Scranton victory would be unfair: he hadn't done anything to earn it; he was being handed the governorship just because of who he was and what he'd inherited. But Bill Scranton was moderate and pro-choice, exactly the kind of Republican Pennsylvanians tended to elect.[3]

After years writing campaign speeches for Democratic notables like George McGovern and Ted Kennedy, Shrum had entered the political ad-making business just one year earlier when he and his partners scored a win in the Virginia governor's race. Now, in 1986, business for their new firm was good; in addition to Casey, the firm was handling the advertising in US Senate races in Maryland and California.

In Pennsylvania, Shrum's new firm was facing the established and respected partnership of Doug Bailey and John Deardourff, who had a successful track record of electing mainstream Republicans like Bill Scranton. While Shrum was developing a reputation for the deft use of negative TV ads, Bailey and Deardourff shared a reluctance to go negative.[4] Two weeks before the election, Scranton announced that he was taking all his negative ads off the air, a move that earned him favorable press coverage and boosted him to an eight-point lead over Casey in tracking surveys taken by Casey's pollster Pat Caddell.

Behind in the polls with election day fast approaching, campaign manager Chet and the rest of the Casey team had been put on the defensive by Scranton's pledge to forego any attacks on Casey. The reason for Scranton's move, according to Shrum, was that Casey might be forced to take his anti-Scranton ads off the air. The ads had worked, damaging Scranton's image and helping Casey erase most of Scranton's early lead, said Shrum:

We tied Scranton's thin record to his privileged background. After college, the ad said, his family bought him a chain of small-town newspapers—and the photo of a long-haired Scranton filled the screen—"but he stopped going to work and the newspapers failed." Then as lieutenant governor, he'd missed meeting after meeting of the state commissions he was on—one of his only real duties in that office. The spot concluded with, "They gave him the job because of his father's name; the least he could do was show up for work."[5]

Chet and Shrum needed to unleash a new attack ad on Scranton but were worried by a possible backlash from the state's news media. Some people close to Casey were advocating that the campaign produce an ad to remind people of Scranton's 1978 admission of past illegal substance use, an issue that had remained largely dormant in 1986. Such a spot might pull conservative Democrats and rural voters back into the Casey camp. But Casey himself had publically promised not to do so. Chet's hands were tied, particularly in light of Scranton's recent no-negatives pledge.

Suddenly, on a Saturday afternoon nine days before the election, Chet got the break he needed. A field staffer called to report he had a copy of a mailing from the Republican Party of Pennsylvania that attacked Casey. The mailing had been in the pipeline before Scranton made his pledge not to attack Casey. Details like that weren't a problem for Chet, who immediately had a copy of the mailer hand-delivered to a leading political reporter at the *Philadelphia Inquirer*. The story ran the next day, a Sunday. Chet and the Casey campaign could claim that Scranton had broken his no-negatives pledge and that Casey would be justified in launching another attack of his own. Shrum recalled how they crafted the ad, which later became known as "the guru" spot:

> We had to claw our way back with one last and nuclear attack on Scranton. We had discussed and rejected the option of an ad about his past drug use. I hated the idea. It was too risky. Instead, Caddell [the pollster] and I scripted an ad that skirted the line but didn't go over it—except visually. Scranton had been a devotee of TM (transcendental meditation) and had traveled the world with the Maharishi Mahesh Yogi. TM might be harmless, but it didn't sound that way to voters in the blue-collar precincts of mainstream Pennsylvania. With our editor Tony Peist, I was at Modern Video adding in Ravi Shankar-like sitar music to accompany the side-by-side pictures of the long-haired Scranton and the long-haired Maharishi when [Chet] walked in the studio to look at the spot.[6]

Chet agreed it was too risky to bring up the marijuana issue so late in the campaign. He also wanted to make sure that the new spot was not too subtle to get the message out in the last few days of the campaign. So Chet went rogue. Without telling Shrum or candidate Casey, Chet leaked—through a third party—a rumor that Shrum was producing a spot about Scranton using marijuana. When the press clamored to know if the story was true, Chet said that he and Shrum had wanted to make the spot but that Casey was against it. Casey looked like the good actor, while Chet got fresh press coverage about the old story of Scranton's supposed marijuana use in college. The spot hadn't even aired yet, but Chet and Shrum were already generating free message impressions in the news media. Now all they needed to do was to convince Casey to put the guru spot on the air.

With Chet on board, media consultant Shrum took the lead on selling the spot to Casey. Casey was on the campaign trail and, in those pre-Internet and pre-cell phone days, there was no quick way to show the candidate the actual spot. In an interview with the authors, Shrum said he got Casey on the phone while he was in a Mexican restaurant about four blocks from the Philadelphia video studio where the spot was being edited. Like many campaign decisions about advertising, this one was taking place at the last possible moment. "It was the Wednesday or Thursday

The "Guru Spot." The highly controversial 1986 TV spot was produced by Bob Shrum for Pennsylvania Democratic gubernatorial candidate Bob Casey. It used grainy still photos to tie the young, mustachioed Republican Bill Scranton to the Maharishi Mahesh Yogi with whom Scranton had studied transcendental meditation. "The spot is mild by today's standards," Shrum said in an interview with the authors. See the spot at www.nytimes.com/video/weekinreview/1194817112035/the-guru-ad.html.

before the election, and we had to get the spot hand-delivered to TV stations Friday morning," said Shrum.[7] If the spot was not delivered by Friday, it would not air over the critical pre-election weekend. Shrum remembered the conversation:

> Casey was skittish about it. He was on the road. There was no way to show him the finished ad. I described it to him. He fretted that it might seem like we were bringing up drugs. The script never mentioned drugs, I said. I didn't say that the look of the spot could evoke the drug issue without mentioning it. To defend the ad's relevance, I went on, we had included a Scranton quote that he wanted to bring transcendental meditation to state government.[8]

Despite Shrum's prodding, Casey remained skittish. Casey told Shrum that his family was strongly opposed to running the spot, particularly his eight children who were now mostly young adults. At Casey's instruction, Shrum called one of his daughters:

> She was worried sick that the spot would defeat her dad and destroy his reputation. As we talked, I realized that there were other Caseys on the call. I said bluntly that if we didn't run the ad, her dad was going to lose. Was I sure the spot would work? one of the Caseys asked. No, but it was our best shot. Would I take responsibility for it? Yes, I said, knowing that if Casey lost, his "unscrupulous" consultants would be excoriated anyway.[9]

Shortly after his call with Casey's children, Shrum got the word: the candidate had approved the spot. The final edits were made, and videotape copies of the spot were rushed to television stations on Friday morning.

James Carville's First Win

Casey's campaign manager—whom we've been calling Chet—was in fact Chester James Carville (to learn more about his career, see Chapter 9). Thanks to Carville and Shrum, the closing days of the campaign were dominated by talk about Casey's guru spot and by news stories about Scranton's drug use. On Tuesday afternoon at Casey headquarters in Scranton, while Pennsylvania voters were going to polls, Carville got some bad news: the first early round of network exit polls showed Casey behind. Carville ordered that Casey supporters who were driving to Scranton for the election night party should be diverted to Philadelphia, a Casey stronghold, where they could knock on doors and boost turnout. Carville knew this would make little or no difference, but he had to do something.

The extra canvassing in Philadelphia turned out to be unnecessary, and Casey's election night party in Scranton was a good one. Over the course of a couple of weeks, Casey had gone from being eight points behind in his own polling to winning on election day by two points. Ten years later, after he had successfully managed Bill Clinton's 1992 presidential campaign, Carville wrote about how he felt that Pennsylvania election night in 1986:

> What I felt was not in any way the ecstasy of victory. It was just the sheer relief that I could go home Christmas and not be embarrassed. I called my mother. "Mama we did it! We did it!" Governor of Pennsylvania, that was big. It dawned on me that I wasn't always going to be a failure.[10]

Carville says Casey was successful because all of his campaign's messaging revolved around a consistent central theme:

> To me, the campaign turned into this heroic struggle between the son of a coal miner and the son of a coal mine owner, between people who were tenacious and resilient and those who had everything given to them. Holy Cross [Casey] versus Yale [Scranton]. This was a race of significance. Everything got viewed through that filter, and anything that didn't fit I just defined as information that the elites and the privileged class were trying to force-feed the populace.[11]

Shrum told us that the guru spot was successful because, on the eve of the election, it reinforced the campaign's central message as described above by Carville. After the campaign was over, according to Shrum, Governor Casey developed a lifelong aversion to hearing or talking about the guru spot: "[He] especially resented statements like one in *Wikipedia* that it 'depicted Scranton as a dope-smoking hippie.' It didn't, but that was a technical truth."[12]

Did the guru spot make a difference between losing and winning? "I believe the spot made a difference. In a race that close, everything makes a difference," answered Shrum. Years later, John Deardourff, Scranton's media consultant, recalled that the guru spot represented a watershed for campaign manager James Carville as well. "In a way," Deardourff said, "it launched Carville on the idea that this negative stuff worked. It continues to work."

What Do We Tell Voters?

Campaign managers must build a messaging portfolio that includes both positive and negative content. They must also anticipate their opponent's messaging. In 2002, Graham Shafer, who ran Republican Van Hilleary's campaign for Tennessee governor, developed a "message grid" that consisted of some basic questions. The questions sum up how most campaigns approach decisions about messaging. The questions included the following: "What's your candidate going to say about themselves? What's your candidate going to say about the opponent? What's the opponent going to say about your candidate? And what is the opponent going to say about the opponent?" During the campaign itself, when Shafer and his team ran negative ads, they were sure to check what their ads were saying against the themes featured in their message grid. They had to be sure that they were sticking to their core arguments and issues.[13]

"Where do we meet that intersection of what we say about ourselves and what we're going to say about the opponent?" he and his colleagues asked themselves. "And what they're going to say about themselves?" Shafer's team also returned to glance at the message grid whenever their opponents launched attacks against Hilleary. "I'm a big fan of the counterpunch when it comes to negative advertising," Shafer assured us. He argued that "a lot of times that counterpunch can be much more effective than the initial punch." But the punches thrown—the war about the campaigns' messages—were largely conditioned and driven by the message grid that Shafer and his team had initially developed.[14]

The typical campaign message grid or box looks something like this (see Table 6.1):

TABLE 6.1 Campaign Message Grid/Box

	Us	Them
Us	What do we say about us?	What do we say about them?
Them	What do they say about us?	What do they say about themselves?

There is no magic formula that managers have when crafting an effective message grid. In fact, almost every campaign starts out with a blank message board. Rarely, campaign managers told us, do they have preordained messages that they have successfully hammered out before the campaign is even launched. The general political environment in a particular year and a particular state or district sets the context and the campaign manager must work with his or her team and the candidate to figure out what they are going to tell the voters—what they will say about themselves and what they will say about their opponents.

As our campaign flowchart showed you (Chapter 1), all campaigns have to answer some variation of the five core questions—(1) Who do we need? (2) How do we reach them? (3) What do we tell them? (4) How are they doing? (5) How are we doing? Once a campaign manager has done the math and figured out how his team is going to reach the targeted voters, they need to figure out what goes inside the campaign's communications box. What, in other words, are they going to tell the people?

The campaign message is really the stuff in the message box—what the campaign says about the candidate and what the campaign tells voters about their opponent. While the box is supposed to offer campaigns a consistent message and a rubric that instills "message discipline," all messages must be at least a bit fluid too, in response to how their side is faring in the race and what the opposition is saying and how it is performing.

It's also true that microtargeting—which has recently become a prized tool of most campaigns—makes little sense if there's no relevant message reaching targeted voters. So the message box can be and often is multidimensional. It is both the box writ large for the entire campaign and the box that features the messages targeted to specific groups that the campaign is trying to mobilize and sway. Let's say a Democratic campaign manager is trying to peel off a handful of Republican voters. Well, she needs to figure out what the campaign is going to say to persuade these skeptical voters to support her side. Now let's say a Republican campaign manager is attempting to increase turnout among her side's partisans. She needs to figure out which messages will be the most effective way of boosting turnout.

In Chapter 2, we showed you that campaigns can get to 50 plus one by some combination of turning out their own partisan supporters, persuading fence-sitters to vote for their side, depressing the other side's turnout, peeling off some of their supporters, or expanding the size of the electorate in ways that favor them. Thus, the messages can be calibrated according to which of these five strategies the campaign is using. Put differently, campaigns figure out what they will tell voters after assessing the five options for achieving victory that are available to them. Campaign managers understand that messaging, like campaigns overall, are fluid, and that they must also continually ask, "How are we doing?" and "What are they doing?"— and if necessary readjust their messages and strategies based on the answers to these core questions.

Still, it'd be a mistake if students finished this chapter thinking that the message is totally malleable. It's not. Most campaign managers don't want a message that drastically shifts depending on who's being targeted or what's happening in the world. According to the campaign managers we surveyed, campaigns lacking a consistent message are often losing campaigns.

Campaigns, as Michael Bloomberg's 2005 campaign manager Kevin Sheekey told us, need a "story arc." And on that race, he "started developing themes early." Sheekey had "to figure out who our electorate was and how we were going to target them and how we were going to move them." Sheekey and his team went so far as to design attack ads themselves to simulate what they thought their opponents would throw at them—so they could anticipate the most effective responses.[15]

As we noted previously, campaign managers prize message discipline—with good reason. If they can force voters and the media to focus on the issues that most advantage their side, they then increase their odds of influencing elections on the margins—and it's the marginal variance that often determines who loses and wins the election.

Some political professionals (including us!) are wary of consultants who use a simplistic "box" to demonstrate how they are going to win the election. While as a rule it's smart to beware of consultants wielding their boxes (and we try to spare you the use of many boxes in this book), the message box is a case of a box that actually makes some strategic sense, and it is often effective. Above all, though, a message box is used by many campaigns as they determine what they are going to tell voters—and attempt to stay "on message" during the ups and downs of the contest.

As Shafer argued, a message grid can help the campaign stick to the issues that resonate with voters and on which they perform well. Further, a grid can enable campaigns to anticipate what their opponent will be saying with regard to those same issues—and how to respond swiftly and forcefully.

Once an effective message box is set and the themes are in place, a campaign can then combine that message box with its various demographic targets. This will help a campaign make sure they are better on the issues that are most important to the people in the areas where it counts the most.

Let's keep in mind that determining the message is a dynamic process. In most campaigns, each side must decide for itself what the campaign is going to be about. Oftentimes, they agree on the terms of the message wars. During George W. Bush's 2004 election contest, for example, both the Kerry and Bush campaigns concluded that the campaign was going to be about Kerry, the challenger, rather than the incumbent, Bush.[16] This seemed like an odd conclusion at first blush, but it actually made perfect sense. In 2004, President George W. Bush had approval ratings that were virtually impossible to move. He was well known and admired by many Republicans and disliked by many Democrats. At the same time, Kerry, despite being a long-serving senator, was still relatively unknown to the American electorate.

The Bush team set out to define Kerry for the voters before Kerry could define himself. Their goal was to portray Kerry as a flip-flopping liberal who couldn't be trusted in times of crisis. Thus, the two campaigns agreed that the message war wasn't about Bush but about Kerry. Kerry pollster Mark Mellman explained that "Kerry was the variable. He was the thing that could be changed . . . and therefore, even though the election is not primarily about John Kerry, what gets communicated in the campaign is primarily about John Kerry because that's the one place where there's room for change."[17]

The 2004 ad-tracking data demonstrate how the negative messaging was focused much more on Kerry's statements and qualifications than on Bush's. Only 2.4 percent of Kerry's ads focused solely on George W. Bush, while 59.5 percent of Bush's ads focused solely on John Kerry. The Kerry campaign spent 61.8 percent of its advertising talking about Kerry's benefits, while the Bush campaign spent only 26.9 percent of its advertising talking about its candidate's positive characteristics.[18]

But did any of this back and forth even matter? Kerry lost to Bush by nearly 120,000 votes in Ohio, which, had it gone for Kerry, would have flipped the election. Bush's campaign ran an ad showing Kerry windsurfing as a narrator highlighted Kerry's inconsistencies on the Iraq War among other key issues. A third-party group, Swift Boat Veterans for Truth, also questioned Kerry's war credentials and his patriotism. These negative ads did not by themselves win the election for Bush. But in a tight contest, they mattered, raising enough doubts about Kerry that made it harder for him to gain separation from Bush. If Bush hadn't defined Kerry first, could Kerry have won the election? We'll never know, but it's not unthinkable.

How the Message Matters

Here, we need to ask if the message matters, and if it does matter, how does it matter? How do campaigns determine what they are going to tell voters? Is negative advertising effective? If so, how? When does it backfire? What do America's campaign managers think?

Some communications theory holds that political messages have little to no impact on campaigns and election results. Even much-discussed negative ads, scholars say, don't really affect who wins and who loses elections. According to this theory, each campaign is so well armed that typically their ad barrage is equal in firepower and offsets the other side. Scholars argue that even if this were not true, partisans tuned in to Rush Limbaugh or Rachel Maddow on MSNBC are not going to be persuaded to vote in a different way than their partisan predisposition. And ads that reach less ideological voters rarely penetrate so much that they turn out unlikely voters and persuade voters to vote a particular way, other scholars have said.[19]

Meanwhile, pundits see in political ads and message moments a series of game changers that determine the election's outcome. Popular culture, as well, is equally off base when films and TV shows depict political advertising wizards working under the cloak of night to manipulate the masses into voting for a candidate based on fundamental deceptions. Consider, for instance, Robert De Niro's character in *Wag the Dog*, in which this message maven orchestrates a fake war with Albania to distract attention from a president up for reelection who is caught in a sex scandal.

Neither the scholarly theories nor the popular image fully captures the true impact messages can, and do, have on the electorate during the closest races. If the margins matter, then messages matter. But they don't always matter; don't necessarily matter in the same way on every race; and have different effects, depending on the circumstances. Still, there is no better way to affect a campaign's share and performance during a hard-fought election than to use smart messages targeted at the right voters, backed up by the right amount of resources, to help campaigns reach their vote goal of 50 percent plus one. And, as we saw in Chapter 5, paid television advertising remains the overwhelming focus of such efforts.

Candidate speeches, press releases, e-mails, tweets, and yard signs can all motivate people to donate money, volunteer, and vote. But it is the televised ads that come over broadcast (and cable, to a lesser extent) channels that have the most significant effect on the all-important margins of the electorate. Messages communicated through televised ads enable candidates to define their opponents (as Bush did with Kerry), defend their own records, connect their biographies to voters' lives, and articulate what they would do in office.

But what is a campaign message? At its simplest, a message includes what a campaign is going to say about itself and what it's going to say about the opposition. But the "what do we tell them?" question hardly elicits a simple set of prearranged, cookie-cutter answers.

Almost all campaigns come down to a debate in which one side is for change and the other is for the status quo—as Barack Obama's 2008 campaign famously framed it, "hope and change" vs. the status quo. James Carville told us that electoral politics has long been about this basic change vs. more of the same proposition. "The first guy that stood up in the town square in Athens said something to the effect that this election's really a choice, you know, between somebody that wants to do this and I want to do that," Carville explained. "And the campaign fifty years from now is going to be that."[20]

A message is also part of an extended argument over which side is best suited to be entrusted with holding office and wielding power. One campaign manager we spoke to asserted that in order to win over "a persuadable voter . . . you need somebody that has argument and an agenda that will win them over," and that means "having a . . . sound message, a good agenda, and a person at the top that people can believe in and trust."[21]

Now, let's turn to the matter of how campaign messages get developed. Contrary to impressions fostered by *House of Cards* and other popular TV shows, messages are not created by a single Machiavellian campaign brain; rather, as campaign managers told us, mostly messages get developed through a series of conversations held between candidates, their families, campaign managers, pollsters, and media advisers. There is no formula that all campaign managers follow when they go about figuring out "what we tell them." Still, as a rule of thumb, drafts of messages get tested in focus and dial groups and are refined through field experiments, with polls and Internet surveys, and opposition research and counter-opposition research. Not all campaign messages have the same audience, either.

Some messages are particularly aimed at mobilizing one side's partisans to show up and vote, while others target so-called swing voters who are unsure which candidate they support but are likely to show up and vote on election day. And a campaign's message can be adjusted over time, depending on what opponents are doing and what third-party groups (mostly super PACs [political action committees]) are doing. Achieving message discipline while also retaining sufficient flexibility to adjust when needed is a key to many successful campaign operations.

Why Campaigns "Go Negative"

And let's recall that not all campaign messages are bleak and harsh; in fact, some are more inspirational (think *West Wing*, the TV series) than cynical (*House of*

Cards). Some of the campaign managers we talked to argued that a forward-looking message—defining their own brand, their own agenda, what they would do in office—was as important as "going negative" on the opposition. Campaigns that lacked what former President George H. W. Bush called "the vision thing" typically deprive themselves of a positive rationale for winning the job. Franklin Roosevelt's 1932 pledge to enact a "New Deal" was a potent catchall that rallied Americans fearful during a great economic collapse. Ronald Reagan's 1980 reminder of America as "a shining city on a hill" evoked national greatness and called for a return to prosperity.

But, if close campaigns must make the race about choices, then they must almost all go negative at some stage of the race in order to underscore differences and gain separation from opponents. And let's not forget that negative ads are not all created alike. They have distinct tone, themes, and emphases. Some negative messages are contrast spots that highlight the differences between the candidates on particular issues (contrast ads), while other negative ads are efforts to eviscerate the opponent's character, making her unelectable. While some Americans believe that campaigns have become harsher, more personal in recent years, since the nation's founding, campaigns have been focused on gaining separation from one's opponent to affect the vote total at the margins. Rick Ridder, who managed Colorado Democrat Diana Degette's congressional races, told us the following:

> If I got it right, within the first few chapters of the Bible, God goes pretty negative on Adam and Eve. I think it's how you go negative. You have to make sure that it's accurate and you have to make sure that you detail precisely what it is. You know, when they uncovered Pompeii, they found on a wall that had been covered in rubble for a thousand years the words, "Crassus is a crook." Crassus had turned out to be a local mayor. And as early as that time, you know, 100 A.D. or whatever, they were going negative on their politicians.[22]

Indeed, the early Republic was replete with examples of negative campaigning, making it something of a national pastime. In 1796, Federalist John Adams attacked Democrat Thomas Jefferson as an "atheist," "anarchist," "demagogue," "coward," and "trickster." In 1800, Jefferson's supporters started a rumor that John Adams, Jefferson's presidential campaign opponent, intended to marry his son off to George III's daughter and restore British rule to the Americas. Adams' supporters then cast Jefferson as "the son of a half-breed Indian squaw, sired by a Virginia mulatto father . . . raised wholly on hoe-cake made of coarse-ground southern corn, bacon and hominy, with an occasional change of frecassed bullfrog." (George W. Bush never accused John Kerry of eating "hoe-cake.") In 1828, Andrew Jackson and John Quincy Adams ran against each other for president and ended up attacking each other's wives; Jackson's supporters claimed that Louisa Adams was an illegitimate child who had been having sex with Adams before marriage. Adams' supporters charged that Rachel Jackson married Jackson before her previous marriage had legally ended.[23] In 1884, Republican James Blaine suffered attacks when he refused

An anti-Andrew Jackson editorial from 1828—an early example of negative messaging.

to distance himself from a Protestant minister's anti-Catholic slurs, including that the Democrats were the party of "Rum, Romanism, and Rebellion."[24] Grover Cleveland, his opponent, was assailed for having fathered an illegitimate child, leading to Blaine's campaign slogan, "Ma, ma, where's my pa?"[25]

But why do campaigns still use negative messages and advertising in particular? And how do such messages affect the election at the vote margins? Do these messages truly matter? How so? Campaign managers argued that simply by affixing the negative label to an ad, it is another way of saying, "any ad run by my opponent that I don't like." But calling a message "negative" reveals little about its taste, accuracy, or purpose. Some positive ads are wildly misleading, while some negative ads are calm, factual critiques of an opponent's record.

Negative ads, campaign managers told us, serve several purposes though. They often feature more truthful information than positive ads. They give voters information about the key differences among the campaigns and signal to voters that the stakes are high and the election is consequential. In 2008, Hillary Clinton ran the "3:00 a.m. phone call" ad that questioned Barack Obama's experience in international politics.[26] The message was deemed a "negative" ad—yet was it a disservice to the public to challenge the qualifications of the man who would later become the leader of the free world?[27] Similarly, during the 2008 campaign between Obama and McCain, was it "negative" of Obama to question McCain's apparent lack of interest in the economy?[28]

Most campaign managers agree that positive ads—although important—are often less impactful than negative spots. According to Vanderbilt political scientist John Geer, "If we only listen to the candidates' positive advertising, we would believe we have a choice among these perfect candidates who are going to balance all budgets, solve all educational problems, and end the problem of global warming within four years."[29] Geer, who authored a book called *In Defense of Negativity*, added, "That's a preposterous position. You need the other side of the coin. And the other side comes from these attack ads."[30] And most campaign managers agree with that.

Campaign managers are also acutely aware that much of the public has a love-hate relationship to negative televised advertising. But managers told us that these ads could be highly effective in focus groups and at least partly responsible for why they both lost and won particular races. Steven Law, who managed Mitch McConnell's 1990 Kentucky Senate campaign, described how he and his campaign team cut a series of negative spots and tested them on focus groups. He was surprised when he learned how voters responded, "by giving a high believability score to our most negative ad, which was what we ended up putting on the air. The most negative ad had the most concrete information and that's what [the voters] responded to. It was the hard information in the ad rather than the harsher tone."[31] One southern campaign manager said that negative ads were essential to informing voters about the choices they faced. "I would be perfectly happy if every voter out there would just take it upon themselves to go to the candidates' websites, to read the articles about them, do their own research on it and make up their own minds," this manager told us. "But they're not. I mean, we're lucky if we get 50 percent of the electorate to actually turn out to vote, let alone how much smaller the person that actually takes the time to research their own candidates before they vote, as opposed to those who just vote straight ticket as to the ones you actually can affect with your own advertising. So, you know, you pull out every weapon in your arsenal [including] . . . running negative ads."

"A Hugging Contest?": Why Negative Ads Affect Election Margins

Managers further said that negative ads were often highly effective at contrasting their campaigns against their opponents', gaining separation for their candidates in small and crucial ways on the electoral margins.

Casey Phillips, who managed Delbert Hosemann's 2007 Mississippi Secretary of State campaign, spoke for other managers when he called negative advertising "a necessary evil." "Every campaign that is behind has to use it to close the gap," he told us. Phillips added that "there's really no such thing" as going too negative. "In this country, I am convinced that people secretly love gossip and negative and nasty campaigns but they just can't admit it to themselves. Football games and boxing matches draw huge crowds and they are rough; how many people could you pack into a stadium for a hugging contest? The future of our country is at stake, don't be afraid to figuratively punch your opponent in the face."[32]

Again, it's important to recall that not every negative message is the same. Based on our survey of the campaign managers, there is no iron law about how campaigns are best able to use negative ads and negative messages. It really depends on the circumstances, as we showed you in the 2004 case of Bush and Kerry. What's surprising is that numerous campaign managers reported to us that in their extensive experience, candidates were reluctant to "go negative" on their opponents. They had little affection for the jugular. Yet they also tended to relax their inhibitions once they came under attack from the other side.

Mike Hamilton ran Alabama Republican Martha Roby's 2010 congressional campaign, and he revealed that Roby was opposed to running "harsh negative ads from the get-go. . . . Martha's test was that, 'I want to be able to go to the Publix grocery store with my kids after the elections and still be able to have a smile on and have people respect me.'" So, Hamilton says, the campaign never unleashed harshly negative spots, although he was able to persuade Roby to nationalize the race by running "a harder-hitting contrast ad" against her opponent Bobby Bright, a Democrat who had voted for Nancy Pelosi to be the House Speaker. "Very few [candidates] start off a race saying, 'Hey, I want to go for the jugular,'" Hamilton concluded.[33] Roby won 51 percent on election day, hitting her campaign's goal of 50 percent plus one. The ad helped Roby gain separation, nationalizing the contest, enabling her to unseat a Democratic incumbent in an anti-Democratic year.

Campaign manager Casey Phillips echoed Hamilton's observation. "As a campaign manager, the hardest thing about negative advertising is getting your candidate to go along with it, because if you're a journeyman like me, you can be out the door and on the next state and the next race the day after the election," Phillips told us. "The candidate and his or her family have to continue to exist in those communities and make a living win or lose. . . . It's a game . . . with real life consequences."[34]

There is no formula for creating messages that affect the margins that often decide elections. Some ads that are expected to be effective ultimately fizzle, while others, which might seem odd at first blush, ultimately resonate. In 2010, Republican California Senate candidate Carly Fiorina ran what has since come to be known as the "Demon Sheep" ad against her primary opponent, Tom Campbell. In order to make the case that Campbell was a "fiscal conservative in name only (FCINO)," Fiorina's ad featured an individual dressed as a sheep with glowing red eyes, crawling on all fours among other actual sheep. While the ad puzzled political

Carly Fiorina produced a famous ad against primary opponent Tom Campbell that featured "demon sheep."

professionals, political newcomer Fiorina was able to defeat former congressman Campbell before losing in the general election to her opponent US Sen. Barbara Boxer, a longtime Democrat. Did the ad, which never actually aired on television, change the primary election outcome? Probably not. But trailing Campbell in the polls, Fiorina spent millions of her own fortune on ads that helped persuade Republican primary voters that she was authentically conservative. The demon sheep spot earned news coverage and shored up her credentials while calling Campbell's into question.[35]

Other factors compel campaign managers to endorse and convince candidates to accept the fact that they must sooner or later in tight races "go negative." For example, some campaigns deliberately make the election a "mud fest" right out of the gate, in order to bait their opponents into getting into the mud with them. Some campaign managers believe that mud fests leave voters unhappy with both sides and lead to a low turnout election that aids the incumbent; if fewer new voters turn out, there is less chance of a surprise.

In 2008, when Democrats swept to power across the country, Missouri Republican Rep. Sam Graves faced Democratic challenger Kay Barnes in what was expected to be a tough election fight. Yet Graves' campaign was led by Jeff Roe, Graves' former chief of staff who was no stranger to flinging mud. In 2006, Roe and Graves had charged that a sixty-three-year-old grandmother who was running against Graves was actually a pornographer on the theory that she had once sold advertising for the science magazine *Omni*, which at the time was owned by *Penthouse*.[36] In 2008, Roe was again able to lure the opposition, this time Kay Barnes, into a negative slugfest.

The strategy was effective. Graves likened Barnes to House Speaker Nancy Pelosi with ads denouncing the "San Francisco lifestyle" and one spot that accused Pelosi of "throwing a party for Kay Barnes."[37] Barnes, for her part, ran an ad that called Graves "pathetic." Election day wasn't even close. In a very good year for Democrats, the Republican, Graves, crushed Barnes, 59.4 percent to 36.9 percent.[38] By going negative early and turning the campaign into a mud fight, Graves was able to tarnish both sides and do what he needed to do to hold on to his job. It may have been winning ugly, but the negative onslaught worked.

In 2008, Sen. Mary Landrieu, a Louisiana Democrat, and her campaign manager Jay Howser followed an even more complicated playbook that involved negative messaging. They mixed positive and negative advertising to gain separation from her opponent—and won in a tough state for a Democrat. Landrieu's reelection was far from assured, and Howser approached the message decision methodically. In late 2007, he and the campaign did some polling and focus groups to learn both how they should position Landrieu and attack their opponent, John Kennedy. "Actually, we figured a lot out in that little bit of research," Howser recalled.[39]

They next cut some television ads, with the scripts approved by both Hoswer and Landrieu. They shot the ads in February. As the campaign unfolded, they conducted more polls to test lines of attack against their opponent. They also tested three of their positive ads and one of their negative ads. "We wanted to figure out how we were going to start the campaign against him," Howser told us. Ultimately, Howser concluded that Landrieu could win the state but only "if we defined him first," rather than Kennedy defining himself or defining Landrieu first. Howser assumed that if either of these things happened, they were probably going to lose.[40]

So in mid-July, Howser and Landrieu gambled. They decided to go on the air with some positive ads that described how Landrieu had fought for Louisiana and delivered federal funding to residents, and they had the airwaves all to themselves. In 2008, there were no super PACs to go up on the air and counter Landrieu's message. Then, around August 1, their campaign unleashed a negative ad against Kennedy that Kennedy's campaign never refuted or answered. Instead, Kennedy ran a positive ad that Howser interpreted as a spot that they had planned to air all along.[41]

"We were up on the air negative from August 1st for the rest of the campaign," Howser told us. In June, Howser had commissioned a poll showing a dead heat, but by late August, he had a new poll showing Landrieu had opened a twenty-point lead, thanks in part to their messaging strategy. "We basically had put the race semi-away," Howser proudly remembered. Landrieu, a Democrat, won 52.1 percent to 45.8 percent in a rock-solid Republican state.[42]

Then there are the spots that directly assail the opponents' character, in the hopes of making them unelectable and depressing the other side's turnout and persuading swing voters to vote against them. The 2008 ad run by Rep. Lincoln Diaz-Balart, R-FL, against his opponent, Democrat Raul Martinez, former Hialeah mayor, underscores the point. In 1999, a group of Miami-area protesters had blocked the busy Palmetto Expressway in order to protest the US Coast Guard's treatment of Cuban rafters. A video camera rolled as twenty-one-year-old protester

A 2008 Lincoln Diaz-Balart ad featured video of his opponent, Raul Martinez, choking and punching an anti-Cuba protester in Miami.

Ernesto Mirabal was choked and punched repeatedly by the 6'4", 275-pound Mayor Raul Martinez. The twenty-second video shows police trying to pull Martinez off the young protester.[43]

It is the type of video an opposing campaign dreams of, and Diaz-Balart made the most of it. He ran numerous ads with footage of the assault, including one ominously titled "Horrifying." Other Diaz-Balart ads accused Martinez of spitting in a rival's eye, of threatening a city employee's life, and of "disrespecting women."[44] Diaz-Balart bucked the strong anti-Republican trend in 2008 and won by a comfortable 58 percent to 42 percent margin, whereas Barack Obama lost the same district to John McCain by only two percentage points.[45] In other words, Obama performed seven points better than Martinez, his fellow Democrat. Diaz-Balart's campaign mattered, and his negative messages influenced the election results.

When Going Negative Backfires

Just as no sure formula exists for going negative, sometimes negative messages also backfire. Mike Hamilton argued that "harsh" and "personal" attack ads were more politically dangerous to run than "issue-based," "contrast" ads. "You can go over the line and it can backfire," he told us.[46] Other managers argued that if one candidate is ahead in the polls, running negative ads can have an adverse effect on the election results. Michael Sullivan, who ran Republican Patrick Hughes' losing 2010 US Senate primary race, argued that going negative when a campaign led in the polls can boost the name ID of the opposition. Sullivan recalled working on a campaign where the campaign manager wanted to go negative, and Sullivan opposed doing so. Going negative, he argued, would raise the opponent's name ID and remind voters that they had "another option." Another lesson Sullivan has learned is that when campaigns turn negative, the campaign becomes a tussle over "who can seem the least dirty." "You can win on good advertising and a good candidate," he concluded.[47]

Negative ads are also held to a higher standard, and that's a positive development overall in the world of campaigns, argued campaign manager Steven Law.[48] Today's press corps, Law reasoned, will not allow campaigns to "just run a spurious ad" and get away with it. Law hypothesized this about voters:

[They have become] much more sophisticated consumers of political information than they used to [be] largely because of the Internet. . . . I think it's harder to move people than it used to be because they have information sources that they're shaped by that your advertising may impact or may not. . . . I think it's much more of an art than it used to be when you could just run 1,000 points behind a negative ad and you could—as [the late Republican ad maker] Greg Stevens used to joke, "We'll make it true."[49]

He added that "the old . . . three negative points on a graph with an ugly picture of your opponent doesn't work anymore." Voters don't necessarily know all of the facts, Law said, "but they have deeply ingrained perceptions that shape and condition how they view things."[50]

Another check against unrestrained negativity is the voters themselves—if a candidate attacks in an overly personal manner, crosses an ethical line, or blatantly lies, their campaigns can be engulfed in negative attention, and they can suffer at the polls. One example of breaching such boundaries occurred in the 2010 California congressional race, when Republican state assemblyman Van Tran came up with a novel way to turn voters against his opponent, Sen. Loretta Sanchez, D-CA. Tran sent out mailers with the words, "Open for a fragrance sample of 'Loretta, The Scent Of Washington'" printed on the outside.[51] When the recipient opened the mail piece, they were assaulted with the smell of human feces, and "Something smells rotten about Loretta. It's the stench of Washington."[52] (One GOP staffer told the Atlantic Monthly "it is a horrible odor—like a combination of five or six of the worst possible scents you can imagine.")[53] When the mailer hit voters' doors (and olfactory senses), they were aghast. Many complained that it even made their house smell foul while sitting in the trash. Tran ended up losing to Sanchez 51 percent to 42 percent in a district that used to be reliably Republican (although it is now 69 percent Hispanic, a mostly Democratic voting bloc).[54] Had Tran's mailer never existed, Sanchez still might have won the election, but the margin probably would have been tighter than 9 percent.

Perhaps the best-known recent case of a negative ad backfiring occurred in Orlando, Florida, in 2010. Some ads are so sensational and so egregiously wrong that they affect not only the electoral margins but can move voters to vote against their preferred party's candidate. In 2008, flamboyant attorney Alan Grayson had ridden the Democratic electoral wave and defeated four-term incumbent Republican Ric Keller in the race for Florida's 8th congressional seat. Quickly after taking office, Grayson earned a reputation as an aggressive liberal politician. He described the Republican health care plan as "die quickly" and compared the American health care system to the Holocaust. The *New York Times* reported that "Mr. Grayson has catapulted himself to national renown for outlandish rhetoric and a pugilistic political style that makes him seem less staid lawmaker than a character on the lam from one of his Orlando district's theme parks."[55]

In 2010, Grayson lived up to his reputation. He was challenged by former Florida Speaker of the House Daniel Webster, and although Grayson was leading in the polls in September, he began running an ad against Webster called "Taliban Dan."[56] The ad compared Webster's Christian beliefs to the fundamentalist beliefs of Islamic terrorists, showing out-of-context video taken from a speech Webster previously had given to a Christian organization. In the video clip, Webster says "wives, submit yourself to your own husband" and "so she should submit to me."[57]

In fact, Webster was quoting the passage from the Bible to warn husbands to avoid taking that passage literally—saying the opposite of what Grayson had alleged. Grayson's ad earned him a stiff rebuke from the *Orlando Sentinel* newspaper.[58] Grayson's support quickly eroded. Shortly after the ad began running, polls began to show Webster pulling ahead, 43 percent to Grayson's 35 percent. The candidates refused to debate, with Webster calling Grayson's tactics "gutter politics" and Grayson labeling Webster a "religious nut" and a "draft dodger."[59] On election day, Webster carried the seat 56 percent to 38 percent, contributing to the sixty-three seat Republican pickup in the US House. Webster was the beneficiary of a Republican wave in 2010, but the size of his 22 percent victory margin was partly a function of his casting Grayson's attacks as unfair and immoral, using a negative ad run by his opponent to gain meaningful separation in the message wars. While Grayson's ad didn't by itself sink his reelection chances, it did help seal his fate.

Negative advertising—this time by a third-party group—arguably did even more damage to a candidate in a race for a seat on Wisconsin's Supreme Court. Recall that the campaign manager plays many roles and that the campaigns are seeking to answer the five core questions to affect the election at the margins. But it's equally important to note that much remains beyond any campaign's control, and that's become especially true with the rise of super PACs, which are essentially third-party groups funded by anonymous donors that engage in mobilization and persuasion activities (through television advertising) yet aren't allowed to coordinate with the official campaigns. As super PACs were gaining traction, in February 2011, Wisconsin was turned upside down when Republican governor Scott Walker proposed a plan to virtually eliminate public sector collective bargaining. This prompted hundreds of thousands of protesters to descend on the State Capitol in Madison, marching and banging drums for weeks on end.

In April, conservative Supreme Court Justice David Prosser was set to defend his seat in a statewide election. And while Supreme Court elections in Wisconsin are

Alan Grayson for Florida Congress, 2010.

Alan Grayson's attempts to paint Daniel Webster as a religious fundamentalist backfired.

generally sleepy affairs, the race became a statewide referendum on Walker's collective bargaining proposal. Prosser's challenger, liberal attorney JoAnne Kloppenburg, subtly signaled that she would vote to overturn Walker's law, while it was assumed Prosser would side with the Republican governor.

Two weeks before the election, it appeared that the sixty-nine-year-old Prosser was struggling. Internal polls had the incumbent justice down 7 percentage points and fading, due in large part to Walker's unpopularity. (Bumper stickers in the Madison area read "PROSSER = WALKER.")

On March 23, however, the liberal Greater Wisconsin Committee, an independent group believed to be funded by organized labor, began running an attack ad against Prosser that revived Prosser's fortunes.[60] The ad criticized Prosser for a sexual abuse case he had handled as a district attorney in 1978, claiming the following:

> A priest sexually abuses children for thirty years across Wisconsin. A mother tells DA David Prosser her two young sons were sexually assaulted. What does Prosser do? Prosser refuses to prosecute—doesn't even ask the police to investigate. Instead, Prosser meets with the bishop. To avoid scandal, they send the priest to another community and the assaults continue. Tell David Prosser: Judges should protect our children, not sex offenders.[61]

The Greater Wisconsin Committee accused Justice David Prosser of being soft on pedophiles in this 2011 ad.

According to Prosser, there was not enough evidence to convict the priest at the time and that further revelations about the behavior only came to light in 2002 when more victims came forward.[62] Yet despite the lack of hard evidence, Prosser met with the bishop at the time, who agreed to move the priest.

Most importantly in the defense of Prosser, the abuse victims came forward and backed him in the 2011 election—effectively refuting the charge of the third-party attack ad. They called the ad "offensive, inaccurate, and out of context," with one brother even cutting his own television ad to rebut the one being run against Prosser. In the ad, Troy Merryfield claimed he was being "victimized again" by JoAnne Kloppenburg and her allies, publicly disclosing that he had previously urged them not to run the original pedophile ad.[63]

On April 5, Prosser beat Kloppenburg by .47 percent, or 7,004 votes statewide— another stark reminder that even in a race for a state Supreme Court seat, the margins matter, and, in this case, the message mattered. Many political observers credited the negative ad run by Kloppenburg's supporters with providing Prosser the platform he needed to eke out a win in an election he just recently had seemed fated to lose. (And elections, lest anybody forget, have consequences: Once Prosser reassumed his office, the 4-3 conservative majority upheld Governor Walker's collective bargaining legislation, with Prosser siding with Walker.)

Of course, the most negative ads run in the 2011 Prosser-Kloppenburg race were run by third parties, not by the candidates themselves, raising other questions on the campaign flowchart—"What are my allies doing?" and "What are the third parties saying?" Indeed, when independent groups run negative ads, they are typically more sensational than the spots candidates run. Oftentimes, voters can't tell when an ad is run by candidates or one of their surrogates, so blowback from an ad can fall on candidates even if they aren't responsible for the content.

The most glaring instance of a third-party ad that backfired happened during a 2011 special election for a Los Angeles–area congressional district. In June, a group called Right Turn USA created a controversial web video charging that Democratic candidate Janice Hahn supported a program that allowed former gang members to receive time off prison sentences for mentoring current gang members.[64]

Yet the video, which some have labeled the most offensive campaign ad of all time, featured two black males shooting machine guns into the air while stuffing dollar bills into a stripper's underwear. There is simulated oral sex, while the lyrics "give me your cash, bitch!" play over a hip-hop beat. Pictures of famous outlaws (including, for some reason, Charles Manson) pop up on the screen, insinuating that Hahn's support of the mentoring program meant she favored sending taxpayer money to violent criminals.[65]

Naturally, the web video created a firestorm of controversy, generating nearly a half million views in its first week online. Hahn's Republican challenger, Craig Huey, quickly denounced the ad and attempted to distance himself from it. But his comments had no impact. In a shrewd political move, Hahn actually tried to keep the web ad in the news, filing an official complaint with the Federal Election Commission (FEC) tying Huey's campaign to it.[66]

The web video's producer, a controversial filmmaker named Ladd Ehlinger Jr., who on his website compares himself to filmmaker Orson Welles, complained

Right Turn USA.

Two alleged "gangsters" stuff money into a stripper's underwear in this 2010 anti–Janice Hahn ad run by Right Turn USA.

that Huey was "missing an opportunity" by not embracing his message.[67] The controversy undercut Huey's image and helped sink his chances. On July 13, Hahn defeated Huey by a 55 percent to 45 percent margin. The third-party ads are clear cases when campaigns managers lacked control over what outside groups were doing. They serve as stark reminders that as much as campaign managers seek to influence share and performance, they sometimes have little control over the actions of third parties and events in a city, state, or country that nobody controls.

In another recent case, a candidate actually ended up apologizing for the negative tone of his campaign ads. In 2008, Republican Greg Davis challenged Democrat Travis Childers for Mississippi's open 1st Congressional District. The candidates would actually meet in three elections in 2008; a special election for the open seat, a runoff to serve the remainder of the term, and the November general election.

Childers won the April 22 special election but failed to garner the 50 percent of the votes he needed to avoid a runoff. In the May 13 runoff, Childers defeated Davis, meaning he would be running as the incumbent in the November election. In advance of the fall election, Davis began attacking Childers, attempting to tie him to Barack Obama and Obama's controversial pastor, Jeremiah Wright. Davis also tried to link Childers to 2004 Democratic presidential candidate John Kerry, who had lost the district by 25 percentage points.[68]

Additionally, the National Republican Congressional Committee (NRCC) began running television ads attacking Childers for owning substandard nursing homes.[69] Yet those ads also backfired, as they were based on faulty research. Mississippi campaign manager Casey Phillips, who worked as a field representative for the NRCC in 2008, recalled this:

2008 was a bad year for Republicans in general and people were getting very tired of George W. Bush, but we still lost races we shouldn't have. In a special election I was assigned to in Mississippi, the NRCC [Independent Expenditure] unit came in with an attack ad against Travis Childers talking about how he owned nursing homes that were substandard. Their source was basically a user generated, online rating site that did not carry much credibility.

Their second mistake was not finding out that the opponent's mother lived in that nursing home. Three days later, Childers hit back with a response ad that said, "Obviously my opponent is lying about my nursing homes, if this place was so bad, would I put my own mother here?" The electorate just basically said, "No, I don't believe he would put his mother in substandard care." And the voters tied the ad to the Greg Davis campaign and not the NRCC IE unit. That little exchange absolutely flipped the poll numbers, and we lost a seat we should have won. An entire congressional seat that went south on a little bad research, it shows how close these things can be.[70]

The ads from Davis and the NRCC played so badly that Davis actually issued an apology to voters for the negative (and untrue) nature of the messages. Davis went on to lose the November election, 54 percent to 44 percent. In each of the three Childers versus Davis elections, Childers increased his margin of victory with each subsequent election. In the same district, John McCain defeated Barack Obama by a 61 percent to 38 percent margin. The differential in partisan outcomes—a landslide Obama defeat; a substantial Childers victory—is partly explicable due to the NRCC independent ad, showing how, as Phillips said, "a little bad research" can help flip an entire congressional seat from one party to the other.

One northeastern campaign manager told us that negative ads backfiring were a growing problem, and he approached his campaigns by sticking to some advice he received when he was starting his career.

The first person to ever tell me about messaging said, "Don't ever lie in a negative attack because that'll actually hurt you more than it hurts them." And so I've never put anything out there that's untruthful. I've never put anything out that's completely slanderous or just making stuff up.

Going Negative in a Primary

How the message matters differs from a primary to a general election. In a general election, going negative on an opponent is like checkers. One side attacks and hopes the opponent's voters either switch to that side's candidate, decide not to vote at all, or their partisans are even more motivated to vote. But going negative in a crowded primary is more like chess than checkers. If one candidate attacks another candidate, there's no guarantee voters will switch over to the candidate responsible for the ad—they may have a number of other moves they can make. Furthermore, when a candidate attacks another candidate in a primary, it's typically true that the person is attacking someone with many of the same policy positions that the attacker holds. The result is that both attacker and the object of the attack end up getting tarnished in the eyes of the primary electorate. And primaries tend to be such low turnout affairs that the margins, at times, can matter even more than in some general elections.

Chris Durlak, who ran Chuck Volpe's state senate campaign in Pennsylvania in 2010, explained the problem of developing a message and engaging in contrast during a party with multiple candidates running. For example, he said, "In a six-way primary, it's hard to be aggressive. We wanted to be aggressive. We knew we needed to be aggressive, but the problem in a six-way primary is if you attack someone else, they don't necessarily come to you. They have multiple other places to go." He cited the 2004 Democratic presidential primary, arguing that Howard Dean was winning Iowa when he unleashed an attack on former House minority leader Dick Gephardt. Gephardt then turned around and attacked Dean. "They start fighting on TV. What happens? John Kerry and John Edwards one and two, Howard Dean three, distant three, Dick Gephardt four. It's murder-suicide."[71]

Thanks to Volpe's own wealth, Durlak's campaign had the most money and ultimately spent more than $600,000 on a single state senate seat in Pennsylvania. Durlak said the question hanging over Volpe's race was this: When are you going to attack this guy? In the end, their strategy came up just short.

Volpe lost to a dark-horse candidate, John Blake, by fewer than 800 votes. The inability to launch an effective attack in a six-person primary was a blow to Volpe's campaign, and Durlak's story is a reminder that money matters and the message matters but money by itself does not buy elections.[72]

Responding to Negative Attacks

Finally, recalling the question, "How are they doing?" campaigns must also figure out how they respond when they are hit with a negative attack. If a candidate is in a competitive race, chances are high the opponent will go negative eventually. And the closer the race is, the more the margins matter and the nastier the attacks may become as campaigns fight for every last vote. Campaign managers argued that the best defense against such attacks was to be prepared. One of the first tasks of any campaign was to research one's own candidate and anticipate how the opposition is going to attack one's side, they consistently stressed.

Some attacks, however, are so far out of the blue that they can't be anticipated. One campaign manager who wished to remain anonymous described a particularly odd attack their candidate faced:

It was a really hardcore attack. And I remember very vividly it actually accused—this is actually something I use as an example all the time in my work right now. It accused my candidate of using Chinese-bought pencils in his role at the Michigan lottery. Chinese pencils. I mean, they showed the pencils on the TV. Chinese pencils. You just can never forget that, right?

That was the first negative ad. There were three. And so, you know, I think that we all came together as a team and had to really decide, "What do we do?" Because you never want to react on their message. You want to always be on your message and communicate on your terms, right? So we didn't want to change what we were talking about to go react to what they were talking about. And we needed to decide, well, do we make a decision to change what we're talking about because we think that what they're saying is going to so affect voters that we need to change what we're talking about? And we made a decision that it didn't. We made a decision that we were communicating with voters enough with a message that we didn't need to change what we were talking about.[73]

If an opponent is spending money on advertising that doesn't make a dent, campaign consultant Evan Tracey argued that campaigns are better off just ignoring the attacks. "Never interrupt your enemy when he's making a mistake. Very good political advice. Too many people try and come in when someone else is self-destructing. Just resist the urge. Seriously, resist the urge and let them do it themselves."[74]

When former member of Congress Charlie Melancon first ran for the US House, he was surprised by one attack he received. Melancon's opponent, Republican Billy Tauzin III, began running an ad accusing Melancon of supporting sex education for third graders while a member of the state legislature.[75] Melancon's campaign manager, Brad Beychok, described how his campaign reacted to the sensational charge.

> The first instinct when you see an ad on TV that says he voted for sex education for third graders is, "Where's the research?" Like you yell for your researcher to come in here and tell you why this is not true. Or if we didn't see it was coming, well, how did we miss this? And it's never a good conversation if they're like, "I got to get back to you." They'll give you an answer within seconds. If they can't give you an answer within seconds, you're in deep shit.
>
> Now see, we had this in 2004, they ran an ad against us, against Melancon, that said that he voted for sex education for third graders. The firm that did our self-research, it was not in our book. He voted in the state legislature on some goofy bill that somehow had some sort of money for third graders to have sex education. And that was something you'd like to have caught. I think you have to be prepared.[76]
>
> Bradley Beychok, campaign manager,
> Charlie Melancon for Senate, 2010 (LA)

In the course of researching one's own candidate, campaign managers wanted to tie up any loose ends the research finds. Beychok explained that during another campaign he ran, the candidate had to quickly resolve some tax issues before their opponent made them an issue:

> So I'll give you another example. I've done self-research on a candidate where we took—after we did our own research, we found out that our candidate taken a homestead exemption in both Washington and the state that we worked in. And it was an honest mistake of a CPA not realizing that they took an exemption in both areas. But it was one that would come back and bite you in the ass.

So in that sense, speed is important because what do you do? You go back to the D.C. tax office, say, "Hey, I owe this much money according to my records and taxes, I made a mistake." You clear it up, and then that issue is over, dealt with, and done.

If you let someone come to you and say, "We think you took two home exemptions, didn't go pay it," you say, "I took care of it," you've gotten busted. And so it's very important I think to do your own research on yourself and know what those attacks are going to be.[77]

Bradley Beychock, campaign manager,
Charlie Melancon for Senate, 2010 (LA)

If campaigns know a specific attack is coming, they then often try to break the news on their own terms. In July of 2010, for example, Republican US Senate candidate Ron Johnson told a luncheon that Social Security was run like a "Ponzi scheme." "What did Bernie Madoff do? . . . He took money in from investors. He paid some of the older investors off, and he spent the rest of the money. The money was spent, it's gone," he told the crowd. "You just tell me how [Social Security is] different from a Ponzi scheme," Johnson added.[78]

Johnson's campaign knew incumbent Sen. Russ Feingold, D-WI, would use that statement against him. So Johnson's campaign cut a simple television ad, with the candidate speaking directly to the camera. "Guess what's coming in Russ Feingold's negative campaign?" he asked. "He's going to tell you I said Washington treats Social Security like a Ponzi scheme. And you know what? I did say that. Because it's true."[79]

Johnson continued by saying the following:

Russ Feingold and politicians of both parties raided the Social Security trust fund of trillions, and left seniors an I.O.U. They spent the money. It's gone. I'll fight to keep every nickel of Social Security for retirees, and I'll respect you enough to tell you the truth.[80]

With that one ad, Johnson commandeered the Social Security issue away from Feingold. Johnson had taken what had traditionally been a strong anti-Republican talking point and made it a strength for his campaign and in the process inured the public to his "Ponzi scheme" comment. Johnson would go on to defeat the incumbent by 5 percentage points in November.

During the 2011 Republican presidential primary, Texas governor Rick Perry would also call Social Security a "Ponzi scheme." But Perry wasn't as prepared as Johnson for any backlash. One of Perry's opponents, Mitt Romney, shredded Perry for wanting to "eliminate" Social Security. Where Johnson's strategy had been to explain that Social Security had to be fixed to be solvent, Perry was simply made to look like he disliked the program and wanted to gut it. Perry faded quickly and never seriously challenged for the GOP nomination.

Conclusion

"What do we tell them?" is the core question guiding the message development of almost all campaigns. And most campaign managers explained that if done artfully and under the right circumstances, it was fair and responsible to run ads showing why the other side's positions would do damage to their constituents. Campaigns, ultimately, are about choices—"change vs. more of the same." Campaign managers said they wanted to inform the voters with credible information so voters could make the best-informed choices, could know that the stakes were high, and that every vote mattered.

Campaigns have long been fueled by efforts to define the opposition. And while the means by which campaigns deliver their messages have evolved through the decades, the fundamental messages coming from campaigns have not changed much at all. The next chapter is also about "What do we tell them?" It explores how campaign managers use "earned media" to deliver their messages and how they navigate an increasingly complex media landscape that's speedier, more fraught, and more exciting for campaign managers than it has ever been.

Notes

1. C. Phillips, personal communication, October 18, 2011.
2. Robert Shrum, *No Excuses: Concessions of a Serial Campaigner* (New York: Simon & Schuster, June 5, 2007), Kindle ed., 162–163.
3. Ibid.
4. D. Bailey, personal communication.
5. Shrum, *No Excuses*, 163–166.
6. Ibid.
7. R. Shrum, personal communication, September 17, 2015.
8. Shrum, *No Excuses*, 163–166.
9. Ibid.
10. Mary Matalin and James Carville, *All's Fair: Love, War, and Running for President* (New York: Simon & Schuster, 1995), 41.
11. Ibid., 35
12. Shrum, *No Excuses*, 163–166.
13. G. Shafer, personal communication, September 20, 2011.
14. Ibid.
15. K. Sheekey, personal communication, June 20, 2014.

16. Jim Rutenberg, "The 2004 Campaign: The President; 90-Day Strategy by Bush's Aides to Define Kerry," *New York Times*, March 20, 2004, www.nytimes.com/2004/03/20/us/the-2004-campaign-the-president-90-day-strategy-by-bush-s-aides-to-define-kerry.html.

17. Ibid.

18. Dana Milbank and Jim VandeHei, "From Bush, Unprecedented Negativity," *Washington Post*, May 31, 2004, www.washingtonpost.com/wp-dyn/articles/A3222-2004May30.html.

19. Diana C. Mutz, "The Great Divide: Campaign Media in the American Mind," *Daedalus*, Fall 2012, 83-97, https://www.amacad.org/multimedia/pdfs/publications/daedalus/12_fall_mutz.pdf.

20. J. Carville, personal communication, November 9, 2011.

21. Anonymous, personal communication.

22. R. Ridder, personal communication, September 20, 2011.

23. Kerwin Swint, "Founding Fathers' Dirty Campaign, CNN, August 22, 2008, www.cnn.com/2008/LIVING/wayoflife/08/22/mf.campaign.slurs.slogans.

24. Digital History, "The Election of 1884," 2014, http://www.digitalhistory.uh.edu/disp_textbook.cfm?smtid=2&psid=3117.

25. Robert McNamara, "The Election of 1884 Between Cleveland and Blaine Was Marked by Scandals," About.com, 2014, http://history1800s.about.com/od/presidentialcampaigns/a/electionof1884.htm.

26. Brian Montopoli, "Clinton Campaign Releases New '3 AM' Ad," CBS News, April 2, 2008, www.cbsnews.com/news/clinton-campaign-releases-new-3-am-ad.

27. Ibid.

28. Brian Montopoli, "Obama Ad Attacks McCain for Owning Seven Houses," CBS News, August 21, 2008, www.cbsnews.com/news/obama-ad-attacks-mccain-for-owning-seven-houses.

29. Heather LaRoi, "Negative Ads Accentuate the Issues So Says a Professor Who Is Making it His Job to Study the Pot Shots Candidates Take at Each Other," Madison.com, March 30, 2008, http://host.madison.com/news/local/negative-ads-accentuate-the-issues-so-says-a-professor-who/article_97272f1b-7799-594c-9ccb-28c4e53ba47d.html.

30. Ibid.

31. S. Law, personal communication, September 29, 2011.

32. C. Phillips, personal communication, October 18, 2011.

33. M. Hamilton, personal communication, October 3, 2011.

34. C. Phillips, personal communication, October 18, 2011.

35. Kevin Freking, "Carly Fiorina Wins California Republican Senate Primary, Will Face Barbara Boxer," Huffington Post, June 9, 2010, www.huffingtonpost.com/2010/06/08/carly-fiorina-wins-califo_n_605431.html.

36. Pema Levy, "Meet Ted Cruz's Karl Rove: 'He leaves a path of destruction,'" *Mother Jones*, www.motherjones.com/politics/2015/03/meet-ted-cruz-karl-rove-jeff-roe.

37. Kevin Diaz, "Cruz Consultant Jeff Roe Thrives in the School of Hard Hits," *Houston Chronicle*, May 1, 2015, www.houstonchronicle.com/news/houston-texas/houston/article/Cruz-consultant-Jeff-Roe-thrives-in-the-school-of-6236892.php.

38. "Election Results 2008—Missouri," *New York Times*, 2008, http://elections.nytimes.com/2008/results/states/missouri.html.

39. J. Howser, personal communication, November 9, 2011.

40. Ibid.

41. Ibid.

42. Ibid.

43. Hill Staff, "Diaz-Balart Ad Shows Martinez Fighting With Protester," *The Hill*, October 23, 2008, http://itk.thehill.com/blogs/blog-briefing-room/news/campaigns/41424-diaz-balart-ad-shows-martinez-fighting-with-protester.

44. Ibid.

45. "Election Results 2008—Florida," *New York Times*, 2008, http://elections.nytimes.com/2008/results/states/florida.html.

46. M. Hamilton, personal communication, October 3, 2011.

47. M. Sullivan, personal communication, 2011.

48. S. Law, personal communication, September 29, 2011.

49. Ibid.

50. Ibid.

51. Chris Good, "Scratch 'n Sniff Mailers: Loretta Sanchez Smells Bad," *Atlantic Monthly*, October 25, 2010, www.theatlantic.com/politics/archive/2010/10/scratch-n-sniff-mailers-loretta-sanchez-smells-bad/65109.

52. Ibid.

53. Ibid.

54. "Election 2010—California," *New York Times*, 2010, http://elections.nytimes.com/2010/results/california.

55. David M. Herszenhorn, "Alan Grayson, the Liberal's Problem Child," *New York Times*, October 31, 2009, www.nytimes.com/2009/11/01/weekinreview/01herszenhorn.html.

56. Andy Barr, "Rep. Alan Grayson's 'Taliban' Ad Backfires," *Politico*, September 28, 2010, www.politico.com/news/stories/0910/42818.html.

57. Ibid.

58. Ibid.

59. FactCheck.org, "Rep. Grayson Lowers the Bar," September 27, 2010, www.factcheck.org/2010/09/rep-grayson-lowers-the-bar.

60. Tom Kertscher, "Greater Wisconsin Committee Says Supreme Court Justice David Prosser Mishandled Allegation of Sex Abuse by Priest," PolitiFact Wisconsin, March 29, 2011, www.politifact.com/wisconsin/statements/2011/mar/29/greater-wisconsin-political-fund/greater-wisconsin-committee-says-supreme-court-jus.

61. Ibid.

62. Ibid.

63. Ibid.

64. Jeff Winkler, "Turn Right USA's Offensive Attack Ad Against California Democrat Janice Hahn," Daily Caller, http://dailycaller.com/2011/06/14/turn-right-usas-offensive-attack-ad-against-california-democrat-janice-hahn.

65. Ibid.

66. James Oliphant, "Hip-Hop-Themed Janice Hahn Attack Ad Draws FEC Complaint," *Los Angeles Times*, June 17, 2011, http://articles.latimes.com/2011/jun/17/news/la-pn-hahn-ad-complaint-20110617.

67. Ibid.

68. Ben Smith, "Obama Stars in Mississippi Attack Ad," *Politico*, April 27, 2008, retrieved from http://www.politico.com/blogs/bensmith/0408/Obama_stars_in_Mississippi_attack_ad.html.

69. Ibid.

70. C. Phillips, personal communication, October 18, 2011.

71. C. Durlak, personal communication, September 23, 2011.

72. Borys Krawczeniuk, "State Senate 22nd District: Dark Horse Blak Wins Democratic nod," *Times-Tribune*, May 19, 2010, http://thetimes-tribune.com/news/state-senate-22nd-district-dark-horse-blake-wins-democratic-nod-1.794786.

73. Anonymous, personal communication, June 20, 2014.

74. E. Tracey, personal communication.

75. B. Beychok, personal communication, November 8, 2011.

76. Ibid.

77. Ibid.

78. J. Johnson, personal communication, November 2, 2011.

79. Ibid.

80. Ibid.

CHAPTER 7

Spinmeister and Policy Wonk

Navigating the Media Landscape

Defusing Bad Press

In 1998, Republican Jeb Bush ran for governor of Florida against Democratic lieu-tenant governor Buddy MacKay. Bush had lost in 1994 against incumbent governor Lawton Chiles. Before Bush could fully launch his candidacy in 1998, his campaign had a matter to settle with the state's media outlets. Bush had some past business dealings that his campaign knew could be used against him in the campaign—so they quietly began preparing the media for the information to come out.[1]

The Bush campaign collected a team of accountants, attorneys, and people who had worked with him on some private business ventures. For example, Bush had invested in an extremely lucrative company called M&W Pump Company, which built wells in Nigeria.[2]

But Bush's father, George H. W. Bush, had been vice president at the time, and there were State Department cables indicating that the ambassador of Nigeria had been notified that the vice president's son was coming for a visit. Understandably, there were questions about whether or not there had been improper influence used on his behalf to secure some of these deals.

According to members of Bush's 1998 campaign, the Nigeria episode was only one example of many issues related to Bush's business interests that could crop up during what they expected to be a hotly contested race. So the campaign began to identify everyone involved with the company and began their own process of col-lecting information.[3]

The campaign found that with all of the potential issues, there was no wrongdo-ing and no improprieties on Bush's part. They found that Bush was frequently not very hands-on in some of the deals, but recognized that it didn't matter, because he was, at the very least, associated with the dealings. So they had to know every single meeting that he attended, when he attended, and with whom he met. They had to do their own freedom of information request for State Department cables. They had to identify the pilots of the private planes he flew into Nigeria. The campaign collected notebook after notebook on every one of these potential land mines, so the campaign was prepared to deal with them if and when they went off.[4]

From there, they strategized about how to release the information on their own terms. The campaign held long meetings talking about how they were going to alert the media. Due to the complexity of the business deals, they concluded that the average political reporter hadn't had enough exposure to business to understand how the deals worked. Ultimately, they decided to give the information to reporters from the *Wall Street Journal* and other news outlets. They provided the information they had so these national reporters could write the definitive "Jeb Bush and the business deals" story.[5]

Thus, the story went public even before the campaign went public. While the story wasn't flattering for Bush, it wasn't fatal. (Ironically, the *New York Times* ran an in-depth story about Bush's business dealings months before he declared his 2016 presidential candidacy; this, too, seemed to have no impact on his chances in the primary.[6]) Public interest in Bush's Nigerian business dealings died quickly. As a result of the timing and the manner of the story's release, the Bush campaign was able to diffuse what could have become a damaging story line. The Bush team released the story on its own terms, using what is known as "earned" media (rather than "paid" media) to push out its story at a time and place of its choosing.[7] Not coincidentally, Bush went on to win the election 55.3 percent to 44.7 percent over MacKay, and was reelected in 2002. If they had handled the issue poorly, could it have sunk his campaign? Nobody knows the answer to that question, but it's not unthinkable.

Nowadays, campaign managers face a media landscape filled with cliffs and boulders and is undergoing constant upheavals. The landscape makes their jobs trickier; at the same time, they now have many paths they can use to shape the campaign's narrative arc and deliver their messages to their voter targets. The emergence of e-mail, Facebook, and Twitter has forced campaign managers to adapt. They have to play some form of campaign spinmeister, answering the core questions in order to influence the electoral margins—specifically, "What do we tell them?" and "How do we reach them?" But to be effective, campaign spinmeisters need policy wonks on their teams, so they can use the campaign's policy ideas to sharpen differences with opponents and signal to voters their positions on the race's biggest issues. Even if the candidate's policy planks never make it into law, they can nonetheless generate media coverage; frame narratives about each side's plans, ideals, and values; and shade how reporters discuss candidates and their respective governing agendas.

If the campaign's message is delivered through "earned" media, it can provide free publicity for or against a side and influence the election at the margins. And integral to what message is sent is both what a campaign says about itself and what a campaign says about its opponent. Put differently, the campaign's research (self and opposition) shapes and drives the campaign's message, and the message box featured in Chapter 6 gets filled in once the campaign learns something about itself and information about the other person. The message grid is informed by each side's positions on policy issues.

Earned media is complicated by one of the biggest changes campaign managers have faced in recent years—the rise of digital media, birthing a perilous landscape that they all must navigate. And, although TV ads remain the biggest drain on a campaign's budget, earned media can offset some of the impact of television ads by shaping the narrative arc of each side. The messages delivered through "earned" and "unfiltered" media shape the image of the candidates in the public mind and influence the impressions voters develop about each campaign. Earned media can tarnish a candidate's standing, give a campaign credibility, drive voters to the polls, and turn off voters, all depending on the circumstances and type of news coverage a campaign is generating.

The Shifting Character of the Media Landscape

During the early nineteenth century, campaign managers did not need to worry about a multimillion-dollar media budget or how to raise the money to pay for it. For campaign managers, the media was easier to navigate than it is nowadays. Instead, campaign managers focused on winning a communications "air war" fought primarily through printed handbills, newspaper reporting, and word of mouth. And yet, although the delivery vehicles have expanded, campaign managers remain focused on the core questions of "How do we reach them?" and "What do we tell them?"—all in the hopes of improving one's vote total at the margins.

Of course, the media changes of late have some precedent in changes that occurred almost a century ago. During the 1920s and 1930s, radio began to enable presidents to communicate their messages to voters without a filter. Franklin Roosevelt used fireside radio chats to communicate his key messages in easily understood words and imagery. Television's rise during the 1950s marked another breakthrough in the use of technology to deliver the message directly to voters. Richard Nixon's 1952 televised "Checkers" speech, in which he defended himself from charges that he had a personal campaign slush fund, saved his position as the number two on Eisenhower's presidential ticket. Both Ronald Reagan and Barack Obama used unfiltered televised addresses to talk to their partisans directly and launch themselves as plausible presidential candidates—the former in 1964 ("A Time for Choosing"), the latter in 2004 (Democratic Keynote Convention Address).

Much has changed in the past decades since television became a political force. A half-century ago, campaign press releases were hand delivered to the local bureaus of the Associated Press and United Press International, local newspapers, and television and radio news departments. Less time-sensitive press releases were actually mailed, which, in a larger state, could mean hundreds of pieces of first-class mail had to be paid for, addressed, and stuffed by campaign staff and volunteers every week.[8] Cell phones did not exist, so the traveling candidate and his road team stayed in touch with the campaign headquarters by placing collect or credit card calls through pay phones. Before mobile phones, there was no way for the headquarters to reach the candidate or his traveling staff and brief them on a breaking news story or to suggest that the candidate make a statement in response to something said by his opponent. The principal point of communication was the campaign's scheduler who relayed over the telephone information to and from the candidate and his traveling staff or driver.

In the 1970s, however, this world slowly began to quicken and grow more complicated. The Exxon Corporation introduced the Qwip, a first-generation portable fax machine that enabled the campaign headquarters to stay in touch with the candidate on the road. Political professionals also found new ways to reach voters with their direct communications. In 1982, President Reagan started to deliver his weekly radio address in order, he said, "to bring the facts to the people as succinctly as I can cram in five minutes," bypassing the mainstream media that he thought was often misinformed.[9]

Other innovations would soon follow. Bill Clinton's 1992 presidential campaign used live satellite television interviews to target more voters in key markets. Clinton and his surrogates sat in a studio or near a satellite uplink truck where they would conduct back-to-back interviews with local television news reporters and anchors—reaching viewers in critical places where they believed the election would be

1970s Political New Media. Manufactured by Exxon, the Qwip first-generation portable fax machine enabled the campaign headquarters to stay in touch with the candidate on the road.

decided.[10] "The cost of satellite time was about $500 per hour," said Jeff Eller, mastermind of the Clinton effort. "In an hour, I could get $500,000 of free airtime on local television news broadcasts."

Clinton's campaign team also built the first website for a campaign. The site featured some basic information—Clinton's speeches, policies, and biographical material. But it marked an important moment. Of more than 100 campaign managers we surveyed, many of them said the most significant change they've experienced in their careers is the impact of the Internet on campaigns and elections. In 2008, the *New York Times* claimed that Obama's use of the Internet in that year's campaign "Changed Politics" and the conduct of elections—using e-mail to raise money from small donors and mobilizing volunteers in swing states where the outcome would be decided.[11]

The culture of the media also began to shift some forty years ago when the *Washington Post's* Bob Woodward and Carl Bernstein helped uncover the Watergate scandal. Reporters became more suspicious of the politicians they covered; dug more strenuously for wrongdoing; and ultimately began to report on candidates' sex lives, mental and physical health, as well as business backgrounds. Reports of Gary Hart's philandering sunk his 1988 presidential campaign.

The subsequent proliferation of blogs and quasi-news websites ended the days when elite institutions decided what was news and set the national news agenda for the United States. Another turning point occurred in 1998 when iconoclastic blogger Matt Drudge was the first person to reveal on his website that reporters were investigating charges that President Clinton had an affair with a White House intern named Monica Lewinsky. The revelation forced traditional media to begin covering the story, touching off a feeding frenzy that lasted for more than a year.

The landscape of 2016 is even speedier, more fractured, more partisan, and more unforgiving than it was when the Lewinsky scandal broke. Cell phone video recorders are ubiquitous (remember Mitt Romney's 47 percent comment?), and virtually any utterance by a candidate or campaign official is now considered fair game for the press. Gaffes and stumbles can hijack a campaign's message, impeding the manager's ability to build the campaign's narrative and shape the election results on the margins. The managers we talked to described today's media landscape as among their tougher challenges—one that they were still coming to grips with. At the same time, our interviews revealed, campaign managers still have a healthy respect for the press's role in campaigns and elections. They often sought to feed them stories that both benefited their cause and were honest, and they cultivated relationships with reporters and sought to build up mutual trust.

"Your Best Friend or Your Worst Enemy"

This all raises some of the questions at the center of this book: How do campaign managers use earned media to affect the electoral margins? How do their media strategies matter? How do they shape the campaign narrative arc, ultimately seeking to influence one side's share and performance on election day? There's no single, or simple, answer.

Campaign managers revealed that they have two ways of delivering their messages: paid media such as television and radio ads, online advertising, and direct mail; and earned media such as TV, radio, or newspaper interviews, press releases, tweets, speeches, and campaign blog posts that can get picked up by the wider media world and reach voters, mobilize volunteers, and raise money. Campaign managers also said that the raw material affected what they told the press and, ultimately, the voters. This included such information as the campaign's poll numbers, the opposition research, the price of oil, the unemployment rate, and where the Dow stood a month before election day.

Campaigns typically formulated their messages through collaboration between the candidate, the campaign manager, and key aides, their collective goal being to keep the campaign flowing in the right direction, as our campaign model (Chapter 1) illustrates. Reed Galen, Arnold Schwarzenegger's 2006 campaign manager in his California governor's race, told us that earned media mattered because during most campaigns the press "can be your best friend or your worst enemy."[12] He argued that the best campaigns laid out early on "from a campaign's perspective what is it you want the press to cover" and then found ways to get reporters to cover it accordingly—all in the hopes of delivering their core messages to voters and influencing their side's share and performance.[13]

Additionally, earned media was important, managers argued, to blunt storylines that had the potential to depress their side's turnout or offend undecided voters. The reality, campaign managers told us, is that the contemporary press corps is biased not in a partisan direction but rather toward sensational stories and horse-race analysis. Eager to draw as many eyeballs as possible and lure advertisers online, media companies were in a furious competition for readers and clicks that had magnified the coverage given to campaign stumbles.[14]

This was hardly a welcome development in the eyes of the managers we talked to. Galen, for example, told us that most political reporters are searching for "a different angle. They want something interesting to write about."[15] But, managers added, recognizing this reality, they could then develop a feel for what was controversial and stay a step ahead of opponents by feeding the media negative press about foes and finding ways to burnish their side's story.

The Frustrated Policy Wonk

Garnering earned media also involves framing news stories and gaining positive attention for one's side or negative publicity for opponents by spinning policy-related issues. A campaign's policy platform and spinning the media are both threads woven into the fabric of most campaigns. Ultimately, policy is made by elected officials, not by their campaigns. The chief function of a campaign policy wonk is to provide content to the candidate and their spokespersons, who must be able to answer questions on a broad range of policy topics and, ideally, spin the news stories to their liking. Many young people get involved in campaigns because they have strong feelings about an issue or a cause, and they want to do something to affect government outcomes on their issue. As David Axelrod told us, it's very important for campaign staffers to have commitment to the issue positions of the candidate for whom they are working. But many political people who start out with a policy focus soon find themselves doing other kinds of campaign work.

One example is Laura Quinn, the former deputy chief of staff for Vice President Gore and founder of the data analytics firm, Catalist (for more on Catalist, see Chapter 3). Quinn studied international relations and economics and came to Washington ready to do serious policy work. "Frankly, I ended up doing campaign work because . . . the campaign side of things offered more senior jobs more quickly," said Quinn, who started out in politics doing advance work because she'd been told that's where the action was. On her first campaign, L.A. Mayor Tom Bradley's 1982 race for California governor, Quinn reflected that "we lost to George Deukmejian by a very, very tiny margin [1.19 percent]. . . . But having lost by such a narrow margin, that's the most dangerous thing of all because then you really feel like, 'I need to get back in there.'"[16] Additionally, although some politicians prefer governing to campaigning because government is where they can actually change policy, many campaign professionals believe that by helping their candidates win elective office, they are influencing policy decisions and improving people's lives. Gary Peters' 2008 congressional campaign manager Julie Petrick observed, "the best way to effect change is to elect better people. . . . Sometimes, it's 10:30 at night and I've been on the road for three weeks and I'm like, 'Maybe I should go run a food bank.' And then I remember that if I elect somebody that's going to get more funding to that food bank, then that's the better way to do it."[17]

Still, campaigns can be a frustrating place for the committed policy wonk. One problem is that some reporters don't seem to care that much about covering a candidate's issue positions. Brad Todd, a campaign veteran and founding partner at OnMessage, Inc., has a master's degree in journalism, and he argued that campaign managers "can't get the press to write policy-related stories that are on a positive scale." Instead, most reporters were writing "process stories and . . . gotcha stories. And if you got one of those two things to peddle, you could get it." Getting positive press for one's candidate is "very hard, so you end up managing bad news or getting bad news for your opponent."[18]

One example cited by Todd was a gubernatorial campaign on which he consulted.

[We] had policy councils on every area of state policy. And we had rock stars on these policy councils. People who had been cabinet secretaries before, CEOs, generals, you name it. Rock stars. And we would do a press conference with these people who were—really you were looking at the face of the future government. You know, you were looking at future cabinet people, future commissioners, future chief advisers, and something very newsworthy. And

> they were sitting there talking about potential policy options. We did six or
> seven of these policy council press conferences and got maybe one or two
> stories out of all of them. And it was substantive, significant news, but there's
> just—a journalist can't sell that to his editor anymore. The news hole shrunk
> and they just can't sell it.[19]
>
> Brad Todd, OnMessage, Inc.

At times, then, campaign managers found that the message and media-driven policy debate were simply out of their control. In his book *Out of Order*, Thomas E. Patterson observed that the media's appetite for controversy defined Vice President Dan Quayle's effort to help George H. W. Bush win a second term during the 1992 campaign. Early in 1992, Quayle was set to give a speech on family values that touched on abortion, race, poverty, and work. At the last minute, according to Patterson, Quayle penciled in a line about the television character Murphy Brown, a single working mother portrayed by Candice Bergen. "It doesn't help matters when prime-time TV has Murphy Brown . . . mocking the importance of fathers by bearing a child alone and calling it just another 'lifestyle choice,'" Quayle said.[20]

That sentence produced an unintended firestorm. Every other element of Quayle's speech was ignored, but his Murphy Brown comment produced headline after headline in national newspapers, because it was socially provocative. Patterson argued that "the sensational is favored over the routine." (Patterson added that during the 1980 campaign, the media offered up seven times as many stories about President Carter's oft-inebriated brother Billy than they did about the Strategic Arms Limitations Talks between the United States and the Soviet Union).[21]

But did the media coverage matter? According to the campaign managers we talked to, yes. It mattered by shaping how voters regarded the candidates and how they understood the arguments from both sides about why they deserved to win elected office. The real driver of campaign coverage, managers told us, was horse race-related tidbits, poll results, fundraising news, endorsements, and gaffes. Reporters, lamented some interviewees, had become Monday morning quarterbacks, picking over what went wrong and why campaigns failed. "The suppressed desire of most journalists is to be a campaign manager now," Rick Ridder, Democrat Diana Degette's longtime Colorado congressional campaign manager, told us.[22]

> They all want to sit around and try to figure out whether or not this is the
> right spot, or this was—or, you know, gee, I don't know if he should have said
> this. I swear, I spend most of my time with journalists on the phone walking
> through the rationale for the campaign activity as opposed to covering what
> did happen.[23]

Rather than seeing stories after an election such as, "Senator Smith defeated Congressman Pacheco in the US Senate race for East Pacheesas by 35,000 votes," Ridder reads breathless analyses of how "Smith's attack on Pacheco backfired" and what "John Pundit for hire" has to say about why the attack didn't work.

From the vantage point of campaign managers, who are trying to push their policy stances and tar the opposition through earned media, there were too few political reporters, with too little experience on the trail. And, they said, the fierce competition for speed and eyeballs resulted in stories that were increasingly sensational. One campaign manager told us that "there's too much news and too few reporters," who, on the whole, give credence to all arguments whether or not they were even based in fact. Brad Todd echoed that campaign reporters were young and "stretched . . . thin. . . . The press corps as a whole," he said, "does not have the level of experience, campaign exposure, and expertise that we had several years ago. And that is a real problem for campaigns, especially if you're trying to communicate something complicated."[24]

Campaign managers were somewhat divided about the effects of traditional media coverage on their election chances at the margins. Harris, for one, argued that by shedding the extremist label from Toomey's name in the media, the stories ultimately helped Toomey prevail on election day (see Chapter 2).[25] Todd, in contrast, cited one statewide campaign he did in which his side received terrible press; still, "there was no evidence it made a bit of difference" in the polls.[26] Ultimately, though, a sizable majority of campaign managers argued that media coverage mattered. They cared about what the media wrote and said about their campaigns, because they believed it affected their share and performance in the electorate.

Their most effective strategies for generating news coverage, they said, involved creative ploys that would pique the interest of editors and reporters. But the tricks had to underscore some aspect of the campaign's core message or issue positions; they couldn't simply be divorced from what the campaigns were telling the voters. Creative stunts enabled campaign managers to "break through."

Cell Phones and Earned Media

Take, for example, Casey Phillips' gimmick when he managed Delbert Hosemann's 2007 Mississippi secretary of state campaign. Hosemann had proposed a sweeping reform of the state's business laws, which hadn't been updated for decades and were woefully inadequate to the task at hand. It was an issue about which Hosemann was passionate. So, armed with a six-page white paper and a deep knowledge of the policy, he crisscrossed Mississippi, talking to editorial boards, seeking to gain coverage for his reform idea. Reporters and editors greeted his proposal with a collective yawn; the idea, they told Phillips, simply wasn't terribly exciting. That's when Phillips came up with a strategy: he went on eBay. He told us he "bought a 1983 Nokia cell phone that came with a backpack basically and a charger and . . . this crank." And he gave the old phone to Hosemann along with an iPhone, and the candidate began to hold up the Nokia phone and say, "This was business in '83." Then, he'd hold up the iPhone and say, "This is business today. This is why it needs to [change]." The gimmick, Phillips recalled, "actually got us some stories." The key to making a message or policy proposal stick, said Phillips, was to find a novel way to generate public attention—to give local newspapers and other outlets sexy and engaging ways to convey the campaign's substantive policies and message. During a different race Phillips managed, he actually had a "college Republican [dress up] as a giant waffle." The student followed their opponent around—to cement his image as "Waffle Man." That stunt, too, helped Phillips break through in a highly competitive media climate.[27]

Other campaign managers tried to affect the vote margins by cultivating local newspapers and local radio and television stations in order to expand a candidate's name ID and show voters that she knew about the issues that mattered to them in their towns, hamlets, and cities. Graham Shafer, Van Hilleary's campaign manager in the 2002 Tennessee governor's race, was seeking to depict Hilleary as "a pretty normal guy." In order to communicate that message in ways that garnered earned media, the campaign sent the candidate on twenty-four-hour tours of local communities—a 1:00 a.m. diner stop, a 5:00 a.m. hand-shaking with factory workers arriving for their shifts. The media was invited and often followed Hilleary on these stops, and Shafer also made a point of focusing on local editors and reporters and weekly local papers, community radio stations, and local events including moon pie, tomato, and RC Cola festivals—all of which led to positive coverage in local media venues.[28]

Shafer recalled that Hilleary was one of the first candidates "to use a stock car NASCAR-type sponsorship" to garner earned media and promote the campaign's average Joe message. The campaign gave the driver "a $10,000 donation that paid for his tires for the season," Shafer told us. And with that modest investment, "we got signage over the whole vehicle, on the side panels, on the back, on the roof, everything. And so we actually used that in a lot of situations." He said that "ultimately we put the car and the driver in the [campaign] ad using the tagline with Van, saying, . . . 'We'll get Tennessee fixed in no time flat.'"[29]

These weren't just empty-headed gimmicks. As Shafer pointed out, the near single-minded focus on local events and local media, and by using a sport that Tennesseans loved, Hilleary gained an edge in the quest to influence the election results. He used these strategies to show voters that he understood their lives and that he was like them, which helped voters identify with him and helped Hilleary compete statewide. Even though he lost that race by around 50,000 votes out of more than 1.5 million votes cast, Hilleary arguably would have suffered a bigger defeat had he and Shafer not cultivated the local press through their aggressive earned media strategies. Even though they were narrowly defeated, their earned media was effective on the campaign's margins.[30]

Other campaign managers described similar stunts that rooted their candidates in their local communities, linked them to popular issue positions, and identified them as candidates in touch with people's lives. Karl Koch, who ran Democrat

Lawton Chiles' 1994 Florida governor's race, recalled that when "Chiles first ran for United States Senate in 1970," he "walked the length of Florida from Pensacola to Key West. And so ever since then, he was known as Walking Lawton. And . . . we literally walk. We'd go in a community and he'd walk from point A to point B and 200, 300 people would follow him everywhere he went." Although Koch admitted it was a "gimmick," Walking Lawton became "his campaign trademark that was guaranteed to build a crowd, guaranteed to get media"—and it delivered their message to undecided voters and Chiles' partisans at the same time. Branding Chiles as somebody who knew Florida's communities and understood its diverse neighborhoods and peoples was instrumental in cementing his reputation as a major figure in Florida elections.[31]

Because campaigns are seeking to affect the margins of the vote, some campaign managers described micro-events, targeting relatively small numbers of voters who they hoped would be difference-makers on election day. Even a handful of voters were important to some statewide campaigns. Thus, Mary Landrieu's 2008 campaign manager Jay Howser told us that in Louisiana they developed a "community dinner program that . . . was a great tool for our field staff" in helping turn out their reliable supporters. "What we would do is target voters in some parish or in some town or a subset of voters and have a free community dinner," he went on to explain.[32]

And we would cater the food and we would have our field staff call those people and while they're calling, they also ID them and invite them. And we would get between . . . 75 and 150 people there at these dinners. It was a great kind of field effort . . . in places like Lafayette parish or . . . Lake Charles parish. It was great field, it was great political, and the local newspaper and TV showed up as well.[33]

These dinners typically garnered favorable coverage for Landrieu's campaign—a series of small events earning positive free news and affecting the electorate a handful of votes at a time. Running in a deep red state, Landrieu needed every conceivable vote in order to win her race.

Charlie Melancon's Louisiana US Senate campaign piggybacked on a much-publicized National Football League controversy involving the New Orleans Saints as a strategy to sign up volunteers and generate positive earned media. The NFL ordered shops in New Orleans to stop selling clothes with the Saints tagline, "Who Dat?," claiming that the NFL held the rights to the popular phrase. Bradley Beychok explained that when he ran Melancon's campaign, his side launched a petition urging the NFL to let Louisianans use the phrase on their apparel. The petition generated some 75,000 signatures and gave the campaign "a bump" with voters and helped break through Louisiana's cluttered media landscape. Beychok further recalled that Melancon visited small-town newspapers and took pictures with editors and ultimately garnered "noncontentious" stories and interviews about the candidate's policy goals and priorities. Such earned media coverage is invaluable at reaching local voters in these communities. And finally, when Beychok heard from local reporters that they weren't interested in a story Beychok deemed important, his strategy was to peddle the story to national political media such as *Politico*, Talking Points Memo, and cable news shows; then, once the story ran, he'd tell the local editor, "You got to cover this." Beychok's media strategy is simple: "Local is best."[34] But he described the "new class of media" as a key way to generate stories that pressured local and state media to ape their coverage, thus influencing share and performance.[35]

"The Blogs Will Pick It Up Immediately" (Speed)

Virtually all campaign managers are seeking to tilt the media's narrative about their races just slightly to their advantage, but the answer to "How do we reach them?" increasingly comes down to a single word: blogs. Campaigns continue to rely on standard techniques such as press releases that reporters can quote when writing their stories, as well as stump speeches and news interviews yielding sound bites that reporters can drop into their radio and television spots. Handling newer forms of political media, such as bloggers, has been a much more vexing challenge for most of the campaign managers we surveyed. Yet blogs have also become increasingly vital to spreading the campaign's message. As Brad Todd observed, campaign managers now have the power to "give it to a blog" and "move things through the press and what we call earned media." He explained the rationale: "You give to a blog first, then you take the blog to a more mainstream reporter and say, 'See, the blogs are beating you on this. Better cover it.'"[36]

That has indeed become a go-to strategy for many of the professionals we interviewed. Kelly Evans, who managed Christine Gregoire's 2008 Washington governor's race, argued that traditional news sources were still "really important." But she also remarked that reporters are clearly reading political blogs, adding, "getting your stuff up on political blogs is sometimes the first thing" she liked to do. Evans had Gregoire "spend time talking to bloggers," and she described a full-bore media campaign seeking to disseminate their side's message in the hopes of shaping voters' impressions of the race and, ultimately, using the media to influence who people voted for. "We did everything," Evans told us.[37]

> We did traditional press conferences. We sent out press releases, whether it was positive or negative stuff. The state party did most of the attacking of our opponent. But we made web videos that got posted. The party did that. Or they'd make web videos about our opponent. And we'd post those and try to get attention to those. . . . We tried to use all the tools that were available to us at the time. We did regular weekly communications to the press that went out via e-mail. The governor would spend one-on-one time with reporters.[38]

"And we thought it was necessary" to try to shape the media narrative and give Gregoire a slight advantage in what was widely seen as a closely contested race for governor—but the blogs were a vital component of the overall media strategy to drive the campaign's message to the public.[39]

Yet it wasn't simply the rise of blogs that have empowered campaign managers to garner earned media and influence the election's margins. The news cycle's warp speed had also posed a set of complicated challenges for political pros seeking to control their message and keep the campaign on a winning course. Even legacy media such as the *New York Times* and NBC News are continually updating their websites with breaking news, and the cliché is true—the news cycle truly is nonstop. News outlets have to cover breaking stories twenty-four hours a day, and cable news outlets have more time they need to fill. There are more stories to cover and more time to cover them. "Each cycle gets faster and faster," Shafer, Van Hilleary's campaign manager, observed, "to the point where . . . you almost feel like you don't have a news cycle." Campaigns, he explained, needed "to be on top of a story the minute it breaks with traditional and social media tools." Equally challenging, Shafer argued, was that the message—or a message harmful to a campaign—can be delivered in a "multiple of ways" at blinding speed, and campaigns are facing off against "bloggers . . . who are not trained. When I mean trained, I mean educated journalists. They're educated people, but they didn't go to school for media or journalism. They're you and I, and they have the power to turn on a computer, Facebook, tweet, and Instagram a message." That's why Shafer insists that communicating his side's message to those bloggers is crucial; "they take sides, [and] they've got their jersey on." Shafer is determined to "cultivate a relationship with them in real time, where they're feeding you information and you're feeding them information. And a lot of times you now deliver stories into blogs rather than going into direct news media", likely because the blogs will pick it up immediately.[40]

Working the Refs (Credibility)

Behind the scenes, campaign managers are engaged in a fierce jockeying to deliver their messages to the voters in ways that will gain a small advantage for their candidates. Bloggers and reporters alike enjoy attention and appreciate help doing their job, and campaigns need them to spread their messages and policy ideas. Thus, the managers we surveyed almost all cultivated bloggers, reporters, and editors whom they thought could be helpful in getting their message to targeted voters. Matt McDonald, who helped run Democrat Elia Pirozzi's 1998 California congressional race, explained how his campaign "reap[ed] a lot of benefits" by being "forthright, friendly," and generating goodwill with reporters "just by returning calls and having accurate information and following through with very simple commitments to reporters. They'll treat you better if they feel like you're treating them with respect."[41] He added this:

> The inclination particularly in Republican circles is to tell the media to take a flying leap and that's absolutely the wrong strategy because, as much as you

might think that they're out to get you, yeah, they are, they're out to get everyone. I mean, they're out to get your opponent too. They're out for a good story, no matter what. And you're not going to change that by hiding in a hole and pretending that they aren't there because, guess what, they buy their ink by a barrel and don't go to war against somebody who buys ink by the barrel. You're going to lose.[42]

Campaign managers were critical of the press, but they neither loathed nor feared the reporters who covered their races. More often than not, they actually valued their role in the democratic process, notwithstanding the press corps' sizable warts. Martha McKenna, who learned her trade at EMILY's List, said her approach as a campaign manager was to "be in touch with the media all the time." She added that some managers were unjustifiably "afraid of the press" and worried that reporters were "going to screw them at every turn and . . . write bad stories about you." But, she echoed McDonald, reporters for the most part were simply trying to do their jobs and didn't "have a political ax to grind," and they needed to be treated fairly. Managers, she argued, had to build relationships with reporters, "give them leads, pitch them stories," and give them access to their candidates in order to give their side the best shot at influencing the election's margins. Managers, she concluded, "have a responsibility to their candidate to have relationships with reporters in the district and to be representing them well."[43]

McKenna didn't see a formula for certain success, for sure; however, she argued, by giving reporters access and cementing those relationships, a campaign increased its chances that the stories would at least be fair and that their side of the policy argument and message would get aired—giving her campaign the best shot to inspire its partisans and persuade swing voters to support her side.[44]

Democrat Screven Watson, who ran Rod Smith's 2006 Florida gubernatorial campaign, agreed that in order to improve his candidates' chances, campaign managers had to continually work the referees. "You've got to be . . . proactive with the press," he told us. Reporters, he explained, are sitting at their desks, reading blogs, texts, e-mails, and tweets, and in today's environment they were hard pressed to dig for stories and launch their own investigations. Watson argued that by building rapport with the press and looking for a series of little stories that helped his side's argument, his campaign could find success. People in politics, he said, "want to have the front page [story] that I've got a company relocated to Tampa that's going to create 1,000 jobs. Great. If you can do it, I'm not saying don't do it. But if you do a bunch of little things—working the press," being honest with them, building relationships, and feeding them usable nuggets—it can get a campaign's message out on earned media. The little victories, he concluded, added up to bigger ones that can affect election results.[45]

Trust, honesty, and relationship building also defined Raul Labrador's earned media strategy, according to his 2010 Idaho congressional campaign manager China Gum. Gum told us that their goal was to make their campaign the honest brokers in the race. They knew that their opponents were sending out multiple press releases daily, spinning relentlessly, sending reporters "on a lot of goose chases." Gum realized that Labrador's campaign was best served by being trustworthy and giving the media "the honest, straight-up answer, and that when we gave them something, they could trust that it was what we truly believed and we weren't trying to stretch anything. . . . That was really important to Raul. He wanted us to be the trustworthy ones."[46] Gum observed the following:

> Some campaigns will put out multiple press releases throughout the day with misinformation to see what they could get to stick. We never did that. We only sent out press releases when there was something totally legitimate going on. . . . So the media tended to trust what we had happening. If we said something about our opponent, it came with footnotes and facts, not a wild goose chase. So I had a great relationship with the media.[47]

Labrador went on to score a big upset over his Republican primary opponent, and then he bested his general election foe, a Democratic incumbent, by nearly 10 percent. Their strategy wasn't the lone difference-maker, but it helped put Labrador in position to become a member of Congress.

Earned Media: An Imperfect Tool

Some managers mourned the loss of multiple, traditional press outlets such as the demise of local newspapers. Fifteen or twenty years ago, such papers would enable campaigns to microtarget voters through earned media. Democrat Chris Kelly's California attorney general campaign manager, Katie Merrill, pointed out the following:

> In the Bay Area, you used to have the *San Jose Mercury News, San Francisco Chronicle, Oakland Tribune*, the *Contra Costa Times*. And now the *Contra Costa Times*, the *Oakland Tribune*, and the *San Jose Mercury News* are all one paper. So instead of having all these mini-markets within a media market, mini-newspaper markets in the media markets to try to pitch your stories, now you've got two instead of four.[48]

That contraction made it much harder for her to get their message heard through the local press. "It's just very, very difficult to get stories written," Merrill explained. "You don't have as many reporters to pitch to. And there [are] a lot of young, inexperienced reporters as the older reporters have taken buyouts" due to the downsizing of media companies.[49]

The result for campaigns is that "whereas you really could do microtargeting with your earned media, . . . you just can't anymore. . . . And it's unfortunate because it just makes it more difficult to communicate with voters without having to pay for it," especially in a state as sprawling and populous as California. Thus, during Kelly's 2010 run, Merrill decided to target the Sacramento press corps in the hopes of "getting stories written that would . . . frame the campaign" and "get Chris viable" in Sacramento "as a means of then getting him viable to the voters." She was pleased with the results. Her campaign was able to push the "truth about the front-runner's [Kamala Harris] record," in addition to burnishing Kelly's credentials, and "we were just slamming it all the time on the earned media side." While Kelly came in virtually tied for second in the Democratic primary, his campaign was ultimately credible, breaking through a crowded, seven-person field and theoretically setting him up for a future run at statewide office. Even though he lost, his earned media strategy elevated his visibility and deepened his political credibility.[50]

Other campaign managers whose side was leading in the polls opted to take their feet off the pedal as much as possible. Their goal was to keep their campaign out of the media's glare and deprive their lesser-known rivals of garnering free publicity. They wanted the dynamic to remain static. Campaign manager Michael Sullivan told us that during Todd Rokita's 2010 Indiana campaign for Congress, his goal was "to be very quiet because if we made noise, the media would notice."[51] Attention, in this case, was the last thing the front-runner desired. Sullivan hoped to keep the contest low profile and controversy-free in order to cement his position in first place. Their strategy paid off. Rokita took 42 percent of the vote in a thirteen-person Republican primary, becoming his party's nominee, and he easily won the general election in the heavily Republican district.

Garnering earned media can also help qualify candidates as legitimate contenders simply because they are featured in stories. In Barack Obama's 2004 Illinois Senate primary run, the future president had trouble garnering earned media attention in the early going. His campaign manager James Cauley said he just kept "throwing it at the board and praying," but, he recalled, "We couldn't get on the news to save our ass." He said, "Chicago media was a tough nut to crack. And I don't know that we did it that well. Again, we were at 16 percent, and we didn't move till we went on TV. Then we went on TV and we moved." But once they started generating more earned media coverage, the publicity gave Obama's campaign "a certain amount of credibility," which helped inspire his partisans and helped him pass the "credibility threshold."[52]

Showing the voters that an officeholder was working hard in their job to bring them tangible benefits was another rationale for trying to gin up much earned media. When Stuart Roy ran Ben Nighthorse Campbell's 1998 Senate race in Colorado, he welcomed a stream of press releases from Campbell's Senate office trumpeting Campbell's efforts on behalf of his constituents.[53] The releases offered a blend of policy and targeted messaging. His office announced the grants Campbell had secured, votes he had taken, the bills he had sponsored. Some of the releases would be targeted to reporters in Colorado's Larimer County or western Colorado, where voters were especially affected by the senator's action. Thus, incumbents running for reelection not only have advantages in raising money but also in generating earned media by virtue of their official acts that often create positive impressions among the electorate.

The bottom line is that earned media is a highly imperfect tool that campaign managers approach with a wide array of strategies—all with the goal of affecting voters' impressions of the campaign and her issue positions and influencing who turns out and how they decide to vote. From blunting bad news to winning support from swing voters; from building rapport with the electorate to showing that candidates in fact understand people's lives; from microtargeting voters in precincts, parishes, towns, or counties to tying candidates to relevant, popular policies and sharpening distinctions among the candidates, campaign managers employ countless earned media strategies to shape the narrative arc, influence what the media tells voters, and ultimately improve their side's turnout and their performance with swing voters. By using free media to communicate their policies and message, they aim to give their side a marginal advantage that will bring them victory. An imprecise art, spinning the news media helps campaigns answer the question, "What are we going to say?," fueling the behind-the-scenes struggle between campaigns, reporters, bloggers, and other influential voices that often make a meaningful difference on election day.

Notes

1. Personal communication, names withheld by request.
2. Ibid.
3. Ibid.
4. Ibid.
5. Ibid.
6. Steve Eder, "A Balancing Act for Jeb Bush in 1989," *New York Times*, April 16, 2015, http://www.nytimes.com/interactive/2015/04/17/us/politics/bush-trip.html?_r=1.
7. Ibid.
8. The problem of duplicating press releases was solved in the 1960s with the introduction of the Xerox machine. The price of the machines and cost per copy were much higher than they are now, and photocopying was an expensive line item in campaign budgets.
9. Alexander Hopkins, "Ronald Reagan's Presidential Radio Addresses: Themes of Unity," *Student Pulse* 5 (2013), www.studentpulse.com/articles/733/2/ronald-reagans-presidential-radio-addresses-themes-of-unity.
10. Richard L. Berke, "The 1992 Campaign: The Media; Clinton Bus Tour Woos and Wows Local Press," *New York Times*, August 9, 1992, www.nytimes.com/1992/08/09/us/the-1992-campaign-the-media-clinton-bus-tour-woos-and-wows-local-press.html.
11. David Carr, "How Obama Tapped into Social Networks' Power," *New York Times*, November 9, 2008, www.nytimes.com/2008/11/10/business/media/10carr.html.
12. R. Galen, personal communication, September 30, 2011.
13. Ibid.
14. Matthew Gentzkow and Jesse M. Shapiro, "Media Bias and Reputation," *Journal of Political Economy* 114, no. 2 (2006), http://web.stanford.edu/~gentzkow/research/BiasReputation.pdf.
15. R. Galen, personal communication, September 30, 2011.
16. L. Quinn, personal communication, June 1, 2015.

17. J. Petrick, personal communication, November 9, 2011.

18. B. Todd, personal communication, September 9, 2011.

19. Ibid.

20. Thomas E. Patterson, *Out of Order: An Incisive and Boldly Original Critique of the News Media's Domination of America's Political Process* (New York: Random House, 1994).

21. Ibid.

22. R. Ridder, personal communication, September 20, 2011.

23. Ibid.

24. B. Todd, personal communication, September 9, 2011.

25. M. Harris, personal communication, June 20, 2014.

26. B. Todd, personal communication, September 9, 2011.

27. C. Phillips, personal communication, October 18, 2011.

28. G. Shafer, personal communication, September 20, 2011.

29. Ibid.

30. Ibid.

31. K. Koch, personal communication, October 20, 2011.

32. J. Howser, personal communication, November 9, 2011.

33. Ibid.

34. Ibid.

35. B. Beychok, personal communication, November 8, 2011.

36. B. Todd, personal communication, September 9, 2011.

37. K. Evans, personal communication, September 20, 2011.

38. Ibid.

39. Ibid.

40. G. Shafer, personal communication, September 20, 2011.

41. M. McDonald, personal communication, November 7, 2011.

42. Ibid.

43. M. McKenna, personal communication, October 26, 2011.

44. Ibid.

45. S. Watson, personal communication, October 7, 2011.

46. G. China, personal communication, October 17, 2011.

47. Ibid.

48. K. Merrill, personal communication, September 15, 2011.

49. Ibid.

50. Ibid.

51. M. Sullivan, personal communication, 2011.

52. J. Cauley, personal communication, November 1, 2011.

53. S. Roy, personal communication, June 20, 2014.

CHAPTER 8

Field General

Waging the War on the Ground

The country was still at war with terrorists from Afghanistan to Yemen and beyond, and the candidate, a president managing multiple crises, had become a divisive figure in the Oval Office. His signature achievement was deeply unpopular, and polls showed that approximately half the electorate approved of the president's performance, while the other half expressed negative opinions, with some of his fiercest critics calling him un-American.

Running for reelection against a well-funded opponent with outside groups funded by hugely wealthy individuals from the world of finance, the president had assembled a team of skilled loyalists to run his race. His strategy was to eschew professional firms and build up large volunteer grassroots army to contact voters and microtarget messages. Furthermore, the campaign was committed to the use of sophisticated experiments and the latest technology to turn out his core voters and persuade a relatively small number of swing voters to cast their ballots for him.

The election, virtually all polls suggested, was going to be decided by a close margin. The other party had a legitimate shot at victory. Democratic and Republican lawyers were preparing their battle plans if any of the swing states—Ohio or Florida especially—was too close to call on election night.

And then there was the first debate. The incumbent's campaign manager told us that "the president in the first debate was terrible. There was no, 'Well, he had this,' or, 'Well, he had that,' or, 'Well, the press was unfair. The questions were uneven.' He was very bad in the debate. He came across as a guy who didn't seem like he ought to be commander-in-chief, period, end of discussion."[1]

While the first debate unnerved the president's supporters, the campaign stuck to its plan and was confident in its technological advantages and ground game. They knew that whichever side could do a better job at motiving their grassroots activists and getting out their vote was likely to win the White House. The victor was probably going to be the one who took advantage of the most modern tool and had developed the superior ground game.

Barack Obama's reelection campaign in 2012? Well, actually, no. The candidate was George W. Bush, who owned an unpopular war, had middling job approval ratings and was awful in the first debate—and, who, in 2004, used a sophisticated turnout operation to eke out a victory over his Democratic opponent, John Kerry.

Surprised? The Obama campaigns, and 2012, in particular, are legendary for his vaunted mobilization efforts and his ability to expand the American electorate.[2] Using a variety of tools, relentless experimentation, and findings from political scientists,[3] the Obama campaign utilized sophisticated, data-driven get-out-the-vote (GOTV) operations. Still, while phenomenally well done by the Obama team in 2012, such efforts are hardly novel. As the brief vignette just given on the 2004 Bush campaign shows, the science of mobilization was not invented in 2012. Candidates for almost any elective office have always focused on grassroots mobilization as a core activity that can help influence who loses and who wins. Mobilizing voters to go to the polls and cast their ballots for and/or against somebody is still one of the most vital activities in almost any campaign operation.

And in 2004, George W. Bush and his campaign manager Ken Mehlman were bent on improving their performance in this department. "In 2000," as Mehlman told us, "we were crushed when it came to the ground game. Gore did better than we did."[4] Mehlman had no stomach for excuses or rationalizations. He led his team in 2004 to take hard looks at the campaign's performance each week. And each week, the campaign often said, "'We lost this week.' Not, 'The press was unfair.' Not, 'Well, if you look at it this way, we really won it.'"

In 2013, Mehlman said this in an interview with Southern Methodist University:

> There were definitely really big lessons that we learned. I've always thought that, in life—and it's not just in politics; I think about it in business too—what you do wrong is more important than what you do right, in some ways, if you can learn from it. So, often, sustained success can be dangerous, because it can lull you into believing that, in fact, you're so great, when, in fact, often you're just fortunate. And similarly, mistakes or things that don't go as well as you want can be huge opportunities for growth. So if you think about it, we lost the popular vote in 2000, by 500,000 votes. And in the final several days before the election, our numbers went down. And part of that clearly was the DUI revelation. But part of it also, we thought, was we could do a much better job in how we turn out voters. So we came up with a concept we called the seventy-two-hour effort, around the last seventy-two hours of the campaign. And we literally studied every aspect of how you target, how you identify, how you motivate, and how you turn out voters. And we used the 2002 election cycle as a giant laboratory for how we would identify more effective tactics, going forward.[5]

By 2004, Mehlman had concluded that one key to better turnout was the role of "person-to-person" contact, of neighbors persuading neighbors to vote for Bush and against Kerry. Such personal contacts would supplant in part the campaign's reliance on paid calls and paid door knockers. He sought more precise targeting of voters in 2004 (using sophisticated data analytics; for more on data in campaigns, see Chapter 3) as well as a bigger person-to-person grassroots army, which was a direct lesson about the mistakes the Bush campaign had made in 2000.

Refusing to rationalize his side's disappointing GOTV performance in 2000, Mehlman was determined to target better and find new ways to turn out their voters to carry Bush to a second term. Mehlman and his team developed turnout goals. They conducted "a careful analysis of who the swing voters were" and concluded that Hispanics and suburban women were going to decide the election. "We ended up with a larger level of conservative turnout than we had four years before," Mehlman explained, "but if you look at what really moved and changed things, it was our ability to win over Hispanics and suburban women. So the increased Republican turnout was also helpful, but if you said to me what did we spend all day, every day thinking about, it was those two audiences." They had answered the "Who do we need?" question. Now, "How do we reach them?" became their major preoccupation. They had to figure out how to touch them and ensure that they decided to support Bush for reelection.[6]

Their strategy was to appeal to both groups by contrasting "President Bush's steadfast leadership at a time of war with Senator Kerry's changing his position based on the audience, which at a time of war we thought was perilous. That was the argument." And they would use the argument to reach suburban women and Hispanics and perform marginally better with both groups to influence the vote totals in key states. And the best way to reach and influence such voters was through "word of mouth and person-to-person communication."[7]

Mehlman said that anybody who says grassroots organizing is a waste of time was making an "absurd" statement. His 2004 campaign's GOTV efforts provide a case in point. Bush improved his vote totals among Latinos, winning 39 percent in 2000 and 44 percent in 2004. They motivated evangelical voters to go to the polls in swing states such as Ohio, improving on their 2000 performance, when news that a much younger Bush had been arrested for drunk driving dampened evangelical turnout. (There's also some debate about whether evangelicals turned out in higher numbers to vote against same-sex marriage initiatives, which appeared on the ballot in some swing states.) Most importantly, some pollsters said afterward that Bush improved his performance among women voters: In 2000, he lost women to Al Gore by 11 percent; in 2004, his deficit among women against Kerry was only 3 percent.[8]

The 2004 voter mobilization plan was based on years of field experiments and hard work by Republican operatives. The Republican National Committee (RNC) 72-Hour Task Force conducted dozens of organizing experiments during 2001 off-year elections, concluding that door knocking could improve voter turnout for their side by two to three percentage points over, say, stuffing fliers in mailboxes.

The Bush team infused state parties with resources, deployed trained operatives, registered thousands of new Republican voters, and set up GOTV organizations in all of Florida's sixty-seven counties, to cite one example.[9] On election day, Mehlman's team had 85,000 GOTV volunteers, and their job was to talk to voters and ensure that voters turned up and voted for Bush. They held house parties, made phone calls, talked to their neighbors. The campaign's message stressed socially conservative values—anti-same-sex marriage, anti-abortion, pro-religion—and Bush's strong wartime leadership, and their messages resonated with rural voters especially. In Ohio, the key swing state that year, Bush was able to match his 2000 performance in the state's urban areas, and at the same time, he improved his share of the vote in Ohio's rural communities. "Compared with 2000, his vote totals and margins of victory soared all across Ohio's Appalachian southeast and its southern and western farm belt," the *Washington Post* reported shortly after election day. In Ohio, Bush defeated Kerry by just over 200,000 votes. And Bush's win in Ohio carried him to victory in the Electoral College, handing him a second term.[10]

All of these smallish differences added up to victory on election day. Mehlman's mobilization plan was executed, and it worked well.

The 2004 case raises a larger point: voter mobilization, also known as GOTV and voter canvassing, raises a core concern among political scientists and political professionals alike. What motivates people to cast their ballots? Why do they decide to vote for one candidate, or, oftentimes, against another candidate? What's clear is that voting is a two-step process—deciding to vote is the first step; deciding for whom to vote is the second. Based on the scholarly literature and the campaign managers we surveyed, we believe that the strongest motivation to come out and vote is the desire to vote for or against somebody. Campaigns are about maximizing the turnout of those who will vote for you but may not vote and about maximizing the loyalty of those who are sure to vote but may vote for the other person. On Bush's campaign, Mehlman's goal was to maximize the turnout of evangelicals, who fit into the former category, and maximize the loyalty of Latinos and women—two groups that Mehlman saw as the most pliable within an already fairly stable electorate. Mehlman told us that he used polls to learn "where the public is, their attitudes toward your candidate, their attitudes toward the other, what they think [about which] issues are important, what motivates them."[11]

As Mehlman admitted, Obama built on Bush's voter mobilization innovations and elevated them to a new level of sophistication and effectiveness. And Bush, for his part, had been inspired by Howard Dean's voter mobilization activities during the 2004 Democratic primary. Mehlman was impressed with Dean's use of "netroots" to build his campaign network and mobilize his supporters.[12] He called Dean's use of "social media, meet-ups, to mobilize people . . . a very smart move" and said he learned from Dean "about . . . the power of neighbor mobilizing and influencing neighbor. And we tried to adopt similar tactics in our effort."[13]

Yet, although Bush, Obama, and other campaigns have used new technologies and more sophisticated measures of their return on investment to gauge their mobilization progress, campaigns have always been targeted. Voter mobilization is as old as political parties. Yet, in recent years, pundits, political pros, and analysts have all fallen in love with mobilization and grassroots-fueled campaigns, as if the ground game is a shiny new object that campaigns must collect and cash in. But Dean, Bush, and Obama were hardly the first campaigns to target and political scientists conducting experiments at Yale about mobilization activities were not the first people to experiment.

Grassroots activism—battle for victory in the ground game—has a stubborn romantic quality surrounding it. Voter mobilization is often associated with the power of thousands of volunteer-activists who are impassioned for their candidate and the larger cause and who work their guts out to realize their collective vision of reform and national rejuvenation. And by harnessing the power of a movement fueled by grassroots ardor, campaign leaders can lead their army to decisive victory at the polls, bending history toward justice and equality.

How Do We Reach Them?

This version of voter mobilization isn't entirely fiction. Grassroots activism and targeting voters has a long history. In 1960, Matt Reese set up a voter mobilization headquarters in the basement of Charleston, West Virginia's, Kanawha Hotel, spending eighteen hours a day calling voters to ask them to vote for John F. Kennedy in the state's Democratic primary.[14] As the chief organizer of JFK's volunteer operation, Reese helped ensure that Kennedy's supporters voted, giving the candidate a crucial win that propelled him to his party's presidential nomination.

At 350 pounds and 6'5", Reese, a native of West Virginia, spoke with an earthy drawl that hid the pioneering nature of his work in targeting voters on political campaigns. He preferred to target two types of people: voters who were likely to vote for his candidate but weren't sure if they'd actually vote and voters open to arguments for his candidate or against his candidate's opponent. The *Washington Post* once quoted him as saying that he told his field operatives, "If you want to pick cherries, go where the cherries is."[15] Reese helped pioneer and refine the process of voter targeting and canvassing, using demographic data, polls, and other voter information to target particular groups of voters with particular messages that were likely to convince them to go to the polls or to vote for or against a particular candidate.[16]

Decades prior to Reese's innovations, the leader of Tammany Hall, George Washington Plunkitt, refined the art of constituent service and voter mobilization among urban machines. He targeted Italians, Irish Catholics, Russian Jews, and other recent immigrants. Meeting with people in his district to find out what they needed from the machine, he built his power by ensuring strong voter turnout and loyalty to Tammany Hall. "And turnout was a function of relentless outreach and tireless service," historian Terry Golway has written.[17]

Other, more recent examples underscore the degree to which grassroots organizing can power even presidential campaigns. Barry Goldwater's 1964 White House run enjoyed strong support from conservative activists in such groups as Young Americans for Freedom, and such activists ultimately helped put Ronald Reagan in the Oval Office in 1980. Barack Obama drew thousands of mostly youthful volunteers who rallied behind his call to change politics and restore hope to the broken political process. The idea of grassroots movements (Tea Party, Occupy Wall Street) sparking and propelling reform causes and candidates has a hallowed spot in American political history. The media depicts the ground game as, at once, the most prosaic and exhilarating aspect of political campaigning. Volunteers, young and old and fueled by adrenaline, pizza, and booze, are portrayed as sacrificing their careers and family to make America better.

The narrative isn't totally off base. Field organizing and grassroots activism often is grueling, romantic, and impactful; many campaign managers interviewed in this book got their start as grassroots organizers and were inspired to stay in politics by these early experiences. Canvassing taught them invaluable lessons, too. California campaign manager and former grassroots organizer Katie Merrill told us, in fact, that no moment in politics trumps the thrill of a winning campaign that successfully mobilized its grassroots activists. "When you're running a race . . . and you meet the contact goals and you meet your ID goals and you meet your turnout goals and win, it's about the coolest thing in the world," she explained.[18] Campaign managers argued that their grassroots experience unveiled for them how and why voters are persuaded to go to the polls and vote for a certain candidate.

Political scientists have arrived at a long-standing, rough consensus on the importance and impact of voter mobilization in political campaigns. In fact, seventy years before political scientists rediscovered the power of experiments and applied them to voter mobilization, Harold Gosnell, in Chicago, ran some of the first field experiments to measure the impact of voter mobilization on political campaigns. Direct voter contact, he showed then, led to an increase in political participation. Since then, political scientists have consistently demonstrated that direct voter contact (direct mail, door knocking, and phone banking in more recent times) can improve one side's share and performance and influence who votes and whom they decide to vote for and/or vote against. As one of us pointed out in another article, "The vast majority of [academic] studies . . . show that people who are contacted by parties, campaigns, or interest groups are more likely to participate in politics than those who are not."[19]

The decades of findings from the political science literature resonated with the professionals' experiences in running campaigns regardless of the political office. In order to build winning coalitions and affect the election results, campaign managers routinely told us, their field operations—nowadays informed and driven by high-tech tools such as electronic voter lists detailing individuals' preferences and interests—were essential elements in reaching 50 plus 1 percent of the vote.

Grassroots experience is therefore important to the operatives who run campaigns and devise campaign strategies. But what does voter mobilization even entail? How should we define it? How do campaign managers view its role and importance in winning and losing elections?

Political canvassing is best understood as comprising any activity that induces voters to go to the polls and cast their ballots for or against a particular candidate. Again, it's a two-step process—getting people to vote and getting them to vote for or against someone or something. Campaign managers understand that civic-minded appeals to voters aren't enough to get people to vote. The ground game, they know, is about trying to increase the perceived benefits or lower the costs to people who are likely to vote. Either campaigns use mechanics to make it easier for people to vote—registering voters, reminding them about election day, driving them to the polls, sending them absentee ballots; make it seem like there's a cost if they were to avoid voting—making them feel guilty about not voting; or make people see that there's a benefit to them by casting their ballots. Whether campaign managers employ mechanics or messages (or both), all of them are trying to play with this roughly similar turnout equation.

Political mobilization includes both the mechanics of voter contact and messaging, according to campaign managers surveyed here. So mobilization should be seen in broader terms than most scholars typically see it—not only as door knocks, direct mail, and phone banking but also as the messages that campaigns are targeting to discreet blocs of voters. In other words, the messages campaigns send motivate citizens to participate in the political process, and communications should be seen as synonymous with political canvassing and GOTV activities.

In Chapters 5, 6, and 7, we covered the role, delivery, and effects of messaging on campaigns and elections. Although we devote less time in Chapter 8 to analyzing message as a mobilization tool, it's important to remember that GOTV activities do not occur in a political vacuum. Campaigns must wrestle with such forces as competing messages from their opponents (How are they doing?), a political climate shaped by fundamentals (economic, party ID, demographic), available information about persuadable voters, and what outside groups are communicating over the airwaves without technically coordinating with the campaigns themselves.

Thus, voter mobilization is only one among a number of factors that can and do influence vote totals. But there is widespread agreement that direct voter contact has a positive impact on who turns out and for whom they vote. Remember that campaign managers are ultimately seeking to influence share (turnout) and performance (persuasion) to favor their candidate at the margins (Chapter 2); so the messages campaigns communicate, the voters they target, and the grassroots activities they harvest are proven methods for affecting who votes and for whom on the margins. And as we never get tired of saying in this book, the margins can determine who controls Congress, who sits in the Oval Office, which party controls a statehouse.

The Two-Step Process: Deciding to Vote and Voting for or against a Candidate

Voter mobilization is not a one-size-fits-all activity, of course. Just as campaign messages differ based on content, delivery, and volume, mobilization includes volunteers knocking on people's doors, neighborhood block parties, snail-mail landing on voters' doorsteps, phone banking, and targeting particular blocs of voters with particular messages. Which of these activities are most effective? Which ones are least helpful? Is it better to focus campaign's efforts on getting people to the polls or, rather, on persuading them to vote for or against a particular person? The best answer we can give is, it depends. Field means different things depending on the kind of campaign that's being run, where it's occurring, and the type of strategy that the campaign is using. Democratic campaign manager Ashley Spillane argued that "in Washington State that's 100 percent vote by mail, you can't run the traditional 72-hour GOTV campaign. You have to understand each state's voting process to mount an effective political campaign."[20]

More generally, a well-organized ground game can provide a boost to long-shot candidates and aid campaigns that are trailing their opponents in funds raised or ads aired. An army of volunteers attending rallies, knocking on doors, and posting on social media can provide campaigns with much-needed earned media, raise funds from small donors, and help turn out voters on election day. Campaign manager Mark Block, who ran Herman Cain's unorthodox 2012 presidential primary campaign, helped Cain leap to the front of the pack by forging what he called "a nontraditional campaign" powered by a "grassroots citizens' movement" based on the Tea Party.[21] Block's vision was to run a bottom-up campaign. Indeed, while Cain ultimately was defeated, he briefly became a front-runner for the nomination. And more broadly, the Tea Party (albeit often backed by donors with deep pockets) has become a grassroots force in low-turnout Republican primary campaigns to unseat numerous incumbents seen as insufficiently conservative, including former House majority leader Eric Cantor, (R-VA,) and longtime senator Richard Lugar, (R-IN.)

Still, most campaign managers see robocalls, for example, as less effective than neighbors persuading neighbors to go to the polls and vote for their chosen candidate. Person-to-person contact, they tend to say, matters more than impersonal mobilization techniques. And the timing is also not inconsequential. Some managers told us that doing a direct mailing to voters early in a campaign was more beneficial to their candidate than bombarding voters with literature in the campaign's final days, when voters are typically sick of the campaign and more likely to ignore any campaign communications. Some political scientists have argued that person-to-person contact is more effective than phone calls and direct mailings, although the evidence in support of this is iffy.[22] At the same time, scholars have paid too little attention to the role of communications in mobilization—and we argue that message and direct voter contact together should be seen as key elements in any mobilization strategy. A hyper-organized, well-funded ground game that lacks a persuasive, engaging message is more likely than not going to lose. As pollster Mark Mellman has said, "[W]hile organization is vitally important, it is not sufficient. . . . When a campaign claims they are going to win on turnout, they will likely lose."[23] All the organization and mobilization in the world may not make a decisive difference if the campaign lacks a cohesive message that penetrates the targeted voters.

"Old-Fashioned Grunt Work"

We've seen that there's no pure formula dictating to campaign managers how they must use the tools available to them in order to win elections. Campaign managers must identify a winning coalition, build the campaign's infrastructure, raise the right amount of money to conduct campaign activities, develop the right messages, and ensure they reach the right voters at the right moments. Put differently, there simply is no grassroots magic—waves of volunteers appearing out of the blue—that can automatically propel a candidate to a House or Senate seat or even into the Oval Office.

At the same time, campaign managers know that ineffective ground games can put them at a real disadvantage on the electoral margins. They all must decide how they are going to recruit and utilize their volunteers and turn out their voters on election day in the most efficient way possible. Looked at another way, they all need some kind of "field" strategy that can help tilt a tight election in their favor during the course of the contest. A sophisticated field strategy integrates organizing, funding, targeting, and messaging in the hopes of maximizing one side's share of the vote and persuading as many undecided voters as possible. Field activities also help to answer three of the key questions you saw on the campaign flowchart featured in Chapter 1: How do we reach them? What do we tell them? How are we doing?

And indeed, virtually all of the managers we talked to saw field as an important element in their overall toolkit—even in the age of digital communications. Author Sasha Issenberg told us that while direct voter contact remained a central element to contemporary campaigning and now rests firmly on "a high-tech foundation." "The big thing that's happened in the last 15 years in politics is that we've gotten a whole lot smarter about how to knock on doors and have volunteers make phone calls," he argued. While campaign managers don't necessarily know with any precision what impact televised advertisements have on who votes and how they vote, "we do know that there's something that happens when a volunteer knocks on the door of somebody in their neighborhood and has a well-trained, well-structured interaction."[24] Even in the age of the Internet, Issenberg observed the following:

> The most targetable, controlled interactions in politics are at the doorstep or at the mailbox. You know who you're talking to. You know if you got to them or not. And for all the advantages of broadcast or online communications, and there are wonderful media for all sorts of things, you don't have that. You don't have that level of precision, specificity, accountability.[25]

The impact of political canvassing is quantifiable to many campaign managers. Matt McDonald, who served as deputy campaign manager for Elia Pirozzi's 1998 congressional campaign and has taught in campaign schools, said that any effective grassroots plan should aim to "turn out about 10 percent of their entire vote goal." During a campaign's GOTV push, he added, the campaign must figuratively "drive 10 percent of everything they need to the ballot. And all of the grassroots work that they do before that needs to prepare and build toward that goal." He has taken to invoking his mantra that "all grassroots is GOTV"—ensuring that months of organizing pays off on election day. Echoing our argument that campaign activities can be decisive on the margins, McDonald argued that with each side highly motivated, "the only way that you can win [close elections] is by having a ton of organization. And if you don't have that, then you probably lose." He estimated that campaigns had some degree of control over "10 to 15 percent of the final outcome" by implementing "a strong grassroots operation."[26]

Democrats Todd Schulte and Joe Abbey, for their part, estimated that an effective ground game should account for around 2 percent of the overall vote. That's a meager percentage at first blush. But let's remember that campaign managers running competitive races are trying to gain every edge to affect the vote totals. Again, at the risk of sounding like a broken record, the margins matter. Schulte did the math for us.

> I think it's important to filter down past the idea . . . that campaigns should be about moving huge portions of the electorate. They're not. I think that field is really important but field has never been shown, even in super low turnout special elections in the middle of winter, to move more than 5 to 6 percent of the vote. But that's a huge amount if 20 percent of the electorate's the only part that's up for grabs. Most of the time, field is 2 percent, which again is 10 percent of your votes that's up for grabs.[27]

Now let's recall Joe Abbey's decision in Creigh Deeds' primary campaign (Chapter 4) to fire his field organizers and pour all of the campaign's resources into television advertising. Does Abbey's decision mean that field, didn't matter to Deeds' campaign? Hardly. Abbey was making a strategic call that field, as he put it, would get him perhaps 2 percent of the vote but in a low-turnout primary where Deeds' had low name identification, television could move as much as 15 percent of the primary vote. Abbey's gamble, as we now know, was successful.[28] The television blitz helped Deeds pull off a come-from-behind victory to secure the Democratic nomination. But that, too, was a form of mobilization—mobilizing voters and persuading voters to support Deeds' bid over the airwaves.

Most managers we surveyed said that voter mobilization constituted a core element of any winning campaign plan they made. Republican Graham Shafer told us that campaigns are only in position to catch an election year wave if "they've raised enough money to deliver their message" and "found enough volunteers and activists to . . . generate momentum on a grassroots level."[29] Mobilization and message, broadly defined, are lynchpins of many successful campaigns. Another campaign manager said that a good field campaign can absolutely move the needle for a candidate and help the campaign assemble a winning coalition.[30]

Republican Steve Bell, who ran Heather Wilson's 1998 congressional race in New Mexico, described campaigns now as little-changed from campaigns run in the early nineteenth century. Campaigns need to identify every person that is going to vote for their side and ensure that the person casts a ballot. "Not much has changed," he said. The core questions he always asks when managing a campaign include "What forms the winning coalition? How do we put that coalition together? What theme or two themes, because you can never do more than really two or three themes, what puts those people together? And how can we best reach them?" He added another key question: "How do you make sure they show up?" He stressed that campaigns had to methodically identify their voters "one by one. . . . Where they live, what their zip codes are" and undertake "old-fashioned grunt work" of knocking on doors and delivering fliers in order to assemble their winning coalition.[31]

Campaign managers also seek to mobilize important activist groups on their behalf because they can bring foot soldiers to the campaign and reach voters who are likely to support the candidate and help get them to the polls. Bell reported that the endorsement of the National Rifle Association (NRA) and New Mexico's anti-abortion groups established Wilson as a true conservative in the 1998 Republican primary.[32] Bell's team also used voter lists to target and mobilize people who typically voted in Republican primaries.[33] Adam Bodily, Duane Snow's deputy campaign manager in his race for county supervisor in 2009, described how the Albemarle County GOP gave his campaign "walking lists . . . worth their weight in gold."[34] The lists enabled them to identify, reach, and mobilize strong and weak Republican voters.

But why haven't e-mail, Facebook, and Twitter replaced person-to-person voter contact and mobilization activities? These tools tend to be useful, among other things, for communicating with, motivating, and raising funds from already devout activists who will support the campaign no matter what. Matthew Arnold, who ran Darcy Burner's, D-WA, 2012 congressional campaign, argued that e-mails sent by campaigns were highly effective at talking to the party's activists.[35] On a ten-point scale, he rated e-mail a six as a useful motivation tool.[36] But to turn out a larger percentage of one's potential voters, to register new voters, to persuade undecided voters, and to ensure people actually cast a ballot, such tools as e-mail and social media were of far more limited value.

Ironically, campaigns, for all the advances in technological wizardry, still need door knocking and phone banking programs. Direct mail still matters, too. According to some managers we interviewed, these GOTV activities have become even more vital because digital tools and electronic information enables much more precise targeting of the electorate. In other words, it's easier for campaigns to target voters with particular messages using old-fashioned methods (door knocks, direct mail, etc.). Mitch McConnell's 1990 Senate campaign manager, Steven Law, argued that retail politics—person-to-person contact aimed at persuading swing voters and mobilizing one's partisans—"enjoyed a renaissance during the Bush years with the emphasis on microtargeting techniques and organized door-to-door" contact.[37] Technology enables campaigns to have a wider array of tools to answer the "how do you reach them?" question, however, and it can fuel a GOTV grassroots plan by making targeting and contacts more refined and effective.

Katie Merrill, who started as a field organizer and later became a California media and campaign strategist, underscored this irony. As she entered California politics in 1992, people warned her that "field is dead." They added, "It's all about TV." That prediction turned out to be wrong. Merrill told us that, in fact, "field has made a comeback and it's making a comeback because of the Internet. It's just easier to organize, much easier to call, much easier to recruit volunteers, actually get them to do things for the campaign"—activities that help the campaign turn out their voters and persuade swing voters and affect the race's margins on election day. The Internet, she concluded, has made grassroots organizing and GOTV efforts less labor intensive and "more cost effective."[38]

As we have argued in this book, the campaign's goal is to move the electorate at the margins, in the hopes of securing a relatively small percentage of the vote for their side by persuading voters and turning out loyal partisans. Campaigns are about simple math, share and performance, and all the data-tracking, microtargeting, information-mining tools used by campaigns now still need to be used effectively to reach, persuade, and mobilize the right voters. In 2008, campaign manager Julie Petrick was running Democrat Gary Peters' congressional campaign in the Detroit, Michigan, suburbs. Her goal was to make sure that Democrats "voted down the ballot for our candidate"[39] in a presidential year with expected high Democratic turnout and Obama on the ballot.

Grassroots figured prominently in her strategy. Like Merrill, Petrick believes in the impact of field operations partly because she started out in politics by doing voter mobilization on campaigns. "That was the best training I ever got," she assured us. She learned the most about campaigns "by working on campaigns [at the grassroots level]... and by working for some awesome, talented managers." A Florida native, Petrick worked on two races for student body president at the University of Florida and later learned the nuts and bolts of campaigning as a grassroots organizer on John Kerry's 2004 presidential campaign and as field director on Rep. Ron Klein's, D-FL, 2006 congressional campaign.[40]

In 2008 as Peters' campaign manager, she mounted "a really aggressive direct voter targeting program on both the paid and volunteer sides."[41] The effort was sophisticated and effective. Petrick launched her GOTV operation months ahead of election day. Drawing on the Voter Activation Network (VAN) (which contained a trove of data on voters from Michigan's secretary of state's office), Petrick's team began to identify voter targets for the campaign's mobilization efforts. They focused on Democratic voters because Peters was facing an uphill battle with an entrenched Republican incumbent. While he had been a state senator and barely lost a state-wide race for attorney general (the margin was 5,200 votes)[42] and enjoyed decent name recognition among Democratic voters, he was also squaring off against a sixteen-year GOP incumbent with deep ties to the district. Thus, Petrick focused their grassroots campaign on reaching persuadable, largely Democratic voters. After compiling lists of their voter targets, Petrick launched a door knocking program in March, which continued right on through to election day. Ultimately,

Peters defeated his Republican opponent, Rep. Joe Knollenberg, by a healthy margin—52 to 43 percent. He had the advantage of running in a blue state in a great year for Democrats when Obama was on the ballot nationwide. McCain, Obama's opponent, had also abandoned the state in the campaign's final weeks, giving Democrats a wider opening. And while Petrick's field program did not alone bring Peters' victory, it helped him overcome some of the disadvantages any challenger facing an eight-term incumbent must surmount. Peters is now a US senator, the only freshman Democrat in the 2015 Senate class.

On both the left and right of the spectrum, campaign managers argued, voter mobilization (including person-to-person contact and targeted communications) was still a highly effective means of improving a candidate's shot at victory. Graham Shafer, Van Hilleary's, R-TN, 2002 gubernatorial campaign manager, told us that a venerable test of a campaign's viability is "whether they've found enough volunteers and activists to . . . generate momentum on a grassroots level."[43] Even on a presidential campaign, a grassroots plan implemented effectively can make a big impact. During the 2008 Republican presidential Iowa caucuses, Mitt Romney's team was looking to make their candidate a front-runner for the nomination.

The way to do that, they concluded, was to perform well in Iowa. Romney's Iowa campaign manager Gentry Collins helped craft a particular kind of grassroots strategy: by winning the Ames Straw Poll held many months before the caucuses, Romney, Collins reasoned, would generate the kind of earned media and political momentum that would help him perform well at the caucuses themselves. Collins figured this:

> If we overperformed at Ames, that would put us up on the stage along with the front-runners for the entire period of time between August and January . . . So we set about to do that on a tactical level, meaning, you know, 99 counties in Iowa, you need that county chair not only advocating for you and hosting events for you so people can get to know you as a candidate, but then specifically asking people not just to be a supporter or write a check or vote for you next January, but to get on a bus, . . . go to Ames, participate in the Straw poll, vote for Governor Romney.[44]

Collins had two tasks: He had to recruit enough strong Romney supporters in Iowa who would be persuaded to back Romney and take a bus to Ames and cast their ballot for Romney, and he had to build the infrastructure "into which we could push those [supporters]."[45] He had to achieve both things simultaneously. Collins's faith in his strategy wasn't misplaced. Romney won the straw poll. Ultimately, while he lost the caucuses and the presidential nomination (Mike Huckabee won the former and John McCain the latter), he took second place on caucus night, making himself a leading candidate for the nomination, forcing his chief rivals to reckon more fully with him as a front-runner in the Republican primary.

Losing and Winning on the Ground

If campaigns are about reaching targeted voters with the right messages delivered by persuasive messengers, they are also about persuading voters to volunteer for the campaign, cast ballots on election day, and vote for a particular candidate. The greater the number of grassroots supporters on a campaign, the more tied they are to the district or state, and the more passion they have, the more likely it is that a campaign will reap electoral benefits on the margins. They can field the shock troops enabling them to flush its vote on election day, persuade undecided voters to support the campaign, and eke out a victory in a close contest.

Campaign managers must ask the core questions as they make their voter mobilization plans: How do we reach them? What do we tell them? How are we doing? Field operations amount to direct voter contacts and the messages behind these contacts that enable campaigns to ensure that their core supporters indeed are solidly behind the candidate and will go to the polls. If the voter says they are 100 percent for Jane Smith, but they have no way of getting to their polling station, the campaign can provide a car or bus to take them to the polls. If a voter isn't sure about whether she supports Jane Smith, the campaign's field person can do their best to deliver the message that's hopefully going to persuade this voter to cast a ballot for Smith. Indeed, field matters not only because it can affect the vote totals on the margins; it matters because many campaign managers got their start as grassroots volunteers and field organizers. Mississippi campaign manager Casey Phillips spent crucial time as a field organizer for the National Republican Congressional Committee (NRCC) in 2008, to cite another example.

Voter mobilization is exhilarating, exhausting, and often consequential work. Knocking on people's doors and calling them on their phones to try to make sure they are supporting your side requires stamina, discipline, resources, training, and endless planning. But it is at the grassroots where campaigns are sometimes lost and won. Voter mobilization can provide campaigns with earned media, help campaign managers glean information from the field and thereby assess their progress, motivate partisans, persuade the persuadable, raise funds for other campaign activities, and influence the vote total at the margins—making the difference between losing and winning.

Notes

1. K. Mehlman, personal communication, November 9, 2011.

2. Sasha Issenberg, "How Obama's Team Used Big Data to Rally Voters," http://www.technologyreview.com/featuredstory/509026/how-obamas-team-used-big-data-to-rally-voters; Dan Balz, "How the Obama Campaign Won the Race for Voter Data," *Washington Post*, http://www.washingtonpost.com/politics/how-the-obama-campaign-won-the-race-for-voter-data/2013/07/28/ad32c7b4-ee4e-11e2-a1f9-ea873b7e0424_story.html.

3. David Nickerson, "Quality Is Job One: Professional and Volunteer Voter Mobilization Calls," *American Journal of Political Science* 51, no. 2 (2007): 269, 282; Sasha Issenberg, *The*

Victory Lab: The Secret Science of Winning Campaigns (New York: Broadway Books, 2012); Donald P. Green and Alan S. Gerber, *Get Out the Vote!: How to Increase Voter Turnout*, 1st ed. (Baltimore: Hopkins Fulfillment Services, 2005).

4. K. Mehlman, personal communication, November 9, 2011.

5. "Ken Mehlman Interview," Center for Presidential History, Southern Methodist University, The Election of 2004 Collective Memory Project, December 13, 2013, http://cphcmp.smu.edu/2004election/interview-with-ken-mehlman.

6. Ibid.

7. Ibid.

8. Lisa Trei, "Pollsters Dissect Bush Election Win," *Stanford News*, November 17, 2004, http://news.stanford.edu/news/2004/november17/polls-1117.html.

9. Garance Franke-Ruta, "The GOP Deploys," *The American Prospect*, January 15, 2004, http://prospect.org/article/gop-deploys.

10. Paul Farhi and James V. Grimaldi, "GOP Won With Accent on Rural and Traditional," *Washington Post*, November 4, 2004, www.washingtonpost.com/wp-dyn/articles/A23754-2004Nov3.html.

11. K. Mehlman, personal communication, November 9, 2011.

12. Ibid.

13. Ibid.

14. Bart Barnes, "Matt Reese, Veteran Political Consultant, Dies at 71," *Washington Post*, December 3, 1998, www.washingtonpost.com/wp-srv/politics/campaigns/junkie/links/reese.htm.

15. Ibid.

16. Ibid.

17. Terry Golway, "The Forgotten Virtues of Tammany Hall," *New York Times*, January 17, 2014, www.nytimes.com/2014/01/18/opinion/the-forgotten-virtues-of-tammany-hall.html?_r=1&gwh=2CF5EB2A29121BED38E85D29E29E6499&gwt=pay&assetType=opinion.

18. K. Merrill, personal communication, September 15, 2011.

19. Kenneth M. Goldstein and Matthew Holleque, "Getting Up Off the Canvass: Rethinking the Study of Mobilization," in *The Oxford Handbook of American Elections and Political Behavior*, ed. Jan E. Leighley (Oxford, UK: Oxford University Press, 2010).

20. A. Spillane, personal communication, September 30, 2011.

21. M. Block, personal communication, November 2011.

22. Alan S. Gerber and Donald P. Green, "The Effects of Canvassing, Telephone Calls, and Direct Mail on Voter Turnout: A Field Experiment," *American Political Science Review* 94, no. 3 (2000): 653–663, www.jstor.org/stable/2585837.

23. Mark Mellman, "Myths and Facts in Iowa," *The Hill*, October 24, 2007, http://thehill.com/opinion/columnists/mark-mellman/8597-myths-and-facts-in-iowa.

24. S. Issenberg, personal communication, April 17, 2013.

25. Ibid.

26. M. McDonald, personal communication, November 7, 2011.

27. T. Schulte, personal communication, November 9, 2011.

28. J. Abbey, personal communication, November 18, 2011.

29. G. Shafer, personal communication, September 20, 2011.

30. Anonymous, personal communication.

31. S. Bell, personal communication, June 20, 2014.

32. Ibid.

33. Ibid.

34. A. Bodily, personal communication, September 30, 2011.

35. M. Arnold, personal communication, October 25, 2011.

36. Ibid.

37. S. Law, personal communication, September 29, 2011.

38. K. Merrill, personal communication, September 15, 2011.

39. J. Petrick, personal communication, November 9, 2011.

40. Ibid.

41. Ibid.

42. David Enders, "Midwest: Michigan: Candidate Won't Seek Recount," *New York Times,* November 26, 2002.

43. G. Shafer, personal communication, September 20, 2011.

44. G. Collins, personal communication, October 1, 2011.

45. Ibid.

CHAPTER 9

Strategy Enforcer and Team Builder

Keeping a Day-to-Day Focus on the Long-Term Path to Victory

It's the economy, stupid![1]

James Carville, campaign manager,
Bill Clinton for President, 1992

James Carville: Losing Before Winning

Political campaigns are full of daily distractions punctuated by periodic crises. These can make it hard for managers to keep a campaign focused on its long-term strategy for winning. Few campaign managers have faced more distraction than James Carville did while running the red-hot 1992 Clinton-Gore campaign from their national headquarters in Little Rock, Arkansas.

While some Clinton-Gore staffers from "up north" took a while to adjust to the slow-paced Arkansas capital city, Carville was close to home. An unabashed Southerner and LSU football fan, James Carville grew up in a political household in tiny Carville, Louisiana, just north of Baton Rouge on the Mississippi River.[2] Like other southern hamlets, the town of Carville was named for a postmaster who, in this case, happened to be James's grandfather, Louis Arthur Carville.[3] To this day, Carville's favorite TV program remains *The Andy Griffith Show*, a 1960s sitcom about the elected sheriff of a small southern town.[4]

Politics started early for Carville. "It was just always a topic of conversation at my house. I never remember not talking or hearing about politics," said Carville, who

"I always had my desk in an open room. . . . I don't like closed doors." James Carville wears Mardi Gras colors in the 1992 Little Rock, Arkansas, headquarters of the Clinton-Gore presidential campaign.

started out as teenage campaign volunteer in local campaigns before he was old enough to get his driver's license. "Candidates used to do signs on telephone poles back then," he remembered. "I was tearing the other guys' signs down," said Carville, who is still known for his aggressive political style. At LSU, Carville got involved in the Young Democrats, then did a stint in the Marines (a fact that has been rarely reported since Carville became a political celebrity) before heading to law school.[5]

Carville found a job at a Baton Rouge political consulting firm doing local races. When his candidate won the mayor's office, Carville worked in city hall for about a year and a half before deciding that being on the municipal government payroll wasn't for him.[6] "I had three choices: to go crazy, go to jail, or go somewhere else."[7] Where Carville went was back into electoral politics. Pollster Peter Hart helped him get a job in a Virginia campaign, and Carville started working in a series of races that would culminate in the 1992 Clinton White House victory.

Despite his fame from the successful Clinton campaign, Carville was thirty-three years old before he ever visited Washington or New York. Even more surprising, although he had been involved in campaigns since receiving his driver's license, he didn't win his first race until 1986 at the age of 42.[8] In fact, he chalked up a lengthy losing streak that would have persuaded less hardy souls to find a different profession. But his winning streak began when he signed on to manage Democrat Robert Casey's gubernatorial race in Pennsylvania (for more on that campaign, see Chapter 6).[9] By April 1991, Pennsylvania's senior senator, H. John Heinz III, died in a plane accident, and Carville managed Harris Wofford's race against Dick Thornburgh, the former governor and US attorney general.[10] Early polls showed Wofford trailing Thornburgh by almost forty points.[11] Yet, improbably, Wofford won the election, a victory that brought Carville and his partner Paul Begala to national prominence. Carville went on from there to manage Bill Clinton's 1992 campaign. He brought with him some of the lessons he had learned on those earlier races. He concluded that the manager had to enforce the campaign's strategy and build a campaign culture and team spirit that could enact the strategy effectively. He envisioned a unified set of campaign hands all pushing in the same direction toward their shared goal.

Clinton-Gore 1992: "The Best Campaign Ever"

Under Carville's leadership, Clinton's 1992 effort came to be seen as the next step in the evolution of modern electioneering. A team of documentary filmmakers camped out in the Little Rock headquarters and produced a film that starred not the candidate but Carville and his campaign staffers.[12] The news media was attracted to youngish Clinton personalities like Carville and his communications director George Stephanopoulos, who discovered that they could make news themselves by changing the way campaigns were run.[13]

Carville's 1992 campaign innovations were destined to become staples of today's campaigns including the rapid-response "war room," the candidate family bus tour, and presidential candidate appearances on late-night talk shows, which were previously regarded as unpresidential. "It was the most culturally significant political campaign in modern American history," claimed Carville, with only a little exaggeration.[14]

The most lasting of their innovations was the Little Rock "war room," where young press operatives constantly talked to reporters, monitored news coverage—which was much more difficult in pre-Internet 1992—and crafted rapid response statements to shape breaking news coverage for Clinton's benefit. The Clinton war room was born out of necessity. From the beginning, the Clinton campaign was bombarded—first by his Democratic primary opponents and then by the Republicans. The war room fended off stories about Bill Clinton's escape from the Vietnam draft and travels to Moscow as well as charges about Hillary's business dealings as a Little Rock lawyer. Most potentially damaging were news accounts of the married Bill Clinton's past relationships with women. These stories came to be known as "bimbo eruptions," and the irresistible combination of sex and politics drew heavy media attention.[15] Carville's campaign staff was getting distracted and in danger of spending too much time fighting the eruptions and not enough time playing offense.

Keeping the Campaign Team on Strategy

It is not easy to unseat an incumbent president. In order to win, the Clinton campaign targeted "Reagan Democrats" and independents who voted for Bush in 1988 but had become disenchanted with the lackluster economic conditions of 1992. The core message was summed up by Sen. Al Gore, vice presidential nominee, at the Democrats' New York convention:

> Unemployment around the country has gone up; the number of jobs has gone down. The trade deficit has gone up; personal income has gone down. The budget deficit has gone up; consumer confidence has gone down. Poverty has gone up; the number of jobs has gone down. Bankruptcies have gone up, jobs, down; fear, up; hope, down; everything that oughta be down is up, everything that should be up is down; they've got it upside down, and we're gonna turn it right side up![16]

To remind staffers that their core message was more important than "bimbo eruptions" and other disruptive crises, Carville began posting what Stephanopoulos called "campaign haikus" on walls and whiteboards.[17] One of these, "It's the economy, stupid," became not only the driving management directive inside Clinton-Gore campaign headquarters across the country but was also repeated outside the campaign by news reporters in their stories about the highly disciplined Clinton team.

Carville said that the strategy exists to be shared with the staff who will then go on to implement it. "I want everyone [in the campaign] to know what the strategy is. It's not a fricking secret. I really want everyone to understand exactly what it is that we're up to," said Carville.[18] He added that many campaigns fail to build an effective team because they keep too many secrets and physically silo campaign staffers off from one another.[19] Carville is a big believer in having an open floor plan at a campaign headquarters and said that an abandoned high school gym would be an ideal location.[20]

"I've heard of campaigns, they want one floor for the managers and another floor is the fundraising and another floor is the research and another floor is this, everything else. You know what I mean? You should be able to walk around and say, 'Hey, what's going on here?'" Carville doesn't like paper shredders and closed doors. "If anybody has anything, just ask me."

According to Carville, the number one organizational enemies of campaigns are meetings: "Discourage meetings . . . discourage meetings at all costs."[21]

Carville's approach to integrating strategy and team building is highlighted in a scene late in *The War Room*. The Little Rock campaign staff is gathered on election eve, and Stephanopoulos is introducing Carville:

Stephanopoulos: And finally, before I give him the floor for what I hope isn't the last time. I think we all know that, besides Bill Clinton, one person really gave this campaign focus. And one person wrote what I call a haiku [scattered laughter] about five months ago: "Change versus more of the same. The economy, stupid." I think if you did a Nexis, it would come up in about a thousand places.

I was kidding James yesterday. I said he was about to pass from a role of regular human being into the role of a legend. [chuckling] And I think he really deserves it . . . because probably for the first time in a generation tomorrow we're gonna win. And that means that more people are gonna have better jobs. People are gonna pay a little less for health care, get better care . . . and more kids are gonna go to better schools.

[Cheering]

Carville: There's a simple doctrine. Outside of a person's love, the most sacred thing that they can give is their labor. And somehow or another along the way, we tend to forget that. And labor is a very precious thing that you have. And any time that you can combine labor with love . . . you've made a merger. And I think we're gonna win tomorrow . . . and I think that the governor is gonna fulfill his promise and change America . . . and I think many of you are gonna go on and help him.

I'm a political professional. That's what I do for a living. I'm proud of it. We changed the way campaigns are run.[22]

Clinton went on to win 43 percent of the popular vote, while George H. W. Bush took 37 percent and independent billionaire candidate Ross Perot garnered 19 percent of the popular vote. Carville helped Clinton achieve victory by executing the campaign's core strategies and infusing his team with a shared sense of mission. Clinton became the first Democrat since Jimmy Carter to win the presidency. One reason that happened was because Carville played his role as strategy enforcer/team builder with moxie, instinct, and an even keel. The Clinton campaign withstood scandal after scandal and kept on its winning course, partly because Carville kept the candidate focused and established a culture that persuaded all staff to feel invested in the strategy.

Inheriting a Team: The Turnaround Manager

Carville and his team built the 1992 Clinton strategy and campaign infrastructure from scratch and had the time to make sure that their strategy and their people were in sync. Not every campaign manager has that luxury. In the worst case, a replacement manager is parachuted into an ongoing campaign—usually one that's in trouble—and charged with turning it around. Not only does the new manager have to evaluate the campaign's strategy but they must also assess and take charge of the campaign staff and volunteers. And they must do all this while building a working relationship with the candidate and their existing entourage of advisers, friends, and donors.

A brand-new campaign manager we'll call Andy found himself in this situation just thirty-five days before the November congressional election. Although only thirty-four years old, Andy was no political novice. Four times he had successfully managed his own campaign for a seat in the Massachusetts House of Representatives—so successfully, in fact, that Andy had no opposition in the upcoming November general election. This congressional race would be much more difficult. Andy's candidate, Tom, was a moderate Republican and a political novice running against a one-term Democratic congressman. By Massachusetts standards, the district was one of the more competitive in the heavily Democratic state, yet Andy knew it would be an uphill fight. However, a recently completed poll suggested they were within striking range, showing the incumbent with 41 percent, Tom with 30 percent, and 29 percent undecided.[23]

The previous campaign manager, a midwestern outsider whom Tom had hired over the phone, had ten days earlier agreed to stay on and run the fundraising operation; he was now located at a different campaign office than Andy and the rest of the staff. Andy had heard that both the campaign field director and the campaign scheduler had been interested in running the campaign without a manager. But the campaign's general consultant, a friend of Andy's, felt the campaign needed a more senior person in charge. Andy certainly was not looking for this job, but his consultant friend talked him into taking it, saying it would be good for the Massachusetts Republican Party and for Andy's own political career.[24]

Andy's first day on the job was a Monday: "I remember it well. I think I was the fifth campaign manager, and I think four of the campaign managers were still employees of the campaign or had an advisory role with the campaign, so it was very awkward." Andy knew he wouldn't have the time or even the authority to put together his own campaign team. "I'm not sure I was given the authority to hire and fire. I didn't feel as if I did. . . . Coming into the campaign that late, you don't really have the opportunity to hire new people," Andy recalled in an interview with the authors. "You can bring in people to fill holes, but you can't create a hole to be filled. So I kind of inherited a team and I had to work with it."[25]

Andy did not know the candidate Tom nearly as well as the others who had been working on the campaign for months, and this further complicated his job. "It was really hard because it wasn't as if I had the complete confidence or trust of the candidate, because I hadn't been around long enough for the candidate to know me or for me to know him. It's the same situation with the candidate's spouse, and candidly, it's the same situation with a lot of the financial backers of the campaign." As Andy put it, he was brought on to get things done, to be a "transactional leader" as opposed to a "transformational leader" who would have changed the whole direction of the campaign. He generally agreed with and was committed to pursuing the strategy that had been laid out in a fifteen-page planning document prepared for Tom in the spring.[26]

It was less about strategy and more about implementation of strategic tactics to get [our] vote. You didn't have time to change the strategy of the campaign or really have an impact on the communication strategy in particular. You had to execute. So you had to motivate people to do a better job, but it wasn't that the job changed, you just had to motivate them to do their job because time was running out and the effort had to produce results in a very short time.

I inherited the policy work and the field expertise, the scheduler, the finance effort basically had been done—there was very little work I did on the fundraising side. It was mostly the execution of a get-out-the-vote (GOTV) effort, scheduling the candidate to be at the right place at the right time with an audience that was strategically relevant. And making sure that the nuts and bolts were there to identify the vote and pull it out on election day. It was not about coming up with a grand strategy for the campaign.

"Andy," Massachusetts Republican campaign manager

One of Andy's key objectives was to generate news coverage of Tom. The suburban district was located on the fringes of the large and very expensive Boston media market.[27] The campaign could afford a modest radio buy, but Boston television advertising would likely be scant or nonexistent. This was going to be an old-school retail style event-to-event campaign, and Andy wanted press coverage of those events. It was tough to generate news coverage of the contest in the major Boston media, but the several small towns in the district had their own local newspapers and radio stations who reported on the race. Most news reporters had taken a liking to Tom, a lawyer from a blue-collar family who had a good way with people and small groups. Andy recalled the following:

[I wanted] the candidate to be very, very visible, to the extent possible, including media outlets in the campaign schedule. So it wasn't just showing up to a plant, or a cocktail party, or a coffee party, or a Rotary Club meeting, there was also [a] plan to get media coverage and editorial board meetings.[28]

Andy's time was also taken up by dealing with the large number of part-time consultants and friendly advisers who would periodically check in to see what was happening and offer their own opinions as to what the campaign should and should not be doing. While he generally respected them and valued their advice, Andy was in execution mode and didn't want the campaign to be slowed down by what he calls "meddling and second guessing." But Andy also realized that part of his job was similar to the constituent service he provided to residents of his district as a state representative. So, like other people-savvy campaign managers, Andy made the time to keep Tom's inner circle briefed, involved, and generally satisfied with the campaign's progress.[29]

Among campaign staffers and volunteers, Andy's people and management skills also paid dividends. The staff remained intact and productive, there were no major blowups, targets were met, and the strategy was enforced. The race was going to be close, and Andy knew the campaign needed a break to put it over the top. There were high hopes for an influence peddling investigation of the incumbent member of Congress related to his previous tenure as a town mayor, but he was cleared of those charges before the election. In November, Tom lost the race by a margin of just 2.7 percent.[30] Still, Andy's deft leadership—his ability to enforce the strategy and achieve buy-in from his team—helped give Tom a shot at victory.

In fact, the campaign Andy managed took place in 1980 and pitted Republican Tom Trimarco against first-term incumbent Democrat Nick Mavroules in the coastal 6th Congressional District north of Boston. Even though they lost, Andy said the campaign ultimately proved to be a step on the way to political success for at least two of his young staffers. Field director Joe Malone was elected Massachusetts state treasurer in 1990 and reelected in 1994.[31] The campaign's research director, Peter Torkildsen, was elected to the Massachusetts state house in 1984.[32] In 1992, Torkildsen was elected to Congress, defeating none other than Nick Mavroules, who was fined $15,000 and sentenced to prison for accepting the free use of a beach house and no-cost leased automobiles while a member of Congress.[33] The break Andy had been looking for in the fall of 1980 came twelve years too late for Trimarco but just in time for Torkildsen.

After the 1980 race, Andy Card's own political career still held in store a couple of hard knocks. In 1982, Andy ran unsuccessfully in the Republican primary for governor. Even while losing, he did impress the winning candidate, who promptly asked Andy to manage his own general election campaign. They lost to Michael Dukakis.[34] Despite three defeats in just two years, Andy's political management skills were recognized in Washington, and he was offered a staff position in the Reagan White House where he rose to director of intergovernmental affairs dealing with governors and other state and local elected officials. Under President George H. W. Bush, who had defeated Dukakis in another "small world" political coincidence, Andy served as deputy chief of staff before being named secretary of transportation. After Bush was defeated by Bill Clinton in 1992, Andy served as

White House representative to the Clinton transition. He then entered the private sector as president of the American Automobile Manufacturers Association. In 2000, Republican presidential nominee George W. Bush asked Andy to manage the Republican National Convention. On November 26, 2000, Andrew L. Card was appointed to be chief of staff for president-elect George W. Bush and is most famously known for whispering news of the September 11, 2001, attacks in the ear of the president as he sat in a Florida elementary school classroom.[35]

Card now serves as president of Franklin Pierce University in Rindge, New Hampshire. Asked to describe his current relationship with politics, Card said the following:

> I still consider myself to be a political figure, I'm active in politics and am not afraid to be. I call for people to participate in politics, but I am not an active candidate nor am I actively engaged in a campaign right now . . . but I will be actively engaged as a partisan.[36]

How Are We Doing?

Strategy enforcement and team building seem at first blush a bit like inside baseball—topics that matter mainly to political junkies and the reporters who cover them. But having a strong strategy enforcer or team builder in the manager's slot enables the campaign to answer, "How are we doing?" as well as, "What are they doing?" and thus give their candidates the best shot possible of winning. Campaign manager Robby Mook, who is Hillary Clinton's 2016 presidential campaign manager, defined the manager's "most important role" as "arriv[ing] at a strategy, and then build[ing] a team and lead[ing] a team to execute that strategy."[37]

Mike Shannon, who worked on George W. Bush's two presidential campaigns, agreed. At the campaign's outset, he said, the manager better "spend a significant amount of time . . . building a strong theory of how [the] candidate can win"—and then inculcate the strategy in the team to keep the campaign on its winning path.[38] Steve Bell, who ran Heather Wilson's congressional campaign from New Mexico in 1998, said that campaigns had to keep a tight focus on such questions as these: "Who do we have to move? Who can we move? How do we move them?"[39] Mitt Romney reported to us that he agreed with his campaign manager's strategic argument that his 2012 campaign should invest heavily in the Republican Iowa caucuses. "Our senior strategist was inclined to not have any role there at all, but our campaign manager disagreed. He argued that we should maintain a presence early on—an office and a few key people—and if things look good down the road, we should make a big effort. His view carried the day." He implemented and enforced the strategy. Romney added, "If ever there were issues of disagreement, I was the final arbitrator. Typically, however, the campaign manager was able to guide the senior team to reach consensus on strategic issues."[40] Without a clear strategy and

In front of a Florida elementary school class, White House chief of staff Andrew Card whispers in President Bush's ear on September 11, 2001. "A second plane has hit the second tower. America is under attack."

collective sense of team-driven mission, the campaign's problems can breed staff infighting and suspicion, draining the campaign's energy, weakening the team's focus on winning the election. Consider what transpired in those times when managers were unable to enforce a clear strategy and failed to ensure that the team was all moving in the same direction. In these instances, the campaigns lost track of their candidate's core identity, and their message discipline unraveled. One member of the Obama team pointed out that the lack of strategy enforcement on Romney's general election campaign meant that Romney's campaign ultimately veered "in a million different directions."[41] His team, she explained, tried to "[soften] him up," turn him into a common man, and depict him as an economic Mr. Fix-It, yet none of the images stuck in the public's mind or were ultimately persuasive to voters.[42] This campaign professional also observed that her team made the same mistake eight years prior when they sent John Kerry hunting and failed to stick to a strategy about who Kerry was and why voters should hire him to replace the incumbent,

George W. Bush.[43] The lack of an enforcer and a team culture made Kerry more vulnerable to charges that he was a flip-flopper and Romney open to being attacked as an out-of-touch plutocrat.

Campaign managers agreed that once a campaign decision had been reached, all team members had to support and execute it to the best of their ability. Any good campaign team, Republican manager Adam Bodily argued, should be working in unison from the very same playbook and ultimately striving "toward the same goals."[44] Chris Durlak, who managed a 2010 state senate race in Pennsylvania, argued that managers who become bogged down amid the advice and comments "from the candidate, from the press," and criticisms from their opponents risked losing sight of "the big picture."[45] He said that in some cases managers got so immersed in the campaign's daily problems that they were "going native," failing to see the treetops while running from one crisis to the next.[46]

Another campaign manager stressed that his job was to steer the campaign down the right path. As a manager, he had to ensure all of the campaign's resources—the candidate's time, his time, staff time, volunteer efforts, and money—were all propelling them the same direction. Almost everybody associated with the campaign, including the candidate, was going to have strong ideas on how the campaign's resources should be allocated. With millions of dollars at stake and

AP Photo/Charlie Neibergall.

In 2004, Democratic presidential nominee John Kerry went goose hunting in order to assure hunters and rural voters that he was not the flip-flopping, weak-kneed liberal that had been depicted by the Bush campaign. This photo came in the final days of the campaign and struck some of Kerry's critics as a desperate, last-minute bid to shift his campaign's strategy and messaging.

much else riding on the election's results, it was the strategy enforcer's job to say "yes" to the right things that advanced their strategic goals and nix those ideas that were at odds with the larger goals of the particular campaign. The manager's office, said one campaign professional, is where good ideas must go to die if a campaign's strategy is going to find success.

Democratic campaign manager Raiyan Syed explained that as the strategy enforcer one of his candidates gave him "a NO button," which, when pressed, announced, "No! No! No!" The gift to Syed from his boss was a less-than-subtle hint that he needed to be disciplined and ensure that the campaign's strategic priorities were not being sacrificed on the altar of every good idea that came his way.[47]

And keeping track of "How are we doing?" is simply harder to do without a strong enforcer at the helm. Campaign managers, Republican Mike Shields said, must "make sure that the campaign stays focused on executing [the campaign] plan on a daily basis and to report back up where the plan is working and where it's not working." Finding the sweet spot is crucial. Campaigns that fail to adjust when conditions warrant often get stuck, single-mindedly wedded to a strategy that needs fine-tuning. Yet campaigns that are ever-shifting with no core rationale or message give late-night comedians, reporters, and political opponents the fodder they need to tag them as hollow, inauthentic flip-floppers or other pejorative labels. Effectively enforcing strategy requires that managers wield another skill—listening intently, consuming information, taking advice. "A really, really good leader . . . doesn't just say, 'Here's what we're going to do,' but tries to be collaborative and listen to other people," Shields told us. And then that leader makes a decision and executes the decision.[48]

Nonetheless, keeping the campaign clear-eyed about its strategy (as Carville did) is actually harder than it might sound. Campaigns are often filled with talented, smart professionals. They bring deep experience and strong opinions about what the winning strategy should be. Consultants are paid much money to advise campaigns on messaging, polling, and grassroots organizing, and guiding and enforcing the strategic decision process requires a delicate balancing act.

Consider the hard enforcement task facing Steven Law and his colleagues, who were working on Sen. Mitch McConnell's 1990 reelection campaign in Kentucky. In late 1989, a mentally ill man carrying an assault rifle entered the Standard Gravure printing factory in Louisville, Kentucky, and murdered eight people. The shooting accelerated the debate about passing an assault weapons ban in Congress, where McConnell was still a first-term senator.

Despite his incumbent status, McConnell's reelection was anything but a slam dunk for Steven Law. McConnell had defeated a Democratic incumbent in 1984 by some 6,000 votes out of more than 1.2 million cast, and in 1992, he faced the formidable former Louisville mayor Harvey Sloane.[49] McConnell had a perfect score from the National Rifle Association (NRA), and the group had endorsed him. McConnell and his team were torn.[50] Two advisers argued that McConnell, as Law recalled, "ought to vote for [the ban]" because the national politics had shifted in favor of gun control. But their state director, "who had a strong sense of the state's pro-gun culture, argued passionately" that we should "dance with the one who brung you"—essentially, stick with our allies and vote against the ban. "And that's what we did."[51]

Law recalled this about the vote:

> [It was] absolutely the right decision because people who cared about the issue on the other side weren't going to be for us anyway. And to the NRA, it made our race that much more important, because we stood firm. The realization came home to me when I was driving in Eastern Kentucky in October and heard pro-McConnell radio ads blanketing the airwaves, sponsored by the NRA.[52]

As the strategy enforcer, Law had to ensure that every view was aired and that once the strategy was set, the campaign stuck to its script and vigorously defended McConnell's vote. They believed that they had a winning strategy. And they were right. McConnell won by less than 5 percent of the vote in 1992, and the robust support from the NRA helped ensure McConnell's reelection.

Strategy Enforcer in the Age of Super Political Action Committees

One of the greatest recent challenges facing campaign managers tasked with enforcing strategy has been the advent of super PACs (political action committees), following the Supreme Court's *Citizens United* decision in January 2010. The Court's ruling said that spending on political campaigns was protected by the First Amendment's free-speech clause, and as such, it could not be restricted. Under this law, deep-pocketed donors are permitted to donate millions of dollars to independent committees that were set up with the express purpose of running ads in support of a particular cause or candidate.

At the same time, under *Citizens United*, super PACs are not legally permitted to coordinate with the candidates' campaigns, draining some of the power and authority from the campaigns. Super PACs spent tens of millions on television advertisements during the 2012 and 2014 election cycles—and the arms race is only growing exponentially.[53] In the run-up to the 2016 presidential campaign, super PACs were assuming the character of shadow campaigns, raising far more money in some cases than the campaigns themselves. That development has big implications for campaigns and campaign managers. Led by strategists who have close ties to the candidates, the 2016 super PACs have become vehicles for candidates to raise unlimited sums from a small number of donors without adhering to fundraising restrictions that the official campaigns must follow. For example, Jeb Bush's super PAC, Right to Rise, had raised a whopping $103 million by July 2015—nearly ten times what his official campaign had raised up until then. One of Bush's closest strategists, Mike Murphy, is the man running Right to Rise, while Hillary Clinton's super PAC is likewise being managed as of this writing by her 2008 campaign political director, Guy Cecil. "Super PAC donations totally change the game," NPR reported after fundraising totals began to be released in mid-2015.[54]

The campaign managers couldn't have agreed more. They pointed out that in answering the campaign question "What are they doing?," they must pay attention not just to their political opponents but also now more than ever to the outside groups that are raising and spending tens of millions of dollars to deliver messages directly to voters in the hopes of affecting election results. Thus, enforcing the strategy has become vastly more complicated since *Citizens United*. Campaign managers must pay rapt attention to what ads' outside groups, over which they supposedly have no direct control, are running on television and other media platforms. Campaign managers, in short, were groping for a way to enforce their own campaign's strategy without getting sidetracked by what the super PACs were doing. "You can't overstate how [much super PACs affect] these campaigns," manager Brad Beychock explained.[55] He said that if campaigns spent between $6 and $15 million on a US Senate race in a midsize state, outside groups such as American Crossroads or Americans for Prosperity would "dwarf th[at] campaign spending."[56] Ultimately, he added, these groups had an impact on public policy and how members of Congress vote. "It's only growing every day with *Citizens United*," he lamented.[57]

On a less existential level, super PACs (also known as "independent expenditures") make it harder for campaign managers to ensure that the campaign is reaching its targeted voters with a clear and forceful message. Republican campaign manager Gentry Collins described the conundrum created by super PACs. He called it "a friendly fire problem."[58] He explained that a "campaign manager . . . can say, 'Look . . . in this particular state or district, we want the message to be about . . . growing the economy and creating jobs. That's what our messaging is going to be about.'"[59] But then, this happens:

All of a sudden, you have a third-party group who's running ads . . . on immigration. And now you have a problem because what they may be saying on that or any particular issue . . . may excite base turnout, but may be a big turnoff to some other part of the electorate, independents or moderates or swing voters.[60]

Those charged with leading the independent expenditure campaigns at the Republican Governor's Association, National Republican Congressional Committee (NRCC), National Republican Senatorial Committee (NRSC), and on the Democratic side try to "first do no harm" with their outside-group spending,

Collins explained. But, because the groups are barred from coordinating with the campaigns, doing no harm is easier to say rather than follow, he added.[61]

Super PAC spending on television ads can breed strategic confusion within a campaign environment, as Republican manager Matt McDonald fretted. "I'm scared to death of somebody who is not on the inside of the campaign making decisions that affect the outcome of my race. . . . It increases the number of players in the process" and sowed a lot of uncertainty that was "a dynamic I don't want."[62] Campaign managers had few concrete answers for how to keep their campaigns on track strategically in the face of substantial super PAC spending. And some managers expressed a deepening gloom and even cynicism about the political process due to super PACs' influence. Ashley Spillane pointed out that independent expenditures from third parties are almost completely focused on negative advertising. "I don't remember running any positive ads at the [Democratic Congressional Campaign Committee (DCCC) Independent Expenditure] in 2010," she admitted. The candidates, saddled with limited resources, are asked to do the brunt of the positive messaging, while outside groups are increasingly expected to "beat the crap out of the other side."[63]

Although their power to control super PACs' messaging is circumscribed by the law, managers agreed that at bare minimum they needed to pay close attention to what the outside groups were doing with their messaging. Jarryd Gonzales told us that as the enforcer his plan was to "find out who's buying . . . airtime . . . who's using certain printers, . . . because . . . your resources are limited and the more you can find out about what's going on, the better you can allocate your own resources" and adjust the campaign's strategy, if necessary.[64] So far, some campaigns have been slow to recalibrate based on what super PACs were doing in a race. Zac Moffatt, who worked on Mitt Romney's 2012 presidential campaign, argued that super PACs injected a degree of unpredictability that "hurt Mitt more than they helped him" during the primary.[65]

Moffatt pointed out that had it not been for super PAC spending, Newt Gingrich would have had to end his run after the Nevada primaries, and Rick Santorum also would have folded his campaign much earlier than he ultimately did. The super PACs "allowed people to stay in the race who had no campaign," Moffatt pointed out.[66] They gave Romney's rivals cover from outside spending in which millions of dollars were devoted to destroying Romney. The super PAC spending harmed Romney's image, softening him up for Obama, and forced him to devote limited time and resources to fending off his GOP rivals.

The worst mistake a manager could make on this score was to ignore the super PACs as if they were nonexistent, as Paul Tencher told us: "You have to win a campaign based on what's the reality." Tencher, who managed Joe Donnelly's successful 2012 Democratic Senate bid from Indiana, revealed that when it became clear that super PACs were about to air ads attacking Donnelly, he and his team "made the [strategic] gamble right away to go up on television very, very early." That unorthodox decision was necessitated by what the outside groups were doing, forcing him to shift course mid-campaign and then enforce the strategy shift on his campaign team.[67]

Team Builder: "A Big Cheerleader"

It's virtually impossible to be an effective enforcer without also building a harmonious team that embraces the strategy and works hard to achieving the campaign's strategic goals. It is hardly ever enough simply for managers to hire good staff (for more on hiring, see Chapter 4: Entrepreneur and Chief Financial Officer) and let them tackle their jobs. Team building requires campaign managers to adopt various personas during the course of the race, depending on the manager's style, the candidate, and the type of culture they're building. Graham Shafer told us that team building required him to function as "a big cheerleader" for his staff because he's "seen so many campaigns that just have an awful vibe because a campaign manager has an awful attitude."[68] When running Van Hilleary's Tennessee governor's campaign, Shafer tried to use positive reinforcement in order to motivate his team and make them feel invested in the mission. "The campaign manager drives the entire strategy process, convening the strategy team, drawing out the candidate's perspective, and making sure that a compelling strategy is in place. Then the manager becomes the implementer in chief of that strategy. In my presidential campaign, that's the way it worked," Mitt Romney told us. "The campaign manager . . . is also responsible for the morale and spirit of the campaign. No one else can do that with the exception of the candidate, but typically the candidate is away from the office campaigning," he added. "At critical times, particularly following one of the inevitable losses or dissapointments, the campaign manager is the one to rally the troops, to restore enthusiasm and to remind them of the importance of the task ahead."[69]

On many losing campaigns, the team building frays, the staff bickers ad nauseam, and the campaign is listing off course as a result. Internal rifts, stoked by opinionated, intransigent personalities, can center on spending decisions, hiring decisions, the proper role of the candidate's family, and debates about which team members should fill which roles, just to name a few examples. But whatever the friction's roots, such tension can wreak havoc inside and outside a campaign. The inner tension can foster a toxic climate for a campaign team and even filter into the news media that can turn the campaign into Exhibit A of how not to run a campaign. When that happens, not only is the candidate's image as a strong leader eroded but campaign donors and volunteers tend to be less willing to support a campaign that's perceived as sputtering. Answering the "How are we doing?" question becomes an extended, debilitating exercise in crisis management and damage control.

While this level of acrimony and negative press can occasionally be overcome by campaigns, fractured teams are a distraction to the candidate, the managers, and every other team member, diverting their focus from the campaign's strategic priorities. Instead of defining their opponents and delivering their message about the candidate's good character and leadership skills, friction-filled campaigns must devote energy and resources to fixing the impression of dysfunction and disarray that has engulfed it. Hillary Clinton's 2008 campaign became known for chief strategist Mark Penn's imperious approach as well as staff discord, strategy disputes, and an inner-circle shielding Clinton from outside advice and projecting a haughty air of electoral invincibility. These negative impressions became part of the narrative about her presidential run, while the esprit de corps of Obama's team offered pundits a ready-made contrast to the dysfunction of Hillary Clinton's operation. Her team's dynamics, at least on the margins, damaged her chances in the Democratic primary.

Other examples of dysfunctional teams retarding campaign progress abound. Early in the 2004 presidential campaign, John Kerry had both a Boston- and Washington-based campaign staff that vied for control over the campaign's direction. The war within became part of the news cycle, and during the primary campaign, Kerry was ultimately forced to fire a number of senior staffers to try to fix his flailing campaign. In this case, Kerry was able to overcome the negative publicity and staff infighting, the lack of team harmony and strategic accord, yet the feel of acrimony never entirely left Kerry's side, and it wasn't clear that his staff felt particular loyalty to the candidate or that the team was absolutely committed to his election. Kerry is hardly alone. Early in the 2008 Republican primary race, John McCain was forced to revamp his own team because the discord among his staff had grown so corrosive. While he eventually became his party's nominee, a poorly managed staff process was partially responsible for the lack of vetting of Alaska governor Sarah Palin before he picked her as his running mate. Palin's selection gave the campaign an initial bump in the polls. But the team's inability to function smoothly left the impression that the candidate was unreliable and inconsistent.

Other instances of campaign infighting can divert the campaign's message, sap its energy, and damage the candidate's public image of strength and leadership. In 2015, *Politico* ran a story headlined "Inside Rand Paul's Downward Spiral," chronicling staff infighting, a listless candidate, campaign indirection, and an overall dispirited organization.[70] This is hardly the kind of publicity that, campaign managers told us, further their causes; rather, such press tends to dampen donor ardor for the candidate and create a media feeding frenzy leading to a downward spiral. Losing campaign managers sometimes get desperate, resorting to tricks to keep their staff motivated. Casey Phillips, who ran Delbert Hosemann's 2007 Mississippi campaign for secretary of state, described how when he worked as political director on a different campaign, he found a poll that the campaign manager had commissioned and, it seemed, accidentally left on the printer. The poll showed the campaign running neck and neck; when Phillips found the poll, he went and told his entire campaign team that "the campaign manager . . . forgot to pick up this poll," which showed, he predicted, that their campaign was heading for victory. Yet, he recalled, on election day "we just got slaughtered." Much later, the campaign manager told Phillips "that he [left the poll on the printer] on purpose knowing that I'd find it and knowing that I would keep everybody going."[71]

Ideally, of course, campaigns need not resort to such tricks to keep the team operating on the same strategic page and focused on the same goal. Beychok said his duty was to assemble a team that functioned harmoniously and worked together to persuade and mobilize voters. He described some campaigns he's worked on where the pollster, media consultant, and direct mail consultant are all "big personalit[ies]," and the collection of "big brains" and "big egos" sowed "confusion and dissension." So Beychok strives to hire people whom he knows well and who have a reputation for being team players. Then he works hard to fashion the staff into a team that moves in unison toward the same direction.[72]

Even the best-run campaigns have challenges building the right teams and keeping the campaign driving towards its strategic goals. Every campaign experiences some level of internal friction, as not every team member always agrees on every issue. And, with the stakes high for the candidates and their senior staff, debates often get heated. But Republican manager Mike Shields described that on his campaigns he has a rule that "once a decision is made, you have to execute it even if you disagreed with it so that you're not dividing."[73] The team has to agree to disagree and immediately implement the plan to keep the campaign on its winning path.

Team building requires managers and their staff to put the campaign's priorities ahead of their own egos and ideas as well. They must subordinate their self-pride and financial interests to the campaign's strategic interests and the candidate's agenda. Brandon Waters, who ran Rick Clayburgh's 2002 North Dakota campaign for Congress, described a race in Pennsylvania he worked where a consultant suggested running a particular TV spot. The campaign's TV consultant dissented. Instead, he replied, "I think that's a better message for mail."[74] Waters recalled thinking that he knew then that he "truly had a team of professionals" because his TV consultant was the one saying, "No, we shouldn't do a TV ad on that. That should be delivered through mail because it can be better targeted to the correct audience."[75] The consultant was more interested in furthering the campaign's cause than in lining his own pocket and accruing more power in his own hands.

Team building also was synonymous with campaign managers taking a share of responsibility for the well-being of their staff—and their post-campaign professional lives. David Axelrod described well-run campaigns as having an almost "familial feel" and stressed the need to help campaign staff find good jobs in politics once the campaign had ended.[76] James Cauley told us that on an unnamed campaign he came to the aid of one of his young staffers who had had his driver's license suspended after he got a speeding ticket. Cauley sent "somebody to go pick [the staffer] up and bring him to work every day for a month" because he was his key Internet adviser. Cauley felt loyalty to all the "little . . . souls" working nonstop on behalf of the candidate.[77]

Democratic manager Raiyan Syed told us that when he assembles his campaign team, he puts a sign on the door or the wall that in its own way echoes Carville's signage. The sign says, "The Can-do Club." Syed instills the notion that negative attitudes—"can't work" or "won't work"—are anathema to building the campaign's team spirit. "If there's a thing we want to do, we can do it."[78]

Managing Consultants

Unlike some workplaces, campaigns have both full-time staff and part-time consultants, and managing consultants can pose a distinct challenge to keeping the team unified in support of the campaign's strategy. Consultants often are carrying multiple clients, yet they can have enormous sway over the campaign's strategic decisions. Managing both full- and part-time staff forces managers to serve in the role of boss, mentor, colleague, taskmaster, and cheerleader all at the same time in some cases, and integrating the consultants into the team is also an exercise in diplomacy, finesse, and other interpersonal skills. Syed's approach to team building was to integrate his consultants into the mission by getting them invested in the strategy long before election day. He has held weekly sixty- or ninety-minute calls with the candidate and the consultants to review the strategy and discuss how the other side was doing: "Politically, media, here's what's happening, here's what's going on. Candidate, do you have any questions? What are you thinking? What are your thoughts?"[79]

His staff sent the consultants news clips and talked to individual consultants, sometimes daily, discussing such topics as which issues they should jump on, which ones to watch, and sought their input on a press release or policy rollout. Syed also weaved his consultants into the campaign's culture by using the media consultant as the candidate's media trainer. He described bringing the media person to a retreat to "have them spend time with the candidate, have them coach the candidate on messaging, on just the whole presentation. You're going to have a big TV interview, this is how you pivot, this is your body language. We do mock . . . interviews, show it to them." And, he added, "debate prep is huge," offering another team-building opportunity. "You need your research firm, you need your pollster, you need your media consultant, you need mock debates, [including] a set of questions," and the consultants ideally became deeply invested in the process, the candidate, and the strategy. His best method to build a true team of professionals is to hire consultants whose track records as team players are spotless.[80]

Building the team's morale (and shared sense of mission) also rests on the candidate's preferences and the type of race that's being run. Kelly Evans, who managed Christine Gregoire's 2008 reelection campaign for Washington governor, relayed how the governor had little appetite for listening to internal strategy debates and preferred to have "streamlined recommendations to come to her" so the process was efficient. Evans and her campaign team squabbled amongst themselves about which recommendations they would make, but they resolved their differences before putting Gregoire on the phone. Evans explained that the governor had no "time to listen to [our internal debates], nor did she really want to listen to all of us argue about details and nuance." In its own small way, the process enabled Gregoire to focus on what mattered most and Evans to build a team culture that ultimately maximized the odds that their candidate win another term.[81]

Building team spirit and managing strong personalities also meant, campaign managers said, establishing clear lines of authority within the campaign. "The worst campaigns are full of gray area on who's supposed in be in charge of what," Republican manager Scott Reed argued.[82] Republican manager Mike Shields explained his preferred method of "delegate[ing] [to his staff] with clarity."[83] Former Richard Nixon adviser Roger Stone went even further. He argued that the best-run campaigns with the strongest teams tend to be the dictatorships, and he quoted Gen. Douglas MacArthur's axiom that "war councils breed defeat."[84] Stone saw firsthand that when Nixon micromanaged the strategic decisions during his 1960 presidential bid, the campaign turned into "an abysmal disaster."[85] Stone recalled that Nixon refused to "take any advice," antagonizing his staff.[86] By entrusting key decisions in the hands of a single staff person (ideally, the campaign manager), campaigns, Stone reasoned, would exude a can-do attitude, a sense of forward motion, and instill confidence in the mission.

On Arnold Schwarzenegger's 2006 California gubernatorial campaign, deputy manager Reed Galen concluded that one reason the team functioned so well was that everybody knew and remained in their lanes. Schwarzenegger's manager Steve Schmidt's role was to look "up and out," while Galen was charged with managing the campaign's finances and day-to-day operations. Schmidt told staff who had finance-related questions, "This is what I pay Reed for." Galen felt that the division of labor between them helped build an effective team, where each person felt empowered to do his or her job and knew exactly where they fit into the campaign structure.[87]

"The Right Kind of Culture"

Although he's only thirty-five, Robby Mook, Hillary Clinton's campaign manager, provided insights that had eluded even some veteran campaign managers. Mook told us that every campaign had a culture and that the culture varied from one campaign to the next. But, he pointed out, "it is the responsibility of a manger to establish a culture within the campaign. It's important to be deliberate about that culture."[88] He went on to say the following:

> Some campaign managers try to be thrifty. Some campaign managers try to maximize the amount of work people are doing. I think setting the right kind of *culture* in the organization is [vital], and so what I personally look for are people who are going to be loyal to the candidate and to the organization, people who are going to be self-motivated to work really hard. I'm not looking for people who are interested in being on the campaign for the purpose of going on to do something else. I want to know that they're going to work hard right now for this campaign.[89]

Mook said that the most important thing in terms of getting culture right for the campaign is for people to have the mind-set that the team is "there to win" and "[be] successful in the campaign" above all other considerations.[90] In Mook's mind, strategy plus team offers the best chance for success.

James Carville has learned his share of lessons by losing campaign after campaign before he finally began to win elections. He has worked on less-happy campaign teams than Clinton's 1992 undertaking. By 1992, he had decided that Clinton's campaign was going to do some things differently. For one, he opted against having a separate campaign team for the campaign trail. He had seen campaigns where the team on the road thinks its "doing all the work and the people back at the headquarters are just sitting there, drinking and fooling and talking to reporters."[91] Such divisions festered and became "destructive," he told us, with people shouting at each other because each side regarded the other as incompetent and untrustworthy. In 1992, Carville integrated the road staff in the overall organization and "worked hard on having a good relationship with the road." And he did something else that built the team and strategy into one thing: he made sure that Clinton did not look "at the campaign as just something I'm raising money for them to go out and drink beer and have sex," and that the campaign team did not come to "[look] at the candidate as a giant pain in the ass." Despite the political crises, Carville says of 1992, "the culture [of the campaign] was we had a great candidate." The campaign was professionally run, and it acquired a winning vibe. "If you can't walk in to a campaign and assess immediately what these people are about, what the energy level is, what they all do, you're missing something. . . . I'm trying to get out about 100 million voters. I want everybody here to know what the strategy is."[92]

On that campaign, of course, he succeeded as both strategy enforcer and team builder. By fusing the strategic vision and the campaign team into a unified whole, the strategy and the team became, in essence, a singular force. As Carville's experience shows us, when that merger happens on campaigns and when the staff is all striving to reach the same goal, it is an elegant thing for campaigns and the people who run them.

A strong team buffeted by a clear strategy gives almost any campaign the ability to give a strong answer to the core question from the campaign flowchart, "How are we doing?" At a minimum, the team at that time can know that it is addressing with unity and focus the fundamental factors shaping the electoral terrain (i.e., the economy, presidential popularity, the state of the world). A shared strategy and unified team enable operatives to focus on mobilizing their most partisan voters and persuading their undecided targets as well as free the candidate from any turmoil within to perform at his or her strategic best. When the team and the strategy become one thing, the campaign manager knows that while little in politics is guaranteed, at least they had prevented internal dissent from damaging the candidate's brand and knocking the campaign off its plotted course. Managers who can play these overlapping roles give their campaigns an edge on the margins, a better chance of responding effectively to what their opponents and outside groups are doing, while making sure the campaign is performing as well as possible under whatever circumstances they are facing.

Notes

1. J. Carville, personal communication, November 9, 2011.
2. Ibid.
3. "L. A. Carville from Carville, La.," Published by Early Colonial Families of Louisiana, www.mylouisianafamily.com/histories/Carville,%20Louis%20Arthur%20short%20biography.pdf.
4. J. Carville, personal communication, November 9, 2011.
5. Ibid.
6. Ibid.
7. Ibid.
8. "The Office of James Carville," The Official Website of James Carville, 2008, www.carville.info.
9. Ibid.
10. Ibid.
11. Ibid.
12. *The War Room* was released in 1993 and nominated for an Academy Award. More about the film and the film's trailer are available at www.imdb.com/title/tt0108515.
13. J. Carville, personal communication, November 9, 2011.
14. Ibid.
15. The term *bimbo eruption* was coined by the political director of the Bush campaign, Mary Matalin. Surprisingly, while they attacked each other's candidate, Carville and Matalin had been dating semisecretly during the 1992 campaign. They were married in 1993. Their story is told in *All's Fair: Love, War, and Running for President* published by Random House in 1995.
16. R. J. Cutler, Wendy Ettinger, and Frazer Pennebaker, *The War Room*, directed by Chris Hegedus and D. A. Pennebaker, 1993 (New York: Criterion Collection, 2012), DVD.
17. Ibid.
18. Ibid.
19. Ibid.
20. J. Carville, personal communication, November 9, 2011.
21. Ibid.
22. R. J. Cutler et al., *The War Room*.
23. A. Card, personal communication, August 24, 2015.
24. Ibid.
25. Ibid.
26. Ibid.
27. Ibid.
28. Ibid.
29. Ibid.
30. "Massachusetts Election Statistics," http://electionstats.state.ma.us/elections/search/year_from:1980/year_to:1980/office_id:5.
31. "Former State Treasurer, Republican Joe Malone Jumps the GOP Ship," *Cape Cod Today*, October 21, 2013, www.capecodtoday.com/article/2013/10/21/22278-Malone-jumps-ship-Coakley-aide-wants-her-job.
32. Peter G. Torkildsen, "Massachusetts Election Statistics," http://electionstats.state.ma.us/candidates/view/Peter-G-Torkildsen.
33. Ibid.

34. A. Card, personal communication, August 24, 2015.

35. "Andrew H. Card, Jr. Former White House Chief of Staff," The White House, http://georgewbush-whitehouse.archives.gov/government/card-bio.html.

36. A. Card, personal communication, August 24, 2015.

37. R. Mook, personal communication, March 14, 2013.

38. M. Shannon, personal communication, May 7, 2013.

39. S. Bell, personal communication, June 20, 2014.

40. M. Romney, personal communication.

41. Anonymous, personal communication.

42. Ibid.

43. Jodi Wilgoren, "Kerry on Hunting Photo-Op to Help Image," *New York Times*, October 22, 2004.

44. A. Bodily, personal communication, September 30, 2011.

45. C. Durlak, personal communication, September 23, 2011.

46. Ibid.

47. R. Syed, personal communication, June 20, 2014.

48. M. Shields, personal communication, November 9, 2011.

49. Kentucky State Board of Elections, "1984 Primary and General Election Results," 2015, http://elect.ky.gov/SiteCollectionDocuments/Election%20Results/1980-1989/1984/84ussenate5.txt.

50. S. Law, personal communication, September 29, 2011.

51. Ibid.

52. Ibid.

53. Jaime Fuller, "Who Needs a Presidential Campaign? Outside Spending in 2014 Could Rival 2012's," *Washington Post*, July 10, 2014, www.washingtonpost.com/news/the-fix/wp/2014/07/10/there-are-a-lot-of-super-PACs-spending-money-in-2014-a-lot.

54. Danielle Kurtzleben, "5 Things We've Learned about 2016 Presidential Fundraising," NPR, July 16, 2015, www.npr.org/sections/itsallpolitics/2015/07/16/423358905/5-things-weve-learned-about-2016-presidential-fundraising.

55. B. Beychok, personal communication, November 8, 2011.

56. Ibid.

57. Ibid.

58. G. Collins, personal communication, October 1, 2011.

59. Ibid.

60. Ibid.

61. Ibid.

62. M. McDonald, personal communication, November 7, 2011

63. A. Spillane, personal communication, September 30, 2011.

64. J. Gonzales, personal communication, November 18, 2011.

65. Z. Moffatt, personal communication.

66. Ibid.

67. P. Tencher, personal communication, February 13, 2013.

68. G. Shafer, personal communication, September 20, 2011.

69. M. Romney, personal communication.

70. Alex Isenstadt, "Inside Rand Paul's Downward Spiral," *Politico*, July 28, 2015, www.politico.com/story/2015/07/rand-paul-2016-downward-spiral-gop-campaign-120716.html.

71. C. Phillips, personal communication, October 18, 2011.

72. B. Beychok, personal communication, November 8, 2011.

73. M. Shields, personal communication, November 9, 2011.
74. B. Waters, personal communication, November 17, 2011.
75. Ibid.
76. D. Axelrod, personal communication, March 14, 2013.
77. J. Carville, personal communication, November 9, 2011.
78. R. Syed, personal communication, June 20, 2014.
79. Ibid.
80. Ibid.
81. K. Evans, personal communication, September 20, 2011.
82. S. Reed, personal communication, June 20, 2014.
83. M. Shields, personal communication, November 9, 2011.
84. R. Stone, personal communication.
85. Ibid.
86. Ibid.
87. R. Galen, personal communication, September 30, 2011.
88. R. Mook, personal communication, March 14, 2013.
89. Ibid.
90. Ibid.
91. R. J. Cutler et al., *The War Room*.
92. Ibid.

Candidate Caretaker and Confidant

Handling Details and Building Trust

> [The candidate-manager relationship is] very important. You have to be the person that he or she trusts the most in their whole orbit. You can't be afraid to tell them no, you can't be afraid to disagree with them, and you can't be afraid to really hold your ground on an issue that you do strongly disagree with him. At the end of the day, it's their name on the ballot and they have to do what they want to do but they need one truly honest broker who's not advising him to do something because they're going to make money off of it or because there's some personal benefit to them. They need someone whose only goal and only objective is the success of the campaign, and that's the role that the manager fills.[1]
>
> Jon Reedy, campaign manager, Scott Bruun for Congress, 2010 (OR)

In film and on television, the campaign manager is frequently romanticized as a sage candidate whisperer. Imagine the close-up of the earnest campaign manager holding his candidate's elbow as she prepares to take the debate stage, leaning in close and saying something like, "It won't be popular with some big donors, but it's true. For the last time, you've got to say it!" The candidate grimaces but she listens intently because over the years she and the manager have developed a high level of trust and the ability to honestly disagree with one another. The candidate quietly and seriously considers his advice because she knows the manager has only her best interests at heart. Finally she nods, puts her hand on his shoulder, and whispers back, "You're right. Let's do it."

Our campaign managers didn't tell us about any scenes like this. What they did tell us, however, suggests that Hollywood gets the important part right because mutual trust and the ability to confide in one another are key ingredients in the successful candidate-campaign manager relationship. While each relationship will be unique and can depend to a large extent on basic personal chemistry, campaign managers share some common beliefs about managing their relationship with the candidate, including the need to serve as a trusted confidant.

As we talked with experienced campaign pros, however, it became clear that, before a manager can rise to the level of candidate confidant, there is a related caretaking or fixer role that campaign managers must first master. The candidate is the focus, but managers say the caretaking role must often be enlarged to include the extended circle of the candidate's family, advisers, donors, volunteers, and friends. Much less glamorous than confidant, caretaker can mean taking care of larger needs, like briefing the candidate on his next campaign stop, or handling smaller details like reservations, laundry, a couple of extra head table seats at the fundraiser, or any of the other dozens of little requests and questions that find their way to the campaign manager's desk. Managers and staffers who can take care of the details become indispensable to one another and to the candidate.

Becoming Indispensable

Campaigns are built out of many small moving pieces and mundane tasks that must be managed if the campaign is to move forward. No matter how compelling the candidate is or how brilliant the strategy, the devil is still in the details—the copier needs toner, the candidate's cell phone is dead, or the PowerPoint presentation isn't updated. The candidate hires a campaign manager and staff to take care of these details so they don't have to do it themselves, and the best managers, staffers, and even volunteers will make themselves indispensable if they can handle these tasks for the candidate and for others involved in the campaign.

Becoming indispensable is a fast path to increased responsibility and stature for junior campaign staffers. Roger Stone, now best known as the sometimes political confidant to Donald Trump, learned this as a teenager volunteering in the mayor's race in his hometown of Norwalk, Connecticut. It was his first campaign experience and, instead of simply stuffing envelopes, ambitious young Roger wanted to do and learn more. In his case, the key was simply having the key:

> At the Republican headquarters, they had all these wooden folding chairs. And when they weren't being used, they were all kept in this closet. There were about forty of them, and they were in this closet. And I noticed that the closet door had a lock on it, so I got a key to the lock. Now if anybody wanted the chairs, they had to call me. So I [had] made myself indispensable. I was there for every meeting because I had to unlock the closet so they could get the chairs. I would set them up, and then I would take them down after the meeting was over. But that way I was included in every meeting.[2]
>
> Roger Stone, former adviser to presidential candidate Donald Trump

Another story about becoming indispensable in a campaign was told to us by Mike Shannon, now a senior partner at Vianovo, a business management consultancy in Austin. As an undergraduate at Vanderbilt, Shannon knew he wanted to get an MBA. The top-tier business schools like to admit students with at least two years of work experience, so Shannon—after graduating from college in 1997—got a job working in corporate finance for a large energy company based in Texas. By 1999, Shannon was ready to get his MBA but considered putting it off for another year so he could do something he had always wanted to do.

"I decided to scratch an itch before going to graduate school," said Shannon. "I always wanted to work on a campaign."[3] Shannon went up to Washington to scout for opportunities, including possibly by starting out in an office on Capitol Hill. People told him he should go back to Texas and try to get a job in Gov. George W. Bush's presidential campaign, which was in the middle of the 2000 Republican primary season and gearing up for the general election. "That's where all the action is"[4] is how Shannon described the advice he heard. Shannon remembered his tough job search:

> I knew a guy who knew a guy who knew Israel Hernandez [a Bush campaign staffer], who was in the strategy group. And I just kept calling him until he said he would have lunch with me. We have lunch, and at the end of lunch he says, "We are looking for someone to start as a volunteer. You'll have to work your way onto staff. I need to talk to Karl [Rove], but I think you'd be a good fit. Can you start on Monday?" That was on a Wednesday. I said okay and slept on Israel's couch for the next six weeks.[5]
>
> Mike Shannon, Vianovo

The campaign headquarters was in a sleek Austin high-rise just down the street from Governor Bush's official residence in the state capital. Shannon quickly learned that the Bush campaign ran on a very tight budget when he was given an eight-year-old Apple computer. The computer was so old it could not connect to the Internet. "When I did any work, I had to put it on a floppy disk to get it to somebody. That's how important I was when I started," remembered Shannon. "Then one day, Karl Rove stuck his head out of his office and asked if anyone knew how to do PowerPoint. I said I did."[6] Shannon got a new computer and went to work.

It was kind of this crazy roller coaster like everybody has on campaigns. You know, one minute I'm filing and answering phones, and the next thing you know, on a Wednesday, I'm at the [Republican National] Convention in Philadelphia, with Karl giving me a bunch of marching orders to take our strategy presentation and add twenty slides to it. And I work all night, and all of a sudden, on Thursday I'm up in [Dick] Cheney's suite for the strategy briefing. And it was one of those surreal how did I get from there to here? situations."[7]

After Shannon had become Rove's indispensable PowerPoint clerk, another senior staffer started asking Shannon for help on projects. "I didn't know who he was, but it turned out to be Matthew Dowd [the campaign pollster and media manager]," said Shannon. Dowd ended up moving into an office next to Rove's while Shannon sat outside in the bullpen. "I was doing all of Karl's [PowerPoint] presentations, and I started helping Matthew track all the polls and track all the media buys."[8]

Becoming indispensable worked out well for Shannon. When Bush became president, Shannon did an eighteen-month stint in the Office of Strategic Initiatives (jokingly known inside the White House as the "strategery" group, in a reference to a *Saturday Night Live* skit) before retiring from politics and heading off to enter the MBA program at Northwestern's Kellogg School of Management. But politics wasn't finished with Shannon. While interning at a management consulting firm in 2003 between his first and second years, the call came from Dowd. "He said he needed me for the 2004 reelection starting in January," recalled Shannon. "I said I wouldn't be finished with my MBA and he said, 'Well, that's when I need you.'"

At the end of 2003 fall semester, Shannon took a leave of absence to begin a yearlong job as director of media planning. There, he managed the campaign's advertising and media budgets, reporting to Dowd and campaign manager Ken Mehlman (profiled in Chapter 4.) After the election, political analysts, as well as those inside the campaign, would credit Bush's advertising operation as one of the campaign's strengths. Shannon retired from campaign work a second time, finished his MBA, and got the job he wanted at a leading management consulting firm.

The Buffer and the Concierge

In presidential campaigns, a manager like Ken Mehlman will have a stable of staffers like Shannon. Most campaigns don't, and managers find themselves taking care of things they'd rather not have to handle. One of these is listening to unsolicited campaign advice from the candidate's inner circle. "[The campaign manager] has a very difficult job because he has to fend off a candidate's family and friends and supporters, with a smile, and keep them doing the grassroots stuff that you want them to do and not worry about campaign strategy," said Roger Stone, the former Trump adviser. "A thousand friends of the candidate are trying to get through with their idea which will win the election. Stop them—friends and donors and family."[9]

The job is comparable to that of a hotel concierge, said Stone. "You need something from the candidate, you come to me, and I arrange it if it's worth arranging. If you just want to give him a book or a letter, just give it to me. It needs handling—the handling of the friends and family—so the candidate can stay in the cocoon and stay on message."[10]

The concierge analogy also fits when it comes to taking care of the candidate's needs and those of his immediate household family, especially family members who are active as surrogate campaigners. With the campaign schedule controlling and consuming their time, the candidate and their partner often look to the campaign for help in managing the day-to-day details of life. For assistance, campaign managers look to the campaign's scheduler, who in many campaigns also functions as the candidate's personal assistant, and to the candidate's traveling staff person who is commonly called the "body man." The manager has the ultimate responsibility for keeping everyone happy, and in smaller, low-budget campaigns, it's the managers themselves who end up playing caretaker. Sometimes the manager has to help the candidate park his car before they become a trusted confidant.

Building Trust: "Jimmy, Here's What We Need to Do"

In July 2003, James "Jimmy" Cauley met Barack Obama for the first time in a coffee shop across the street from Obama's US Senate campaign headquarters. Cauley, a veteran campaign manager, was serving as chief of staff to newly elected Rep. Dutch Ruppersberger, D-MD. Obama, as noted in Chapter 4, was running in a crowded, seven-person Democratic primary and was hardly a shoo-in to be his party's nominee, let alone to win the Senate seat. Cauley doubted that Obama's campaign was the campaign for him. He went in to the meeting more interested in the free trip to Chicago than in the prospect of running an iffy Senate bid. Obama's race wasn't high profile and seemed like a bit of a long shot. Cauley was unenthused.[11]

The meeting went well. Cauley was blunt with the candidate about the kind of race he would run if he managed his campaign. If Obama wanted to run a campaign targeting a broad constituency, Cauley told him, he could do that, and he knew how to win. But if he wanted to restrict his focus to mobilizing African American voters and fail to build a big coalition, Cauley said he wasn't the right fit. Obama assured him that building a broad coalition and winning the election were his highest priorities, and he quickly won over Cauley with his charisma, savvy, and political intelligence.[12] Cauley was persuaded to move to Chicago and go to work for Barack Obama.

It's hard to imagine an odder pairing than the caustic Cauley managing the campaign of the preternaturally calm and cerebral Obama. Cauley was a working-class white political operative from the Appalachian hill country in Kentucky who graduated from the University of Kentucky. He habitually salted his sentences with f-bombs. Obama, in contrast, was an African American Harvard Law graduate who was raised in Hawaii. He was back then an Illinois state senator with a reformist bent who taught constitutional law at the University of Chicago.

But over the coming months, at a time when few Americans had heard of Barack Obama, Cauley and the future president formed a bond, primarily professional but also one with a distinctly personal touch. They reached a kind of unspoken understanding. Obama developed trust in Cauley's discretion and judgment, while Cauley learned to respect Obama's quirks, harness his political talents, and meet the candidate's needs and handle his family and friends with Kentucky bluntness and diplomatic niceties. Cauley said that on a lot of campaigns, his job was to let the candidate vent "when they've had a bad day. . . . But that also means that when I'm getting yelled at, they've got my back, which leads to trust. So you [need to] have that relationship where you can speak your mind in private."[13]

Campaign managers, Cauley told us, "deal with people and their problems." That was certainly true during Obama's 2004 Senate run. At first, Obama refused to let a driver take him to Springfield because he had wanted to preserve "his alone time." Cauley was frustrated that Obama would lose thirty minutes here and thirty there as the candidate searched for his own parking spot. "It was a huge fight to get him to take a driver in the car," Cauley explained. When he finally convinced Obama to let somebody drive him to campaign events, he then learned that Obama was still getting lost.[14]

Cauley asked the driver, "How can you get lost with GPS?"

"Well, Barack don't like to turn it on," the driver replied.

Apoplectic, Cauley feared the driver was becoming "Barack's best friend and not working for me." Cauley warned him, "I didn't hire you to make him happy. I hired you to get him from A to B at the right time." If Obama kept getting delayed to events and meetings, Cauley felt, the schedule would be out of whack, and the campaign would miss some opportunities to raise money and win votes.[15]

But the hardest part of his job, Cauley told us, was managing the candidate's friends, especially their constant advice, anxieties, and their dire predictions about the campaign's losing direction. About four or five weeks before the primary, Obama's friends called and said, according to Cauley, "Oh my God, you're losing. You got to get on the air. We'd done all this work and raised all this money, you've got to get on the air." At first, Obama felt confident in the campaign's plan and didn't let the warnings shake him. Their plan was based on their budget: they were to start advertising around three weeks prior to election day. But before long, Obama started wavering, and Cauley bore the brunt of the candidate's second-guessing. Obama suggested to Cauley that they spend $200,000 in the Chicago media market right away, which would have upended their television strategy. "You know what 200 grand in the Chicago media market is?" Cauley asked. "You might as well take that money out in the yard and burn that shit."[16]

"Dude, we're going to go up when we can go up," Cauley assured the candidate. Cauley explained that at week five, Obama "was behind me. Week four, he started wavering. And we got on the air week three or he'd probably fire me and spent the money." Their plan succeeded.

Ultimately, Obama won the primary. Obama retained faith in the advertising strategy and had confidence in Cauley's judgment. Cauley managed to persuade the candidate that he understood more about spending the campaign's resources wisely to reach their targeted voters with the campaign's message than his informal circle of adviser-friends.

And yet, the challenge of managing Obama's friends didn't end there. Obama's law school friends urged Obama to wade deep into policy during the campaign.

Cauley considered their prescriptions a path to defeat and refused to be dragooned into letting the campaign veer off course.

> There's a whole cubby of Harvard fucks around me, oh, everywhere. Oh, they would come in and tell me, "Jimmy, here's what we need to do. We need to do a white paper on Israel." And I'm like, "You know what? Here's a stack of literature. You need to go down the neighborhood and knock on some damn doors. Get out of my face." But around him, there's always a circle of Harvard freaks. And they all think they're goddamn geniuses, and they all think they made the world spin by themselves. And if I don't listen to them, he's going to lose this race. And that's what they'd tell me to my face. And I'd be like, "Here's some lit. There's a street. Here's a map. Go hit some doors."[17]

Obama occasionally grew upset with Cauley for paying too little attention to policy, but Cauley ultimately won this battle, too. Obama's friends would "all sit in a room and just . . . talk policy . . . for hours," alarming Cauley, who wanted them to "go raise some money or knock on a door, do something that moves our ball down the field."[18] Cauley understood that door knocks were more valuable than producing white papers and helped ensure that the ground game remained intact.

Managing the candidate's spouse is another delicate challenge, as Cauley knows firsthand. One day, he recounted, Michelle Obama phoned Cauley. Mrs. Obama was upset that Barack had missed one of Malia and Sasha's parent-teacher conferences at the Lab School in Chicago. "He missed it. He and his dumbass driver missed it," Cauley recalled. "He told her it was [my fault]. So she calls me up that afternoon and she blisters me, and you know what I did, as the manager, I took it. . . . I adore [Michelle] . . . because she basically left me alone. She was raising her kids and she was making money and she was holding up the homestead. She was a very pleasant spouse to work with. . . . But what I realized was . . . he used me as the weapon with which to fend her off. So I just smiled and took it on the chin like a good manager."[19] Cauley simply promised her it wouldn't happen again.

As campaign manager, Cauley felt responsible for Obama's schedule, the budget, making sure the campaign ran smoothly, that his family had enough time with him, and that the overall plan was being enacted in the right way. His relationship with Obama was important to achieving all of these goals. Without having Obama's loyalty and winning his trust, the campaign's strategic plan could collapse. Other decision makers could step in to the void and upend the strategy. Infighting would ensue. Cauley knew that he should try to lessen the strain on Obama and that their mutual respect was going to help keep the campaign on track to reach its goals.

Mutual respect built on trust is among the most vital elements in any robust candidate-manager relationship. Consider how some of our respondents described the impact of trust in their relationships with their candidates on their campaigns:

I think there has to be like a sibling relationship. I think you need to know each other well like siblings do, but also siblings aren't afraid to call each other out.[20]

> Adam Bodily, Duane Snow for Supervisor, 2009 (VA);
> Mitt Romney for President, 2008

I think the most important factor is to have [an] unparalleled level of trust and understanding between the candidate and the manager.[21]

> Brad Beychok, Charlie Melancon for US Senate, 2010 (LA)

The best campaign managers in the world have that kind of back and forth where they can tell their candidate they're wrong. But they've built enough trust to where they really think that the candidate believes them. The worst campaign managers in the world are the ones that think they're always right.[22]

> Casey Phillips,
> Van Taylor for Congress, 2006 (TX)

You have to have the candidate buy into what you want to do. . . . If you need to persuade a candidate, you must work with their closest friends, family, spouse, etc., to help them sell your point of view.[23]

> Graham Shafer, Michael Steele for US Senate, 2006 (MD);
> Van Hilleary for Governor, 2002 (TN)

There has to be mutual understanding. The campaign manager needs to understand that this is the candidate's campaign, with her credibility on the line. And the candidate needs to trust the campaign manager to do what he was hired to do: use his expertise to manage a successful campaign.[24]

> Jarryd Gonzales,
> Gloria Matta Tuchman for Congress, 2000 (CA)

Without having established a level of mutual respect, candidates have trouble performing at the top of their abilities and sticking to the critical elements of the campaign's plan. Josh Ginsberg, who ran Chris Dudley's near-miss 2010 Republican gubernatorial race in Oregon, argued that the campaign's "most important commodity . . . is the candidate and his time. So with the candidate feeling comfortable with the decisions that are being made, it just means he's going to be better out there on the campaign trail because he doesn't have to worry about the little things."[25]

Michael Bloomberg's campaign manager Kevin Sheekey told us that the candidate running for reelection needs "to be focused on being someone in that job" and "let the campaign do all the dirty work. The candidate has to have complete trust in the campaign manager to make those decisions and run it. And I've almost never met a candidate who I thought had any aptitude for running a campaign."[26] And the campaigns that aren't well run, he added, "are ones that don't have a clear manager and have a series of people" arguing over decisions.[27]

Building the Relationship

In order to answer the "How are we doing?" and "What are they doing?" questions, campaign managers must have achieved a level of trust with their candidates to tell them how they are performing on the stump, how their opponents are faring, and what needs to be tweaked. The campaign manager needs the moral authority to be able to tell the candidate whether or not they have met their fundraising, outreach, and advertising goals and what they should do differently to hit their targets.

Survey respondents almost universally agreed that the candidate-manager relationship affected the quality of the campaign and even election outcomes, albeit indirectly. Almost all campaign activities—shaping the candidate's image, delivering the message, making budget decisions, fundraising, microtargeting, canvassing, having debate prep, to name a few—are affected by the manager-candidate relationship. Thus, the ability of candidates to make their case to the voters, to perform well at town halls and during debates, and to avoid gaffes that distract the campaign from core tasks is crucial. While bad candidates such as Kansas's Pat Roberts sometimes win their races and while good candidates such as North Carolina's Kay Hagan sometimes lose theirs, strong candidates can sometimes win close elections, and the converse is true for bad candidates—and how the campaign performs can rest, at least in part, on the candidate's confidence in and comfort level with their manager.

Consider what some of the managers said. Travis Worl, Sanford Bishop's 2012 Georgia congressional campaign manager, argued that candidates who trust their managers can more easily let their managers make strategic decisions. Candidates, he said, are "going to ask you your opinion on those issues and also what you recommend that they should do." While many decisions won't determine the outcome, "some decisions about message, about what a candidate should say in an interview, about a candidate being on call-time . . . are critical."[28] He added the following:

And if your candidate won't do call time and you won't just call them and say, "You need to get into the call-time room right now," then you're not doing your job for them. And if there's something that your candidate wants to say and feels like they need to say but you feel like if they say it, it's going to be terrible for the campaign, you need to make that known. It's one of those critical times, if you do not stick to your guns and say, "You know, I think this is going to destroy your campaign," and if they decided "Okay then, you know, I don't want you for this campaign . . ." that's your job. I've been fired from campaigns, but I was so because we disagreed about which way the campaign should go. . . . I'm not going to spend $50,000 on fucking yard signs."[29]

He refused to be the manager who said, "'Okay, spend it all on lapel and bumper stickers' just so I can keep my job and everyone else can be happy. My job is to manage a campaign to win."[30]

In order to have candidates performing at the top of their games, Brad Beychok, who ran Democrat Charlie Melancon's 2010 Louisiana campaign for US Senate, revealed that as the manager his goal was to let candidates "focus on what they're good at," whether it's retail politics, giving speeches, or other activities. His goal was to make sure that they had the space and support to "concentrate on the hardest job, which is to be the candidate."[31]

One of the manager's hardest tasks is getting the candidate to buy into the strategy. Managers have to persuade candidates to do what's needed to keep the campaign on a winning course, balancing the candidate's preferences with the campaign's strategic priorities. Indeed, some survey respondents told us that serving as a candidate confidant was the single most important task they had. Most candidates need to be provoked, cajoled, inspired, and reasoned with. It is their name on the ballot, and they feel the most pressure—and the manager needs to inject sanity into the relationship and the political process.

The absence of trust can disrupt a campaign and lead to strategic chaos. While the media often hypes the importance of internecine campaign warfare, internal campaign dynamics, according to our survey respondents, affect campaign trajectories. The activities that affect the vote totals become harder to execute when the manager-candidate relationship is based not on trust but on suspicion. Michael Sullivan, who managed Republican Patrick Hughes' 2010 Illinois campaign for US Senate, said the manager's "number one job is managing the candidate"—especially their expectations of money, polls, and votes.[32] "Anything they hear about the campaign should probably come through you," he argued. Jarryd Gonzales, who ran the Republican Gloria Matta Tuchman for Congress 2000 campaign in California, agreed that managers and candidates had to be aligned on the strategy, the candidates' roles, and the families' roles.[33]

Partners in a campaign firm, Democratic managers Jen Pihlaja and Martha McKenna, approached the manager-candidate relationship through a similar lens. McKenna told us that candidates were doing one of "the most brave and courageous thing[s]" imaginable. Being the campaign manager, she added, means that "you're entrusted with that person's name and reputation," and "that comes with a seriousness and a responsibility that both is important and exhilarating."[34]

Pihlaja stressed that managers who became confidants were able to execute the campaign plan more effectively and give their candidates a better shot at victory.

The most important thing is to win the candidate's trust by doing whatever the candidate needs you to do, whether it's some candidates need you to go out with them on the stump and spend time with them, and some candidates would rather you never come out with them on the stump, but instead make their kitchen cabinet feel important. The most important thing in my mind is establishing the trust that you need.[35]

While cynicism about politics and politicians is axiomatic nowadays, many of the managers interviewed for this book felt inspired by their candidates—and the ideas and causes for which they were fighting. Managing somebody's campaign, Pihlaja said, is "amazing for all the right reasons."[36] Thus, the managers we talked to were not all, by any stretch, hired guns, roving from race to race, regardless of the candidate or the issues. Contrary to popular [belief], and overwhelmingly negative impressions of electoral politics, as David Axelrod told us, the best managers forged candidate relationships "rooted in absolute trust."[37] Axelrod added the following:

I'm always cognizant of the fact that when candidates run for office . . . this is their life. . . . And often, . . . you're risking your reputation, you're jeopardizing your future, at least in politics. And you need to have a sense of trust in your manager that they're, A, going to be consistent with your values, and, B, that they're going to be strategically and tactically sound. And see that they're going to be able to manage those under them effectively. And if you have those three elements, you have the makings of a strong manager and a strong manager-candidate relationship.[38]

Nothing is more damaging to a candidate than being branded as inauthentic. The manager-candidate relationship can influence the candidate's image. Managers must become a confidant to run a campaign that, Brad Todd, from OnMessage, Inc., told us, "looks, feels, and smells like the candidate."[39] Managers must know their candidates well enough to help them develop a message that's true to who they are and what they believe. When that doesn't happen, the campaign winds up playing defense. When Vice President Al Gore ran for president in 2000, word leaked that he had hired image consultants, who counseled him to wear more "earth tones" to soften his public persona. This followed Gore's previous assertion that he had helped invent the Internet. While Gore's missteps can't be blamed on his campaign manager alone, the manager's inability to stop the campaign from reinventing itself hurt their cause. In June 2000, five months before the general election, Al Gore replaced his ailing campaign chairman Tony Coelho with Commerce Secretary William Daley. One person close to Coelho told the *New York Times* that "Tony and Al Gore never really liked each other. There's little mutual respect and no affection. They're very different people."[40] Gore had little faith in Coelho, and, the *Times* reported, was consulting other aides behind Coelho's back.[41] The absence of harmony at the top fueled the narrative that Gore didn't stand for anything and that his campaign was at sea.

Trust-based relationships enable the manager to keep morale high in tough times. Ashley Spillane, who ran Tim Walz's Minnesota congressional race in 2010, said the following:

> Keeping morale high in the middle of running lots of negative ads and having your candidate hit on negative ads is [particularly] challenging. I personally watch the ads and think, "Oh God, their poor wife and kids that have to see this." But as a manager, you have to stay focused, keep the candidate's morale high, keep your staff's morale high, keep them motivated and working as hard as they are.[42]

Sometimes, even the best campaign managers are unable to control candidates who refuse to do the grunt work that it takes to win the election. In the late 1990s, for example, John Schulze was running a legislative race in northern Wisconsin and was badgering his candidate to get out and start knocking on doors. While very few candidates like to spend time on the doors, this candidate had a particular disdain for the practice.

It was typical of this candidate to disappear for days on end—literally hide so he did not need to attend fundraisers, make phone calls, or knock on doors. One day close to the election, Schulze was unable to find the candidate at his usual haunts, so he went to the candidate's house. After a thorough search of the premises, Schulze found the candidate hiding from him under his daughter's bed. The candidate sheepishly tried to explain to Schulze that he was reattaching the headboard of his daughter's bed. No matter what Schulze did, the candidate clearly wasn't going to become a politician who enjoyed hand shaking and door knocking. There is no one-size-fits-all relationship; trust, in other words, assumes distinct forms.

In 2006, Jay Howser (who would go on to run Louisiana senator Mary Landrieu's reelection campaign in 2008) managed the successful Brad Ellsworth for Congress race in Indiana's 8th Congressional District. When Ellsworth announced his candidacy, he was a local sheriff. Howser explained how he had to take a different approach to preparing an incumbent like Landrieu than a challenger like Ellsworth. But his relationships with both candidates were also effective. The Ellsworth campaign, he said, required "a lot more of coaching than in 2008, when he felt like he was more focused on "managing the pieces." During the Ellsworth race, Howser's advising the candidate created some friction. "But it was good for him, and it was good for me, and it was good for the campaign," Howser concluded. "And he was always worried about being coached on the issues and thought he had to know every federal issue. And I was more like, 'Actually, the fact that you don't know every federal issue and you are more like a regular person actually helps you.'" Ellsworth proved to be a fast learner. "He was one of those guys that you told him to say this and he said that. And it was fantastic. You don't get many of those [candidates]. So at the end of the day, he was a fantastic candidate who all he needed was a little bit of push to work a little harder and I think I gave him . . . that."[43]

Indeed, not every candidate walks into a campaign a sparkling, polished diamond. According to 2008 Mitt Romney advance representative Adam Bodily, the best candidate "edits his own speeches up to the last minute. You know, think Bill Clinton or other people like that . . . gives the teleprompter operators a heart attack, that's a good candidate."[44] But not all candidates can hit the ground running—especially if they are entering politics from the private sector or making the leap from local to national office. Especially if a candidate is running for public office for the first time, there is a reasonable chance they won't be as knowledgeable about state and national issues as the incumbent. They will need public speaking practice, issue briefings, and debate preparation all provided by the campaign. The manager must be able to direct all of these activities and help the candidate become a better candidate.

Honesty

One of the toughest aspects of the confidant relationship is knowing how to help the candidate navigate political attacks on her record and leveling with her about the campaign's direction. This includes helping the candidate deflect arrows thrown by opponents at the candidate's character. Honesty, campaign managers routinely told us, is a crucial ingredient in building the candidate's confidence and running a winning campaign.

Often, a candidate will have ideas about the direction of the campaign that run counter to the goals managers have set. They will be hearing from friends that say the message is all wrong, that the campaign's colors should be different, that she should be spending more money on golf pin flags advertising the campaign (true story), and so on. The candidate, wanting to please everyone, will lay this at the doorstep of the campaign manager, who will need to be strong enough to say no. The manager will have to be honest about the hard choices facing the candidate and the campaign team.

This isn't easy. Oftentimes, candidates are either incumbents that are used to having full staffs who accommodate their wishes or they are wealthy businesspeople who aren't used to being told no.

A campaign manager who preferred not to be identified said the following:

[You need to be able to] sit there and shoot the shit but then also talk about the campaign—at the same time like when he has a bad idea or is doing something wrong, be able to be very stern and almost . . . like a father scolding a child. So . . . they've got to think you're their friend, but you've got to know you're not. You're almost their boss.

It is vital that a candidate get accurate, timely information from their campaign manager. As one Democratic congressional campaign manager told us, campaigns are full of people who want jobs with the candidate when he or she wins, so they kiss up to the candidate every chance they can get. This manager, who wished to remain anonymous, said his job "is not to be the guy's friend." And he said that getting close to the candidate and hoping for a job if the person wins does a disservice to the campaign. Too often, he said, "People work on campaigns to . . . get the job afterwards. And as a result, . . . you try to almost ingratiate yourself with the candidate. And then you become kind of part of the whole boy's club. . . . You protect your candidate from too much of what they don't want to do." If the candidate wants to cut the fundraising from the schedule, the manager said, "My job is to . . . give it to him straight" and "give my honest opinion of what is the most effective" way to win the election. The manager also said that if he developed "a level of trust with the candidate," then "come October, when I say we need to go do X, he is willing to say, 'Okay, we'll go do this even if it's not something I want to be doing.'"[45]

Many survey respondents stressed the importance of literally being the candidate's confidant on the most intimate of issues. Candor to a degree unusual in most professional settings was often required. "Surprises" on the campaign trail can tarnish the candidate's image and even derail the campaign's strategy. Throughout the process, campaign managers need to know things about the candidate that even the candidate's closest friends or spouse don't know. And being able to prove to a candidate up front that you are capable of handling the most sensitive of information goes a long way in earning a candidate's trust.

Screven Watson, who ran Rod Smith's 2006 Florida governor's race, conveyed the intimacy of the relationship and the role honesty and candor plays in the manager-candidate relationship. Navigating the shoals of politics in an age when any piece of a candidate's (or staff's) personal life is fair game in the blogosphere is complicated. Watson told us the following:

> I've had people tell me things that they've never told their wives. Doesn't mean that I'm Sigmund Freud. I don't care. I'm not going to judge you. . . . But I got to know. I have to know what's out there . . . I had a story with a state senator that I had to tell him that his wife had taken their money and had to default. Watson sat down and told him: "Senator, this isn't easy for me, but I got to tell you this because if I know, they know." And I had to tell him that his wife had blown their money, had lawsuits out the wazoo, [and] had tax liens. And I knew he didn't know. Color drained from his face.[46]

"You have to be a nonjudgmental confidant," Watson argued.[47] One candidate confessed to Watson that he had "an ex-wife that hates me" because he didn't pay child support. Watson had to be prepared for attacks on his candidate's character from opponents, who could use his ex-wife to validate the charges. Watson once had to ask another candidate's ex-wife if she'd be willing to defend the candidate if the campaign needed her to vouch for him.

The confidant relationship also involved the manager leveling with the candidate about activities and decisions that could harm their chances on election day. For example, Watson had candidates who liked to drink, so he strove "to keep them out of those environments" where they might get drunk. The campaign manager has "to be able to keep the candidate away from his or her own weaknesses: of the flesh, of the bottle, of . . . talking too much to the press." Being truthful with the candidate is a crucial way to handling these hard situations. Trust is built, at least in part, on honesty.[48]

According to many of our respondents, the campaign manager also needs to be able to keep candidates from becoming overly involved in internal campaign strategy. This, too, requires a level of straight talk. As Mississippi governor (and former Republican National Committee [RNC] chair) Haley Barbour told us, "you never saw a horse turn around and tell a jockey which way to run." Another survey respondent warned that if the candidate starts running the campaign, "you end up putting up yard signs 24/7." Candidates who lack faith in their campaign managers—who don't think their managers are being up front with them about their campaign—end up wasting precious time and energy on strategic and organizational decisions best left to the manager.[49]

Sometimes, candidate involvement can be much more serious and potentially damaging to the campaign. For instance, changing the campaign's course to settle a score can waste valuable time and money—oftentimes, a candidate will get involved to respond to personal attacks when it isn't warranted. In 2010, former Republican member of Congress Pat Toomey ran against Democratic representative Joe Sestak in a hotly contested Pennsylvania US Senate race. In October, Sestak began running a television ad that criticized Toomey for being too sympathetic to China. While working for a Wall Street firm twenty years ago, Toomey took on a nine-month project that sent him to China to help with economic development. Yet according to Sestak's ad, Toomey was some sort of plant—a Manchurian candidate—secretly trying to send American jobs to China. "Maybe he ought to run for Senate—in China," the ad ended.[50]

The Toomey campaign knew the accusation was going to sting a little. But rather than answer the ad directly, Toomey's staff wanted to attack Sestak in a different area to change the subject.

But the China ad irritated Toomey too much. According to sources, the representative was insistent that they spend money answering the charge that he was plotting to export American jobs to Asia. So the campaign cut an ad of Toomey speaking directly to the camera, explaining that the job he had was twenty years ago, hoping that would mitigate the effect of Sestak's ad. In the ad, Toomey emphasized that he left Wall Street a long time ago and started a family business with his brothers, creating jobs in Pennsylvania.[51]

Yet when the campaign polled on the ad, all the people who saw the ad could remember was that Toomey had once worked on Wall Street. Instead of giving him credit for creating jobs in Pennsylvania, Wall Street was all that resonated. The campaign quickly cut their losses and pulled the ad. Toomey's staff, led by his campaign manager, had to be frank with him that the ad was backfiring. And in a strong Republican year, Toomey managed to win the seat with 51 percent of the vote. (For more on how he won, see Chapter 4.)

Rep. Joe Sestak's ads attacked Pat Toomey for sending jobs to China.

On occasion, a candidate's instincts may be pretty good, and the campaign manager has to figure out how to persuade colleagues that the candidate's judgment is on the mark. In 2004, the Barack Obama for US Senate campaign was set to run a television ad that featured the daughter of former senator Paul Simon, who had passed away in 2003 and whose seat Obama now sought. Prior to his death, Simon had been set to endorse Obama. The campaign, at the urging of adviser David Axelrod (who used to work for Simon), put an ad together that invoked Simon's memory, with his daughter Sheila finishing the ad by saying, "I know Barack Obama will be a US senator in the Paul Simon tradition."[52]

According to Jimmy Cauley, Obama detested the ad, thinking taking advantage of Simon's death was too "weird." But some campaign advisers insisted it be run; eventually, the campaign team ran it by a focus group. "In the summertime, we went back into focus groups, and we showed it in Peoria [outside the Chicago media market] to a group of white male[s]" who were over the age of thirty-five. The focus group, Cauley recalled, just "hated it. Oh, my God, all them white men thought it was just horrible, we're taking advantage of a dead man." Following the focus group, the campaign quickly pulled the ad.[53]

Managing the Candidate's Family

When Republican Indiana governor Mitch Daniels announced in May 2011 that he wouldn't seek the GOP presidential nomination, he chalked it up to his family's

Barack Obama's 2004 US Senate campaign ran an ad tying Obama to recently deceased senator Paul Simon. Obama hated the ad.

reticence about a national run. "In the end," Daniels told supporters, "I was able to resolve every competing consideration but one, but that, the interests and wishes of my family, is the most important consideration of all. If I have disappointed you, I will always be sorry."

Daniels took a lot of flak for laying his decision not to run at the feet of his family, especially since the Republican presidential field appeared to be very weak in early 2011. But to many candidates, the involvement of the family—and especially the candidate's spouse—are vital to the campaign's operation. A number of survey respondents argued that developing a relationship with the candidate's spouse was one of their most important tasks.

Other respondents preferred to fully explain to the candidate's family up front what a rough road lies ahead. They stressed that having an honest conversation with the candidate and their spouse explaining what it will be like for them is a vital step for a supportive family and a candidate performing at his or her best. Across the board, respondents wanted open communication with the candidate and their family and would take calls any time of the day to address their concerns.

Unfortunately, while candidates tend to understand basic political strategy, family members are often less enlightened about the process. Oftentimes, family members don't ask to get involved in politics; they are there only because they have to be. One campaign manager told us part of her job was to visit her candidate's mother once a week to assure her that all the attacks against her son weren't true.

But oftentimes, the lack of political experience won't prevent family members from offering the campaign pointers on any number of topics, including whether the campaign should go negative; or how many yard signs should be out on the street; or in which shopping center parking lot the candidate should shake hands all day, every day. Because in the end, it is their husband or wife, or son or daughter, or father and mother, and they want to be able to brag about their association with the candidate, not have to shy from it, and see their loved one succeed.

Yet while spouses always have an opinion, their input may not always be welcome:

As a campaign manager, the spouse is without a doubt the toughest obstacle to overcome if they turn against you. You can have all the trust of the candidate, but the person that they lay their head down next to at night has the final word. So if you have splintered that relationship—if you lose that trust of either one of them, you're in big trouble. That's how campaign managers manage to get fired.[54]

Casey Phillips, Delbert Hosemann for Secretary of State, 2007 (MS)

Furthermore, spouses will frequently have a say in the campaign's scheduling operation. As Screven Watson told us, "God almighty, scheduling can kill you. It can eat you alive. The spouse of the candidate can get, 'I want him or her home for dinner every night.' Or, you know, his daughter or her daughter's graduating. It means keeping the candidate happy. I mean, it's vitally important."[55]

Losing and Winning: When the Campaign Ends

The final days of the campaign, as frenetic and intense as they are, don't mark the end of the candidate-manager relationship. Managers felt a deep responsibility to their candidates in the event of a loss. Not only can a campaign financially ruin candidates but it can also damage their personal reputations—especially worrisome if they plan on making another run for public office. One manager who requested anonymity told us this about part of his job:

[It] is protecting the candidate from going into debt, taking too great of risks so that if they lose their job and they put 20 percent of their savings or 50 percent of their savings in the campaign, you have to protect them. You have to give them information and toward the end of a campaign, you need to make sure you don't go into debt unless they're willing to. And you have to protect them legally too. . . . [And] whether you win or lose, sometimes the hardest job for the campaign manager is to deliver the news that you've lost and stay with the candidate so . . . they don't do something stupid that embarrasses themselves for down the road.[56]

The manager also has to prepare the candidate "for the fact that election day is not the last day, that you're not going to get a rest for three or four days afterward because the very first thing that needs to happen the next day is the candidate needs to get on the phone and . . . start calling all of the donors and supporters and people who contributed, not just financially, but also emotionally and in terms of time commitment and . . . thank them, whether they win or lose," said Matt McDonald, Elia Pirozzi's deputy campaign manager on his 1998 California congressional race.[57]

If you know you're going to lose, the only thing that you have within your control is the manner in which you go down. Does your candidate go down graciously, earning the respect of the people who fought with him? Or do they go out bitter and small and being somebody that nobody's going to miss the next election?[58]

Although most Americans tell pollsters that they hate politics, campaigns and elections have lasting effects on how we live our lives. Health care, the economy, the environment, and myriad other issues are dependent on competent representation. Even though many of the managers told us that they enjoyed politics less as their careers have developed, they also expressed a surprising degree of optimism about and faith in the democratic process and their roles on the front lines of it. On the whole, these managers treated the voters with respect, admired and took inspiration from their candidates whose careers and reputations were at stake, and believed in the values and policies that their candidates championed. Further, they understood the gravity of their roles—the responsibility for their candidate's name and reputation, for the young people they hired and their futures, and for running a race that they could look back on with pride.

The insights the managers have offered to us recall Winston Churchill's statement that democracy "is the worst form of government, except for all those other forms that have been tried from time to time."[59]

Notes

1. J. Reedy, personal communication, November 11, 2011.
2. R. Stone, personal communication, April, 2013.
3. M. Shannon, personal communication, May 7, 2013.
4. Ibid.
5. Ibid.
6. Ibid.

7. Ibid.
8. Ibid.
9. R. Stone, personal communication, April, 2013.
10. Ibid.
11. J. Cauley, personal communication, November 1, 2011.
12. Ibid.
13. Ibid.
14. Ibid.
15. Ibid.
16. Ibid.
17. Ibid.
18. Ibid.
19. Ibid.
20. A. Bodily, personal communication, September 30, 2011.
21. B. Beychok, personal communication, November 8, 2011.
22. C. Phillips, personal communication, October 18, 2011.
23. G. Shafer, personal communication, September 20, 2011.
24. J. Gonzales, personal communication, November 18, 2011.
25. J. Ginsberg, personal communication, October 19, 2011.
26. K. Sheekey, personal communication, June 20, 2014.
27. Ibid.
28. T. Worl, personal communication, November 2, 2011.
29. Ibid.
30. Ibid.
31. B. Beychok, personal communication, November 8, 2011.
32. M. Sullivan, personal communication, 2011.
33. J. Gonzales, personal communication, November 18, 2011.
34. M. McKenna, personal communication, October 26, 2011.
35. J. Pihlaja, personal communication, October 25, 2011.
36. Ibid.
37. D. Axelrod, personal communication, March 14, 2013.
38. Ibid.
39. B. Todd, personal communication, September 9, 2011.
40. Richard L. Berke and Katharine Q. Seelye, "The 2000 Campaign: The Vice President; in Latest Shift, Gore's Campaign Names New Chief," *New York Times*, June 16, 2000, www.nytimes.com/2000/06/16/us/2000-campaign-vice-president-latest-shift-gore-s-campaign-names-new-chief.html?pagewanted=all.
41. Ibid.
42. A. Spillane, personal communication, September 30, 2011.
43. J. Howser, personal communication, November 9, 2011.
44. A. Bodily, personal communication, September 30, 2011.
45. Anonymous, personal communication.
46. S. Watson, personal communication, October 7, 2011.
47. Ibid.
48. Ibid.
49. H. Barbour, personal communication, October 30, 2011.
50. M. Harris, personal communication, June 20, 2014.

51. Ibid.

52. J. Cauley, personal communication, November 1, 2011.

53. Ibid.

54. C. Phillips, personal communication, October 18, 2011.

55. S. Watson, personal communication, October 7, 2011.

56. J. Cauley, personal communication, November 1, 2011.

57. M. McDonald, personal communication, November 7, 2011.

58. Ibid.

59. Richard Langworth, "Democracy Is the Worst Form of Government . . . ," June 26, 2009, https://richardlangworth.com/worst-form-of-government.

Appendixes

Teaching and Research Resources

The materials in the appendix are based on the authors' classroom experiences while teaching the material covered in the text. In one course, students or student teams were assigned the task of conducting their own original research by interviewing one or more local campaign managers, candidates, or other political professionals. Some students invited their interviewees to class, where they could be asked questions by other students. Interviews were structured using the questionnaire items detailed in the Campaign Manager Survey Questionnaire Library (Appendix A), which includes all the questions most frequently used by the authors and their research team for in-person, telephone, and online interviews from 2011 to 2015.

Based on their research, students are assigned to first prepare an edited transcript of the interview. As an example, Appendix B includes an edited interview with Doug Bailey, a former political ad maker who was also the founder of The Hotline, the first electronically distributed daily political report. The authors considered his interview to be among the most informative and entertaining we've conducted.

After completing their interviews, students can also be assigned to write short profiles. The appendix includes two profiles of campaign managers who appear in the textbook: Katie Merrill (Appendix C) and Reed Galen (Appendix D). In addition to writing profiles, more advanced students can prepare a fully researched and written case study. The case study describes a situation faced by a campaign or campaign manager, describes the decisions or actions taken, and then presents the outcome. Appendix E includes a case study by the authors about Herman Cain's bid for the 2012 Republican presidential nomination and a situation facing campaign manager Mark Block.

Appendix A
Campaign Manager Survey
Questionnaire Library

Preliminary Questionnaire

1. *2011–2015 Campaign Manager Survey Introductory Interview.* Thank you for your interest in participating and for taking five to seven minutes to complete this interview. This survey is being conducted on behalf of a college textbook for SAGE, a leading higher education publisher of political science textbooks and course materials. You will be asked about your campaign experience and your opinion on campaign management. Depending on survey sampling quotas, you may be invited to participate in additional telephone, in-person, or online surveys. All of your opinions and insights will be aggregated and reported anonymously unless we request and receive your prepublication approval. So we can contact you for follow-up, please enter an e-mail address and your first name only. This information will be used only for the purposes of the study and not released to any third party.

   E-mail address: (1)

   Re-type e-mail: (2)

   First name: (3)

2. Which of the following describe your political campaign experience? Check as many as apply to you.

   ❑ Employee of campaign from 2006 to 2015 (1)

   ❑ Employee of campaign prior to 2006 (2)

   ❑ "Senior" employee of campaign from 2006 to 2015 (3)

   ❑ "Senior" employee of campaign prior to 2006 (4)

   ❑ "Campaign manager" of campaign from 2006 to 2015 (5)

   ❑ "Campaign manager" of campaign prior to 2006 (6)

   ❑ "Senior consultant/adviser" to campaign from 2006 to 2015 (7)

   ❑ "Senior consultant/adviser" to campaign prior to 2006 (8)

3. Thinking about the campaigns you've worked in and your other political experiences, what are your areas of particular expertise? Please check all that apply.

- ❏ Direct mail/microtargeting (1)
- ❏ Fundraising (2)
- ❏ General consulting/strategy (3)
- ❏ Grassroots/direct contact/voter ID (4)
- ❏ Internet/social media (5)
- ❏ Legal (6)
- ❏ Media—creative/ad production (7)
- ❏ Media—media buying/placement (8)
- ❏ Opposition research (9)
- ❏ Political/field operations (10)
- ❏ Polling (11)
- ❏ Policy/issue research (12)
- ❏ Press/communications (13)
- ❏ Speech writing (14)
- ❏ Issue research (15)

4. What are some recent campaigns you've worked for? You may list up to three. Please start with what you consider to be the campaign that was most important to you personally.

Candidate or campaign name: (1)

Office sought: (2)

Year election held: (3)

Your position(s): (4)

Your location: (5)

5. Which of the following describe this campaign? Please check all that apply.

- ❏ Incumbent campaign (1)
- ❏ Challenger campaign (2)
- ❏ Open seat campaign (3)

❑ Primary election (4)

❑ General election (5)

❑ Referendum/ballot issue (6)

❑ Democratic campaign (7)

❑ Republican campaign (8)

❑ Third-party/independent (9)

❑ Nonpartisan election (10)

❑ Independent expenditure campaign (11)

6. Feel free to provide any additional details here.

7. Did you start out in politics as a volunteer or in paid position? Choose one.

○ Volunteer/unpaid (1)

○ Paid position (2)

8. What year was that?

9. Briefly describe how you became involved in politics.

10. Approximately how many campaigns have you been involved in?

As a volunteer: (1)

As a paid staffer: (2)

As a campaign manager: (3)

As a senior adviser/consultant: (4)

11. On a scale of "very liberal" to "very conservative," how would you describe your position on social issues?

○ Very liberal (1)

○ (2)

○ (3)

○ Neither liberal nor conservative (4)

○ (5)

○ (6)

○ Very conservative (7)

12. On a scale of "very liberal" to "very conservative," how would you describe your position on economic issues?

   ○ Very liberal (1)

   ○ (2)

   ○ (3)

   ○ Neither liberal nor conservative (4)

   ○ (5)

   ○ (6)

   ○ Very conservative (7)

13. On a scale of "very Democratic" to "very Republican," how would you describe your partisanship?

   ○ Very liberal (1)

   ○ (2)

   ○ (3)

   ○ Neither liberal nor conservative (4)

   ○ (5)

   ○ (6)

   ○ Very conservative (7)

14. If a candidate asked you to serve as their campaign manager, what are two or three of the most important questions you would want to have answered before deciding whether to take the job?

15. In what year were you born?

16. What is your highest level of education? Choose one.

   ○ Less than high school degree (1)

   ○ High school/GED (2)

   ○ Some college (3)

○ 2-year college degree (associate's) (4)

○ 4-year college degree (bachelor's) (5)

○ Master's degree (6)

○ Professional degree (MD, JD) (7)

○ Doctoral degree (8)

17. Gender?

○ Female (1)

○ Male (2)

18. Describe your current job position.

19. Overall, what do you feel is/are the most important job(s) of a successful campaign manager?

20. Before we finish, is there anything else you would like to tell us about your campaign experiences or about your interest in participating in this survey?

21. Lastly, how did you hear about the this survey?

Section A: Interview Information

Interviewee:

Interviewers:

First interview date:

- ○ In person
- ○ Telephone
- ○ Internet

Follow-up interview date:

- ○ In person
- ○ Telephone
- ○ Internet

Other questionnaire modules completed:

Principal campaign discussed in interview (and outcome):

Other campaigns discussed in interview (and outcome):

Other disposition notes and follow-up:

Respondent contact information:

Section P: Campaign Management Practices (in a particular campaign or campaigns)

P-1. I'd like to start out talking about a particular campaign where your experiences might offer some insights to young people who are interested in the campaign field, or it could be a campaign where you held the position of manager or other senior position or just a campaign that was personally important to you. What campaign or campaigns would you like to focus on?

P-2. When did you join the campaign and in what position?

P-3. Did you hold this position throughout the campaign or move into another position?

P-4. After initially being hired for the _____ campaign, what were the first three things you did? What were your top priorities?

P-5. Were you responsible for hiring most of the paid staff in the campaign?

P-6. At the peak, how many paid staff worked in the campaign?

P-7. When putting together a campaign team, what kinds of people and skills were you primarily looking for? Are there any personality attributes that you look for?

P-8. Let's talk about the consultants that your campaign retained. We're interested in how and when they were selected and your role in selecting them. Which kind of consultant did the campaign hire first? (Probe for pollster, media, direct mail, Internet, fundraising, and any others. Include consultant name and/or firm.)

P-9. How do you effectively manage consultants in a campaign?

P-9a. How were your consultants compensated? Was this set by you, by the candidate, or by someone else? (Probe for specific fees, commission percentages, etc.)

P-10. What's generally more true—that you managed your consultants or that your consultants were trying to manage you? Why do you say that?

P-10a. Do you have an example or an anecdote about a situation where you did a particularly good job or poor job of managing a consultant in a campaign?

P-10b. Have you ever had to fire a significant employee or a consultant during a campaign? Can you tell me how you handled it or about any lessons you've learned from your experiences?

P-11. Thinking about the types of media and communications vehicles that are used in campaigns, I'd like you to rate the cost-effectiveness of the following formats on a scale of 0 to 10 (0 = not effective at all and 10 = very effective). If you have no opinion, leave the item blank. (Print as hand card for in-person interview, which is attached at the end of the questionnaire.)

Broadcast TV	0	1	2	3	4	5	6	7	8	9	10
Cable TV	0	1	2	3	4	5	6	7	8	9	10
Radio	0	1	2	3	4	5	6	7	8	9	10
Out-of-home	0	1	2	3	4	5	6	7	8	9	10
Internet Ads	0	1	2	3	4	5	6	7	8	9	10
E-mail	0	1	2	3	4	5	6	7	8	9	10
Direct mail	0	1	2	3	4	5	6	7	8	9	10
Direct contact by phone or in person	0	1	2	3	4	5	6	7	8	9	10
Newspaper	0	1	2	3	4	5	6	7	8	9	10

P-12. Overall, how much money was spent in the _____ campaign? (Use example.)

P-13. How much of that spending was accounted for by the *combined* items in the previous list?

P-14. What were your largest spending categories? Roughly what percentage did you spend for _____? Probe for spending in as many categories as possible, but it is not necessary to get them all.

P-15. Was it part of your campaign strategy to place a special emphasis on any of these areas? Did you think any of these would be the key or keys to winning?

P-16. How did your campaign use the Internet? Probe for the following areas and any others.

P-17. How much of your total fundraising do you attribute to the Internet?

P-18. Not including Internet advertising, how much do you think you spent on all Internet activities such as building your website and maintaining it, and the staff cost of e-mailing, social outreach, and other Internet marketing and communications?

P-19. In 2012, what percentage of total spending in statewide and congressional campaigns will be on the Internet?

P-20. What will this percentage be in 2014?

P-21. Thinking some more about the advertising in the _____ campaign, what was the process for deciding which ads would be produced and aired?

P-22. How often did you do ad testing, and how often did you just rely on instinct and judgment?

P-23. Can you give me an example of a particularly effective ad that was used by your campaign and why you think it worked so well?

P-24. Is there any ad that you used and wished you hadn't?

P-25. How did your campaign use negative advertising? Probe: What are your thoughts on negative advertising?

P-26. What role did third-party or independent expenditure advertising play in your campaign?

P-27. What are the implications of independent expenditure advertising for the job of the campaign manager today?

Section V: Campaign Management Priorities

V-1. Overall, what is the most important job or jobs of a successful campaign manager?

V-2. What are the best ways to find good campaign staff?

V-3. Roughly, what percentage of your total budget was spent for staff salaries?

V-4. What kinds of nonfinancial assistance did you get from the state or national party organizations? From other third-party organizations?

V-5. Talk about your fundraising. Did you raise more or less or about what you thought you'd be able to?

V-6. What's a short version of your overall finance plan?

V-7. What was the mix of individual large donors, small donors, political action committee (PAC), and party donations?

V-7a. Talk about your approach to setting up fundraising events.

V-8. What was the individual contribution strategy—for instance, did you ask people for the maximum allowable contribution up front, or ask for a succession of smaller amounts?

V-9. Describe your direct mail fundraising. What do you think your profit margin was on direct mail?

V-10. How were your direct mail fundraising appeals generally framed? For instance, were they framed as attacks against your candidate's opponent, or were they positive toward your candidate?

V-11. How frequently did you send direct mail to current donors asking for another contribution?

V-12. What kinds of research did the campaign conduct—polling, focus groups, ad testing, online research? Probe for different types of research conducted.

V-13. What's an example of polling, focus groups, or other research affecting your campaign plan or tactics? Can you think of any others?

V-14. What was the process for determining what questions would be asked in your polls?

V-15. When you do research in a campaign, what are some of the key things you're trying to learn? Probe: How well does research help you learn what you need to know? What are some of strengths and limitations of polling, focus groups, and other kinds of campaign research methods?

V-16. Thinking about the relationship your campaign had with the media, how often did your campaign personally contact reporters to provide them with information?

V-17. How many press releases did your campaign issue per week?

V-18. What types of strategies did you use to garner earned media?

V-18a. What is the role of the news media in campaigns today, and how is it changing?

Section C: Concluding Thoughts on Campaigns and Elections

C-1. Sometimes academics say that campaigns have little effect on election outcomes because elections are driven by larger trends and events outside the campaign's control. What effect do you feel the campaign actually has on the outcome of elections?

C-2. Thinking about the _____ campaign, how many percentage points do you think your campaign added to your candidate's vote?

C-3. What are some of the biggest changes you've seen since you started out in politics? What else?

C-4. Overall, would you say you enjoy working in politics more or less since you started out?

C-5. Why is that?

C-6. Have you ever left politics and decided to come back?

C-6a. Please explain the circumstances.

C-7. Is there a time in the future when you plan on leaving politics?

C-8. Here are some things others have said, and I'd like to know if you strongly agree, somewhat agree, neither agree nor disagree, somewhat disagree, or strongly disagree.

C-8a. What are some other statements that you think would be interesting to include in this series? (We are looking for statements that are likely to provoke differences of opinion.) Probe: Do you agree or disagree with the statement?

C-8b. At the beginning of a campaign, how important are the following?

Please rank them in order of importance to the success of a campaign.

C-8c. (Ask of consultants/nonmanagers) Thinking some more about gross rating points (GRPs), what percentage of campaign managers you've worked with could accurately define what GRPs actually are? Has a client ever asked you what GRPs are?

C-8d. (Ask of campaign managers) Thinking some more about GRPs, have you ever asked your media consultant or someone else what GRPs actually are?

C-8e. How comfortable are you with your knowledge about media definitions and terms such as *GRPs, impressions, reach,* and *frequency*? What would you say you are?

C-8f. What are GRPs?

C-8g. In the campaigns you've worked on, what type of GRPs were used for buying and reporting? What demographic group?

C-8h. Thinking about the Internet, how comfortable are you with your knowledge about online media definitions and terms such as *behavioral targeting, cookies, splash page,* and *rich media*? Would you say you are?

C-9. Using the zero to ten scale, how important or critical do you think each of the following types of campaign functions, consultants, and vendors are to the success of a statewide or congressional campaign?

Direct mail/microtargeting

Fundraising

General consultant/strategist

Grassroots/direct contact

Internet/social media

Issue research

Legal

Media consultant—creative/ad production

Media consultant—media buying/placement

Opposition research/counter-opposition research

Political/field operations

Pollster

Press/communications

Scheduler

The candidate's personal aide, driver, or "body person"

Speechwriter

C-10. Are there any other types of important consultants or vendors missing from the previous list? If so, please tell us which ones.

C-11. As we wrap up, overall what would you say are some key principals of successful campaign management and successful campaign managers?

C-12. (Ask if subject has not come up or been addressed in detail.) Tell me your thoughts about the relationship between the campaign manager and the candidate. Probe: How should a campaign manager manage the candidate, or should they even try?

C-13. What about a situation where it is late in a campaign and it's pretty clear you're going to win or going to lose? How does that affect the job of a campaign manager? Do you have any experiences in this kind of a situation?

C-14. (Make this the last question in the interview.) Finally, what advice would you have for a college student or recent college graduate who wants to become a campaign manager?

Appendix B
Interview with Doug Bailey

William J. Feltus, February 2012 by telephone

Feltus: I need your help. I want to summarize like how big of a deal Bailey Deardourff was back then.

Bailey: Well, in its day, it was the biggest Republican consulting firm around. And I think as a practical matter, with Reagan, Black, Manafort, Stone took over that title and they were welcome to it.

Feltus: Yeah. And some of the big names these kids will know that were your clients included?

Bailey: Oh, included like—

Feltus: You say that you started with Rockefeller?

Bailey: Rockefeller, Howard Baker, Ed Brooke, Chuck Percy.

Feltus: Chuck Percy, there you go. Rockefeller's good.

Bailey: Alexander, Lugar.

Feltus: Lamar Alexander, Lugar.

Bailey: John Danforth. I mean, you name them, we had them.

Feltus: Okay. And then you were—and then the Gerald Ford campaign in 1976.

Bailey: Correct.

Feltus: Was there a new media in the Gerald Ford campaign in 1976? Was there a fax machine in 1976?

Bailey: I don't think so.

Feltus: I'm going to say there wasn't.

Bailey: I don't think so.

Feltus: First time I—I became aware of it in the Cochran campaign in 1978 that there was this—you could send a page over a telephone line.

Bailey: You know, you and your Mississippi roots are way ahead of me.

Feltus: Okay. So what other thoughts would you tell a college student these days studying political science or communications and I thought I wanted to get into politics? What would you tell them?

Bailey: Oh, it's probably not relevant for you, but—I mean, it's worth saying. You can say it if you want to. I got out of campaign politics. It couldn't get the politics out of me, but I got out of politics. I got out in the late 1980s because it had gotten so negative. And little did I know how awful it would become. And it just seems to me every cycle it gets worse, and it's just unbelievable this stuff now.

Feltus: In terms of the amount of—

Bailey: The volume of just negative stuff. They have nothing positive to say. I know, I know, negative ads work. I remember the days when we used to worry about whether there was a price you had to pay for running a negative ad, and therefore you never quite did it until you got desperate. And when you got desperate, it's too late because when you did it, everybody said, "Oh, they must be desperate."

Feltus: What's the first negative ad you can remember producing and running?

Bailey: I remember doing some great negative ads that I just wrote one night, a radio ad for a John Deardourff client, but it just struck me that it was right. Deardourff's client was running for the senate. Nelson Gross was his name, running for senate in New Jersey. And he was running against—

Feltus: Case?

Bailey: No, it wasn't Case. It was the other senator. What was his name? Was there a Williams? A Democrat. And that was the point, nobody knew who the hell he was. He'd been there for two terms. And so we made up some— I made up some man in the street radio ads, I mean made them up of people saying, you know, they could never remember. "Tell me about New Jersey's two senators." "Oh yeah, yeah, Cliff Case is great. Cliff Case is great. Let's see. Are you sure we have two senators? Who's the other one? I can't remember who the other one is. Cliff Case is wonderful, but the other guy—" "He's been there for two terms." "I know, I know, I know, I know, I just can't remember his name." Stuff like that. And then there was a series where we went as if we were in the Senate. We brought our microphones to the US Senate to interview the members of the senate about New Jersey's two fine senators. "Pardon me, sir, do you have a view on New Jersey's two senators?" "Oh, yes, yes, I do, I do. Cliff Case, what a wonderful gentleman. What a wonderful, wonderful gentleman. Cliff Case was a great US senator. Now let's see about senator—Cliff Case is a wonderful gentleman. You've got me off balance there. I can't quite remember that other gentleman's name." I can see that you see it's very funny.

Feltus: That's going in the book. So that was a radio—

Bailey: It was a radio ad that Deardourff refused to show, refused to run for Gross, much less Gross making a decision. Deardourff vetoed it. It's always been one of my favorite ads.

Feltus: So that's the first negative ad you can remember writing.

Bailey: Correct.

Feltus: All right, well, you've been very helpful. What are the three key principles of a successful campaign manager?

Bailey: Don't think you have a plan if it isn't written out.

Feltus: Yeah, that's a good quote from you that should go into the planning chapter.

Bailey: The second one is never do something important that your candidate doesn't know about. And the third is the rule to live by . . . do what you say you're going to do. There is nothing very unusual about any of those, but what's disappointing is few campaigns seem to follow those rules.

Feltus: Those are pretty high rules. Kind of reminds me of why I've never been a campaign manager.

Bailey: Yeah, the first one is, to me, the most critical that's generally misunderstood. If you get an idea in the back of your head, it's not a plan. If you have a one-page memo, it's not a plan. Plan it out. Cross the t's, dot the i's. Force yourself to put a budget in and force yourself to fill in your time schedule. Be the master of your own campaign. The only way to do that is to plan it out.

Feltus: So the biggest change you've seen in politics since you started doing this is the negative tone of it?

Bailey: Yeah, and it changes everything. I mean, you hear this a million times, but it's the way I feel about it. It is so easy, so much easier to get a vote against the other guy than it is to get a vote for you that it drives everybody to the negative side. That is to say I've got 30 seconds to work with, but if I'm going to get a vote against you, all I've got to do is communicate one thought, and that may work. But to get a vote for me, I have to communicate a bunch of things. I have to communicate who I am, what my priorities are, and where I stand on issues that are important to you. That's a lot of stuff. You can't get it done in thirty seconds, so why not use your thirty seconds to destroy the other side?

Feltus: That's good. Would you recommend to somebody, a young college kid, that they get into politics these days?

Bailey: I would only if they are really grounded. That is to say, they're willing to set out as a goal from the very first day that they're going to change a system that is broken. And that doesn't mean that they can't work for somebody, but it is their goal to change the system that they know damn well is broken. And if they don't know it's broken, they shouldn't get into it.

Feltus: So they need to be motivated by belief in a principle.

Bailey: Absolutely, absolutely. Or the thing will eat them alive.

Feltus: What about somebody that gets into politics because they really like somebody that's running?

Bailey: Well, that's fine.

Feltus: Is that the same thing?

Bailey: It's the same thing as long as they continue to work for that guy who they really like and don't waver for a moment when people suggest, "Well, we've got to help elect this guy that we really like by doing these nasty, stupid, dumb, negative things."

Feltus: Don't you think a lot of people, young people that get into politics, think that way, but then change how they think?

Bailey: Sure they do. I mean, the whole system is a gotcha system, which is very enticing. You know, oh, I'll only do it this time. And then it worked. Hmm, hmm, maybe we can do that over here. You know, it's very gotcha. People get into it because they love the power and excitement and all that, so that's very gotcha too. But my god, look at what we built. We built a political system that is just—that elevates the phonies and that considers politics more important than governing. I mean, that's another aspect of it that I feel is important, that governing, what you do in office, is a hell of a lot more important than getting there. But that doesn't seem to be the priority that dominates the system.

Feltus: Politics for the sake of politics.

Bailey: You know, it's easy to say if I don't win, I can't get anything done, so that justifies anything. That justifies running the kind of campaign that you run. In order to win, you destroy the other side. You throw away things that are important to you. And then you get there and you've lost your soul. I mean, you're talking to a guy who really is not very pleased about the nature—

Feltus: Current state of the game.

Bailey: It's just awful, and it continues to get worse. When a super committee can do nothing and a super PAC can do anything, we've got a problem.

Feltus: I think the one thing that's screwed up politics so much is the election law stuff. If you go back, every time they change the election law, they try to do something about this. Because it's emasculated the parties. There is no calm, central power source that can, you know, use a whip to kind of tame any excesses anymore. That's because of the way they regulate the money.

Bailey: That's part of it, certainly a large part of it. But every time they change the law, all you do is figure out new ways of getting around it. And the Supreme Court is likely to approve anything.

Feltus: Well, I can see free speech. If some rich, crazy guy in Las Vegas wants to run negative ads against Mitt Romney, he can do that.

Bailey: Yeah, what about this rule? I'm not trying to write a chapter in your book, by the way, but here's a very simple thought that I don't hear expressed very often. It's really radical and maybe can only be accomplished by a constitutional amendment. But if you can't vote for the person, why should you be allowed to contribute to the person or against the person? Think about that. That means no money from corporations, no money from special interest PACs, no money from lobbyists unless the lobbyist happens to be registered in that particular congressional district. That doesn't mean that the corporations and the PACs and the special interests and the lobbyists can't go to the district and try to raise money for a particular candidate.

Feltus: But the donors would have to be registered voters and in the jurisdiction of the election.

Bailey: At least they have to live in the jurisdiction of the election. Probably registered voters, why not? I mean, it just seems to me that it's so simple. I know, I know that some are favorite special interests, whatever they are. You'd like to make an exception for them because they're special, they're good guys. But my sense is when most members of Congress, incumbents, get more money from outside their district than they get from inside the district, there's something really wrong.

Feltus: Yeah. I see that point. It depends—the thing I don't like about that is that there are wealthy districts and there are poor districts.

Bailey: Yeah, but what's true for one person in a poor district is true for another person in a poor district. It's not as if you're [in a] poor district—some guy in a poor district versus some guy in a rich district. You're not. What's good for the goose is good for the gander. You can quote me on that if you want.

Feltus: It disadvantages the challenger. That's a problem with any of these rules is that, you know—

Bailey: It's not a disadvantage to the challenger. The challenger is disadvantaged, Will, by the fact that any incumbent in Washington can go down on K Street and raise all the money in the world, which the challenger basically cannot raise.

Feltus: But even under the district rule, the challenger would still be able to raise so much more money in the district.

Bailey: Yeah, there's no question about that.

Feltus: So you've got some challenger who's like a hot commodity that, hey, we want to embrace this guy. You know, he's running against an entrenched incumbent.

Bailey: How about a hot challenger in the district who people in the district want to embrace this guy? You know as well as I do that incumbents raise money in Washington in order to drive challengers away from ever challenging.

Feltus: Yeah.

Bailey: I'm not saying it's a perfect solution, but for god's sake, what in god's name are we doing with corporations being able to spend unlimited amounts of money through super PACs and nobody even knows that they're contributing? It's crazy. You can quote me on that. I don't think that this is going to get into your book.

Feltus: No, it could well get into the book. I'm not paying as much attention to the fundraising, but it's an important—I mean, the book is—we're definitely going to address this negativity in the campaign issue. And you know, we'll touch on the money stuff, but we can't—you know, the book is not about—

Bailey: Of course, of course.

Feltus: The system. You know, you've got twenty professors writing books who are basically saying what you're saying. Our book is more about this is what campaign managers have done book and how they think about it. Have you ever managed a campaign?

Bailey: No, thank god. I'd be terrible at it.

Feltus: Let's recount briefly the story of how you—Harvard and then Rockefeller—how you got into politics.

Bailey: I was in graduate school. I went to graduate school to get out of the army early. And I stayed in graduate school because I had no idea what I wanted to do, so I kept staying on, getting more degrees and more degrees and more degrees. Finally I'm working very slowly on my PhD and I had no job. I'm going to Fletcher School at Tufts, and I had no job. I didn't know what I wanted to do. But I had a sort of part-time job as an assistant to the dean, and the dean calls me in one day and says, and this is in June of 1960—

Feltus: And young Bailey is how old?

Bailey: And young Bailey is twenty-seven.

Feltus: Oh, so you are wandering aimlessly through the halls of academia.

Bailey: Oh, yeah. And I'd spent a couple years in the army and all that kind of stuff. And I'm finishing up a PhD, but going very slowly at it because I had nowhere to go. And the dean calls me in and says, "Doug, do we have anybody waiting for their foreign service orals or anybody just waiting here during this summer for their foreign service assignment or something like that? I just got a call from Henry Kissinger, who said that Governor Rockefeller wants to be briefed on every conceivable issue that he might confront as secretary of state, secretary of defense under a Nixon administration if Nixon wins in November." And I said, "Well, I'll think about it, but I think I can come up with somebody." And so I applied for that job myself and went to New York. That is the result of the 5th Avenue Compact if you remember such a thing. Nixon and Rockefeller met, and Rockefeller promised not to run for the Republican nomination. He had just been elected governor of New York in 1958, and he promised not to run for the nomination if Nixon would promise to appoint him either secretary of state or secretary of defense. And so Nixon made that promise. And Rockefeller, typical Rockefeller came back from the meeting, called Henry Kissinger, and said, "Henry, I want to know everything there is to know about every issue I might confront as the secretary of state or secretary of defense."

Feltus: How did Rockefeller know Kissinger?

Bailey: They had known each other from the mid-1950s on. You know, Rockefeller had spent some time in the 1950s in the defense department, and he had made a point to reach out to Kissinger. And they knew each other through the Council on Foreign Relations or something like that. But in any event, Kissinger was obviously going to be Rockefeller's guy when it came to foreign policy in terms of his presidential ambitions. So I went to New York and spent the next three months until November, four months until November writing position papers on everything.

Feltus: For Nelson Rockefeller with Kissinger's guidance.

Bailey: Right. And Kissinger then said, "Okay Bailey, finish your PhD at Fletcher. Get it done, for god's sake, and then come over and be my teaching assistant at Harvard, and we'll plan Rockefeller's 1964 presidential campaign together and we'll do it together."

Feltus: And that's how young Bailey the academic ended up in politics.

Bailey: That's how young Bailey the academic became the number two guy in the foreign policy research side and met—in the Rockefeller campaign—and met a guy named Deardourff, funny spelling, who was the number two guy in the domestic policy research side, having worked for a congress-woman, two members of Congress. But he ended up number two on the domestic policy research side. So that's where we met, in the Rockefeller campaign. And we decided after the 1964 campaign to go do something, invent a new world. And we had this vision of a consulting firm. There was no such thing. There were some consulting firms. There were one or two consultants on the Democratic side and there were some in California, but there was no such thing as a national Republican consulting firm, so we founded one. And we didn't know what we were doing, but we did pretty well.

Feltus: Who was your first client? So you founded it in 1965 basically.

Bailey: Well, 1965, right. I went down to Washington, worked as a staff director of the Wednesday Group in the House of Representatives just to get to know people who were likely to run for the Senate later.

Feltus: So you were a house congressional staffer.

Bailey: I was a house congressional staffer. And John was the executive director of the party in New York. And he would go to all the seminars around the country, the Republican seminars around the country, and we would pick off clients. We had a third partner named Dave Goldberg in Boston, and he recruited Ed Brooke as a client, so our first client was 1966, when we helped Ed Brooke, the first black man ever to serve in the US Senate since reconstruction. And that was our first client.

Feltus: Was that an open seat? What was that Brooke election? What was he before that?

Bailey: He was the attorney general of Massachusetts.

Feltus: I can Google all this, but since you're on the phone.

Bailey: And it was an open seat. I think that was Leverett Saltonstall's seat, and he was stepping down.

Feltus: And our other senator from Massachusetts then was—

Bailey: Was Ted Kennedy.

Feltus: Ted Kennedy, okay.

Bailey: And then in 1967, we really got on the map. We wrote some wonder-ful cartoon ads which ran throughout the state of New Jersey that changed—1967—that helped change a two to one Democratic majority in both houses of the state legislature to a three to one Republican majority in both houses of the state legislature. And, by god, from that point on we were hot stuff.

Feltus: Were those negative? I mean, were those cartoons in those days—

Bailey: They were cartoons. I don't think they were perceived as negative. Of course they were negative, and that's sort of the first time we learned that, you know, you can say all kinds of things if you get people smiling when they see it if it's not nasty.

Feltus: What's the best TV ad that you ever made?

Bailey: You're not going to like this answer. It's one that your boss and my friend killed. 1976, Gerald Ford, what I call the cherry bomb ad. Five minutes at the end of the campaign. I didn't disagree with the decision to kill it, but it's the best campaign ad for its purpose that I think we ever made.

Feltus: Was it produced?

Bailey: Absolutely it was produced. And it shocked everybody. But the whole purpose was he was going to lose, so why not shock everybody and shake everything up? And Bob had it focus grouped in Detroit. And because— well, there were a variety of reasons. Almost everybody that went into that focus group, there were some who were pro-Carter, some who were pro-Ford, and some who were undecided. And after watching the ad, everybody was undecided. We lost the Ford people, we lost the Carter people. Everybody was—but that was the goal, that was the purpose of the ad.

Feltus: So why didn't Bob think that was a good idea?

Bailey: He thought—for two reasons, and I understand this. And I don't disagree with the decision. In fact, I agreed with the decision at the time. And thinking back, it's still the best thing I ever did. But one reason Bob had was he was so convinced that the University of Michigan audience, which was the audience that was shown in the spot, would have turned the state of Ohio off. I mean, I come from Ohio. I come from Ohio. I know the intensity, but I think that's crazy. I think that's really crazy. I don't think that's the reason. The reason was that, remember, we were closing a point a day or a half a point a day. And it was very clear in the polls that we were closing and closing and closing, and this has been designed for a run in the last week when we thought or we were fairly certain that we were going to lose.

Feltus: No, I was the Ford-Dole communications director in Mississippi, and I remember that we thought we could actually pull this thing out.

Bailey: Well, and the Saturday, if you remember, the Saturday before the election, a Gallup poll had us a point ahead. So it was pulled in that sense that—

Feltus: You had the momentum and maybe—

Bailey: It was an unnecessary risk. Obviously it was a risk, but it was designed to meet a condition which they didn't feel they were in.

Feltus: So describe the spot.

Bailey: The spot was one of those four-and-a-half-minute spots that you could do then. And it opened with a regular, forward music and people on the street. And they were all saying nice things and so forth and the basic message of the campaign. And then it said—and then it shifted to saying something about Ford, the remarkable, steady hand at a time of great turmoil for the country or something like that. The stress was the steady, steady hand. And it showed him speaking to an audience at the University of Michigan. And Betty Ford was there on stage listening, and he was saying all the right things about the nature of leadership and so forth, and it was a good segment of the speech. But the important part was that he got to the key part of the speech and there's a gunshot. For all the world, it sounds like a gunshot. And he looks up into the balcony and he looks back down, and he keeps delivering his speech. And he keeps looking up into the balcony, and everybody is just shocked by what is happening. And then the announcer comes back on and says, "Not even the cherry bombs of a misguided prankster can keep this steady hand from—" I mean, remember now, this is 1976. This is after assassinations. I mean, Ford himself—

Feltus: Had been shot.

Bailey: Had been shot at. And so, I mean, it's just plain shocking. And then it said something to the effect that a change has come over America where the president can now travel again in an open car through the streets of Dallas. And there's footage of Ford with an enormous, enormous bulletproof vest on and waving to the crowds and getting out of the car and shaking hands and so forth. There has been a change that's come over America. And the whole point was to say, "Look, you know, we've been through Watergate. We know that. And now the country is in better shape for it because we have a steady, calm, deliberative, brave human being running the show."

Feltus: So it was morning in America before morning in America.

Bailey: Yeah. It was really—it was very, very emotional.

Feltus: So has this spot been seen? Is the spot around? Is this a spot that could be on our book website?

Bailey: Could be.

Feltus: But you have the spot.

Bailey: Sure. I have it in the version that never ran, and then we cleaned it up in the sense of took Dallas out because Jim Baker was afraid we'd lose Texas. Well, of course we lost Texas by half a million votes. And we took the cherry bomb out.

Feltus: You took the cherry bomb out? That's the whole point. Might as well take Jerry Ford out.

Bailey: That was my attitude too.

Feltus: What are some rules, as a campaign manager, how you manage your consultants in a campaign?

Bailey: Yeah, to me there's a big conflict. You know, when we started out, there weren't twenty consultants to a campaign. There was one. You know, and so it was easy for there to be a manager, a consultant, and a candidate. And the three could easily coordinate. And we always felt that it was very difficult for a consultant, particularly if you get the advertising, very difficult for the consultant to do a good job if he didn't have real access to the candidate and understood who the hell the candidate was.

Feltus: Say the part about the consultant and the advertising again.

Bailey: We felt that at a time when there was only one consultant to the campaign, it was easy for the consultant, the manager, and the candidate to form a team. And we always felt that if the consultant also did the advertising that it was really important that the consultant have a personal relationship with the candidate and really, really understand who the hell the candidate is. And so a manager that gets between the candidate and the consultants. Sometimes that's necessary, I understand that, but sometimes it's very much to the detriment of the campaign, I think particularly in the advertising world. Because I just don't believe you can do effective advertising. Maybe that's all changed, Will, I don't know, but I don't think you can do effective advertising without knowing who the candidate is and really parting the curtains and letting the candidate be seen as he actually is rather than just slapping something up there because you need a new ad. And I think that's a very difficult relationship. And frankly, there have been—in most campaigns now there are I don't know how many—a dozen consultants of one form or another. Not all of them need to have access to the candidate. My sense is that the advertising people do, but maybe that's an old thought as well.

Feltus: So the campaign manager has to have the confidence in his relationship with the candidate that he doesn't allow—so he will allow the consultant to have a direct relationship with the candidate without having to go through the manager.

Bailey: That's correct. But that also takes a judgment on the consultant. I mean, you have to both have—the manager has to make a judgment that a personal relationship between the candidate and the consultant is not likely to undo the campaign. It could undo the campaign in either way. I mean, either because of the candidate or because of the consultant. The manager

Feltus: has to be in charge of the operation so that that relationship—ideally so that that relationship—if it would help, between the candidate and the consultant is permitted but also so that that relationship can be stopped if it isn't going to help.

Feltus: Okay. Can you recall an anecdote where you and the campaign manager disagreed, and he said, "Okay, will you come try to persuade the candidate of this and we'll let him be the tiebreaker?"

Bailey: Let me give you—it's not quite that way. In 1978, Chuck Percy, Illinois. He's running for reelection. He's considered by everybody to be a shoo-in. But there are some people concerned in the state that he's sort of maybe getting a little too big for his britches or something.

Feltus: Taking it for granted.

Bailey: Right. And I can't remember the guy's name, but a nobody that nobody ever heard of was running against him. And suddenly out comes the *Chicago Sun-Times* poll, which is a really memorable event in Illinois politics. It comes out twenty days before the election, and there's a new portion of it every day. Very strange thing. It's almost like a tracker, but each portion for the first ten days covers a different part of the state. There's nothing quite like it. And then after those ten days, they go back and they repeat it, same thing again. Well, so the poll comes out and for god's sake, Percy is behind, behind! Inconceivable, impossible. And so we all assumed that's going to be corrected the next day. Well, the next day it got worse, and then it got worse, and then it got worse. And at the end of there's now ten days left, so the first statewide poll is completed and, you know, many, many thousands of interviews now. This is no light thing. This is just gigantic news. And Percy is, you know, like ten points behind. Holy mother.

Feltus: So that's like when I couldn't get Teeter on the phone from Jackson.

Bailey: Right.

Feltus: Because he was freaking out because he had a poll that showed you ahead, and you had the *Chicago Sun-Times* poll showing you behind.

Bailey: Yeah. And it was just amazing. But there was no particular reason to think that the *Chicago Sun-Times* poll was not correct. I mean, it really was a shocker because the way it's done sort of every day helped to reconfirm what we had been seeing. So we had to figure out what to do. And we did a number of things and they're all interesting, but the one that is relevant here is that I concluded that Percy—this was big news in Illinois. I mean really big news. It was the big story every day in every paper across the state. Percy, for god's sakes, is going to lose! And so I had to convince him, I thought, that he needed to sit down in front of a camera and give kind of a mea culpa apology to the people of Illinois and in effect say, "I've been too big for my britches, but I hear you and I don't want to lose, so help me out. I promise to be a good boy." Now the language was a lot better than that. But he absolutely didn't want to do that. And his family didn't want him to do that. And so I finally convinced him that, okay, let's take all the good ideas that everybody's got as to what you ought to say. I mean, clearly he ought to look into the camera and say something. And it ought to be the ad that runs over the last four or five days. Let's take all the ideas that anybody's got. You write whatever you want to say, and Irene can write whatever she thinks you ought to say, and everybody else can write whatever they want to say, and I'll write what I think you ought to say. And then we'll cut them all and then we'll go test them. And we'll run the one—

Feltus: Make multiple spots. Yeah, okay.

Bailey: And he agrees to that, and he does it. And I think maybe there were three. I think there were four spots that were cut. And the mea culpa spot, we tested it and he hired his good friend who ran—what is that firm in Chicago? Marketing research firm. Doesn't do any politics but his good friend ran it. And that guy and I agreed that he should test them, and he tested them.

Feltus: And that consumer research firm in Chicago tested them?

Bailey: And the mea culpa spot came in second, but it was very close. And we agreed to report back to Percy that the mea culpa spot was it, let's go.

Feltus: After massaging the results.

Bailey: Yeah, it was so close that it was meaningless. But of course, he won. And in fact, the second series of *Sun-Times* poll, the last ten days kept showing the race getting closer and closer and closer. And so by the election day, it sometimes had it as a dead heat. And he ended up winning by eight or nine points. And I think it is because the people of Illinois didn't want him to lose. They just wanted to spank him. You know, they really didn't—and they certainly didn't like his opponent. And they wanted to scare him. It was frankly the same reason that I had encouraged him to want to have a primary in the spring, let people get the sort of negative attitude out of their system early. In any event, that was very difficult and sufficiently difficult that he did not really hire us. And we'd been his polling firm in 1972 and again in 1978. And in 1984 when he ran for reelection, he did not hire us. He hired Roger Ailes, and he lost to Paul Simon.

Feltus: Okay, well, I think that's a good stopping point. That's a good story. You've got a lot of good stories.

Bailey: I've outtalked you.

Feltus: All right, Dr. Bailey. Well, I appreciate your time.

Bailey: Okay. Well, good luck to you.

Appendix C
Manager Profile—Katie Merrill

Managing in the California Big Leagues

Katie Merrill's career in California politics began in 1991. "I always knew I wanted to work in politics," she told us. "I got involved in a local LGBT Democratic Club, which led to volunteering on campaigns, which led to a paid position on a campaign."[1] Merrill has described her personal politics as very liberal on social issues and somewhat liberal on economic issues. She figures she has worked on more than twenty-five campaigns and been the manager or general consultant on fifteen of them. Not only candidates but stakeholders in ballot initiatives—very big business in California politics—have turned to Merrill for her political management skills. Her wins include the successful 2010 campaign against Proposition 23—that is, the campaign to uphold California's greenhouse emissions standards.[2]

Like all seasoned campaign professionals, Merrill also has seen her share of high-profile disappointments, including Democrat Phil Angelides' unsuccessful 2006 challenge to California governor Arnold Schwarzenegger. Schwarzenegger had looked vulnerable at the beginning of the election year. But while Angelides was coming from behind to win the Democratic nomination, the governor's campaign team was raising and spending money to boost his approval rating in the polls. In the general election, the Angelides campaign never really broke through, and the governor was reelected in a landslide with 55.9 percent of the vote.

Not only did Angelides lose but after the loss a leading Democratic consultant who had worked for his primary opponent wrote an op-ed that partly blamed Angelides' defeat on his known impulse to dominate his managers and run his own campaigns.

"Don't Run Your Own Campaign"[3]

Like the lawyer who represents himself, the candidate who manages his own campaign has a fool for a client. Especially at the level of governor, truly smart candidates hire talented, experienced advisers and pay heed to their counsel.

> But not the supposedly brilliant Angelides. One of the worst-kept secrets about the two-term treasurer . . . is that he always runs his own campaigns, down to every tactical decision and the last tedious detail. In the last couple of weeks before the election, major daily newspapers were filled with head-shaking stories from current and former Angelides campaign workers about the ludicrous extent of his micromanagement.[4]
>
> Gary South, former adviser to Phil Angelides

Ahead in the polls in 2006, Gov. Arnold Schwarzenegger agreed to only a single Saturday night October debate with Democrat Phil Angelides (right). Many Californians were more interested in watching college football or the baseball playoffs, according to the *San Francisco Chronicle.*[5]

Showing the wise restraint of an experienced pro, Merrill declined to discuss the pros and cons of her former boss's management style. But she did talk generally about the difficulty of managing staff in a campaign when all the polling says your candidate is almost certain to lose, which was the case for Angelides. As she pointed out, managers also face certain challenges when everyone thinks you're going to win—namely that there is no sense of urgency inside the campaign: "And so what you have is a bunch of horses chomping at the bit, and they're bored."

Grassroots Organizer Learns about California Media

When asked about the irony of running media campaigns in California after having started as a grassroots organizer, Merrill admitted that the psychological boost from successful grassroots organizing and fieldwork is still greater than the boost from successful advertising gamesmanship:

> When you're running a race . . . and you meet the contact goals and you meet your ID goals and you meet your turnout goals and win, it's about the coolest thing in the world. It's a hell of a lot more interesting than, you know, "I put 1,000 points on L.A. TV and got two ads in the NBA finals and won."

More from Katie Merrill's Interview

Q. What are you looking for in the personalities of the young people you hire in campaigns?

A. One of the questions I always ask is, do you play any sports? Because I think it's critical to have the ability to work as a team member. And which doesn't mean that I don't hire people who haven't played team sports. But if they have, they know about two things. One, they know about working on a team. Two, they've got a competitive spirit. And I think both of those things, those personality attributes, are critical to being successful at campaign work.

Q. So you want them to cooperate inside the campaign and be competitive on the outside?

A. Yes, exactly . . . I'm not interested in egos. And you see it all the time. Like a presidential campaign—every time a book's written about a presidential campaign, you hear about people undercutting each other and spending so much time trying to become the director of this or the head of that that they lose focus and often lose the race. I think that [ego] is toxic on any kind of campaign whether you're doing a local ballot initiative or whether you're in the big, big race.

Q. What are some of the biggest changes you've seen since you started out in politics?

A. Well, obviously technology and the Internet have changed politics inexorably. And interestingly enough, in California what they have done is they've made the old new again. When I got into California politics, statewide politics in 1992, people said to me, "Field is dead. It's all about TV." Well, guess what? Field has made a comeback, and it's making a comeback because of the Internet. It's just easier to organize, much easier to call, much easier to recruit volunteers, actually get them to do stuff.

You know, ultimately, until voting becomes an online activity, you have to figure out how to translate online into the offline. And we really weren't able to do it until 2008. The Obama campaign did it. They had brick-and-mortar offices. How did they get people there? They used the Internet. How did they go places where they didn't have brick-and-mortar offices? How did they get people to do stuff? The Internet. When they wanted people to make calls, and Hillary did this too, into primary states but you were out of state, how did they have you make calls? The Internet. I sat at my computer and got on the phone, and they just patched me through to voters. So that's what the Internet has done to allow the field, which is so labor intensive and costly, to become more cost effective.

Q.   What about the relationship between the campaign manager and the candidate? Do you manage the candidate?

A.   You hope that you have a relationship with the candidate. You know, it's not about managing the candidate, but it's about sort of having a kind of partnership. You respect the candidate. You each understand what your roles are. And you respect those boundaries. You're in constant communication. You understand what decisions you're going to make, what decisions the candidate will make, and you operate based on those agreements. . . . Some candidates are aware they have [quirks] and are willing to work in partnership, work around them, and some of them aren't. But I think if you go into it thinking you're going to manage the candidate, you're going to encounter a world of heartache.

Q.   What advice would you have for a young person who might want to get into politics and someday become a campaign manager?

A.   Go volunteer on a campaign right now! If you're interested in politics, this is how democracy functions, right? So, if you want to see how it really works, go volunteer on a campaign and see the bones of it and the ins and outs of it. That's how you find out whether you really want a job in politics. As soon as you volunteer on a campaign, and if you're excited and you do a good job, then you get hired later on in the campaign, or in the next one. It really does start your career.

Notes

1. Katie Merrill, personal communication, September 15, 2011, for this quote and all other Katie Merrill quotes in this appendix.

2. For more background on Proposition 23, see http://ballotpedia.org/wiki/index.php/California_Proposition_23,_the_Suspension_of_AB_32_(2010).

3. Garry South is a Democratic strategist who ran Gray Davis' successful gubernatorial campaigns in 1998 and 2002 and was senior adviser to the Steve Westly campaign for governor in the 2006 Democratic primary.

4. Garry South, "Why Phil Angelides Lost," *San Francisco Chronicle*, November 8, 2006, www.sfgate.com/opinion/article/Why-Phil-Angelides-lost-2467030.php.

5. Carla Marinucci and Tom Chorneau, "Schwarzenegger, Angelides Also Spar on College Costs in Only Meeting of Campaign," October 8, 2006, *San Francisco Chronicle*, www.sfgate.com/politics/article/CAMPAIGN-2006-Gubernatorial-Race-Candidates-2468443.php.

Appendix D Manager Profile—Reed Galen

Just Say No

Reed Galen is a Republican political strategist in California. He served as deputy campaign manager for Gov. Arnold Schwarzenegger's 2006 reelection campaign and served as the deputy campaign manager for Sen. John McCain's presidential campaign through July of 2007. Galen also served as executive director for the inaugural committee.

Getting Started

The biggest challenge facing Reed when he joined Arnold Schwarzenegger's 2006 gubernatorial campaign was that Schwarzenegger was coming off a rousing defeat in his 2005 special election on his four government reform measures.[1] As a result, Arnold was down in the polls approximately 36 percent. The campaign account was half a million dollars in debt and there was no reelection campaign to speak of.

The campaign was in disarray at the start with no organizational structure. Even the state Republican Party, where the campaign was initially headquartered, lacked a fundraising plan, press list, or any basic coalition. It was literally as if Arnold had never run for office.

Given these challenges, Galen and the campaign manager, Steve Schmidt, had a daunting task. They split responsibilities to ensure efficiency and effectiveness during the campaign. "Steve looked up and out, and I looked down and in, and that's the reason why I was able to be so successful as the hammer," explained Galen.

Assembling a Team

Galen and Schmidt were responsible for hiring the campaign's staff. Galen looked for staffers who lived in Sacramento or were willing to move to there. While he looked for skilled people, availability was key. Regarding senior staff picks, Galen explained, "We wanted people who either in Steve's mind had a subject matter expertise that was sort of transferrable anywhere. And if it wasn't that, then you know, a senior person who knew California very well." On middle management and junior staff, Reed explained, "As you go down . . . it was really who's available?

Who's good? How quickly can we hire them? Again, because we had nothing, you know, we had to get something going quickly." Availability was key. Because by the end of the campaign, between the campaign itself and the state party, the campaign had over 100 people on staff, and raised and spent $85.5 million.

Financing the Campaign

The campaign's finance plan was significant at $40 to $50 million. Campaign finance regulations permitted donations of $22,300 per individual per cycle to a candidate—allowing an individual to contribute almost $45,000 total in the primary and general. Individuals could also give a maximum of $25,000 per individual per cycle to the state party, which helped fund the campaign. Given the state's finance laws, the Schwarzenegger campaign sought to secure maximum donations early. The campaign hosted fundraisers as well as used direct mail and the Internet to fund the campaign's war chest. Fundraisers were very effective, but direct mail did not yield the results the campaign had hoped. On direct mail fundraising, Galen said, "I mean, if I had to do it over again, I never even would have done it. But you know, there were some things that were sort of vestiges of the old regime that we couldn't get rid of, and that program was one of them." The state party was a major asset as they were allowed to directly transfer funds to Arnold's campaign.

Research and Messaging

The Schwarzenegger campaign hired Basilik from Austin, Texas, as its pollster. Early in the 2006 campaign, the campaign conducted research to determine whether or not the electorate had forgiven Arnold for the 2005 special. Arnold came out and apologized, which proved to be very valuable. Research showed that while Californians were angry with Arnold, they still liked him personally and did not blame the state's dysfunction on him.

The campaign used research to frame and drive the campaign's messaging, which focused on the economy, lower taxes, and investment in California's future. The core message was framed as a binary choice: Arnold was going to take California forward while Phil Angelides was moving California backward. Supporting messages were tailored to the campaign's target audiences. Anti-tax messaging appealed to the Republican base, while investment messaging around Arnold's sweeping cap and trade bill appealed to moderate Democrats and Independents. To keep a pulse on the electorate and the effectiveness of messaging throughout the campaign, Basilik conducted baseline quantitative surveys, and during the post-Labor Day period, tracking polls were widely used.

By about October 1, the data showed that Arnold was so far ahead and the dynamics of the race were so set that the campaign started campaigning on behalf of ongoing legislative initiatives such as infrastructure bonds to address the state's housing bubble and transportation troubles. Infrastructure bonds were something Arnold strongly believed in and wanted to get passed.

Media and Communication Vehicles

Direct mail and direct contact were most important to reach voters in the campaign, followed by television advertising. Direct mail and direct contact became most important in the campaign's GOTV operation, which the campaign spent about $20 million on. Galen said the following:

> We had phone centers. If we didn't have a phone center in every county, we were darn close. And we had a hell of a volunteer operation making four, five, six contacts into people. You know, very sophisticated (for the time) VoIP phones. You know, crossing people off if they said I'm not going to vote. And Arnold won by seventeen points in a terrible year. Now again, he's the most popular person on the planet and we spent $85 million. Twenty of that again was on a direct GOTV contact program.

The campaign spent approximately another $25 million on television advertising. The campaign faced a unique challenge with a movie star and the camera. Galen explained, "We didn't shoot Arnold two-camera once in the entire campaign, not one time. We used b-roll from events, stock footage or footage the campaign already owned because, and this is something really unique to Arnold, the cost of filming him was so prohibitive because it had to be basically Hollywood quality, movie quality production." As a result, Schwarzenegger's team ran only about four or five ads throughout the campaign.

The campaign's advertising prominently featured Arnold as moving the state forward and Phil moving things backward. That theme ran throughout all of the advertising with subtleties like birds walking backward. "It was the same basic concept I think for all our ads except the point when we did the scroll for all the endorsements," said Galen. Negative advertising also proved effective—primarily pointing out that Schwarzenegger's opponent, Phil Angelides, was going to raise your taxes $17 billion.

All of the campaign's advertising and media buying was targeted to specific audiences on particular networks. Maria Shriver would say, "I've never seen any of Arnold's commercials. Why is Arnold not on the air in L.A.?" The reality is that Arnold was on the air in L.A., just not on anything Maria was ever going to watch. Media buying is like putting up campaign signs on poles where you know the candidate is going to drive.

Galen argues that advertising, the campaign's largest expenditure, is king for now—although, he predicts we will see a shift. Galen explained the following:

> I think with things like DVR, the fact that more and more folks are now unhooking their cable or their satellite in order to just have very high speed

Internet, where they're going to watch their TV shows on Netflix or Hulu or whatever they're going to watch. They may still communicate via that medium. Maybe Hulu opens itself up to political ads or Netflix does, but there will come a point where folks are getting the content they want—and not necessarily because it's on channel four. And I think campaigns are going to have to figure out, you know, if they're not going to watch channel four anymore, how are we going to get to them?

Moreover, third party or independent expenditure advertising played an important role. The US Chamber of Commerce created an ad on the governor's behalf early in 2006 to lay the groundwork for the campaign. Naturally, the campaign had no say or influence over the ad. In addition, the campaign benefited greatly from the fact that California election law permitted the state parties to raise money in unlimited dollars. Thus, Galen said, "The bulk of the TV spending actually came out of the state party, not out of the campaign proper."

The campaign did not use digital and social media much. Galen estimated the campaign allocated only about 5 percent of funds to digital. Galen explained the following:

For us in 2006, we could never figure out where the Internet belonged. I will say it was the most underutilized and most underfunded piece of the campaign. Again, we didn't know enough about how to use it correctly.

Weathering the Storm

Dealing with the media and reporters is a twenty-four-hour challenge in any campaign. Reporters are always looking for the next juicy campaign story. The Schwarzenegger campaign was no exception. Around Labor Day weekend, a story came out about Arnold and comments that were recorded off-the-record by his speechwriter, Gary Delson. Because of Arnold's unique syntax, Delson would record their brainstorming conversations before he wrote his speeches to help learn Arnold's voice. He would upload them to what was perceived to be a secure server for viewing. However, someone gained access to these files and leaked one of the recordings to the press. In the leaked recording, Arnold referenced Latina assemblywoman Bonnie Garcia's temperament as being "very hot" due to her "black blood mixed with Latino blood."

Galen explained, "Thankfully, the woman about whom he was speaking adores Arnold, so that was one of those situations where the Angelides campaign leaked these things. You know, the entire place goes into four alarm, five alarm fire drill. The response people are getting their stuff up and running." Arnold apologized to Garcia and the campaign set up an event with Arnold at the L.A. chamber the next morning to respond. Assemblywoman Garcia appeared by Arnold's side and said she was not offended by the governor's comments. Garcia even said that she often calls herself a "hot-blooded Latina." In addition, Latino and African American supporters were calling the leaked recording dirty politics.

The question remained of who got access to the recording. Galen explained the following:

> And then in a true great campaign pivot . . . we walked it back and it turned out the IP address that had access to that particular page on the governor's website could be directly linked back to the Angelides campaign. And the campaign officially asked the CHP to launch an investigation. And before he knew it, everybody had forgotten about the fact that Arnold had talked about the hot blood of a Latina legislator and everybody was talking about how Angelides was a crook.

"For the Angelides campaign, it was a Hail Mary. They had to do something. And if it had been anybody but Arnold, it might have worked," said Galen. But the Hail Mary turned out to be a boomerang, and the story fired back on them. Arnold's rapid response team successfully weathered the storm, and he went on to win reelection.

Note

1. Source information for Appendix D is from R. Galen, personal communication, September 30, 2011.

Appendix E
The Audacity of Smoke

The Rise and Fall of the Unorthodox Herman Cain Campaign

Mark Block has experienced the highs and lows a campaign manager goes through. But unlike most managers, Block's roller coaster rocketed him to the top, then dropped his campaign into a dizzying vertigo in the space of just two weeks.

Block had signed on with an improbable long shot, a businessman and former radio host with a booming voice and the ability to capture a crowd, but with no actual electoral experience, save a failed bid for a US Senate seat in which he was little more than an afterthought. Now, Herman Cain believed he could be president of the United States of America—and Cain wanted Block to get him there.

Cain started out as an asterisk, an afterthought. In debates, when the candidates were arranged by their poll numbers, Cain would be all the way on the left or right, nearly offstage. But Cain's dogged devotion to a simple, easy-to-remember sound bite—simplify the tax code by levying a 9 percent income tax, a 9 percent capital gains tax, and a 9 percent federal sales tax—started winning him fans and admirers. In a whack-a-mole primary campaign in which seemingly every candidate enjoyed their brief moment in the sun, Cain's time came in late October 2011, just as Gov. Rick Perry from Texas watched his numbers start to tank.

Then Mark Block became the story.

Sometime around Halloween in 2011, Mark Block became one of the most successful and best-known campaign managers in America—at least by the numbers. His candidate, Herman Cain, had been at the bottom of the national surveys ten months before. Now as Cain found himself in a statistical dead heat with front-runner Mitt Romney for the Republican presidential nomination, an in-house video posted on Cain's website went viral on YouTube.[1] Within ten days, 1 million people had tuned in so they could catch the closing shot of the fifty-seven-year-old Block taking an ad-libbed drag on a Marlboro Light.

The video, originally envisioned as a pep talk for Cain volunteers, helped bring an unexpected $3 million influx of online contributions to the low-budget operation.[2] Some now dubbed the high-momentum campaign the "Cain Train," and Block was the engineer.

Like most campaign managers surveyed, Block preferred to leave the job of talking to the press to the campaign's small communications staff. He had remained largely behind the scenes and out of the news since January 2011, when he signed on as manager.[3]

But Block's anonymity went up in smoke on October 19 when the surging Cain campaign posted a sixty-second video featuring Block on the official campaign website titled "Now is the time for action!" Looking directly into the camera in close-up, Block said, "We've run a campaign like no one has ever seen" and urged Cain supporters to get involved.[4] It looked like any other inexpensively produced campaign video intended to recruit and motivate volunteers and donors—except for the cigarette used to punctuate his pitch in the final frames. Block took a drag and then exhaled into the camera. The unexpected juxtaposition of smoking and presidential politics made the video instant fodder for cable news networks and a media hungry for a race. Not only did their coverage drive more people online to watch Block smoke his cigarette, but it drove still more press coverage. Reporters and the bookers who arrange appearances on television and radio shows were nearly as interested in talking to the star of the "Smoking Man" video as they were in talking to his candidate. Block was suddenly making news, something that most campaign managers assiduously avoid. In the ten days after the video was released, ninety-two news stories ran about Block, according to a search of the Nexis news database; over the previous nine months, there had been only seven.[5]

To Democrats, Cain and his campaign manager were just another sideshow, an unexpected challenge, a welcome one to Democrats, that the front-running Republican Romney had to deal with. "If that guy wasn't drunk, I haven't taken a drink in my life," said James Carville on ABC's *Good Morning America*. "He was drunk or stoned. Some kind of chemical, I guarantee you that."[6] (Block maintains that he doesn't drink.)

But many conservative commentators admired the video's blatant disregard for political correctness. Describing Block's performance as "accidental brilliance," nationally syndicated columnist Kathleen Parker wrote, "Herman Cain's craggy-faced chief of staff Mark Block took a drag off a cigarette, blew smoke at the camera, and sent the political class into coughing fits."[7] No one thought Cain would be the Republican nominee—but his campaign had somehow struck viral gold, using little more than a cloud of cigarette smoke.

Looking back, Block agreed that the video's success was accidental. "[We] didn't go out there saying, 'Hey, let's make this smoking video and see whether we can get more press.' It just happened."[8] After staying behind the camera for months, Block began appearing on cable news to explain the video. He told CNN the Cain campaign's fundraising total had jumped to $3 million in October, in part because of the video: "That's what we're seeing in our grassroots activism growth and obviously in the YouTube thing."[9] In an interview with the Fox News Channel, Block said the following:

> I tell you, you walk into a veterans' bar in Iowa, and they're sitting around smoking and you know we are resonating with them. I'm not the only one that smokes in America for God's sake. It was a choice I made, and it was at

Herman Cain for President, 2012.

The audacity of smoke. Mark Block, the manager of Herman Cain's presidential campaign, smokes in the last few seconds of a video posted by the Cain campaign on October 19, 2011. The video set off a media frenzy and went viral with nearly 1 million views in ten days.

the end of the ad. The real message that we're trying to get through was the Cain train is on a roll.[10]

It's not clear how many of those patrons of a veterans' bar in Iowa are clicking through YouTube. But a new generation of libertarian Republicanism was on the rise, and Cain had tapped a vein.

The video was produced on October 19, the day after a Republican presidential debate in Las Vegas. The Cain campaign team was still in town at the Wynn hotel on the Las Vegas strip. Traveling with them was the campaign's videographer, Chris Burgard, who produced short videos of Cain for posting on the campaign's website. Block says the campaign had been talking for some time about the need to produce a video of him addressing Cain's supporters online about the campaign's surging momentum.

The Internet had been a key tool for the relatively low-budget, grassroots-directed Cain campaign. Curious voters had been flocking to Cain's website after seeing or hearing one of his many media appearances in which he talked about his tax plan—"9-9-9," in his oft-repeated baritone.

Cain could be an entertaining interview and had been invited as a guest on the late-night talk shows hosted by David Letterman and Jay Leno, where he reached new audiences outside the television news box. "We had a standing invitation to appear on just about every television show," Block said. He added that Cain wanted to appear at least once on as many shows as possible.[11] This differed sharply from

Herman Cain became a celebrity candidate: Like Donald Trump in 2015–2016, presidential candidate Herman Cain in 2011 was in high demand as a guest on nationally televised talk shows. Below, Cain appears on The *Tonight Show, David Letterman, The View*, and *Jimmy Kimmel Live!*

the approach of Mitt Romney, the other front-runner for the Republican nomination, who accepted only a small number of national media requests and focused more on local media in the early primary states.

Block's smoking at the end of the video was a spur-of-the-moment decision on the recommendation of videographer Burgard. Before the edited video was posted to the campaign's official website, it was circulated for approval by Cain and top campaign staff. "No one said, 'Take out the smoking,'" remembered Block.[12] After the video was launched on the website, early reactions from Cain supporters were negative, and some members of the field team urged that the video be taken down.

But the campaign staffers closest to the volunteers, the lifeblood of any presidential campaign, had a different take: "After about 24 to 48 hours, it began to turn around, and our people became very positive on the video," said Block. As more and more people came to the campaign website to watch it—with many lingering on the site to register or contribute—the campaign's servers were overwhelmed and crashed. Ironically, the popularity of the smoking video was costing the campaign money by slowing down the website, said Block, who then decided to post the video on YouTube. The campaign's internal servers were then able to process more volunteer sign-ups and campaign contributions.[13]

As Block claimed in the video, the Cain campaign was on a roll by the end of October. Just eight weeks earlier, Cain was averaging only 4.8 percent in national primary trial heats, well behind Rick Perry's 26.3 percent and Romney's 16.5 percent. But as Perry's support collapsed to 10.5 percent, largely because of widespread media coverage of his debate gaffes, Cain and Block were glad to pick up the slack. By Halloween, Cain had surged to 25 percent nationally, into a statistical dead heat with Romney's 24.3 percent.[14]

Apparently, Cain's "campaign like no one has ever seen" was working. Block was now managing a front-running campaign for the Republican presidential nomination. "Only in America," said Block.[15]

Mark Block, Chief Operating Officer and Chief of Staff

As the engineer of the speeding Cain Train, the 57-year-old Block was indeed an unlikely choice to manage a major presidential campaign.[16] "Most of the people that are running presidential campaigns don't act like I act," said an understated Block in an October 30 in-depth profile on the front page of the Sunday print edition of the *Milwaukee Journal Sentinel*, his hometown newspaper.[17]

Block had been in politics all his life, but he was a newcomer to presidential politics. His previous experience was largely limited to state and local races in his native Wisconsin. He was not the typical campaign hired gun but owed his position at the top of the Cain organization to his close personal and political relationship with the candidate. Block met Cain in 2005 while Block was running the Wisconsin chapter of a national free markets advocacy organization, Americans for Prosperity, funded by the conservative billionaire brothers David and Charles Koch. Block described how he and Cain got to know one another:

> I had just become the state director of Americans for Prosperity grassroots organization in Wisconsin. Wisconsin became the fourth state chapter of Americans for Prosperity. . . . And Mr. Herman Cain was here to help launch chapters. I brought him into Wisconsin. I think we did like nine meetings around the state in a two-and-a-half day time frame. And that was the beginning, and then Americans for Prosperity asked me to open up Michigan and Ohio. So I had brought Cain into those states and spent a lot of time in a car driving around those states. So if you can imagine, if you spend time in a car with somebody, you get to know him pretty well. And we became pretty good friends.
>
> As we traveled those six, five years ago, almost every time he spoke, people would say, 'You got to run for president. You got to run for president,' so we talked at great length about it, but then two things happened. He got cancer and then obviously pulled out from everything he was doing just to fight for his life. And the second thing is the growth of Americans for Prosperity throughout the United States.

So fast-forward then four years and Americans for Prosperity's now in thirty-two states. He beat cancer and put some serious thought into running for president. If Cain had run in 2004, for example, he wouldn't have had the contacts throughout the country into these grassroots organizations or Tea Party groups, which was really one of the strengths of the organization. One of the things that the press never picked up on, and we didn't want to really let the media know, was that we had incredible grassroots organizations in all fifty states.[18]

Campaign managers surveyed for this book say a key trait of a successful manager is the ability to earn and hold the complete trust of the candidate. As a testament to his faith in Block, Cain said he talked to three people before deciding to enter the presidential race in January 2011: "My wife, my minister, and Mark Block."[19] The bond of trust between Cain and Block was about to be tested by events that began to unfold on Sunday, October 30, the same day Block's profile ran on the front page of the *Milwaukee Journal Sentinel*.

From Campaign Manager to Crisis Manager

That day, Cain was in Washington, D.C., at the bureau of CBS News, the lone guest on *Face the Nation*. Accompanying the candidate in the pre-interview green room were Mrs. Cain, Block, and J. D. Gordon, the campaign's vice president of communications. Although the actual viewing audiences are relatively small for Sunday morning programs such as *Face the Nation*, *Meet the Press* (NBC), and *This Week* (ABC), the programs are closely watched by the political intelligentsia and the media. They serve as trials by fire, tests of a candidate's command of the issues and ability to survive intense lines of questioning from the network's hosts. They have an ability to shape the direction of follow-up news coverage that will reach tens of millions of potential voters that few other television shows can claim to match. Appearing on these programs is a major undertaking for presidential candidates, who typically prepare by studying briefing books and participating in mock interviews.

Block said the campaign had accepted the interview three days earlier, a Thursday. "Mr. Cain had been on the program before but not as the only guest." Block recalls that no special preparations were made for Cain's appearance, although a few members of the staff did sit down with him a couple of hours before the interview to discuss the latest news and issue briefing papers that the campaign prepared for Cain on a daily basis.[20]

From 1991 to early 2015, the host of *Face the Nation* was Bob Schieffer, a seventy-four-year-old, highly respected veteran newsman who is known for having a less confrontational style than many younger television news interviewers. What Cain and Block did not know was that Schieffer is a survivor of bladder cancer who believes smoking is dangerous. They also did not know that Schieffer planned to open the broadcast with the Smoking Man video. After a few quick questions about Cain's "9-9-9" tax plan, Schieffer played the video and pounced.

Schieffer: Mr. Cain, I just have to ask you, what is the point of that, having a man smoke a cigarette in a television commercial, for you?

Cain: One of the themes within this campaign is let Herman be Herman. Mark Block is a smoker, and we say let Mark be Mark. That's all we're trying to say, because we believe let people be people. He doesn't deny that he's a smoker. This isn't trying—

Schieffer: Are you a smoker?

Cain: No, I'm not a smoker. But I don't have a problem if that's his choice. So let Herman be Herman; let Mark be Mark. Let people be people. This wasn't intended to send any subliminal signal whatsoever.

Schieffer: But it does. It sends a signal that it's cool to smoke.

Cain: No, it does not. Mark Block smokes. That's all that ad says. We weren't trying to say it's cool to smoke. You have a lot of people in this country that smoke. But what I respect about Mark as a smoker, who is my chief of staff, he never smokes around me or smokes around anyone else. He goes outside.

Schieffer: Well, he smokes on television.

Cain: Well, he smokes on television. But there was no other subliminal message.

Schieffer: Was it meant to be funny?

Cain: It was meant to be informative. If they listen to the message where he said America has never seen a candidate like Herman Cain—that was the main point of it. And the bit on the end, we didn't know whether it was going to be funny to some people or whether they were going to ignore it or whatever the case may be.

Schieffer: Well, let me just tell you, it's not funny to me. I am a cancer survivor like you.

Cain: Right, I am also.

Schieffer: I had cancer that's smoking related.

Cain: Yes.

Schieffer: I don't think it serves the country well—and this is an editorial opinion here—to be showing someone smoking a cigarette. And you're the front-runner now. And it seems to me, as front-runner, you would have a responsibility not to take that kind of a tone in this campaign. I would suggest that perhaps, as the front-runner, you'd want to raise the level of the campaign.

Cain:	We will do that, Bob. And I do respect your objection to the ad. And probably about 30 percent of the feedback was very similar to yours. It was not intended to offend anyone. And being a cancer survivor myself, I am sensitive to that sort of thing.
Schieffer:	Would you take the ad down?
Cain:	Well, it's on the Internet. We didn't run it on TV.
Schieffer:	Why don't you take it off the Internet?
Cain:	It's impossible to do now. Once you put it on the Internet, it goes viral. We could take it off of our website, but there are other sites that have already picked it up. It's nearly impossible to erase that ad from the Internet.
Schieffer:	Have you ever thought of just saying to young people, "Don't smoke; 400,000 people in America die every year from smoking-related—"
Cain:	I will have no problem saying that. And as a matter of fact—
Schieffer:	Well, say it right now.
Cain:	Young people of America, all people, do not smoke. It is hazardous, and it's dangerous to your health. Don't smoke. I've never smoked, and I have encouraged people not to smoke.
Schieffer:	And it's not a cool thing to do.
Cain:	It is not a cool thing to do. And that's not what it was trying to say. Smoking is not a cool thing to do.[21]

The exchange between Schieffer and Cain became the news-making sound bite from the interview and was featured that Sunday evening on network television newscasts, along with clips of Block smoking. But the real news was about to be made after the interview as Cain was leaving the CBS bureau. On the sidewalk, he was confronted by Jonathan Martin, at the time a top reporter for *Politico*, a national political news outlet.

"Have you ever been accused, sir, in your life of harassment by a woman?" asked Martin.[22] According to Martin's story, "[Cain] breathed audibly, glared at the reporter and stayed silent for several seconds. After the question was repeated three times, he responded by asking the reporter, 'Have you ever been accused of sexual harassment?'"[23] In fact, Martin had contacted Cain's campaign several times in the previous days asking for comment on a tip claiming that Cain had been forced to settle complaints of inappropriate behavior when he was president of the National Restaurant Association from late 1996 to mid-1999. Martin had been holding the story while waiting for the Cain campaign's response to *Politico's* inquiries. Frustrated, he made a spur of the moment decision that Sunday morning to drive over to CBS and ask Cain in person. When Martin told Cain the name of one of the women involved, Cain would only respond, "I have no comment on that." Cain returned to his vehicle and left for his hotel with his wife, Block, and a few campaign staffers.

Block remembered that the conversation in the car was less about Martin's questions than about Schieffer's ambush on the Smoking Man video. "We were all saying, 'What was that all about?'" recalled Block. The campaign had known Martin was working on a story but hadn't known exactly what the story would be. "They had been asking us for comment but would not tell us exactly what information they had or where it came from," said Block. Block thought Martin and *Politico* had a strong liberal bias and were working on a "typical liberal media hit piece" on Cain (Block hadn't known that Martin had worked in Republican politics before becoming a journalist).[24]

The campaign had not prepared a response plan: "We couldn't prepare our response until we saw what they had," said Block.[25] The Cain campaign did not have to wait long. That evening at 8:00 p.m., Martin and his investigating team published their exclusive story.[26] By the following morning, no one would care anymore about Block and his smoking.

Cain had a full schedule of media appearances planned, beginning with a stop at the National Press Club, just a few blocks from the White House. Block also had committed to several interviews on cable news channels. The fallout from *Politico*'s story was only beginning to build, as other news organizations raced to confirm the details and add new tidbits of their own. Now, the question was whether Cain and his campaign should go ahead with their media schedule.

There is but one avenue of recourse: Take control of the story by releasing all of the damaging details as quickly as possible. While developing their crisis response, most campaign managers would have curtailed their candidate's media appearances, particularly avoiding news interviews where anchors and reporters would certainly be asking questions about a fast-developing story. But this conventional approach was not the chosen approach for the unconventional Cain, who made the decision himself: The Cain campaign would not go into crisis mode; it would continue with its planned events.

"Herman decided he was going to do the Press Club and keep his full schedule of media interviews," Block told us, adding that he agreed with the boss's decision.[27] After all, the free media had been good so far for Cain and his low-budget campaign, according to Block.[28] The charismatic Cain was a good interview and in constant demand with bookers. The Cain campaign almost never declined a media invitation; talking mostly about his "9-9-9" tax plan, Cain was garnering tens of millions of free and largely favorable impressions with Republican voters. Now, Cain and Block decided not to run away from the media but to turn up the volume and blast their way through the charges of inappropriate sexual behavior.

Making News in Real Time

It was Halloween—Monday, October 31, 2011. By the time evening trick-or-treating had started, Cain and Block found themselves at the center of a full-fledged national media feeding frenzy, a situation neither man had been in before.

"Get all the bad news out quickly" is a mantra frequently repeated by most of the campaign managers we surveyed. But that's not what Cain and Block seemed to be doing. Even worse, it seemed like Cain's campaign didn't have a full grasp of the facts—or that they were intentionally downplaying the seriousness of the charges and omitting key details. In a series of appearances and media interviews, the campaign's versions of events kept evolving, which, in turn, generated an explosive chain reaction: As other news outlets chased *Politico*'s scoop, wave after wave of new, damaging stories about the accusations against Cain came to dominate the race. While a full recounting is beyond the scope of this case study, here are some key highlights as the story blew up during the first week:

Monday afternoon (October 31): On Fox News, Cain told an interviewer that allegations were made against him but insisted he "never sexually harassed anyone." Cain said the National Restaurant Association investigated the charges and found them to be "baseless." He said no cash settlements were made, adding that if the association did give any money, "I wasn't even aware of it."

Monday evening: Back on Fox, this time with Greta Van Susteren, Cain retreated from his claim earlier in the day that no settlements were offered. He now said there was one "agreement," which he estimated to be two or three months' worth of salary "well within the range of what we would do if there was an amicable separation between the association and an employee." He wouldn't say if the cash payment was a direct result of the allegations against him and insisted there was only one "agreement," not two.

Tuesday morning (November 1): Robin Meade, the morning news host on HLN (formerly Headline News), asked Cain to explain the discrepancy between his two statements on Monday about a "settlement." Cain replied with a semantic distinction: "The word *settlement* suggested to me some sort of legal settlement, and as I recalled what happened twelve years ago, I recalled an agreement. I wasn't thinking legal settlement. And so the words have been a flyspecked, and I do recall an agreement." Cain also charged *Politico* with digging up the story to hurt his campaign while he was rising in the polls. He asked Meade, "Are you being used to try and help paint a cloud and help sabotage my candidacy?"

Tuesday afternoon: Back on Fox News, Cain suggested he was being attacked because of his race. Although he said he had no evidence to support that suggestion, Cain told Charles Krauthammer that he may be the victim of a "high-tech lynching." The *New York Times* reported that at least one of the settlements totaled $35,000, or roughly the value of a year's salary and substantially more than the two or three month's pay Cain had suggested on Monday.

Wednesday (November 2): A third woman said she considered filing a sexual harassment complaint, telling the Associated Press that Cain made sexually suggestive comments and invited her back to his apartment while she worked for him at the National Restaurant Association. Meanwhile, a Republican pollster—now working for Cain's Republican primary opponent Rick Perry—said he personally witnessed Cain sexually harassing one of the two women who received settlements. The Cain campaign began suggesting that the Perry campaign was the source of the story. They noted that consultant Curt Anderson, who learned about the allegations when he worked on Cain's unsuccessful 2004 Senate campaign, had joined the rival Perry campaign only one week before *Politico* published their story.

Thursday (November 3): *Politico* reported that the second accuser received a payment of $45,000. The Cain campaign did not respond directly and continued to claim that they were the victim of an "appalling smear campaign" by "inside the Beltway media." In an interview with Fox's Megyn Kelly, Block appeared to back away from his accusation that Anderson had leaked the story to *Politico*. Kelly noted that Anderson had made several media appearances to defend himself, had only nice things to say about Cain, and denied providing any reporter with information about the sexual allegations. Block's tone toward Anderson became conciliatory, but he continued to suggest the Perry campaign was culpable. Commenting on the interview, one media blogger wrote the following:

[Block's] appearance reasserts the growing concern among many political pundits that the more damning issue with this harassment story is not the pattern of behavior it may or may not suggest of the candidate, but in the inept handling of the allegations at every possible turn.[29]

Friday (November 4): Block, again on Fox News, said he would no longer be answering questions about the sexual harassment complaints: "This is the last time that I'll be addressing the issue." Block also said the *Politico* reporters who broke the story should be fired for poor journalism and hinted that the Cain campaign was discussing a lawsuit. The week before, Cain had dominated the news that came out of the Sunday talk shows. Now, his campaign was again the central focus—but for exactly the wrong reason. Mississippi governor and former Republican National Committee chairman Haley Barbour said Cain might survive but must "get all the facts out as quickly as possible." Other commentators are harsher. "He's not going to be the nominee, if I can just be honest here. He was never going to be the nominee," *Weekly Standard* editor William Kristol said on *Fox News Sunday*. Ed Rollins, Michele Bachmann's former campaign manager, told *Politico* that was over: "This guy knows nothing about foreign policy, '9-9-9' has been ripped apart, the girl problem is not going away and his beating up the media shows a thin skin that will get him in trouble. You combine that with no real campaign and his days are limited."

Monday (November 7): The first woman to use her name and tell her story in detail claimed that Cain attempted to put his hand up her skirt when she was seeking employment advice from him. Sharon Bialek, a registered Republican, said she had been an admirer of Cain's while she worked at the educational foundation of the National Restaurant Association for nine years before she lost her job in 1997. When she asked Cain for advice on finding another position in the association, Cain invited her to dinner in Washington and then touched her afterward in Cain's car. She claimed that when she asked him to stop, Cain told her, "You want a job, right?" The Cain campaign issued a statement: "All allegations of harassment against Mr. Cain are completely false. Mr. Cain has never harassed anyone." That night, Cain told late-night comedy show host Jimmy Kimmel, "The feelings that you have [when] you know that all of this is totally fabricated—you go from anger, then you get disgusted."[30]

Tuesday (November 8): Karen Kraushaar, one of the two anonymous women in the original *Politico* story, went public. Kraushaar, who received a $45,000 settlement payment, is highly credible—a graduate of Brown with a master's degree from the University of Michigan who now works as a communications professional at the Treasury Department. She suggested that she and three other women jointly hold a press conference.[31] Block appeared on Fox and said that the Cain campaign has confirmed that Kraushaar's son works at *Politico*—another claim that turned out to be false.[32]

Cain's campaign went from a front-running position to a disastrous spiral, one that virtually guaranteed he—and the allegations against him—would be the focus of every cable channel and political reporter in the country. If they could, Block and the Cain campaign needed to break the 24/7 news cycle in which they found themselves trapped. In an effort to do so, they added well-known celebrity attorney Lin Wood to their team and called a press conference—Cain's first since the *Politico* story broke—for Tuesday, November 8.[33]

Lin introduced Cain at the late afternoon event at the Scottsdale Plaza Resort. Cain said the charges against him are false, and he blamed the Democratic Party. "The Democrat machine in America has brought forth a troubled woman to make accusations, many of which exceed common sense," he said. "And they certainly exceed the standards of decency in America." Cain suggested he might be willing to take a lie detector test and vowed to stay in the race. "We are not going to allow Washington or politics to deny me the opportunity to represent this great nation," Cain said. "As far as these accusations to cause me to back off or maybe withdraw from this primary race, [that] ain't going to happen. I'm doing this for the American people and for their children and their grandchildren."[34]

Campaign managers faced with harshly negative stories about their candidates almost universally told us that getting the facts out quickly—and completely—is essential. A one-week story is survivable; a monthlong story filled with dribs and drabs of extra information allows reporters covering the campaign to rehash the initial bad news again and again, reminding voters of the story while undermining a campaign's credibility with important influencers, in the media and the community. Whether or not *Politico* had an agenda in pursuing claims about Cain's behavior toward women—and few observers outside the Cain campaign thought the paper had any such agenda—the facts told a story all their own. Cain's campaign lost valuable oxygen—and their front-runner position—by sticking to a story they should have known was unsustainable.

As it turned out, Cain would stay in the race for only twenty-four more days. After the press conference, and with no new accusers coming forward, it initially appeared that the Cain Train might be able to get moving again. "I think if you go back [to the press conference], the story did begin to wane from that point forward. We were attempting to get back on message, and the message was the '9-9-9' economic vision for America," recalled Block.[35] But the story came back with a vengeance on November 28 when an Atlanta businesswoman, Ginger White, told a local television station that she had carried on a thirteen-year affair with Cain. Instead of waiting ten days as they did after the first accusations, the Cain campaign reacted immediately and issued a denial before the story aired. Block described what happened next and how Cain reached the decision to end his presidential bid:

On Monday evening, [Ginger White] was going to break the story. We had been alerted to it. I had made a strong recommendation to Mr. Cain that he address the issue on Wolf Blitzer's show in the afternoon to get out in front of the story. But as the week drew on, a couple of things became apparent. One, that it was causing great consternation to his family. And Mr. Cain really does put his family first. Number two, what we hadn't seen with the *Politico* story, it was affecting our donations online, which is a real-time indication of your support. The polling showed that we were dropping, but more importantly, as we assessed the situation, it continued [to drop].

Every time that he had an interview, every time that he did a TV appearance, everywhere that he went, he would be asked the same questions over and over again. And it was really death by 1,000 cuts. So can you sustain that and still win the nomination? And as you start putting together the pros and cons, it became apparent that you probably could survive this one. But if it continued and the press was going to continue to do this, that winning the nomination wasn't going to happen.

From a businessman's perspective, Mr. Cain looked at it and said, "We have enough cash on hand to make it through Iowa and into New Hampshire. But if our fundraising dries up, we'll be broke, and we'll not accomplish what I set out to do." And I think that was part of the strong family decision, [and] why he made the decision to suspend the campaign.[36]

In the days following White's Monday revelation, the Cain campaign went into public "reassessment" mode. Enthusiastic crowds of supporters still greeted Cain at campaign events and urged him not to quit, but it was increasingly clear that that the campaign was now in dire straits. The *Des Moines Register* released a poll of likely Iowa Republican caucus-goers showing that Cain had fallen to 8 percent just five weeks after leading the Republican pack with 23 percent at the end of October. Asked which candidate was most likely to have a scandal in the White House, a plurality of 47 percent named Cain. Beyond the sex scandal, the poll showed Cain was perceived as uninformed about issues—27 percent said he was the least knowledgeable candidate in the race. Only 8 percent said Cain was the candidate they would most like to meet in person.[37]

Managing the wrap-up of a "doomed" or losing campaign is a situation many managers face. As Cain and his top team deliberated, Block and others in the Cain camp publicly insisted that Cain would not drop out. "I don't know where they're getting their information," said Cain spokesperson J. D. Gordon when asked about reports that Cain would exit the race. In Iowa, Block met with the state's campaign team. "Mark Block, Herman Cain's chief of staff and chief operating officer, just left a meeting at the Iowa headquarters with all four Iowa staffers," said Lisa Lockwood, communications director for Friends of Herman Cain's Iowa staff. "The emphatic message is that the campaign is full steam ahead. Herman Cain is in it to win it. He always has been and that has not changed."[38]

The Cain campaign had earlier scheduled the opening of its larger new Atlanta headquarters for Saturday, December 3. Instead, joined on the stage by his wife and family, Cain used the ribbon-cutting event to "suspend" his unorthodox campaign just weeks after emerging as a national front-runner for his party's presidential nomination. That day, Mark Block took himself off the payroll along with every other employee except for one bookkeeper to look after the roughly $200,000 surplus that would remain in the official committee account after paying all the bills.[39]

Retrospective

"Victory has 1,000 fathers, but defeat is an orphan," John Kennedy famously said after the 1961 Bay of Pigs debacle. James Carville put it another way: "You know, politics is a lot like being a pilot. You don't get so much credit for doing things right, [but] son of a bitch, you get hurt doing things wrong."[40]

When a political campaign fails, the manager must be braced to endure public blame and after-the-fact finger-pointing, whether deserved or not. Many political professionals felt Block deserved it and were heaping out the criticism before Cain even left the race. "The Eric Fehrnstroms and Dave Carneys of the world are pretty savvy on this stuff," said Ty Matsdorf, spokesperson for the independent Democratic advocacy group American Bridge, referencing top staffers at the Romney and Perry campaigns. "I can't imagine that their response strategy would have been the same as what Mark Block and Herman Cain have been doing." Matsdorf said his group might have jumped in if the Romney or Perry campaigns had found themselves in trouble, but in Cain's case it wasn't necessary. "From our standpoint, to be totally honest with you, Herman Cain is doing our job for us," Matsdorf said. "If our job is to highlight Republicans' flip-flops or missteps—he's doing it himself, so there's not a lot of room for us to do anything even if we wanted to."[41]

A few campaign managers speculated to us that Cain and Block were less than prepared for their crisis because they never expected their long shot, low-budget presidential bid would find itself leading the field, at least not in October. They pointed to Block's failure to build a traditional campaign organization as evidence that Cain never expected to win. "The campaign probably started out as a way to sell Cain's speeches and books, raise his profile and maybe get a gig on Fox News," one told us.

"Bullshit," said Block when asked about this characterization. Before Cain announced his long shot candidacy, he and Block had prepared a written plan and budget that charted a way for Cain to win the nomination based on a bottom-up, grassroots campaign instead of the conventional top-down, hierarchical model. "The campaign plan was lifted off of *The Audacity to Win*," said Block, referring to the book by David Plouffe, manager of the 2008 Obama presidential campaign. Their plan was smart and successful, insisted Block, pointing to Cain's rise to the top of the national polls in October as evidence. Block is dismissive of his critics: "Have they ever run a campaign that went from nowhere to first in the national polls?"[42]

Block's detractors say Cain wasted time with his visits to late-primary states like Tennessee and Alabama, instead of focusing on Iowa and New Hampshire. Again, answered Block, these critics did not understand how the Cain bottom-up campaign operated differently from traditional presidential campaigns. "We were running a national campaign," said Block, who said they were targeting Tea Party sympathizers across the country and wanted to be the first to start grassroots organizations in as many different states as possible.[43]

Iowa, New Hampshire, South Carolina, Florida, and Nevada were important. Contrary to what was written [in the press], we didn't ignore those states. In fact, if you go back and take a look at how many times Cain visited those states versus the other candidates, we were second or third. The difference was we went into those states early and built a network of grassroots activists, stepped back and said, "You know what? We pretty much got our act together there, so we're going to go places where others haven't been."[44]

Candidate scheduling is usually strictly controlled by headquarters, but the low-budget Cain campaign schedule was determined differently, with more input from state campaign offices. "We had organizations in states that were raising money and could fund a bus trip into Tennessee and a bus trip into Alabama," said Block.[45]

Block said much of the criticism of the Cain campaign comes from established political consultants and their friends in the media who did not understand Cain's "unconventional" bottom-up organization. Block remains proud that the campaign hired no major political consultants or firms, not even a pollster. "One of the reasons that Rick Perry flamed out is that his consultants put so much crap in his head before the debates that he couldn't process it all."[46] Block also faults Michele Bachmann's professional management team, saying they took her from a first-place finish in the quadrennial August straw poll in Ames, Iowa, to a poor, campaign-ending performance in the January caucuses: "[You] see a transformation of Michele Bachmann from a pretty good candidate to a very controlled-by-consultants candidate." Block said their campaign took the opposite approach: "We let Herman be Herman."[47]

But traditional campaigns that follow well-trod paths win for a reason, and letting Herman be Herman may not have been the best way to manage a national real-time media feeding frenzy. Block conceded they could have employed some more conventional public relations tactics: "You know, probably in hindsight, when that [first sexual harassment] story broke on Sunday night, we probably should have a held a press conference Monday morning and said that these are baseless accusations with no merit. That's what we should have done. But again, we didn't know at that point what the accusations were because Jonathan Martin didn't give us anything." Should Block have used their press spokesman as the primary first responder? "Good question. But I think it's retrospective because Mr. Cain wanted to handle it all himself," said Block.[48]

The campaign underestimated how overwhelming the story would become, admitted Block. No one can really prepare themselves for the fire hydrant of coverage when a big controversy takes hold in today's accelerated 24/7 news cycle, he said. "Everything you say or do becomes news immediately." Block remembered standing on a street corner in Washington when he got a call from a reporter on his cell phone. "What are you doing in town, is something up?" the reporter asked. "How did he know I was even there? He said someone had just seen me and sent it out on Twitter, so he called me. I couldn't even stand on the street without hearing about it from the press," said Block. The rapid back-and-forth caused the campaign to make some mistakes in haste, including some missteps of his own, said Block.[49]

Two mistakes cited by Block came when the Cain campaign attempted to "attack the messenger." Block said the first was singling out Perry consultant Curt Anderson as *Politico*'s source on the sexual harassment story. "I did apologize to Anderson because he said on national news that he didn't have anything to do with it," said Block, although he still insists that the Perry camp was responsible: "We still have some pretty good information that Perry's folks had their fingerprints on this."[50]

In fact, Block was mistaken once again. Advisers close to Jon Huntsman, the former Utah governor and ambassador to China, eventually told the journalists Mark Halperin and John Heilemann the Huntsman campaign had been behind the Cain story. After watching so many other candidates'—former Minnesota governor Tim Pawlenty, then Bachmann, then Perry, then Cain—rise and fall, Huntsman's team believed they would benefit from the fall of another also-ran.

Another mistake was falsely claiming that one of Cain's accusers, Karen Kraushaar, had a son who was a *Politico* reporter. Like the smoking video, this was a last-minute improvisation by Block. "It was like two minutes before I was going on the air that I was shown, on the Internet, that this gentleman had worked at *Politico* and had the same last name of one of the women who had just come out," said Block.[51]

> I'm thinking, "Let's connect the dots here." But it proved to be false. A bit of advice I would give anybody reading this [is to] make sure you've got your facts straight. It was quite embarrassing because I had just spent days telling the press that they should have their facts straight.[52]

Even if Block had spent the time getting his facts straight, it is doubtful whether any presidential campaign—conventional top-down or unconventional bottom-up—could have survived the accusations against Cain, Block believes. But he would do it all again and feels privileged for the rare opportunity to have run a presidential campaign.

Here's a poor boy from Weyauwega, Wisconsin, population 678, going to school at Weyauwega-Fremont High School, single mom on welfare, and then I get to be one of, what, a couple of hundred people in history to run a national [presidential] campaign? I say this in all sincerity—only in America can somebody from where I came from tell that story.[53]

Case Teaching Topics

- Could Block and Cain have managed their way out of the controversy? Or were they unavoidably overwhelmed by events beyond the campaign's control?
- Overall, what's your opinion about Block's management of the Cain campaign (a) before October 30 and (b) after October 30? Did the campaign plan help Cain to the top of the national polls, or was it simply good luck after Perry's poll numbers began to drop?
- What plan would you have recommended to Cain on the evening of October 30?
- What are the advantages and disadvantages to running a "conventional" top-down presidential campaign organization versus an "unconventional" bottom-up campaign?
- The only recent presidential campaign to successfully navigate a sex scandal was Bill Clinton's in 1992. Given today's numerous cable news channels and Internet-driven media environment, could Clinton have survived such a story in 2012?
- Before the sex scandal broke, what was the 0-to-100 probability that Cain could have won the Republican nomination? What was the probability when Cain launched his campaign in February 2011?
- Based on your own research, what other potential problems and accusations were facing the Cain campaign in October and November 2011? What is the post-campaign relationship between Block and Cain?

Notes

1. M. Block, personal communication, November 2011.
2. Ibid.
3. Ibid.
4. Ibid.
5. A LexisNexis search for Mark Block mentioned in stories with Herman Cain, January 1 through October 18 and October 19 through October 30, 2011.

6. MJ Lee, "James Carville: Cain Aide 'Drunk or Stoned,'" *Politico*, October 27, 2011, www.politico.com/news/stories/1011/66975.html.

7. Kathleen Parker, "Herman Cain's Smoking Gun," *Washington Post*, October 28, 2011, https://www.washingtonpost.com/opinions/herman-cains-smoking-gun/2011/10/28/gIQA ugLQQM_story.html.

8. M. Block, personal communication, November 2011.

9. Beth Fouhy, "New Cain Internet Ad Shines Focus on Viral Videos," Associated Press, October 31, 2011.

10. Lindsey Boerma, "Cain's Smoking Chief of Staff Defends Video Ad," *National Journal*, October 26, 2011, www.nationaljournal.com/2012-presidential-campaign/cain-s-smoking-chief-of-staff-defends-video-ad-20111025.

11. M. Block, personal communication, November 2011.

12. Ibid.

13. Ibid.

14. "2012 Republican Presidential Nomination," *Real Clear Politics*, 2012, www.realclear politics.com/epolls/2012/president/us/republican_presidential_nomination-1452.html.

15. M. Block, personal communication, November 2011.

16. Consistent with his business background, Cain insisted on using corporate titles in his campaign organization. Cain referred to Block not as his campaign manager but as his chief of staff. The campaign's organization chart also gave him the title of chief operating officer.

17. M. Block, personal communication, November 2011.

18. Ibid.

19. Ibid.

20. Ibid.

21. CBS News, "*Face the Nation* Transcript: October 30, 2011," October 30, 2011, www .cbsnews.com/news/face-the-nation-transcript-october-30-2011.

22. Jonathan Martin et al., "Herman Cain Accused by Two Women of Inappropriate Behavior," *Politico*, October 31, 2011, www.politico.com/news/stories/1011/67194.html.

23. Ibid.

24. M. Block, personal communication, November 2011.

25. Ibid.

26. Martin et al., "Herman Cain."

27. M. Block, personal communication, November 2011.

28. *Free media* is a term used to describe news media coverage of a candidate. Unlike paid advertising, news media coverage has a relatively low cost to a campaign.

29. Mediaite, November 4, 2011.

30. IBTimes Staff Reporter, "Herman Cain Press Conference: A Full Timeline of the Harassment Allegations," *International Business Times*, November 8, 2011, www.ibtimes .com/herman-cain-press-conference-full-timeline-harassment-allegations-367050.

31. *Politico*, November 8, 2011. Kraushaar's attorney attempted to arrange a press conference but it never took place.

32. The former *Politico* reporter, Josh Kraushaar, denied the charge by tweeting that he and Karen Kraushaar have the same last name but are not related; *Washington Post*, "A Timeline of Herman Cain's Troubles," November 4, 2011, www.washingtonpost.com/politics/a-timeline-of-herman-cains-troubles/2011/11/04/gIQA7BBfnM_story.html.

33. Lin is an Atlanta lawyer who has represented the wrongly accused 1996 Olympics bomber Richard Jewell, as well as former California representative Gary Condit and the parents of JonBenet Ramsey.

34. Reid J. Epstein and Juana Summers, "For Herman Cain, Two Named Accusers, One Flat Denial," *Politico*, November 8, 2001, www.politico.com/news/stories/1111/67887.html.

35. M. Block, personal communication, November 2011.

36. Ibid.

37. Jennifer Jacobs, "Iowa Poll: Herman Cain Support in Iowa Takes Nose Dive," *Des Moines Register*, December 2, 2011, http://caucuses.desmoinesregister.com/2011/12/02/iowa-poll-cain-support-in-iowa-takes-nose-dive.

38. CNN Wire Staff, "Cain to Make Campaign Announcement Saturday," CNN, December 2, 2011, www.cnn.com/2011/12/02/politics/cain-accusation-affair.

39. Federal Election Commission, "Report of Receipts and Disbursements—Friends of Herman Cain," 2011, http://docquery.fec.gov/pdf/249/12951401249/12951401249.pdf.

40. J. Carville, personal communication, November 9, 2011.

41. Alexander Burns, "Foes Count on Herman Cain to Self-Destruct," *Politico*, November 7, 2011, www.politico.com/news/stories/1111/67728.html.

42. M. Block, personal communication, November 2011.

43. Ibid.

44. Ibid.

45. Ibid.

46. Ibid.

47. Ibid.

48. Ibid.

49. Ibid.

50. Ibid.

51. Ibid.

52. Ibid.

53. Ibid.

Index

About the Authors

William J. Feltus is senior vice-president at National Media Research Planning and Placement LLC, an advertising and media agency in Alexandria, Virginia, where he manages political, corporate, and not-for-profit clients. Mr. Feltus is recognized as an innovator in the application of media research data to political and public affairs marketing. Providing polling, communications, and advertising services, he has worked for eight presidential campaigns and for gubernatorial, Senate and Congressional clients in forty-four states. Feltus has been a press secretary in the U.S. Senate, deputy campaign manager of President George H. W. Bush's unsuccessful 1992 re-election bid, and staff director of the U.S. Senate Republican Conference. He received his B.A. from Yale and his M.B.A. from the Harvard Graduate School of Business Administration. Feltus has been an adjunct instructor at Graduate School of Political Management at George Washington University and the University of San Francisco.

Kenneth M. Goldstein is a professor of politics at the University of San Francisco (USF) and faculty director of the USF in DC program. He taught previously at the University of Wisconsin, where he won the Kellett Award for career research accomplishments and the Chancellor's Excellence in Teaching Award. Goldstein is one of the country's premier experts on the use and impact of political advertising. He has authored or coauthored four books and thirty book chapters and refereed journal articles. During the 2012 election cycle, he served as president of Kantar Media CMAG—a nonpartisan political consulting firm that tracks television advertising. Goldstein is currently a consultant for the ABC News elections unit and a member of their election night decision team. He has worked on network election night coverage in every U.S. federal election since 1988. He is also the polling and political ad analyst for Bloomberg Politics.

Matthew Dallek (Ph.D., Columbia University) is an assistant professor of political management in the Graduate School of Political Management at George Washington University, where he teaches courses on political leadership, the presidency, and Washington's political culture. He is the author of *The Right Moment: Ronald Reagan's First Victory and the Decisive Turning Point in American Politics* (Oxford University Press, 2004) and the forthcoming *Defenseless Under the Night: The Roosevelt Years and the Origins of Homeland Security* (Oxford University Press, 2016). His articles and reviews have appeared in many scholarly and popular publications including the Forum, the Journal of Policy History, the *Washington Post*, the

Los Angeles Times, and Politico. In addition, he has been a fellow at the Woodrow Wilson International Center for Scholars and a visiting scholar at Stanford University's Bill Lane Center for the American West. He served as a speechwriter for House minority leader Richard A. Gephardt as well as William E. Kennard, chairman of the Federal Communications Commission.